LIKE CHILDREN

PERFORMANCE AND AMERICAN CULTURES

General Editors: Stephanie Batiste, Robin Bernstein, and Brian Herrera

This book series harnesses American studies and performance studies and directs them toward each other, publishing books that use performance to think historically.

The Art of Confession: The Performance of Self from Robert Lowell to Reality TV
Christopher Grobe

Realist Ecstasy: Religion, Race, and Performance in American Literature
Lindsay V. Reckson

The Queer Nuyorican: Racialized Sexualities and Aesthetics in Loisaida
Karen Jaime

Black Patience: Performance, Civil Rights, and the Unfinished Project of Emancipation
Julius B. Fleming Jr.

Disability Works: US Performance after Rehabilitation
Patrick McKelvey

Like Children: Black Prodigy and the Measure of the Human in America
Camille Owens

Like Children

Black Prodigy and the Measure of the Human in America

Camille Owens

NEW YORK UNIVERSITY PRESS
New York

NEW YORK UNIVERSITY PRESS
New York
www.nyupress.org

© 2024 by New York University
All rights reserved

Library of Congress Cataloging-in-Publication Data

Names: Owens, Camille, author.
Title: Like children : Black prodigy and the measure of the human in America / Camille Owens.
Other titles: Black prodigy and the measure of the human in America
Description: New York : New York University Press, [2024] | Series: Performance and American cultures | Includes bibliographical references and index. | Summary: "A history of childhood that revises the story of manhood, race, and human hierarchy in America"— Provided by publisher.
Identifiers: LCCN 2023040771 (print) | LCCN 2023040772 (ebook) | ISBN 9781479812912 (hardback) | ISBN 9781479812929 (paperback) | ISBN 9781479812943 (ebook other) | ISBN 9781479812950 (ebook)
Subjects: LCSH: Gifted African American children—History. | African American children—History. | African American children—Social conditions. | African Americans—History. | African Americans—Social conditions. | United States—Race relations. | United States—Social conditions.
Classification: LCC E185.86 .O935 2024 (print) | LCC E185.86 (ebook) | DDC 305.23/089/96073—dc23/eng/20240126
LC record available at https://lccn.loc.gov/2023040771
LC ebook record available at https://lccn.loc.gov/2023040772

ISBN: 978-1-4798-1291-2 (hardback)
ISBN: 978-1-4798-1292-9 (paperback)
ISBN: 978-1-4798-1294-3 (library ebook)
ISBN: 978-1-4798-1295-0 (consumer ebook)

This book is printed on acid-free paper, and its binding materials are chosen for strength and durability. We strive to use environmentally responsible suppliers and materials to the greatest extent possible in publishing our books.

Manufactured in the United States of America

10 9 8 7 6 5 4 3 2 1

Also available as an ebook

CONTENTS

Acknowledgments   vii

Introduction: A Black History of Prodigy, a New View on Man   1

1. "Babe Belov'd": Phillis Wheatley and the Grammar of Early American Childhood   33

2. "Wilt Thou Bring My Baby Home?": Tom Wiggins and the Unending Antebellum Family   67

3. The Anatomy of Sammy Tubbs: Black Emancipation and the Human's Reconstruction   103

4. "Oscar Moore Can Tell You": Unbinding Brightness in the Archive of a Wonderful Boy   143

5. "This is the end of the story no it isint": Anarranging Philippa Schuyler's Scrapbook Archive   177

Epilogue: "To Be Held, Free"   219

Notes   227

Bibliography   267

Index   313

About the Author   325

Color illustrations appear as an insert following page 118

ACKNOWLEDGMENTS

It is an honor to acknowledge the many scholars who have shaped this book through their advising, editing, and mentorship. Thank you, foremost, to Jacqueline Goldsby, who has supported and deepened my thinking at every step of this project. Your craft as a scholar, writer, and teacher has profoundly informed the kinds of questions I pursue, how, and why. I extend immense gratitude as well to Daphne Brooks and Crystal Feimster for your support. Thank you for pushing this project further in both historical depth and theoretical ambition and for helping me calibrate the interdisciplinarity necessary to do so. What a monumental privilege to have begun this work in the Audre Lorde Room at 81 Wall Street among the three of you.

Many other faculty stewarded this project while I was a graduate student at Yale. Thank you, Hazel Carby and Glenda Gilmore, for crucial lessons about archives and storytelling. My great thanks as well to Matt Jacobson, Ed Rugemer, Greta LaFleur, Laura Wexler, Beverly Gage, Mary Lui, and Joanne Meyerowitz for critical lessons in your classrooms and in conversation. And thank you, Jodie Stewart-Moore, Lisa Monroe, and Susan Shand, for the roles you played in making African American studies and American studies such vital and collaborative homes.

The Beinecke Rare Book and Manuscript Library at Yale was another home, or origin point, for this project. Thank you to curator Melissa Barton for the fateful suggestion to look at the Randolph Linsly Simpson collection and for the many forms of guidance you have provided me with since. From my first explorations of the Beinecke onward, archives and the curators who make them available have been the backbone of this project. I am grateful to curator Laura Wasowicz and vice president Nan Wolverton for facilitating my time at the American Antiquarian Society (AAS). It is a great pleasure to reproduce several images from the AAS Children's Literature Collection in this book. I am thankful, too, to the New England Regional Fellowships Consortium for supporting my research at several other institutions. My gratitude to the curatorial staff at the Massachusetts Historical Society, the Schomburg Center for Research in Black Culture, the Special Collections Research Center at Syracuse University, the Dolph Briscoe Center at the University of Texas at Austin, the National Library of Medicine, and several other institutions.

My term at the Harvard Society of Fellows provided incredible latitude to think through and write this book. Thank you to outgoing chair Wally Gilbert and current chair Noah Feldman for the immense privilege to work with intensity but without urgency. Thank you, Ana Novak and Sarah Magagna, for the care you take in everything. And thank you to María Méndez Gutiérrez, Mireille Kamariza, Rediet Abebe, Sarah Derbew, Rachel Kolb, Chris Spaide, Eliza Holmes, Matylda Figlerowicz, Tania Bhattacharyya, Anna Seigal, Salil Bhate, Tara Menon, Jason Ferguson, Annika Schmeding, Levent Alpöge, Pedro Regalado, and many others for your intellectual generosity and wonderful company.

Writing much of this book at Harvard led me to reflect often on the tremendous impact of my undergraduate education there. Thank you, Robin Bernstein, for giving me—in my first semester of college—a set of critical tools that I am still using today and for your ongoing role as a mentor and friend in sharpening them. I am so grateful for your encouragement, close readership, and reminders about how to do things with words. Thank you, Glenda Carpio, for making the subversive possibilities of black literature and performance come alive for me. Thank you to Stephen Vider and Wendy Lee for your excellent teaching and mentorship. My gratitude to Deidre Lynch, Durba Mitra, and Joe Rezek for your generosity and support at pivotal points this past year.

Thank you to my colleagues in the English Department at McGill and to chair Erin Hurley for welcoming me, and this project, so warmly. Ara Osterweil, Alexander Manshel, and Amber Rose Johnson, you have made Montreal the best place to finish this work.

Though this project has been informed by many, my editor at NYU Press, Eric Zinner, and editorial assistant Furqan Sayeed have refined this work into monograph form. I extend my gratitude to them; to the editors of the Performance and American Cultures Series, Robin Bernstein, Stephanie Batiste, and Brian Herrera, and to my anonymous reviewers for their invaluable feedback. Material in the first and fifth chapters of this book have appeared, in different form, in essays. Parts of chapter 1 were adapted from my article "'I, Young in Life': Phillis Wheatley and the Invention of American Childhood," originally published in *Early American Literature* 57, no. 3 (Winter 2022). Parts of chapter 5 were adapted from my article "'Fine Discords': Anarranging the Archives of Philippa Schuyler," originally published in *American Quarterly* 73 no. 2 (Summer 2021). Thank you to the University of North Carolina Press and Johns Hopkins University Press, respectively, for permission to include these selections here. Writing and revising this manuscript would simply not have been possible without the encouragement, steadiness, and support of my writing group. Thank you, Virginia Thomas and Kristen Maye, for always taking so much care with my work, for lending critical vision to it, and for offering your friendship to me for many years.

Thank you, Bridget Darby, Carolyn Chou, Sharon Cho, Maryam Parhizkar, Katie Choi, Bianca Dang, Jenny Ye, Liz Jacobs, Isabel Osgood-Roach, Zoe Walsh, Asad Syrkett, Grant Quigley, Hannah Warren, Molly Krifka, Grace Winship, Elizabeth Woolf, Sue Pierre, Suzanna Bobadilla, Pip Lipkin, Ellora Vilkin, Hannah Kerman, Jess Feldman, Danielle Bainbridge, Christofer Rodelo, Sarah Robbins, Jo Ayuso, and Bristol Maryott. My great thanks to the Raymond-Kolkers. Thank you, Nikole Barnes. Thank you to my parents; my older sisters and younger brothers; my wonderful nieces, nephews, and niblings; and the memory of my grandparents, Maxine Hampton Owens and General Miles Owens. Thank you, B, family always. Thank you, Minna, my heart. And thank you, too, to the memory of Trina Schart Hyman, whose intergenerational friendship was, I have no doubt, the beginning of all of this.

I finished the dissertation that became the basis for this book in March 2020, a day or two before the first lockdown of the COVID-19 pandemic. Though only about four years separate that date from the publication of this book, the period in which I wrote this manuscript was dramatically different from the time that came before. Thus, this book is something different than I could have imagined before, underwritten by more glaring urgencies about community care, the organization of family under capitalism, antiblack violence, the future that lies ahead of children, and the vulnerability of children—and all people—now. If shaped by exigencies, this book has taken inspiration from people I know, and people I do not know, practicing forms of abolition and community care and daring to question the shapes that our relations, like family, take. I hope that this book reflects back some of their daring and questioning. Despite making the present's imprint on my writing explicit, I hope that this book remains true to the figures of the past who are its subjects: Phillis Wheatley, Thomas Wiggins, Oscar Moore, and Philippa Schuyler. I believe that their stories contain daring questions too. Though this is an imperfect offering, and one made when none can either refuse or refute it, this book is for them.

Introduction

A Black History of Prodigy, a New View on Man

Figure I.1. "Bright" Oscar Moore, Cabinet Card, January 1889, Randolph Linsly Simpson Collection, Beinecke Rare Book and Manuscript Library.

A small black boy leans his body and one hand on a little desk of carved wood. His other hand rests on his knee, covered in the velvet of an elaborate suit. On his tiny feet shine shoes of patent leather. Because he is leaning, one foot hovers in the air while the other rests atop a large book beneath him. The boy's face, eyes, and slightly opened mouth turn downward. His expression is quiet and impassive. As the label on the bottom of this photograph tells us, the boy in this image is Oscar Moore, or "Bright" Oscar Moore. With this information, we might begin to piece together a story about him. With the use of basic search tools, we could quickly learn something of his identity: that he was the youngest son of formerly enslaved parents, that he was blind, and that he was three years old in this photograph. We could find out, too, when this photograph was taken—in 1889—and for what purpose: as a performance token of Moore's "brightness," or the extraordinary mental precocity that Moore demonstrated for audiences by feats of memorization and mathematics. If spare, this story is enough to contextualize Moore within American performance history—as a prodigy—and to write a catalog entry for this piece of ephemera. But not enough to put this image back down.[1]

Something embedded in this photograph demands further attention and begins another story. Upon closer study, Moore's position between the desk and the book appears propped up by a third object: a thin wooden rod that juts from the lower left corner of the frame to the bottom of Moore's suspended foot. The rod's status is as ambiguous as it is interruptive. It raises, by its appearance, the question of whether it is meant to be seen at all. The rod might be a prop within the scene: perhaps a cane meant to point to Moore's blindness. If it is a cane, however, its placement, not in Moore's hand but held by an invisible one, points away from Moore. Once noticed, the rod invites the viewer's curiosity to travel from Moore's foot, to the edge of the image, and out of it. To follow the rod is to follow a question: Who was it on the other end, and why did they seek to keep Moore so carefully posed?[2]

An answer to the question of whom, and the beginning of why, can be found in the signature that sits beneath Moore's name on the label: David H. Anderson, the man who took this photograph.[3] An address, 785 Broadway, also printed there, locates this photograph as having been taken in Anderson's studio at Astor Place in Manhattan. As a very young black child, Moore was an exception among the white adults who typically passed before Anderson's camera and also within the history of the studio, which had formerly belonged to a much more well-known photographer, Mathew Brady, the US Civil War documentarian and the portrait photographer of Abraham Lincoln, Jefferson Davis, and several other white men of state and at least one black one—Frederick Douglass.[4] Though Anderson was behind the camera and these men in the contextual background, there was another man, the white "showman" who stood to profit from Moore's career, most directly behind the rod.[5] Perceiving the visual, cultural, and financial ties connecting these men to Moore alters this picture and the story we can tell from it. This can no longer *only* be a performance history or a story of Oscar Moore alone. Indeed, this portrait, thus reframed, articulates the central claim of this book: that the power of American manhood has historically been tied to children and that we can see the workings of this relation through the efforts of white men to hold black children in place.

In the nineteenth century, the places of white men and black children in the American social order were, at the surface, diametrically opposed. Based on the American system of hereditary slavery and its afterlife, on the patriarchal organization of family, and on the gendered, age-based, and racial limits of US political enfranchisement, we might easily say that white men occupied a place of power and that black children existed in a state of power's lack. Yet while acknowledging the extremity of this power dichotomy, this book—like this photograph—nevertheless highlights a question: Why did white men often go to great lengths to demonstrate their power over and connection to black children? In raising this question, this book arrives at its driving assertion: that we might not know the place of black children in the American social order as well as we have thought.

If we follow the rod back into the portrait, we can begin to reapproach and defamiliarize that place. The clothing Moore wears is, like the rod, referential yet ambiguous. Upon close examination, Moore's velvet suit appears just like that worn by the titular character of Frances Hodgson Burnett's popular novel and play *Little Lord Fauntleroy* (1886).[6] Calling forth a character beloved by white audiences both for his childhood innocence and for his upright development of manliness, the suit is an index of a powerful child and of the cultural power of childhood in the nineteenth century. Worn by a black child who entertained white audiences by his divergence from childhood's expected development, the meaning of the Fauntleroy suit fits him strangely.[7] Indeed, Moore's relationship to Fauntleroy, as distant as a sentimental story from a staged spectacle or a plot of inheritance from lived exploitation—and yet as close as velvet on skin—materializes a larger relationship between the cultural and social places of black and white children across Moore's period, before him, and after. For while white Americans defined black and white children by legal, social, and cultural distinctions, they nevertheless generated power from the rub between black and white.

Held in the suit's friction and kept still by the rod, it is the *measure* of childhood that forms the last unseen scaffolding holding Moore's portrait—and the performance of prodigy—together. For as this book shows, between the early American period and Moore's late nineteenth-century performances, Americans increasingly came to understand childhood as a measure or gauge: of lacking capacities of reason, rudimentary ability, and incremental intelligence. This is what made it possible to discern the modern prodigy as a figure not only distinct but also off course from the normative child's progress. Yet the human developmental schema that emerged across this period not only distinguished the prodigy from the child; it made it possible to chart how, when, and also *if* one achieved the rational personhood, discipline, and political power that separated children from men. This book, then, is a history of how Americans learned to measure the child and measure *with* the child and also how this understanding became, over time, natural and common sense. As I contend, what the culture and measure of childhood made invisible, the history of black prodigy can make visible, spectacularly.

Through Moore's story and a longer lineage of black children made to perform as childhood's figures of exception, this book examines how childhood's nature was produced in culture, empirical sciences, pedagogy, and law and also how seemingly natural qualities of children, when applied to others, became key supports of white supremacist and patriarchal power. As a conduit of such power, childhood was also the site of ongoing contest and change. The acts of black Americans to assert their freedom and protect their families were often central to this change, and so were the cultural and intellectual acts of black children themselves. Taken together, the chapters of this book demonstrate that the black prodigy's history was not exceptional or minor. From the late eighteenth-century "wonder" Phillis Wheatley, to the late nineteenth-century "Bright" Oscar Moore, to the twentieth-century "Harlem prodigy" Philippa Schuyler, prodigy comprised a pattern, a continuous thread, and a site of repeated negotiation between black children who troubled the measure of childhood and white men who sought to control, exploit, and contain their deviations.[8] White men did so, not as a demonstration of their power, but because their power depended on it.

The Child Is Father of the Man

The pathway that this book takes to reach its subjects is encumbered by the same power relations it seeks to illuminate. For indeed, locating Moore and the other black child subjects of this book in archival evidence requires finding them in the utterances of white adult audiences, often recorded as uncanny "enigma[s]," entertaining "piccaninn[ies]," or "accident[s]."[9] Yet even while appearances of such black children in American archives may only be brief and enigmatic, they can nevertheless be "incisive," articulating power, as Michel Foucault famously explained, through their "instantaneous contact" with it.[10] The contacts with power that this book articulates, however, are more encompassing than instantaneous, characterized more by the "excess" and "everywhere" violence Saidiya Hartman ascribes to archives of slavery and its afterlife than by the "competing passions and interests" Foucault could locate in "the lives of infamous men."[11] In fact, it is the contact of black children like Moore with the interests of infamous and ordinary men that the story of black prodigy in American culture explicates.

The black prodigy's history, then, cannot be told as a series of biographies that fully render each subject, nor can it comprise a true history from below. Rather, it is a history told from "between," its insights arising from asymmetrical forms of contact: the financial contracts, bills of sale, custody rulings, scientific reports, stories, and stage props that impelled black children like Moore to perform certain forms of labor, knowledge production, and entertainment for the profit of some and the enjoyment of many.[12] Examining what mediated the relationships of particular black children and white men primarily illuminates the conditions that immediately surrounded them—yet I contend that it also reframes larger, more generalizable systems of power. For as I show, while finding white men exerting power over black children is unremarkable in American archives, tracing the patterns of their effort reveals something about their purpose: that white men derived power from the value they could extract, and the authority they could take, from children. Staging this argument in the relations of American slavery and its afterlife in the nineteenth and early twentieth century, I proceed toward a larger scale of implication: that considering the child fundamentally changes how we understand the more global power of Man and the episteme of humanism.

While transcending the boundaries of US cultural and intellectual history, abstractions of "Man" and "the human" developed distinctly American cultural lives and social histories by their extension into the political frameworks, scientific knowledge, and narratives of self-making that tied the US to the Enlightenment's wider reverberations and European origins. Indeed, as Sylvia Wynter articulates, Man was not a fully formed figure who traveled into the Americas from Europe but was born from the integration of the Enlightenment, empire, and slavery—that is, the same conditions from which the US came to be. As a "natural being" and a rational civic subject, Man embodied order's reconstitution outside of religious authority and the turn of European thinkers to empiricism and liberal governance.[13] And if given new status, Man was also given new personification: as the reflection of those European men who gained authority through the extension of their knowledge, ideals, commerce, and government into the "new world" from the early modern period onward.[14] It was by this extension that, according to Wynter, Man came to "overrepresent" the human, subjecting enslaved and colonized people to an unresolved status, and becoming, himself, "the measuring stick through which all other forms of being" were evaluated.[15]

The material, ontological, and ongoing problems of this "overrepresentation" are articulated and troubled in multiple critiques of humanism advanced in black studies and adjacent fields.[16] Yet within the extensive realm of this critical conversation and across the examination of the geographical, gendered, and biocentric facets of Man's power, the status of Man *as* a measure has remained relatively unexamined. I argue, however, that if we look for Man's measure, we find it beside him: in the space between him and the child. Over time, as I show across this book, the child's measure became more psychologically, legally, and culturally elaborate—more subtle and also more contradictory. Yet it was a relatively simple rubric—of reason and children's lack of it—that provided initial stabilization to Man's authority in early America.

When white men in early America established their colonial and US constitutional rights, they did so on the basis of their capacity for reason and within the humanist proposition that legitimate democratic government depended on reason. If government was to be democratic, English colonial subjects contended, it was to arise out of the rational "consent of the governed."[17] Expressed in multiple strains of Enlightenment thought, it was John Locke who most firmly entrenched reason as consent's precondition.[18] In making reason the source of democracy's possibility, however, Locke retracted democratic eligibility from a certain group—children—whose mind's he imagined as "white Paper, void of all Characters, without any *Ideas*."[19] In Locke's framing, manhood was a measure of rational, literate distance from the infant's metaphoric blank slate; Man's rights, the reward for one's edification out of childhood. Defining children beneath reason not only precipitated children's loss of political power. As Caroline Levander notes, children's separation from "civic life" inversely helped "constitute and buttress" the meaning of civic life, the civic subject, and the state.[20] Moreover, as Holly Brewer demonstrates, children's abstract exclusion from civic life ceded practical authority to white men, who gained greater power of contract, consent, and custody over their children.[21] For as she details, whereas children in sixteenth- and seventeenth-century England—including those under ten—could contract their labor, marry, vote, hold property, testify in court, or rule a kingdom, by the late eighteenth and early nineteenth century in England and Anglo America, these exercises of power were ceded to fathers' authority, made questions for "family law" to adjudicate, or retracted altogether.[22] This shift was not only philosophical and legal, however; nor was it uniform. While Locke held outsize influence in defining children's political status, his influence crossed with the ascending cultural force of eighteenth-century figures like Jean Jacques Rousseau, whose notion of childhood—not as a lack state demanding society's inculcation but as a state of nature more perfect than society itself—influenced alternative strains of pedagogy and romantic literature and culture.[23] Always in flux, the meaning ascribed to white childhood, attitudes toward white children, and the treatment of white children were not as uniformly organized as their Lockean, Rousseauan, or other ideals.[24] Yet when English romantic poet William Wordsworth wrote in 1802 that "the Child is father of the Man," he communicated the power of childhood's different strains as they braided together: as a symbolic construction and social subject, it was the child who delivered Man's meaning and shaped his power.[25]

I argue that the child's naturalized status yet malleable meaning made childhood a uniquely powerful tool in shaping racial power. Across the eighteenth and nineteenth centuries, white men marshaled childhood's significance toward the formation of race itself, staking the claim that the African and African-descended people they enslaved were unequipped for freedom because, like children, they were devoid of reason. Considered natural dependents on this basis, black people could be incorporated into what Anne McClintock has deemed the human family's "hierarchy within unity."[26] The power of this hierarchy, and the reach of this claim, extended past proslavery arguments and past slavery, as I demonstrate in each chapter of this book.[27] It was etched into law, drawn and performed in caricature, and inseparable from the modern construction of ableism. It was established in antebellum medical practice and in the post-Emancipation sciences of evolution and eugenics.[28] Across the same period, it was also written into antislavery arguments and Reconstruction pedagogies. By the early twentieth century, the simile of black childlikeness—and the attribution of natural childlikeness to a global notion of "lower races"—existed as more than an argument or axiom.[29] Recognized by scholars such as Corinne Field as the political weapon of infantilization, the idea of black childlikeness represented a structuring premise of Man's power and struggles over it.[30] Yet the label of infantilization fails to explicate the process that politically disqualified "the infant" while making a political weapon of them. It also misses the doubleness of such a weapon. As I show, the likening of black adults to white children shaped both.

In the comparison of white children and black adults, black children's place appears troubled, suspended, or exceptionalized, like the prodigy's. This ambiguous suspension illuminates something other than black children's categorical exclusion from childhood, however. As I argue, it prompts instead the need to reassess how terms of inclusion and exclusion have shaped, and limited, our view. By mapping the relations of the black prodigy to the child, the childlike, and the human, this book reveals black children's place not in the margins of American childhood but at the center and thus at the center of the larger structure of American humanism. As I show, even as white Americans enslaved, exploited, caricatured, and harmed black children across the nineteenth century and beyond, they did not place black children outside of childhood. They attempted to incorporate, contain, and bind them to it.

In claiming black children's signal importance and value to the American social and political order, I contravene the tendency to write black children's history as a story of their exclusion, disregard, and dehumanization. Locating black children's place in the margins or outside the boundaries of American childhood has made sense in the observation of overwhelming evidence: that black children have been segregated from white children's resources, that they have been monstrously caricatured in childhood's dominant culture, and that they have been endangered outside of white childhood's protections.[31] The narrative of black children's historical exclusion from childhood often joins with another claim: that of black children's "adultification" in the present or their subjection to a weapon inverse and opposite to black adults' infantilization.[32] This claim is staked on equally compelling evidence: that black children are disparately disciplined in schools, criminalized by the state, and misrecognized by whites as older than their chronological ages.[33] Yet just as infantilization demands finer historical inspection, so do narratives of adultification, dehumanization, and exclusion. As Zakiyyah Jackson argues, dehumanization fails to apprehend the "imposition" of humanness upon black people, and the subsequent "appropriation" and abuse of that humanness, *as* the source of humanism's "ontologizing violence."[34] In framing exclusion and adultification as our ills, we invite inclusion in childhood, and in the human, as our remedies.[35] I argue that in doing so, we miss the violence internal to childhood and black children's long-standing negotiation of it. We miss, too, black children's history of identifying and unsettling the human order from inside.

Placing black children at the center of American childhood's history, I diagram the internal violence that black children have encountered and subverted there. I also identify the source of such violence in white Americans' persistent effort to extract material value and affective, cultural, and intellectual power from black children. I argue that they did so not to demarcate the boundaries of childhood but to produce and regulate childhood's meaning and not to define the boundaries of the human but to fill them. Contravening the prodigy's assumed role as an exception to a larger rule, I tell the story of black prodigy as a rule or pattern itself. I locate a beginning to this pattern in the poet Phillis Wheatley's remembrance as a "wonder" of the early American age.[36] I follow it forward through the music of Tom Wiggins, whose enslavement to white enjoyment outlasted slavery. I trace a pattern of black prodigy's pedagogical use through Sammy Tubbs, a fictional anatomy instructor to white children. Oscar Moore's performance of brightness bends the prodigy's pattern over the nineteenth century's end. Philippa Schuyler's twentieth-century performance of giftedness provides an ending, though not the end, to the story. Told in this forward chronology, the pattern of prodigy also moves in a circle: around the endangered yet insurgent place of black children in the circuit between child and Man. In making this circuit visible, this book revises how we theorize the racial boundaries of the child and the human, where we recognize black children's power within them, and how we read the history of American childhood as a whole. American childhood's primary texts are the essential starting point for such a revision.

The American Grammar Book

In the early seventeenth century, the children of English settlers, of enslaved Africans, and of Indigenous peoples existed in various states of indenture, slavery, and limited freedom under British colonial rule. These statuses were ill defined, as were the racial categories assigned to them.[37] By the end of the seventeenth century, however, English settlers demanded a definition of "whose child could be enslaved" and whose child could not be.[38] Staking the foundation for their future freedom, property, and whiteness, English colonists resolved that white children were not enslaveable and that black children inherently were. Yet to define white children's freedom from black children's bondage, colonists also needed to differentiate white from black. They did so by joining race, freedom, and property in a novel mechanism of black-or-white inheritance. Leaving the status of Indigenous children in a separate and shifting danger, colonists attached a bond-or-free dyad to black and white children by way of their mothers. As Jennifer Morgan writes, this was the basis for "hereditary racial slavery."[39] And as I argue, it also marked the beginning of modern American childhood.

Writing this resolution into law in 1662, Virginians located the "condition of the mother" as, and at, the crux of race. Understood and enforced far beyond its Virginian codification, this law became known as the American doctrine of *Partus sequitur ventrem*: "Whereas some doubts have arisen whether children got by any Englishman upon a negro woman should be slave or free, *Be it therefore enacted and declared by this present grand assembly*, that all children borne in this country shalbe held bond or free only according to the condition of the mother, *And* that if any Christian shall commit fornication with a negro man or woman, hee or shee soe offending shall pay double the fines imposed by the former acts."[40]

Partus invoked black and white children, mothers and fathers. But its impetus lay in the doubt it cast over the status of children born of English fathers and African mothers. Attached to such doubt was an unnamed desire: white men's wish to have free sexual access to enslaved black women, to control black women's reproductive lives, and to make capital of their children. In support of such desire, the law radically removed a father's capacity to pass his status to his child and instead linked a mother's status—enslaved *or* free—to her child. As Morgan writes, in this arrangement, "no white man's *child* could be enslaved," but "all black women's *issue* could."[41] This dynamic, or what Hortense Spillers captured in her field-shaping essay "Mama's Baby, Papa's Maybe," forms what Spillers deems the "originary narrative and judicial principle" of the US symbolic order, or its "American Grammar Book."[42]

Grammars function by the sense they allow and disallow and by what they make legible and illegible. If well mastered, grammars seamlessly incorporate themselves into the acts of reading, writing, and speech, becoming isomorphic with sense and meaning itself. Over time, *Partus* aptly functioned as a social grammar by making certain subjects and relations legible while marking others outside of sense. And in naturalizing the relations it installed, it disappeared the acts and maintenance of their installation. By this process, *Partus*'s innovation of white matrilineal freedom—and the novel significance thus granted to white mothers—disappeared behind the larger authority of white fathers and the naturalized freedom of white children. By the same logic, a white father passing his black child down as property became normative, while a black child inheriting freedom, let alone property, from a white father became, if not impossible, then outrageous. In fact, it was a 1655 suit by a black woman named Elizabeth Keye for freedom on the basis of her white patrilineage that, as Morgan explicates, formed an immediate impetus for *Partus*.[43]

If black children's potential to raise doubts about white family and property precipitated *Partus*'s installation, it was the ongoing life of that disruptive potential, despite *Partus*, that invites reading the law's grammar rather than reading with it.[44] Indeed, the critical force that Spillers offers to the history of childhood is her attention not only to what slavery's laws settled or symbolically carved as "hieroglyphics" in black "flesh" but also to the "severe disjunctures" that remained alive within slavery's system of domination.[45] For Spillers, the violence of the American Grammar was not its wholesale denial of the categories of "mother" or "child" to the enslaved but rather the contradictory imposition of such categories and their "inva[sion]" by "property relations" at once.[46] If we suspend focus on *Partus*'s effect—making black children synonymous with property—we can identify the paradoxical operations by which this effect was accomplished. For while gutting black mothers' claims to their children, *Partus* first invoked black mothers *as* "mother[s]" and black children *not* as "issue" but among the plural entity, "all children," whom it sought to regulate within "this country."[47]

Spillers baby/maybe couplet is a neat crystallization of the inscription and violation that threw black kinship and black childhood into crisis.[48] Yet the incongruence of the common noun *baby* and uncertain adverb *maybe* also expresses something else: a level of symbolic instability from which anagrammatical meanings, and alternative relations, could also arise. The archive of enslaved kinships, resistance, and sociality not only suggests this as a symbolic possibility but confirms it as a historical reality. It was by the extension of "alternative grammars" that enslaved people formed networks of care for children other than their own, maintained or mourned kinships across forced separation, performed gender and family outside of patriarchal order, and sometimes "refus[ed] to relinquish a child to the market," even when that market's capture of that child was a foregone conclusion.[49]

Such refusals formed pieces in the "rewrit[ing]" of a "radically different text" than that which the American Grammar enforced.⁵⁰ Yet arising from historical actors without recourse to legal or social authority, these pieces never proceeded toward a synthetic, contending grammar book, nor should we read them, in the present, as coalescing into the total rejection of the American Grammar's categories of mother, woman, child, father, man, or human. Indeed, the collective pursuit of African American freedom, citizenship, and equality was often, and remains, deeply invested in claiming these categories.⁵¹ Nevertheless, what Spillers identified as "the insurgent ground" found in "*claiming* the monstrosity" of the "different social subject" who exists "on the boundary" is not a theoretical proposition without its own history.⁵² It can be located in genealogies of black gender transgression, black pursuits of reproductive autonomy, and "deviant" black sociality.⁵³ And it is, in many ways, the history of the black prodigy, the figure suspended on the baby/maybe boundary, for whom "monstrosity" was not only a symbolic marking but a spectacular label.

Prodigy is both an unavoidable history and an etymological link between the "monstrosity" Spillers identifies in *Partus*'s reproductive order and the notion of reproductive monstrosity salient to those who wrote *Partus*. For within the cultural spheres of early modern England and Europe from which the drafters of the law came, the term *prodigy* connoted a "monstrous person, freak, wonder, [or] marvel" of "disputed origin."⁵⁴ Describing children whose physical differences or disabilities caused disturbances in their home, to the church, and within God's order, stories and images of prodigies often circulated for prurient enjoyment. But as Lorraine Daston and Katharine Park write, they were not trivial.⁵⁵ To give birth to a prodigy was to give birth to an omen, a sign of a greater disturbance to come. The ability to *forget* prodigy's monstrous meaning in the present, however, highlights that it was a series of secularizing, scientific, and racial—not supernatural—disturbances that followed the early modern prodigy. By the early twentieth century, the ableist construct of "gifted childhood," not a notion of deviance or disability, dominated prodigy's meaning and its performance by white children.⁵⁶

This recasting only gains context within childhood's racialization over the intervening period and in relation to the black prodigy. Indeed, the emergence of the black prodigy marks both a displacement of difference and the recruitment of new monsters in the making of the modern child and the human. Shakespeare's Caliban, the monstrous Caribbean child of an African witch, arises as an early modern appearance of black prodigy in *The Tempest*: "The son that she did litter here, / A freckled whelp, hag-born," whom Prospero describes as "not honored with / A human shape."[57] This new transatlantic imaginary also conscripted living black children into its fictions. In the seventeenth and early eighteenth centuries, European enslavers and colonial agents made a pattern of displaying certain black children—those born with freckled skin pigment patterns of albinism and "piebaldism"—as prodigies who disturbed their new epidermal and reproductive organization of race.[58] By their exhibition, Europeans alchemized the anxiety that these black children produced into something that whites, newly self-conscious of their whiteness, could enjoy.

When read against this history, the black prodigy performances I follow across modern American stages appear less as minor acts in other genres and more as part of their own long lineage. They are, in this sense, repeating figures. And they are also figures of symbolic redundancy. For if we identify the location of black children in the American Grammar as being on the "boundary," the label "black prodigy" appears to enunciate that boundary again, marking a subject twice in excess of the free, legitimate child.[59] This double excess underlines a core argument of this book: that black prodigies represented not just exceptions to the rule (system of measure) of childhood but a disturbance to the rule (system of dominance) that childhood secured. Despite their spectacular singularity, black prodigies were not exceptions but cultural metonyms for value that escaped Man's reproductive system. Indeed, though marked as outliers, the black prodigies that this book follows embodied a collective, not rare, form of excess: the potential of black children to disturb an order written for their capture.

The first and second chapters of this book detail strategies that black children and adults undertook to rewrite this order. As I discuss in chapter 1, Phillis Wheatley wielded her mastery of the literal Anglo-American grammar to create the social conditions for her early American freedom. Moreover, the poet imagined her own notion of a free black family—and black children's protection within it—in literature and in the law. As chapter 2 details, a formerly enslaved woman named

Charity Wiggins made strategic use of nineteenth-century family law to fight for the freedom of her son, the neurodivergent musician Tom Wiggins. Both chapters supply evidence that using the law's letter did not always succeed in challenging its underlying grammar, however. Indeed, the cases discussed in these chapters underscore that black family, freedom, and childhood remained vulnerable to "invas[ion] by property relations" even after manumission or the event of Emancipation.[60] Yet in each thwarted attempt to imagine a notion of family and childhood premised on freedom, *not* property, these stories highlight something plain yet crucial: that the freedom securely attached to white children by family was not itself unencumbered by property but staked upon it.

For even as "pricelessness" became the dominant appraisal of white children's value over time, white children's freedom never transcended property or price.[61] Across the eighteenth, nineteenth, twentieth, and twenty-first centuries, white children's social value and freedom remained tied to the concept of property and to its material transfer through white families. Property, and a man's right to its protection, was at the heart of the democratic freedom that Americans took from Locke's writings and installed in law.[62] When seventeenth-century colonists established white children's freedom in Virginian law, they did so explicitly to protect their property from descending to black people. Routing the future of freedom through the white family, they installed a grammatical slippage wherein white family, white freedom, and white property each depended on the other and where their discrete meanings bled together.

Indeed, white childhood—despite its disappearance as the unmarked, naturalized, and free category in the American Grammar—ultimately requires equal attention to its grammatical installation. Under *Partus*, white children's freedom was not only attached to black children's bonded status by opposition; it was also "held" by a party unnamed by the use of passive language. In one sense, "held . . . free" before the law, white children's freedom was more directly held by their fathers, who also rightfully held black children in bondage. Indeed, it was white men's status as "freeholders"—outright possessors of stolen land and other forms of real property—that made them eligible civic participants in American freedom as it developed in Virginia.[63] No freedom, in this system, was untied from property or from theft.

The priceless, unblemished, innocent child, then, was enmeshed in a structure of property and race and property *in* race. To note this is not to claim a similarity of condition between enslaved black children held as property and white children who possessed what Cheryl Harris deems "whiteness as property," which they could inherit, possess, and convey.[64] Indeed, white children's relationship to property made them, as Morgan writes, "subjects whose identities were coterminous with the political and economic project of the nation, rather than objects whose value fueled it."[65] Yet the more we understand white men's property as the hinge that held black and white children together rather than as a line that has separated the bonded from free, the better we perceive white childhood, not as the unmarked category beside heavily laden black childhood—or Locke's "White Paper, void of All Characters" beside Spillers's "hieroglyphics" carved "in the flesh"—but as a category whose characters, too, require knowledge of the American Grammar to decipher and that, once read, belie all apparent blankness.[66] Indeed, situating white childhood within the American Grammar not only makes it possible to read Locke's "blank slate" but, more importantly, makes the relationship of blankness to blackness the unmistakable fulcrum of American childhood's story.

Rereading the Blank Slate

In telling the story of American childhood, the "blank slate" is often posed as an unavoidable first text—though it is purportedly blank, though it is not technically a text, and though it was an abstraction. Reading the child's blank slate, *tabula rasa*, or "White paper," has remained essential in the field of childhood studies, because, as Seth Lerer writes, it has arguably been "the governing epistemology of children's literature, since the early eighteenth century."[67] And because, as Gillian Brown shows, Locke's blank slate fostered the grounds not only for children's literary imagination but for their sense of self and citizenship.[68] If the blank slate forms the substrate of American childhood's history, early America's literal grammar books, primers, and spellers have been an important next layer, both as archives of early American pedagogy and as sites where American social and religious mores can be read in their instructions. Upon this foundation, the nineteenth century's mass proliferation of children's literature, and its sentimental literary depictions of children, personify and acculturate American childhood's history. It is here that writers and readers encircled the vulnerable, innocent white child in the domestic sphere and also where coming of age became the journey out of childhood's enclosure.[69] Producing the story of the child, American literary history also *follows* it, charting a near parallel journey toward the novel's psychological maturation and, indeed, building the novel on the paradigmatic structure of coming of age.[70] In the American Grammar, the white child and the book form another metonymy.[71]

The overlap in childhood's history and literary history are rooted in archive and in episteme, because children's literature, books about children, and children's marks upon books are an incredible resource for understanding children and the construction of childhood in the past and because, as Patricia Crain writes, the "so-called invention of childhood was also an invention of a new relation to books and reading."[72] The implication of this new relation extends far beyond children's books and outside the purview of literary history, however. What Crain identifies as literacy's production of a child's "self-possession" and what Courtney Weikle-Mills articulates as literacy's role in children's "imaginary citizenship" were both facets in the child's ascent and incorporation into the project of Man.[73] When white children encountered books, internalized their pedagogies, and practiced their grammars, they participated in a collective "autopoiesis," finding their place in the order of things and forming their humanness through narrative encounters with humanity.[74] Indeed, the ease with which "the story of humanism" can be told as a "coming-of-age story," as David Scott points out, is not coincidental.[75] It derives precisely from the role of stories, books, and children's reading in mediating the space between the child and Man.

For this reason, books are essential for recognizing children's important place in the history of humanism, rendering the human's construction in grammar, as told in conduct tales, narrated in novels, and learned from anatomy textbooks. In this book, I read each of these sources as pedagogies in being human and as archives where we can closely encounter white children's conscription—and potential defiance—in reproducing the American Grammar's whiteness, power, property, and status. In doing so, I advance the child—and archives of childhood—from a peripheral place in black studies to the center of black studies' interrogation of the human. Yet for the same reason, I seek to trouble the book as the center of American childhood's history. Indeed, the intervention of this book—to place black children at the center of American childhood's history—requires this troubling. Not because black children did not read, write, or write in books, nor because they did not appear in children's books, but because the same books that map a feedback loop between white childhood and the human confound black children's place in the story. In the book-child relation, black children often appear as competitors for access to literature—and thus for access to the human—or as conduits for the development of white humanness.

Chapter 3 focalizes this dynamic by dissecting an 1874 anatomy textbook that invited white child readers to understand their human bodies through an invented black child. Written by a white physician, Edward Bliss Foote, *Science in Story* taught white children about their anatomy and physiology through the developing story of Sammy Tubbs, a fictional black boy doctor. Sammy's use for instilling white children's "knowledge of [them]selves" reflects a much wider and patterned use of prodigy, black childhood, and blackness as the source and substance of white children's humanity.[76] As I argue in this chapter, reading nineteenth-century children's literature reveals the construction of humanness through blackness, not against it. Disclosing black dehumanization as an error in terms, I argue that the white literary practice that Toni Morrison deemed "playing in the dark" was, in itself, a process of inscribing, or inking, the blank slate.[77] Locating the essential use of blackness in the formation of the human, the substance and status of humanness as pure and unvariegated whiteness comes into question. Identifying blackness as a key conduit for white self-knowledge of the human, however, does not in itself illuminate black children's subjectivities, histories, or humanness. At least not in the same stories.

Yet as scholars such as Nazera Wright, Brigitte Fielder, Crystal Webster, Katharine Capshaw, and Anna Mae Duane have shown, and as the field of African American children's literature attests, there is incredible richness to be found in literary archives of black childhood. Nineteenth- and twentieth-century African American literature demonstrates the commitment and creativity of black adults and children to write black children into literature and to write for black children as readers.[78] And indeed, children figure centrally in the black history of literacy and in African Americans' use of the written word as a site of self-making and self-manumission. The "self-taught" enslaved literacies that Heather Williams locates reveal how black children learned to read, write, and conceive of their own selfhood through literature.[79] Wheatley is an inaugural figure in this history, as I discuss. Enslaved narrators of the antebellum period chart black literacy's continued pressure on the limits of freedom and personhood in their testimonies of black humanity, suffering, and demands for freedom.[80] In and of itself, black literacy and literature can be understood as a counterhistory of the human, where black people have imagined the form and ethical relations of being human beyond the grammars of child and Man.

I consider black children as key actors in this counterproject. Rather than reconstruct a story of black children's counterclaim upon the book-child metonymy, however, I tell the story of black children's negotiation of their breached, anagrammatical, and excess relationship to it. There is no easy metonymy between the prodigy and the book, and the strangeness or estrangement of this relation is, rather than an obstacle, an opening. For if the book was closely sewn into the production of the white child, the uneasiness of black children's relationships to books is an opportunity to examine the processes of the child's production at its seams or another way of reading at the level of social grammar rather than reading the social meaning that grammar has produced. The figures in this book staged radical and imaginative challenges to the measure of being human outlined between the child and Man. Some of them acted through literature. Some of them lacked literacy. Not all of them attained self-possession, personhood, or freedom on Man's terms. Yet their stories, read in their differences and in their patterns, produce an important insight: that lacking literacy did not exclude black children from negotiating with, or acting upon, or even *reading* the books that shaped American childhood and that mastering literacy did not necessarily resolve black children's relationships to books, to the child, or to the human. Across different modalities of knowledge and access to the written word, the children that this book follows acted upon the literal and social grammars around them and staged new relations to the texts, terms, and books imposed upon them. Their acts, performed in literary anagrammars, sonic discords, and irreducible brightness, trouble binaries of literacy/illiteracy and inclusion/exclusion by continuously moving across them. As they coalesce together, their movements unravel the workings of the book-child relation, performing in the space between.

Black Performance Unbinds the Book

As a staged repertoire, an imaginative construction, and a metonym for a larger social grammar, the pattern of black prodigy requires methods of both performance studies and literary studies for its narration and deconstruction. The archival material that this book draws upon—from stage ephemera, literary caricature, and poetry to legal statutes and scientific models—necessitates both of these methodologies and more. Methods of cultural and intellectual history, and a materialist approach to them, support this book's historicization of childhood as constructed in scientific, legal, and economic structures and in literature and culture. To understand the forms of insurgency that prodigies staged upon this conceptual terrain, however, requires a more incisive than broad methodological approach. I find this approach by leveraging black performance methods upon literary and textual sources, allowing their pressure to unbind the primacy of the book as a container for childhood, its development, and its history.

The uneasy place of black children in early American archives and nineteenth-century children's books invites such an approach. The *Hand-Book of the Wonderful Boy, a Few Things of What the Little Blind Two Year Old Boy, Prof. Oscar Moore, Can Tell You*, or the souvenir companion to Oscar Moore's photograph, instructs as to why. A physically small pamphlet that could be purchased at Moore's performances, the *Hand-Book* contained hundreds of questions that audience members could pose to Moore. As such, it is a remarkable source for understanding the contents of Moore's repertoire of "brightness." It is also a site of epistemic and ethical crisis, for how can a handbook—in other words, a user's manual—tell the story, or produce the subject, of Oscar Moore? Chapter 4 confronts this question, reckoning with the failure of the *Hand-Book* to textually archive anything about Moore except his subjection yet identifying other properties in the *Hand-Book*—theatrical, ephemeral, and physical—that might tell more.

Because "books both *mean* things and *do* things," as Alexandra Gillespie and Deidre Lynch argue, the "physical book" remains an essential "object of humanistic inquiry" and a ready site of performance analysis.[81] Indeed, as works by both Robin Bernstein and Katie Trumpener demonstrate, children's books, in their didacticism, have often explicitly "scripted" or compelled performances from their child readers—by the turning of a page or the unfolding of a pop-up.[82] The relationship of this book's child subjects to books like the *Hand-Book* underscores the role of books not only in compelling but also in coercing performances. Yet they highlight, too, the fact that even the most didactic texts can be subverted or, in the case of the *Hand-Book*, "unbound" by Moore's interruptions and breakdowns and the questions he posed.[83] A heuristic for understanding how Moore negotiated with the scripts, props, and managers of his repertoire, "unbinding" nevertheless encapsulates this book's wider investment in marking black children's performances of anagrammar, nonnormative sense, and discord upon a range of other problematic books and texts: a handed-down *New England Primer*, a sentimental songbook, an anatomy textbook, and a set of scrapbooks. Rather than applying "unbinding" as a unitary method to each, I instead draw on the textual or otherwise evident practices of each chapter's figure, uplifting their creative strategies as critical approaches in themselves. Working from the premise that these black children might have read not only, in Walter Benjamin's essential phrasing, "against the grain" but also against the *form* of the book, I identify alternative forms of literacy—physical, aural, sonic, or imaginative—that supported each figure in making books *mean* things and *do* things of their own devising.[84]

Animating the history of black prodigy from limited archival evidence requires not only elaborating black children's extant and potential relationships with books but also contextualizing their relationships to the stage. For if not *only* a performance history, the history of the black prodigy is embedded in performance and theater. Figures such as Moore and Wiggins shared their nineteenth-century stages and cultural work with the black picaninny choruses, cakewalkers, burlesque dancers, and "avatars" who, as the work of Jayna Brown and Uri McMillan articulate, played key roles in the "shaping of the modern" movements of American repertoires and in carving popular culture's tour routes.[85] Moreover, the tour routes traveled by black prodigies—across sideshow stages and through dime museums—pinpoint the central place of the sideshow performer, the freak, and the monster in giving modernity its shape. For indeed, while precocity increasingly eclipsed monstrosity as prodigy's overt meaning across the nineteenth century, the monstrous, the infamous, and the enigmatic remained live and valuable. Rosemarie Garland-Thomson recognizes this value and the broader currency of the "freak" performer in their ability to mark the boundaries of the "normate" as modernity's proper subject.[86] Yet as Garland-Thomson notes, and as the field of black disability studies addresses, the binary of freak and normate requires racial elaboration.[87] The conjunction black child prodigy—marking freak from normate, prodigy from child, black from white—does not simply call for an analysis of multiple intersections, however. The figure of the black prodigy troubles the notion of intersections as discrete crossings and of value split in binaries. The history of the black prodigy is a lesson in the incorporation of difference, blackness, and monstrous excess into the human. Binary interpretations misapprehend these relations not only because they obscure how multiple intersections cross each other. They collapse because they draw lines of distinction where there were circuits of violent inclusion and imaginative struggle.

The Child, the Prodigy, and the Picaninny

The narrative of black children's exclusion from childhood is a story produced and told through binaries, and for good reason. Across the nineteenth century and beyond, white Americans imprinted vivid differences on the cultural iconography of white childhood and black. They marked these differences in color contrasts of black and white, in moral contrasts of deviance and purity, and in value judgments of cheap and priceless childhoods. These polar differences unavoidably shaped the cultural terrain in which the black prodigy moved. Indeed, the prodigies I follow in this book tangle repeatedly with the nineteenth century's dominant icons of black and white childhood: Eva the "angelic white child" and Topsy, the incorrigible "picaninny" of Harriet Beecher Stowe's antislavery novel *Uncle Tom's Cabin* (1852).[88] In Topsy and Eva, Stowe consolidated a moral and affective economy of black and white childhood already in her sentimental surround. Yet as Robin Bernstein shows, the novel's popularity catapulted its child characters off the page and into performance, material culture, and children's play.[89] The intensity of Eva and Topsy's polarity only heightened in these forms (figure I.2).

288   UNCLE TOM'S CABIN; OR,

But what was to be done with Topsy? Miss Ophelia found the case a puzzler; her rules for bringing up did n't seem to apply. She thought she would take time to think of it; and, by the way of gaining time, and in hopes of some indefinite moral virtues supposed to be inherent in dark closets, Miss Ophelia shut Topsy up in one till she had arranged her ideas further on the subject.

"I don't see," said Miss Ophelia to St. Clare, "how I'm going to manage that child, without whipping her."

"Well, whip her, then, to your heart's content; I'll give you full power to do what you like."

"Children always have to be whipped," said Miss Ophelia; "I never heard of bringing them up without."

"O, well, certainly," said St. Clare; "do as you think best. Only, I'll make one suggestion: I've seen this child whipped with a poker, knocked down with the shovel or tongs, whichever came handiest; and, seeing that she is used to that style of operation, I think your whippings will have to be pretty energetic, to make much impression."

Figure I.2. Eva and Topsy illustration by George Thomas in Harriet Beecher Stowe's *Uncle Tom's Cabin* (London: Nathaniel Cook, 1853), Yale Collection of American Literature, Beinecke Rare Book and Manuscript Library.

"Always dressed in white," with "deep blue eyes" full of "spiritual gravity" and an "airy, innocent playfulness" in her body, Stowe wrote Eva St. Clare, the daughter of an enslaver, in deliberate contrast to Topsy, a "goblin-like," "cringing," thieving, enslaved child.[90] In rendering these children "representatives of the two extremes of society," Stowe indicted slavery's character-deforming consequences upon black children.[91] Yet Stowe's novel and its adaptation more effectively siphoned reader and audience concern *from* enslaved black children like Topsy and toward figures of white vulnerability like Eva. Enacted and retold, Eva's innocence, suffering, and death made her an icon of what Duane deems the dominant trope of "suffering childhood."[92] Beside Eva's recognizable and innocent suffering, crude caricatures of Topsy as "wicked" and invulnerable produced what Bernstein deems the "divergent paths" or "split" of black and white childhood.[93] This is where the sensitive and suffering white child and the noninnocent, "insensate" black child became unrecognizable in likeness.[94] As Bernstein argues, this binary produced and covered violence. Indeed, under these conditions, white children learned to play and perform antiblack violence as part of the repertoire of childhood itself. This pedagogy or performance depended on a "dehumaniz[ing]" myth—that black children were "comically impervious to pain."[95] This was, in Bernstein's terms, a key "alibi" of "racial innocence."[96]

Yet this alibi for overt violence may cover violence of a deeper, more insidious kind. For if we turn from the polar "split" that distinguishes Eva and Topsy along a human/dehumanized axis, we can apprehend an underlying violence: the subjection that gives Eva and Topsy their literary and cultural forms, arising out of humanism's internal, extractive structure. As Bernstein recognizes, "polarity is a form of connection."[97] Plumbing that connection by again looking between, I arrive at a different interpretation of the poles themselves, finding that the white trope of "suffering childhood" was produced not against black children's insensateness but as the recoding of black children's pain. If not visible in their surface coloring, this dynamic appears in Eva and Topsy's underlying conditions, where attention is called to Topsy's thievery while her theft—that which made her property—recedes and where it is somehow Eva, not Topsy, who suffers and dies from slavery. Hartman's articulation of the integral linkage of sentiment and slavery supplies the framing to understand this operation: where the "extension of humanity to the enslaved" formed the basis on which their "feelings and consciousness" could be possessed through the "assimilative character of empathy."[98] As I argue, we find childhood's most iconic figure of whiteness in the middle of a novel about slavery for this reason. Not because antislavery produced the moral content of white innocence, nor because her white innocence reflected off of blackness, but rather because she functioned to absorb black pain around her, "bringing suffering [so] near" as to incorporate it.[99]

The operations of extraction and incorporation beneath Eva and Topsy's outer polarity clarifies other forms of violent intimacy that this book traces—from nineteenth-century literary tropes that enclosed black children in white homes to the racially hybrid repertoires danced by white child star Shirley Temple in the twentieth century. This knowledge returns us, too, to the ambiguous touch of black and white childhood first registered in Oscar Moore's portrait, between him and his suit of velvet. For if styling Moore as a black Fauntleroy was a ploy by his managers to lend Fauntleroy's cultural popularity to Moore, the picture shows something else: a living black child made to lend *his* body, intellect, and labor to white childhood's image, ideal, and fiction.

Fauntleroy's conjuring through Moore's body indexes the intimate relationship between American childhood's blackness and whiteness, its material conditions and its fantasies. Yet the stillness of the portrait—maintained both by the rod and by its photographic capture—makes it possible to miss how Moore, as a performer, might have destabilized the system of meaning contained in his costume. Eva and Topsy are instructive here too. For if Topsy was invented to shoulder the imaginative demands that white Americans wrote into childhood, she also illuminates how those demands could change shape or be renegotiated through performance. Like Eva, Topsy had a wide cultural life taken up by whites who commercialized and embodied her in blackface and yet also by black children and adults who negotiated with her and sometimes reimagined her.[100] As Jayna Brown's writing on black Topsy dancer Ida Forsyne demonstrates, black girls and women inhabited and transformed Topsy's abject role with their inventive movements, repertoires, and feelings. In Forsyne's embodiment, Topsy exceeded the terms of her invention, producing something excess and "unruly."[101] Just as

Forsyne's Topsy demonstrates a black animation, or alteration, of a white invention, the excess she produced points back to the excess that Topsy and the archetypal picaninny were meant to capture. As caricatures intended to debase black children, picaninnies were never reflections of black children. Yet through their distortion, picaninnies reveal what white Americans sought to fix in place: black children's excess and unruly value. Indeed, I argue that the picaninny was a means of concealing black children's value behind another thin alibi: cheapness.

Deriving from the *picayune*, a Spanish coin of small value and wide circulation, a picaninny was a measure of fungibility.[102] Topsy gets "many a stray picayune" out of her enslaver, an exchange in *Uncle Tom's Cabin* that communicates the correspondence between the "little plagues" St. Clare enslaves and the coins he keeps in his pocket.[103] Pages away, Topsy seems to confirm the picaninny's other founding lie: of kinlessness, declaring that she "never was born" but just "grow'd" from the ground.[104] Yet if these are the originary fictions of the picaninny, they bear resemblance to fictions of another figure. In her "goblin-like" appearance, the "odd and unearthly" notes of her singing, her "bright and funny" countenance, her "uncommon verbal memory," the "wild, fantastic sort of time" she keeps while dancing, and the "amazement" she commands from the whites who look upon her, Topsy, the paradigmatic picaninny, begins to appear in close relation to the prodigy. Or more precisely, she closes the space between them.[105]

Like white childhood and black and like the child and the prodigy, the picaninny and the prodigy appear in surface opposition. Noting this opposition, Laura Soderberg describes the prodigy as a figure marked "quite distinctly" from the picaninny in her enumeration of the nineteenth century's plural childhoods.[106] Yet in Topsy, we see this distinction break down. Just as she gives feeling to Eva, the paradigmatic white child, she shares in the characteristic disturbance of the prodigy. The longer we look at Topsy, and if we are willing to look, we see her reflect both the prodigy and the picaninny, two sides of the same coin. Recognizing the value hidden there is not an argument for recuperating or romanticizing either figure. Both the prodigy and picaninny reflect histories of white violence. Yet for that matter, so does another category: the child. As I contend in this book, black children, in their excess, occupied each of them. This book follows what black children did in these spaces and in the connections between them. Their stories reveal that black children did not necessarily struggle for the child's innocence, nor did they seek to travel on the child's arc toward Man. They animated and imagined more.

Overview

I begin this book's revision of American childhood by placing a new figure among its formative authors. In chapter 1, "'Babe Belov'd': Phillis Wheatley and the Grammar of Early American Childhood," I argue for Wheatley's inaugural role in writing white childhood and in claiming black childhood. Reading Wheatley's elegies to white children beside her poetic self-naming as a "babe belov'd," I place her literary claims in conversation with her personal claims to the blank slate, primer, and freedom of white children. Wheatley, I argue, understood that childhood's aesthetics and social politics were linked. Such knowledge shaped her relation to her enslavers and her freedom. Legal documentation of Wheatley's adult life shows that Wheatley and her husband staked their economic freedom on white-black relations of inheritance like those of parents and children. White property's preeminence unraveled those relations. Yet in the legal drama that ensued, I pinpoint one of Wheatley's most audacious acts: her demand that the law address harm against her free black child. If Wheatley's insurgent marks on childhood's culture and law have been forgotten, I locate their disappearance in the poet's memorialization as a never-freed, perpetually precocious child in Margaretta Matilda Odell's 1834 *Memoir and Poems of Phillis Wheatley*. As I show, Wheatley's confinement to a sentimental fiction provides a blueprint for the black prodigy's place in the bonds of antebellum family affection.

Chapter 2, "'Wilt Thou Bring My Baby Home?': Tom Wiggins and the Unending Antebellum Family," begins in the sentimental enclosure mapped by Odell's fiction. Born into heritable slavery in 1849, Wiggins's incredible talent as a pianist and composer was made fungible for white entertainment across the nineteenth century's middle and end. In combination, the unending appetite of white audiences for Wiggins and the law's favor for the Bethune family who enslaved him kept Wiggins in captivity until 1908. Reading the 1865 court case that denied Wiggins's "best interests" as a minor and the 1885 case that suspended his disabled blackness into a childlike legal bind, I demonstrate the link between sentimental childhood's endurance and slavery's afterlife. Indeed, the same cultural logic that transmuted Topsy's suffering into Eva's lent force to popular myths about Wiggins. Yet while suspended in juridical and cultural fictions, Wiggins played and wrote their decomposition. Listening to his discordant music and reading his lyrics—deemed "words without sense"—I argue that Wiggins cast himself and his mother into an unsentimental story of black kinship crossed by captivity.[107]

While Wiggins's story charts slavery's endurance, his music resounds in the reckoning caused by black freedom. Taken together, chapters 3 and 4 diagram strategies that white men undertook to maintain old power and to invent new forms of it after Emancipation. In tracing this reformulation, these chapters offer a cultural biography of Man_2, the figure whom Wynter deems Man's biocentric successor. In chapter 3, "The Anatomy of Sammy Tubbs: Black Emancipation and the Human's Reconstruction," I trace how Dr. Edward Bliss Foote, a northern white physician, facilitated Man's remodeling by teaching it to white children. In his anatomy textbook *Science in Story: Sammy Tubbs, the Boy Doctor, and "Sponsie," the Troublesome Monkey*, he created a conduit for white children to develop science's new literacies of being human. I argue, however, that Foote's protagonist, Sammy Tubbs, communicates another lesson: that white humanness was instructed in black—both in cautionary stories of blackened humanity and in the stolen bodies of black people from whom Foote gained his medical education. While Sammy and his pets (Sponsie 1 and Sponsie 2) serve as resources for the new human, Foote's legacy outside of the story—as a feminist and eugenicist—locates the reproductive empowerment of white women beside Man_2 in the human's new regime.

Chapter 4, "'Oscar Moore Can Tell You': Unbinding Brightness in the Archive of a Wonderful Boy," pieces together the story of Oscar Moore in his captors' archives and then unbinds his place there. Answering the question of who stood outside the frame of Moore's 1889 portrait, I uncover the role of Moore's showman, Hans Peter Neilsen Gammel, first in staging Moore's late nineteenth-century career and later in dissolving evidence of it in the twentieth century. I argue in this chapter that Gammel and several other men exploited Moore because they understood brightness as a value to be captured and as a troubling source of intellectual power to be contained. I read the *Hand-Book*, a set of tickets, Moore's popular reception, and his subjection to scientific examination as evidence of this. I read his eventual disappearance as evidence of something else. Moore's disappearance from the popular stage reflects both the problem of Moore's prodigiousness at the twentieth century's turn and also the reincorporation of that problem in the twentieth century's gifted white child. Yet in the end, I show how Moore's vanishing exceeds both incorporation and erasure. Opening the archives of his captors and refusing evidentiary closure, brightness itself acts to unbind his story.

Chapter 5, "'This is the end of the story no it isint': Anarranging Philippa Schuyler's Scrapbook Archive," follows black prodigy into the era of gifted childhood. From the time of Philippa Schuyler's birth in 1931 forward, her mother, white writer Josephine Schuyler, kept a scrapbook of Philippa's incremental developments and IQ. The same year, Philippa's father, black novelist George Schuyler, published his speculative racial satire *Black No More*. Reading the scrapbooks and novel together, I link the scrapbook's positivist project and the novel's cynical racial forecast as attempts, and failures, to arrange a new racial order in Philippa's favor. Though subjected to her parents' vision of her future glory and archived under the scrapbook's authority, I argue that Philippa nevertheless produced a different account of her value. Reading Philippa's antilinear and "anarranged" storytelling across the visual, sonic, and poetic compositions of her childhood, I locate Philippa in acts of looking back at Josephine and at the project of human worthiness that she imposed.[108] Cast in the press as a black likeness of white child icon Shirley Temple, I read Philippa in a different affiliation: with the characters who deconstruct Temple in Morrison's *Bluest Eye* (1970). Unmasking Temple's theft of blackness and decomposing America's stillstanding grammars, I mark the critical perception of Philippa, and black girls, as a turning point, not an ending.

In the epilogue, "To Be Held, Free," I return to the failure of childhood to protect black children past and present, and I turn to calls led by black children, young people, and abolitionists to reimagine and reorganize kinship, care, and relation. Reckoning with childhood's conceptual limits and historical violence, I draw on new, and very old, grammars of interdependence to orient toward something other than inclusion. I ask what it could mean to be held and free.

Like Children

What are children like? We know because the history of childhood has taught us. Despite the breadth of embodiments, ages, and capacities housed in the category "child," we can still answer the question because we have learned to finely elaborate the child's arc. This book shows childhood to be our major pedagogy, and measure, of being human. As children, we learn, practice, and perform our relation to the human through childhood's lessons, its grammars, its books, and its rubrics. Yet even when we are no longer children, childhood is still instructing us in the human's meaning and measure. Taking apart the cultural, social, legal, and empirical filaments that formed the child's measure, I demonstrate what American childhood's commonsense and apparent nature have upheld: a limited framework of family and freedom; a narrow schema of knowledge, reason, and rights; and a conditional extension of care and protection built on a structure of racialized extraction. In illuminating each of these systems, the history of childhood also connects them, showing how they make up the human's internal parts.

"Slave-children *are* children."[109] The emphasis and demand that Frederick Douglass embedded in these words still rings as urgent 160 years after Emancipation. This book repeats yet revises this statement, varying its emphasis and placing an "and." Black children were, and are, children. And they have been more. As Spillers's baby/maybe instructs us, and as Oscar Moore's suit makes tactile, black children have existed in, and in excess of, the category "child," and they have reshaped it. They have been made prodigies and picaninnies both and simultaneously. They have been exploited at the bottom of the American order, but there, they have also subverted those who ruled at the top. This book locates the subversive power that black children have wielded, not in their essence, nor in their resilience to suffering. Instead, the chapters of this book locate black children's powers of perception, interruption, and interrelation. The "insurgent ground" of the black prodigy is not occupied alone but marked across a collective history, tied between the ordinary and extraordinary, and kept in kinships struggled for, lamented, or imagined.[110] The interdependence within these stories and the relations across them form a collective exposure of independence as Man's most powerful and ruling myth. Indeed, we can see it even in the most ephemeral, isolated evidence. For as much as the rod introduces a history of violence into Oscar Moore's portrait, it is also fundamentally a vector of relation. However much we think we know the power that runs from Man to child, from human to blackness, from white men to black children, this book opens from the premise that we can only understand that power if we perceive the force with which black children have pressed back.

1

"Babe Belov'd"

Phillis Wheatley and the Grammar of Early American Childhood

To P.N.S. & Lady on the death of their infant son.
To Mr. & Mrs. L—on the death of their daughter.
To Dr. L—d and Lady on the death of their son aged 5 years.
To Mr. L—g on the death of his son.
To Capt. F—r on the death of his granddaughter.
To Philandra an Elegy.
—Titles from "Proposals, for Printing by Subscription a Volume of Poems and Letters on Various Subjects, Dedicated to the Right Honourable Benjamin Franklin Esq: One of the Ambassadors of the United States at the Court of France, by Phillis Peters," *Boston Evening Post and General Advertiser*, October 30, 1779

Before her death in 1784, Phillis Wheatley was poised to deliver these poems to her early American and transatlantic readers. Advertising their titles among a manuscript of twenty-six other poems and several letters in the *Boston Evening Post* in late 1779 and again in 1784, Wheatley solicited subscription support from those who had previously enjoyed reading, circulating, and emulating her *Poems on Various Subjects, Religious and Moral* (1773).[1] Readers did not renew their support this time, however, and the manuscript to which these poems belonged went missing.[2] With it, the potential of these poems to extend Wheatley's influence and intervention upon early American culture was mislaid too. As titles alone, these elegies offer little more than suggestion. Yet by their shared form and subject, at least five of these six convey something significant: that Wheatley's second volume would have deepened her imprint on the emerging culture of American childhood. The last elegy—"To Philandra"—may or may not fit among this list, as Philandra's identity remains uncertain: she may have been a real child, or an adult, or a mythic figure (though of Wheatley's invention, not a classical reference). But where this last title may be an outlier, the first clarifies a pattern. Published elsewhere as "To Mr. and Mrs.—on the Death of Their Infant Son," "To P.N.S. & Lady" supplied ample verse to articulate Wheatley's formative role in writing the early American child:

> Behold, a child who rivals op'ning morn,
> When its first beams the eastern hills adorn;
> So sweetly blooming once that lovely boy,
> His father's hope, his mother's only joy,
> Nor charms nor innocence prevail to save,
> From the grim monarch of the gloomy grave!
> —excerpt from "To Mr. and Mrs.—on the Death of Their Infant Son"[3]

"Behold[ing]" the "innocence" of the "lovely boy" and adorning him in nature's beauty and his mother's affection, Wheatley supplied early and evocative lines in modern childhood's social and cultural reformulation. Indeed, Wheatley explicitly placed this child at a new dawning while projecting him forward as his "father's hope."[4] Yet in writing toward American childhood's future, she built upon her own prior contributions to the grammar of early American childhood. Casting this child into earthly and ethereal motifs of "sweetly blooming" infancy, Wheatley deepened the command of language she had previously honed across her several elegies to children in *Poems*. This "infant son" entered an imaginary of childhood already populated with James, a "blooming babe" in heaven who "like a seraph glow[ed]."[5] And, too, with beatific Nancy, the "enraptur'd innocent" who ascended in death above the "tempestuous sea" of worldly "sin, and snares, and pain."[6] While these celestial figurations of white childhood undoubtedly bear relation to the Christian devotion of the author and her audience, these poems also display something else: Wheatley's original, imaginative contributions to American childhood's emerging romantic culture and, too, her anticipation of its sentimental future.

By recognizing the continuous thread of Wheatley's writings on childhood, we gain some suggestion about the contents lost with her second volume and also about those contents' potential reflection of Wheatley's last years—as a free black woman, writer, wife, and mother. Yet beyond providing clues to what remains unknown in Wheatley's literary oeuvre and life, Wheatley's intervention into childhood's known history raises questions unanswerable through a list of titles or lines of verse alone. Wheatley's place as an early author of American childhood troubles any notion that the humanist transition in American childhood's meaning was written exclusively by, and for, white men and women or that it was exclusively about, or for, white children. While the innocence, beauty, and dependence with which early Americans imbued white childhood ultimately supported their order of white patriarchal dominance, recognizing Wheatley as a major cultural architect of childhood allows us to perceive resonances of complexity, contestation, and a young black woman's voice at modern American childhood's opening.

Relative inattention to the minor subjects of Wheatley's commonplaces and greater attention paid to her classical influences have kept scholars from noticing her there. Indeed, scholars have often located Wheatley somewhere between the white men of her neoclassical reading and the elite cadre of white men whose signatures endorsed her writing in the front matter of *Poems*.[7] In Henry Louis Gates Jr.'s influential account, it was her trial before these men that formed the decisive moment in her career, and the "primal scene of African-American letters."[8] However, more recent research has questioned whether this scene ever took place. Finding evidence against such a trial's likelihood, Joanna Brooks has created space to consider the other social stages that scaffolded Wheatley's career and structured her writing. Tracking the circulation of Wheatley's poems within an elite white feminine sphere, Brooks argues that it was bourgeois white women's patronage, more than the scrutiny of white men, that dictated Wheatley's poetic emphasis.[9] Moreover, following Wheatley's departure, rather than derivation from previous poetic traditions, John C. Shields has repositioned Wheatley less as an acolyte to the neoclassicists and more as a progenitor of the nineteenth century's romantics.[10]

Understanding Wheatley's role in writing the culture of early American childhood requires more than a reassessment of her literary lineage, patronage, or subject matter, however. It demands reckoning with the stakes of early American childhood and noticing Wheatley's perceptive maneuvering through them. Wheatley learned the grammar of American childhood from within its racial aporia—and she wrote out of it. Arriving in North America as an enslaved seven-year-old, Wheatley's early life was shaped by the violent negation of qualities of vulnerability, dependence, and preciousness that were transforming white children's social position and value. Moreover, she was pressed into the cohering juridical inscription made upon black and white children wherein the former were encumbered with slavery as their inheritance, the latter, slated for freedom. Wheatley's childhood attainment of an education, her appropriation of an American primer, and her travel upon literacy's "ordinary road" were each trespasses upon white childhood, as upon the value and freedom entailed therein.[11] When Wheatley wrote back into childhood's culture as a young adult, she demonstrated her keen perception that childhood was not a subject of commonplace or minor concern but a major anchor of family, freedom, knowledge, and power. She demonstrated, too, that she could unsettle it.

Following childhood's ascent across her published poems, this chapter places Wheatley's elegiac inventions at the foundation of American childhood's cultural grammar. Yet while establishing Wheatley's uncredited contributions to American childhood's formation, this chapter notes areas of critical divergence between the culture of American childhood that Wheatley opened and the dominant conventions that enclosed childhood after her. Across her elegies, Wheatley's invocation of children's innocence, vulnerability, and preciousness mark her poems as antecedents of sentimental culture's affective and aesthetic formations, prefiguring the angelic, beautiful, and mourned visage of figures such as Eva St. Clare. Yet even if recognizable in their formative influence, Wheatley's writings also delivered white children with qualities of authoritative speech and autonomy that unfixed them from their roles in the solidifying domestic order. In Wheatley's expansive vision of childhood, there was as much room for rearranging the social order as for stabilizing it. And there was room, too, for black children.

Wheatley's poetic reference to her own childhood, her dramatization of her father's love and grief upon her abduction, and her subversive claim to have been "like her [enslaver's] child" each demonstrate that Wheatley inscribed black childhood into American literature and claimed it in life.[12] Indeed, the poem in which she wrote of herself as "I, young in life," locates the poet's personal lament over her enslaved childhood as an equally salient opening to American childhood's culture, placing the recollections of a black woman at modern childhood's beginning and designating Wheatley as both its author and its "babe belov'd."[13] If this is not the commonly recognized dawning of American childhood, it is because the most radical aspects of Wheatley's contributions to childhood were eclipsed by the larger culture into which they both fit and formed a challenge. Yet Wheatley's personal and political endeavors nevertheless register the potential, if mislaid, to have written American childhood, and the American Grammar it anchored, toward different ends. Thus, they also offer the potential to read that grammar differently, attuned to its contingency and other strains of invention.

Wheatley's late eighteenth-century poems might appear too late, too indirect, and too fine of marks to read in relation to *Partus sequitur ventrem*'s seventeenth-century juridical inscription or the symbolic markings that Hortense Spillers maps from it. For black American kinship relations were not at their dawning in Wheatley's time; they had been crossed through by over a century of legal practices and by a longer period of traffic. The unremarkability of Wheatley's own theft from her kin, her sale as property, and her renaming *as* Wheatley each underscore this—that, indeed, she arrived into an Anglo-American system of slavery already engrained in practice and in understanding.[14] And even though slavery's end in Massachusetts coincided with Wheatley's death, slavery's material, social, and cultural effects still impinge upon her legacy. The difficulty of retrieving Wheatley's childhood from its archival void, the disappeared evidence of Wheatley's "lost years" as a free black mother to free black children, and the erasure of Wheatley's formative marks on childhood's culture are direct and indirect results of the American Grammar's shaping of what we can read of, and how we remember, the poet.[15]

Wheatley nevertheless perceived childhood as an inchoate site for altering the American Grammar, despite its sedimentation. She was ultimately made vulnerable to the manifold political meanings she discerned in the child, however. After her death, it was the use of "child" as a labile signifier and simile that came to abridge the meaning of Wheatley's work while making an exception of her life. Thomas Jefferson's claim that Wheatley's verse ran "below the dignity of criticism" indexed, in 1785, the rising use of children's base characteristics to measure the human's lower racial orders.[16] Fifty years later, Margaretta Matilda Odell's *Memoir and Poems of Phillis Wheatley* (1834) signaled the use of children's precocious characteristics to contain insurgency that otherwise spilled out of order. Odell's sentimental narrative of Wheatley's "peculiar" childhood remade Wheatley into an effigy that subsequent critics would recognize, repeat, and redub—"the sooty prodigy."[17] Granting the poet a "singular" and uncommon "genius," Odell and those who retold her story announced the force of Wheatley's imagination while binding it within what Odell described as slavery's "golden links of love" and its "silken bands of gratitude."[18] Odell's reformulation of Wheatley offers a guide to prodigy's enclosure in nineteenth-century culture—beside the white child, inside the white household, and held in the relations of the American social grammar, not outside of it. Yet if reading Odell's abridgment of Wheatley prepares us to understand the cultural performance of prodigy after her, releasing Wheatley from her "peculiar" effigy is essential to understanding the insurgent acts she did, in her time, perform.[19]

To broaden the scope of her legible markings, I follow Wheatley closely on the page and carefully off of it. Wheatley's relation to text requires such an approach, as she succeeded in claiming an author's relationship to books, not only a child's. Indeed, in publishing her *Poems*, she produced a culminating arc of her young life and a solid, permanent archive of it. Yet the other arc of Wheatley's life—into obscurity and toward death—makes clear that the authorial and archival personhood she won could also be lost, as much of her unbound and unpublished writings have been. For this reason, while I closely read Wheatley's bound verse, otherwise extant poems, and letters in conversation, I also consider what is indicated yet nonextant: the likely primer by which Wheatley gained her literacy, the unknown contents of her missing second manuscript, and the potential identities of the unknown Philandra, whom she elegized. Doing so, I trace Wheatley's education in the American Grammar around her while deciphering the various textual forms and social arenas where she tested and, at times, undermined it.

The recent recovery of a series of familial legal actions that unfolded across Wheatley's heretofore "lost years" of adulthood extends the grounds for such deciphering.[20] As Cornelia Dayton has found, Wheatley and her husband, John Peters, spent the early 1780s in a tangle of property disputes over the legitimacy of their kinship ties, inheritance, and social standing within a Massachusetts community of white freeholders.[21] Not only have Dayton's findings enlarged Wheatley's story where Odell described it as "blight[ed]," but they also offer fragmentary evidence that black children were at the center of this drama and at the fore of Wheatley's concern as she revised her second manuscript and reached the end of her life.[22] Indeed, an attempt to legally redress violence done to her infant child—and to protect that child from future harm—arises from this archive as one of Wheatley's last recorded acts.[23] With this different ending to Wheatley's story, something else can emerge: a different beginning to the story of American childhood, written and performed by Wheatley in commonplace verse, in her own grammar, and upon the law.

An American Primer

Ongoing myths of Wheatley's childhood—many arising from Odell's *Memoir*—emphasize the exceptional quality of Wheatley's early life in North America. In Odell's narration, it was seven-year-old Wheatley's purchase by John and Susanna Wheatley in 1761 that set her on a distinguished path of "gentle usage," education, and "ease and contentment."[24] Yet if we regard her capture and purchase as the defining frame for her young life, Wheatley's likeness to other black children in North America, not her distinction from them, supplies a common context from which to begin.[25] The difficulty of recovering more facts about Wheatley's early life in archival evidence underscores this commonness. Textual documentation of Wheatley's life—before she began leaving evidence in the form of her poems—is almost nonextant: her advertisement among captives being sold "cheap for Cash" in the *Boston Evening Post* and the name of the ship whose gruesome conditions she survived, which became her own.[26]

If the meager, violent record of Wheatley's childhood bears commonality with that of other enslaved black children—who appear almost exclusively in ledgers of property and violence during this period—this scarcity bears contrast to the archives of society and culture that contextualize, and sometimes individuate, the lives of white children in early America. By 1761, many Anglo-American children were learning to read and write using primers, spellers, and tokens for children; elites were enjoying the first iterations of modern children's books and handling new material playthings; and they were beginning to make their mark in and upon visual and literary culture in portraits that emphasized their beauty and in poems that exulted their innocence.[27] The asymmetry of white and black children's appearance in early American archives surfaces the deeper divergence of black and white children's material circumstances in this period. Yet rather than reflecting the settled fact of black and white children's disparate value in early America, the development of white children's distinct cultural imprint and the apparent absence of a corollary imprint for black children was in itself the production of this system of value. For despite the power of law to codify slavery's social relations, it did not wholly settle them. The American social grammar was settled into sense not by a single act but by repetition and reinforcement: in a body of law, in commerce, in culture, and in early American lessons.

Making black children commodifiable was not only a process of ascribing cash value—and cheapness—to them. It was also a process of learning to commodify. As Jennifer Morgan writes, seventeenth- and eighteenth-century enslavers did not insert African and African-descended people into an existing economic system. They instead produced their system of economics through the elaboration of slavery's logics of "numeracy," "trade," and "equivalency."[28] Those who staged the sale of black children conscripted those children into these logics, inviting buyers to learn black children's status as property through the transfer of money for their persons. Indeed, the Wheatleys' purchase of Phillis cannot, in any terms, be characterized as her merciful extraction from American slavery, because it was the act that confirmed her entrance into it. As the first (and it seems only) Anglo-American family to purchase Phillis, it was the Wheatleys who confirmed that she *could* be purchased.[29]

If buying and selling black children "cheap for Cash" was one site of social learning, white children's precious value was instilled by another pedagogy: the "ordinary road."[30] A practical method for literacy's instruction, the ordinary road was described by John Locke as the child's progression from the "hornbook, primer, Psalter, [and] Testament" to the Bible. This progression was to be augmented with imaginative excursions into Aesop's *Fables* and *Reynard the Fox* and complemented with writing instruction.³¹ As Jennifer Monaghan writes, the content of the "ordinary road" can "tell us much about the value system of seventeenth-century and early eighteenth-century America."³² That value system is not only to be found in the Christian teachings that filled and framed each text, however. The act of reading and writing impressed on white children the value of learning, affirming their rightful relation to books and their entitlement to learn and join the social world around them. Indeed, even the small act of writing one's name in a book instilled a lesson. As Patricia Crain notes, this was the beginning of proprietorship: children learned that signatories were those entitled to enter into contracts and to own things.³³ While instructing children in the procedures and practices of their social position, the ordinary road reinforced that there was a distance between the rudiments of children's practice and the power of men. Textual and social literacy became the necessary route between Locke's blank slate and his political compact, between subordination to authority and authority's exercise.

When Phillis Wheatley learned to read, to write, and to sign her English name, she appropriated the value of the blank slate as property, as promise, and as contract. To understand her transgression requires another appropriation too. Because where there might be an archive of Wheatley's education—of the primer she held or the copybook she wrote in—there is only another mythology: that her enslavers generously supported her learning and that their daughter, Mary (Polly) Wheatley, was her teacher.³⁴ Boston Congregationalists' promotion of literacy among those they enslaved supports the idea that the Wheatleys did, in fact, permit or even facilitate Phillis's learning.³⁵ Beyond this context, however, there is nothing to fully materialize how, after what hours of labor, over which texts, and toward what ambition Wheatley set herself to the task.

Without lending further significance to Polly's role in the story of Wheatley's education, the young white woman can still offer something to her story, for as both Vincent Carretta and David Waldstreicher note, the context of elite white girls' education offers some proxy of the culture and practice of literacy that most closely surrounded her.³⁶ As an elite white girl roughly ten years older than Phillis, Polly had likely experienced the great privileges and gendered limits of Boston's educational offerings. When Polly began her education, colonists in Massachusetts had some of the highest rates of literacy in British North America; however, their schooling was piecemeal, class based, and centered on educating white male children like her brother, Nathaniel.[37] Nevertheless, by a combination of home instruction and tutoring, Polly and her contemporaries progressed on a version of the ordinary road—first recognizing letters in a hornbook, then deciphering the progressive lessons of the *New England Primer*, the most popular and reprinted primer of the century.[38] Later, they practiced cursive by signing their names, by developing correspondences, and by transcribing popular verse into copybooks.[39]

By imagining Phillis retracing Polly's tracks on the ordinary road, we can materialize the incremental process by which she interpolated herself into the English language and learned the primary grammatical, cultural, and religious lessons of her Anglo-American world. Moreover, by reading in critical conjecture beside Wheatley, we can approach the American Grammar not as a symbolic code but more as the component parts of a pedagogical codex. Read in this manner, the lessons of the *Primer* offer a way to understand what held the American Grammar together at the level of its moveable syllables, parts of speech, and first "chain sentences," or the many tracings and retracings required to etch "hieroglyphics" across a social body over time.[40]

Containing songs and verse by the influential pedagogue Isaac Watts, the *Primer* blended evangelical religious teachings with the secular humanist framework to which Watts was an adherent: Locke's prescription that adults should impress ideas of increasing complexity over the "White paper" of a child's mind.[41] The *Primer*'s contents followed this logic, its early pages advancing from representing letters of the alphabet in sequence and at random, toward the construction of syllables, then words of increasing syllables, then sentences, rhymes, verse, and catechisms that communicated the *Primer*'s Protestant teachings: of salvation in God, dutiful work on earth, and obedience to one's father.[42] Yet as Crain demonstrates, even before culminating in these lessons, the early alphabetized pages of the *Primer* were already "capturing the situation of language in the Puritan world" of New England.[43] Indeed, alphabetization previewed the relations of children, men, women, animals, labor, and value in the seemingly scattershot arraying of nouns, adjectives, and adverbs:

Age   all   are   ape
Babe   beast   best   bold

Fa ther   fa mous   fe male   fu ture

Hei nous   hate ful   hu mane   hus band

A-bu-sing   a-mend-ing   ar-gu-ment
Bar bar ous   be ne fit   beg gar ly
Cal cu late   can dle stick   con foun ded

E di fy ing   e ver last ing   e vi dent ly[44]

Developing literacy from the *Primer* was a process not only of learning to produce meaning from each discrete word but of settling relational meanings between them while closing meaning left open in the space between "Babe" and "beast" and in the apertures of "fa ther," "fe male," "hu mane," and "bar bar ous."[45] If we imagine Polly and her peers as the *Primer*'s readers, we can understand how the textbook's lessons operated within a system of reinforcement wherein the meaning of each word, sentence, or lesson within the *Primer* gained corroboration in the social world outside of it—in each reader's assumption of their social position and in their integration in the larger domestic order, religious community, and colonial project of their surround. As clearly as a white child reader could separate themselves, a "babe," apart from a "beast" in the American landscape, they could materialize "father" as the figure whose authority ruled their domestic sphere. In this way, the *Primer*'s edification of individual children was also a process of building a social edifice—settling relations that had been rearranged in the crossing of English common law into colonial law and anchoring what was unsettled and reorganized in the making of racial slavery and freedom. The *Primer*'s textual reinforcement of the reader's social world depended on who that reader was, however. The interstices between the *Primer*'s words, meanings, and relations might not have closed with such finality for a child whom it neither hailed nor directly represented.

A child orphaned by slavery's violent traffic, who could make no claim upon any Anglo-American "father," and whose racialization endangered her in closer relation to the *Primer*'s "ape" or "beast" than to its "babe," Wheatley might have experienced not meaning's closure but instead an awareness of how meaning had been breached and written over in its travel to North America.[46] Indeed, every word, definition, or relation that the *Primer* presented to her in English was etched over a system of meanings and relations and an entire language that had been taken from Wheatley and that she had been stolen from. Before Wheatley's English literacy, there was not blankness but a translation of words, a shift in grammar, and a violent traffic in her personhood. In her literacy, there was the knowledge that a language, a grammar, and a social structure were linked and that they could be made or unmade together.

To imagine Wheatley reading between or against the *Primer*'s didactic meaning, questioning it, or actively subverting it is perhaps to travel too deeply into the speculative and too far from the extant archive we have of her life and work. Wheatley certainly followed the prescribed lessons of the ordinary road: she mastered the English language, she became a devoted Christian, and she espoused morals resonant with those of the white Puritan society in which she was enslaved. Yet she also, and audaciously, became a poet. Writing and circulating her poetry from at least the age of eleven, Wheatley granted herself authority to claim words unintended for her use, to circulate her own meaning through them, and to alter or altogether break the grammatical form of the sentence by arranging meaning in lines of verse. If the *Primer* was a major tool for disciplining, socializing, and hailing Anglo-American children into their status, property, freedom, and whiteness, Wheatley's simultaneous inculcation and estrangement from its lessons offered a different education: that by understanding the language, grammar, and social structure around her, she might carve a place for herself and that, though deprived of the blank slate, she might claim a blank space as her point of inscription.

More like Her Child

Wheatley's appropriated road to literacy was only the beginning of a more precipitous climb to literary virtuosity, public recognition, and relative mobility in a world beyond her enslaved enclosure. At the age of fourteen or fifteen in 1767, she published her first poem in the *Newport*

Mercury; in 1770, she penned a highly acclaimed elegy to Congregationalist minister George Whitefield, establishing a wide and prominent audience for her work. Out of this success, Wheatley worked methodically to obtain subscribers, attestations of support, and patronage, leading to the publication and wide circulation of her volume *Poems on Various Subjects, Religious and Moral* in 1773.[47]

And within months of publishing *Poems*, the twenty-one-year-old poet managed to secure her freedom. As Carretta posits, Wheatley's freedom was leveraged carefully atop the success of *Poems*, as it extended Wheatley's ties, audience, and backing beyond her enslavers and into an elite antislavery milieu on both sides of the Atlantic.[48] Wheatley's travels to London in 1773 and her acquaintance with antislavery advocates, including Granville Sharp, may have provided her with critical leverage to gain freedom from John Wheatley.[49] However much Wheatley's manumission depended on, and facilitated, her disentanglement from her enslavers, Wheatley did not turn away from them once freed. "Now upon [her] own footing," as she put it, Wheatley nevertheless continued to enunciate an affective connection to the white Wheatley family.[50] When Susanna Wheatley died in 1774, Phillis Wheatley expressed her loss in terms that knit them closer together, describing her grief as like that of a child mourning her parent. Writing to her frequent correspondent, an enslaved woman named Obour Tanner, Wheatley conveyed the affective complexity of her relationship to Susanna while also consolidating its meaning—and legacy—in familial terms:

> I have lately met with a great trial in the death of my mistress, let us imagine the loss of a Parent, Sister, or Brother the tenderness of all these were united in her,—I was a poor little outcast & stranger when she took me in, not only into her house but I presently became, a sharer in their most tender affections, I was treated by her more like her child than her servant, no opportunity was left unimprov'd, of giving me the best of advice, but in terms how tender! how engaging! this I hope ever to keep in remembrance.[51]

Narrativizing her entrance into the Wheatley household as taking refuge in Susanna's "tender" care, Wheatley obscured the deliberate transactions that secured her there as property, eschewing reference to her "slave" status entirely. Instead, Wheatley granted herself the more mutable status of the "little outcast" or "stranger" whose position, she suggested, had been renegotiated by "tender affections." And indeed, the flow of tender affections had reshaped not only her position in the household but Susanna's as well. Lamenting the loss of Susanna as like that of a "Parent, Sister, or Brother," Wheatley underscored her familial tie to Susanna, yet rather than adopting her as "mother" alone, she triply crossed through the title of "mistress" with three familial roles.[52] In Wheatley's characterization, strangers could become family, and the entrance of a stranger could remake family in an unfamiliar form.

While writing a space for herself within the Wheatleys' sphere of "tender affections," however, Wheatley did not entirely efface her enslavement in their household. Placing terms of "servant" and "child" into a relation of simile, Wheatley calibrated her station between the two, attenuating the intimacy of familial bonds by the acknowledgment of her servitude. Moreover, when she suggested to Tanner "let us imagine the loss of a Parent, Sister, or Brother," she raised the real, not imaginative, history of loss that attended her enslavement and Tanner's. Tanner, like Wheatley, could more likely recollect than imagine such a loss of kin.[53]

Wheatley's writing about Susanna can be read as an authentic attempt to describe a relationship established between slavery's structure of subjection and the affection that increasingly bonded white domestic relations. Yet while weighing Wheatley's words to Tanner for what they convey about Wheatley's emotional life, we can also understand them as part of her strategic claims to childhood, family, and freedom. She had been "treated by [Susanna] more like her child than her servant," and this treatment meant something.[54] Closing her musings on Susanna by stating, "This I hope ever to keep in remembrance," Wheatley signaled her effort to maintain ties to the Wheatleys: to be remembered as one of them and to be remembered by them.

The stakes of such remembrance were, as Wheatley likely understood, vital to her survival, because the freedom that Wheatley achieved was, by slavery's design, extremely precarious. Hoping to be remembered "like [Susanna's] child," was, in the context of early black freedom's exigencies, an entreaty to remain in the sphere of obligation, care, and concern that parent-child relations connoted.[55] Placing Wheatley's bid for familial remembrance chronologically after her manumission underscores the critical orientation of her hope: Wheatley was retroactively claiming the status of a free child—to whom concern and inheritance were extended even into adulthood—and not the status of the manumitted bondsperson, to whom nothing was obliged. Susanna had apportioned more affection to her than was due to a servant. In doing so, she had made Wheatley *more like* her child. Wheatley suggested that if this was Susanna's will in life, its implications should be carried forth after her death.

Claiming her place as a "sharer in their most tender affections," did not, however, facilitate her share in the Wheatley inheritance. Despite Wheatley's statements of familial remembrance in this and other correspondence, John Wheatley did not write Phillis into his will.[56] When he died in 1778, Phillis was left with little support beyond her literary royalties.[57] In light of this, Wheatley's 1774 reference to Susanna's death as a "great trial" resounds as an acknowledgment both of emotional turmoil and of the precarity brought about by Susanna's loss. It perhaps conveys Wheatley's knowledge that in the absence of Susanna's favor, her already tenuous status would become even more so. Indeed, taking this as Wheatley's self-described "great trial" underscores again that Wheatley perceived the facilitating power of white women and their domestic relations—as much as the signatures of white men—in gaining, and keeping, her footing.

Wheatley's claim is as instructive in its failure as in its audacity, because, in asserting that she had been "like [her enslaver's] child," she tested her period's settling common sense: that the enslaved were like children. The lack of traction gained by Wheatley's claim, however, clarifies that this common sense did not make the kind of sense one could stand on; moreover, if it was an equivalency, it was not a measure of what obligations, care, or recompense was owed to the enslaved. The claim that black people were like children was not rooted in white childhood's elaborated endowments of affection, care, education, inheritance, freedom, or futurity. Instead, the claim that the enslaved were like children rested on childhood's deficits: what children were said to lack (reason) and what they could therefore be deprived of (consent).[58]

Indeed, the child's usefulness as a measure rested here, in their index of irrationality's political and social consequences, not in the implication of irrationality alone. For white Americans did not necessarily need a reference point for black irrationality; by their geographic origins, alternative systems of knowledge, and different physiognomy, people of African descent were already suspect within Enlightenment and post-Enlightenment conceptions of reason. As Wynter explicates, because Man's reason was so narrowly attached to the European figure "of the mercantile upper bourgeoisie" and so broadly "absolutized" as "reason-in-general," the arena of reason's "lack state" was necessarily wide—as wide, in fact, as the rest of the world and all its human and animal inhabitants other than Man himself.[59] Children, however, nevertheless played a key role in measuring the nonreasoning world and domesticating its relations. White children were *known* to Man. They were subject to his increasing authority in his household and under the law, and they were also, increasingly, the object of his study. As the most fully rendered and least contested figures of reason's lack state, they supplied the "ratiomorphic apparatus" by which to negatively measure "natural reason and the degrees of its possession."[60] Indeed, Locke put children to this purpose in his *Essay concerning Human Understanding*. Stringing "*Children, Ideots, Savages, and the grosly Illiterate*" into an affiliation, he used the child—his subject described in detail and depth—to give schematic coherence to several other groups over whom Man sought to naturalize his authority and from whom he sought to withhold the exercise of power.[61] As children's ignorance formed the basis of their declining political standing over the course of the seventeenth and eighteenth centuries, the consequences of being like children were settling on the same grounds.

Childhood was an unstable, contradictory ground to settle on, however. Even as children defined reason's lack state, they also promised its development. While one could ostensibly secure the social subjection of "ideots, savages, and the grosly illiterate" on the basis of the ignorance they supposedly shared with children, the joining of this collective implied an equal and contrary possibility: that, like children, these groups could develop reason, overcome gross illiteracy, and ascend to Man's political status. To maintain childhood's use as a measure of subjection demanded the nimble choreography of extending and suspending childhood's meanings at once.

When, a year after Wheatley's death, Thomas Jefferson defamed her poetry as "below the dignity of criticism," he invoked and dismissed

Wheatley within such choreography. Placing his comments on Wheatley in the midst of Query XIV of his *Notes on the State of Virginia* (1785), Jefferson affiliated Wheatley with the "faculties of reason" he judged "inferior" among "the blacks" and with the less-than-"elementary" artistry he claimed as hallmarks of her race.[62] In his remarks, Jefferson cast his indictment of black reason into the broader interspecies terrain of reason's lack, marking both deficient reason and excessive sensation as indications of immutable racial inferiority. "In reason much inferior" yet too "ardent" in sexual expression, Jefferson suggested the greater affinity of black people to the "Oranootan" than to Man, whose "natural history" he sought to exile them from.[63]

Jefferson sought to expel black people from Man's political future, too, warning that the republic would be irrevocably "stain[ed]" if a population so "want[ing] of fore-thought" was incorporated as part of the American political body.[64] He enlisted a particular cast of "guardians" to defend against this specter. These guardians were also understood to be ignorant, wanting of forethought, elementary in understanding, and ill equipped to govern. Yet considering their ignorance as blankness, Jefferson saw latent potential upon which the nation's future could be inscribed. To "provide an education adapted to the years, to the capacity, and the condition of every one"—every white child—was the means by which Jefferson sought both to manifest their "freedom and happiness" and to secure the "future order." As he explained, it was by instructing "all the [white] children of the state [in] reading, writing and common arithmetic" that they would become "the ultimate guardians of their own liberty."[65]

In 1788, three years after the first publication of *Notes*, Jefferson negotiated a different formulation of meaning through the linked logic of white children, freedom, childlikeness, and bondage. "To give liberty to, or rather, to abandon persons whose habits have been formed in slavery," would be, Jefferson insisted, "like abandoning children."[66] Here, Jefferson signaled how the common sense of black childlikeness could cover its own contradictions: not by their explanation but by their concealment in childhood's emerging culture of sentiment. Invoking the charged figure of the vulnerable, dependent, and innocent white child—and then abandoning that child—Jefferson made use of white childhood's growing cultural force, diverting the question of black freedom behind the affective drama of white children's suffering. Confusing the two would become one of the most malleable political means of enforcing slavery's perpetuation in the coming antebellum period.

Indeed, even as the child's place, and value, in the early American order sedimented, the meaning attached to childhood remained politically flexible. By shifting its empirical, legal, or cultural emphasis, one could establish or undermine racial hierarchy; make a claim for social recognition or against the exercise of civic power; or conjure, or conceal, abuse. Affiliated with others, cast into the future, or placed in danger, the child could naturalize a range of disparate social relations and could recode slavery's juridical and social inventions as common sense. Between Jefferson's "guardians of liberty" and his "abandon[ed] children," as between Locke's "*Children, Ideots, Savages*" and the *Primer*'s "Age," "ape," "babe," and "beast," the child delivered meaning by proximity, by the lack they represented, or by the future they protected.[67]

To move the child and their attendant meaning required facility in the early American social and cultural grammar—an awareness that discursive flexibility was as essential to racial power as was its legal inscription and violent enforcement. Indeed, to invoke, or locate, the child was to perform a certain poetics within that grammar, as Jefferson's own contortion of terms demonstrates. Undermining Wheatley's status *as* a poet was part of this effort too. It was a strike against her own, and differing, meaning making. Wheatley—the poet whom Jefferson refused to recognize as such—was not only dexterous in the American Grammar but imaginative and daring with its use. Within the child's constellation of increasingly recognizable attributes, sentiments, and relations, Wheatley plotted a different potential and steered childhood toward an alternate future.

Such, Such My Case

Locating childhood in Wheatley's poetry does not require speculative reading or searching for abstracted meaning but instead recognizing the significant presence of children as her subjects and of child-parent relations as some of her central themes. Wheatley's earliest extant poem, composed around the age of eleven, was an elegy to the deceased (adult) children of her neighbor.[68] If we trace her writings on children and parental loss forward, a pattern of imaginative, affective, and political invention appears. The elegies in *Poems*—to Nancy, James, Charles, and unnamed children; her retelling of Apollo's murder of Niobe's children; and her invocation of her own parent's "excruciating" pain upon her enslavement—demonstrate that Wheatley did not take up childhood as a settled or commonplace subject but understood its emergent power and set it to her own use.[69]

The several elegies to white children in *Poems* denote Wheatley's engagement in Puritan discourses on child death and salvation that informed and likely instructed her. As a young reader, Wheatley may have encountered this tradition in *A Token for Children*, a text of related pedagogical use and equal popularity to the *New England Primer*.[70] Adapted by Congregationalist minister Cotton Mather from James Janeway's English text of the same name, *A Token* delivered a series of hagiographies that described children who found salvation before their deaths, leading to their "eternal sabbath."[71] As Diana Pasulka has argued, these texts—intended to cultivate piety in child and adult readers—had the additional effect of laying the groundwork for the cult of white child death in sentimental American literature.[72] Placing Wheatley as an early interlocutor in this lineage, however, reveals the poet's critical contributions and interventions in the making of sentimental childhood.

While centered, too, on children's ascent from their earthly parents to God, Wheatley made the child's journey more capacious and fantastic, granting children greater autonomy and knowledge in their ascent and upon their arrival. And while her lament at the tragedy of severed family ties inversely tightened their cultural import, Wheatley ultimately spilled the family's relations outward, reordering them. Releasing children into the splendor of churning heavens, Wheatley imagined children like Charles Eliot in conditions of radical autonomy and knowledge unimaginable in earthly arrangements:

> Through airy roads he wings his instant flight
> To purer regions of celestial light;
> Enlarg'd he sees unnumber'd systems roll,
> Beneath him sees the universal whole,
> Planets on planets run their destin'd round,
> And circling wonders fill the vast profound

> Th' ethereal now, and now th' empyreal skies
> With growing splendors strike his wond'ring eyes:
> The angels view him with delight unknown,
> Press his soft hand, and seat him on his throne;
> Then smiling thus. "To this divine abode,
> The seat of saints, of seraphs, and of God,
> Thrice welcome thou." The raptur'd babe replies,
> "Thanks to my God, who snatch'd me to the skies,
> E'er vice triumphant had possess'd my heart,
> E'er yet the tempter had beguil'd my heart,
> E'er yet on sin's base actions I was bent,
> E'er yet I knew temptation's dire intent;
> E'er yet the lash for horrid crimes I felt,
> E'er vanity had led my way to guilt,
> But, soon, arriv'd at my celestial goal,
> Full glories rush on my expanding soul."
> Joyful he spoke: exulting cherubs round
> Clapt their glad wings, the heav'nly vaults resound.[73]

In Wheatley's imagining, Charles defies physical limitation, space, and time. From an "enlarged" position, he views "the universal whole," with its "planets on planets," "unnumber'd systems," and "circling wonders."[74] Speaking with exultant rectitude about the mercy of his death, Charles gains a clear voice with which to address the reader, his heavenly audience, and his earthly family. When the poem returns after great length to Charles's parents, the poet offers consolation in the form of an admonition, asking, "Would you tear him from the realms above / By thoughtless wishes, and prepost'rous love?"[75] Positioning herself as arbiter, Wheatley boldly establishes her poetic voice as the mediator between Charles's expansive fate and his parents' desires. In Wheatley's articulation, children were not merely spared worldly sin in death; they were liberated from domestic bonds and developmental logics. Between the conventions of hagiography and elegy, Wheatley crafted a version of childhood that was recognizable in its innocence, preciousness, and piety. But in the celestial heights she ascended, Wheatley created a vast intellectual cognizance for children that defied their social position and, indeed, prefigured the romantic work of figures like Wordsworth, whose mourning of childhood—and its "visionary gleam"—contains shadings of Wheatley.[76] Yet Wheatley's reverent views of childhood contained, and facilitated, something else too: her own voice and the ability to insert it into the tender affections and private grief of white families.

Wheatley's interventions are apparent not only in their departure from the poetic culture of child mourning that *A Token* represented but also in their line-by-line distinction from contemporary poetry composed to mourn *specific* children. Charles Eliot was the son of a prominent Boston family, and just as his death incited Wheatley to verse, it also prompted Ruth Barrell Andrews, Charles's aunt, to compose her own elegy. As Wendy Raphael Roberts notes—based on Andrews's personal correspondence—Andrews demurred to circulate her funeral poem widely within the manuscript circuit that she and Wheatley shared, believing her poem redundant to Wheatley's.[77] Wheatley and Andrews had written very different poems, however. Whereas Wheatley celebrated the widened knowledge of the heavenly "raptur'd babe," Andrews recurrently focalized a different attribute of Charles: the innocence, purity, and whiteness of his "mind" and "soul":

> To me your child was infinitely dear
> As now is witness'd by the falling tear:
> 'Tis for ourselves alone, we breathe these sighs!
> Or find the drops just starting from our eies!
> Think my dear sister that this stroke severe
> Firmly evinces the Almightys care!
> His mind all innocence, no vice could stain,
> The pure ideas of an infant's brain.
> Thus in a state of purity within
> His soul unsullied with the marks of sin
> Our heav'nly father view'd him with delight
> And then withdrew him, from a parents sight.
>
> . . .
>
> Had he still flourish'd to mature age
> His life 'tis possible, on this vast stage
> Had not been equal to the hopes you form'd
> From early beauties which his face adorn'd.

> Had *vanity* o'er Virtue gain'd controul
> And soil'd the snowey whiteness of his soul.
> You in the anguish of your heart had cried
> "Oh! that in infancy my Charles had died!
> When he fair spotless, on my bosom lean'd
> And his young mind with dawning Virtue beam'd."[78]

For Andrews, the "pure ideas" of Charles's "infant's Brain" and the unsoiled "snowey whiteness" of his soul were the features that defined him in life and in death. It was his mother's "anguish" and "crie[s]" that Andrews sought to give voice to, not "fair spotless" Charles himself, who was "withdr[awn]" in silence and eternal purity before any sin could tarnish the "hopes [his mother] form'd" for his future.[79] Though Andrews's poem, like Wheatley's, sends Charles to God's "just" embrace, the poem remains aligned with the domestic relations, concerns, and affects of his family on earth.[80] Andrews, with Charles's parents, shares a "falling tear."[81] Wheatley uses "tear" in a different sense: the act of "prepost'rous love" that would wrench Charles back from God. In this disapproval and elsewhere, Wheatley grants herself an alternative—and elevated—vantage point from which to voice contending authority. In her poem "On the Death of a Young Lady of Five Years of Age," Wheatley—first in "Nancy's" voice and then in her own—"check[s]" the grief of Nancy's parents and directs them to "bow" in God's reverence:[82]

> Her morning sun, which rose divinely bright,
> Was quickly mantled with the gloom of night;
> But hear in heav'n's blest bow'rs your *Nancy* fair
> And learn to imitate her language there.
> "Thou, Lord, whom I behold with glory crown'd,
> By what sweet name, and in what tuneful sound
> Wilt thou be prais'd? Seraphic pow'rs are faint
> Infinite love and majesty to paint.
> To thee let all their grateful voices raise,
> And saints and angels join their songs of praise."
>
> Perfect in bliss she from her heav'nly home
> Looks down, and smiling beckons you to come;

Why then, fond parents, why these fruitless groans?
Restrain your tears, and cease your plaintive moans
Freed from a world of sin, and snares, and pain,
Why would you wish your daughter back again?
No—bow resign'd. Let hope your grief control,
And check the rising tumult of the soul.
Calm in the prosperous, and adverse day,
Adore the God who gives and takes away;
Eye him in all, his holy name revere,
Upright your actions, and your hearts sincere,
Till having sail'd through life's tempestuous sea,
And from its rocks, and boist'rous billows free,
Yourselves, safe landed on the blissful shore
Shall join your happy babe to part no more.[83]

Commanding Nancy's parents to "learn to imitate her language," Wheatley grants Nancy eloquent authority over the meaning of her death and heavenly arrival.[84] Yet while reversing the pedagogical roles of child as imitator and adult as instructor, Wheatley in fact routes her *own* language, instruction, and authority through Nancy's words. And while consoling Nancy's parents with the promise that one day, "safe landed on the blissful shore / Shall join your happy babe to part no more," Wheatley also chides them—as she does the Eliots—to "restrain [their] tears, and cease [their] plaintive moans."[85] While beckoning toward sentimental childhood through Nancy's "enraptur'd innocen[ce]," Wheatley ultimately denies white children the spilling of tears that Andrews's poem gives way to—tears that, as Bernstein explicates, would come to define white children's sentimental power over the next century.[86]

There was one child for whom parental cries and grief were not to be stifled, however. In her poem "To the Right Honourable William, Earl of Dartmouth, His Majesty's Principal Secretary of State for North-America &c," Wheatley crafted an emphatic, ongoing narrative of the grief without end felt by *her* parent after her childhood abduction and enslavement. One of Wheatley's more widely read poems, her address to the Earl of Dartmouth has been viewed as a significant condemnation of slavery and as a welcome counterpoint to her apparent Christian acceptance of it in "On Being Brought from Africa to America."[87] However much attention has been focused on this poem's exaltation of freedom, its coherence around her own stolen, unfree, and mourned childhood is the remarkable crux of the poem's critical import:

> Should you, my lord, while you peruse my song,
> Wonder from whence my love of Freedom sprung,
> Whence flow these wishes for the common good,
> By feeling hearts alone best understood,
> I, young in life, by seeming cruel of fate
> Was snatch'd from Afric's fancy'd happy seat:
> What pangs excruciating must molest,
> What sorrows labour in my parent's breast?
> Steel'd was that soul and by no misery mov'd
> That from a father seized his babe belov'd:
> Such, such my case. And can I then but pray
> Others may never feel tyrannic sway?[88]

Deriving a claim for sovereignty in the colonies from her intimate experience of despotism, Wheatley did not merely reference slavery's tyranny; she dramatized slavery's injustice through its breaking of black parent-child bonds. Sounding the "pangs" and "sorrows" that continued to "molest" and "labour in [her] parent's breast," Wheatley enveloped her reader in endless anguish that could not be remedied.[89] Indeed, the source of her parent's sorrow—Wheatley's kidnapping into slavery—could not be reversed even by her freedom. In Wheatley's telling, this grief was alive, inconsolable, and without resolution. While Nancy's family would reunite on heaven's "blissful shore," the Middle Passage that separated Wheatley from her family could not be meaningfully recrossed in life or, potentially, in death.[90] Having converted to a Christianity not shared with her parents (to her knowledge), Wheatley could not take comfort in a reunion in the "eternal sabbath," guarded, as it was, by redemption in her Lord.[91]

Despite mapping the impossible gulf of her parent's grief, Wheatley's poem also performs acts of reconnection against slavery's estrangement. In shifting from describing her unspecified "parent" to identifying her "father" as the poem's bearer of grief, Wheatley reattached herself to the patrilineage that the American Grammar's juridical apparatus denied her. Calling herself her father's "babe belov'd," she claimed both patrilineage *and* preciousness, the guarded legal and cultural birthrights of elite white American children.⁹² Evidence of Wheatley's revision to this poem demonstrates that she drafted, then deepened, these claims to childhood. Between this poem's publication in the *New York Journal* and in *Poems*, Wheatley moved from referring to "the parent" to "my parent" and from naming herself her father's "much belov'd" to his "babe belov'd."⁹³

Lamenting "Such, such my case," Wheatley narrated the grammatical impossibility of black childhood into Anglo-American legibility and then claimed it for herself.⁹⁴ Indeed, centering her critique of tyrannical power on her own family dispossession, Wheatley layered the personal and political: by connecting the tragedy of her family separation to tyranny, she implied a larger claim that tied black family to freedom. In doing so, she inaugurated a tradition of African American literary claims to childhood that declared the rightful bonds of family as the antithesis of bondage. Like Wheatley, enslaved, fugitive, and free black writers after her would stake abolitionist appeals on interlocking claims of childhood, family, and freedom—a political groundwork that Wheatley had set in verse.

Placing Wheatley's claims for black family and freedom alongside her claim to have been "like [Susanna's] child" underscores Wheatley's adaptive approach to the American Grammar. She understood that to claim the child's place—stolen from a black family or captive within a white—was to make a bid for freedom. Not freedom premised on a myth of independence, but freedom that occasioned reciprocal care, social recognition, and that entailed material security. Indeed, both in her poem "To the Right Honourable William, Earl of Dartmouth" and in her letter mourning Susanna to Tanner, Wheatley directly contravened the US founders' assertion that freedom and independence were synonymous. Just as white men's early American freedom depended on an extensive web of subjection and extraction of those they subordinated, Wheatley's own freedom would depend on her ability to constellate a network of support, or a family, around herself. After the publication of these poems, after her loss of Susanna, and after her lack of remembrance by Susanna's heirs, Wheatley's survival continued to hinge upon, and falter with, the relations of black family and white property on which she established her footing. To survive as a free black writer—and to make a free black family—demanded more than writing into the blank spaces of the American Grammar. It required that she perform radical acts within the domestic sphere and make novel demands before the law.

An Enduring Memoir, a Missing Manuscript

For all the poems we have to reconstruct Wheatley's writing on childhood, some remain critically missing. Her poems to her own children: Did she write about them when they lived, and did she elegize them upon their deaths? Wheatley's maternal grief, the existence of her children's graves, and the names that might mark those graves remain unknown. But now we do know, with greater certainty, that Wheatley gave birth to, and buried, at least two children.[95] We also know, with some likelihood, where. Dayton's discovery of court records pertaining to John Peters and Phillis Wheatley Peters's residence in Middleton, Massachusetts, between 1780 and 1783 has given a location to Wheatley's "lost years" and to the place of her maternal losses.[96] If there are graves, they might be there, in Middleton. This was the place where Wheatley and her husband sought to establish themselves as free black landowners, a place where they immediately faced resistance, and a place from which they were eventually forced out, conceding their land, home, and status.

Evidence of the Peterses' protracted struggle in Middleton opens a long-closed chapter. For not only have these years of Wheatley's life remained without clear documentation; they were also "blight[ed]" by the popular *Memoir* of Wheatley's life written fifty years after her death. Publishing the *Memoir and Poems of Phillis Wheatley, a Native African and a Slave* in 1834, Margaretta Matilda Odell professed intimate knowledge of Wheatley's life based on her status as a "collateral descendant" of the white Wheatley family.[97] As Dayton, Carra Glatt, and others have noted, much of Odell's narrative of Wheatley's life cannot be corroborated.[98] Odell's *Memoir*, nevertheless, became the foundation for Wheatley's remembrance to nineteenth-century readers, and for her biography in the twentieth and twenty-first centuries.[99] In Odell's account, Wheatley's "ill-omened union" with "unworthy," "indolent," and "unsuccessful" Peters in 1778 was the fateful event that precipitated the poet's early death at thirty-one and the years of "misery" and "blight" that preceded it.[100] According to Odell, "little" beyond this "remain[ed] to be told."[101]

Casting Wheatley's self-determined adulthood into obscurity, Odell instead shone sentimental attention on the "early and happy days" Wheatley spent within the home of her enslavers.[102] Explaining that "we cannot ascertain that [Wheatley] ever received any formal manumission," Odell wrote over Wheatley's freedom yet assured readers that "the chains which bound her to her master and mistress were the golden links of love, and the silken bands of gratitude. She had a child's place in their house and in their hearts."[103] It was in this child's place, and "before her mind was matured," that Wheatley's poetic "genius" arose, according to Odell.[104] This "genius" was not, in Odell's estimation, a common product of childhood, nor of its ordinary road. Instead, it was the result of some "peculiar structure of mind," the origins of which could not be traced. This structure was not a blank slate ready for inscription but a faulty one, where impressions did not take. Wheatley, it seems, was never able to retain "impressions" of "her own productions."[105]

According to Odell, Wheatley compensated for her mind's unreliability by writing in feverish fits—lest "one fancy" rush in front of another and cause the prior inscription to vanish from its "occup[ied]" place.[106] Not the product of steady practice, nor was Wheatley's writing the result of a thorough American education. For though she credited Polly as Wheatley's instructor, Odell expressed that she "very much doubt[ed] if [Wheatley] ever had any grammatical instruction or any knowledge of the structure or idiom of the English language," proposing instead that Wheatley's "singular habit of mind" derived from "lack of early discipline."[107] In Odell's story, Wheatley's "literary efforts" were products of an unruly and unusual intellect, not of Wheatley's careful study or grammatical precision. The *Memoir* suggests that without slavery's "golden links" to hold it fast, Wheatley's genius might have dissipated, never marking the page.

Versions of Odell's *Memoir* proliferated in adaptations and republications across the 1830s and 1840s, leading to Wheatley's subsequent epitaph as the "sooty prodigy" and to a broader cultural understanding of the poet as a "curiosity."[108] These narratives not only circulated in published form; they seeped into a private, pedagogical sphere. Transcribed by a young white woman within the pages of a friendship album, Odell's biography was rebound as an object of white women's affective connection and shared practice of literacy. In a copybook kept in the 1830s and 1840s by a Pennsylvania schoolteacher, Deborah B. Smith, a friend or pupil inscribed a "Biographical Sketch of Phillis Wheatly [sic]" between other sentimental poems and prose. Bearing a close resemblance to the *Memoir*, the "Sketch" repeated Odell's claim that "[Wheatley's] powers of memory did not equal her other powers of mind" and further that she was possessed of "no common intellect." The writer of this sketch, like Odell, assured her reader that, though enslaved, Wheatley had been treated by her enslavers "as a child."[109]

That Wheatley would be so assuredly enveloped in a child's place in antebellum white women's imagination is a violent irony. Not only because such claims diminished her adulthood and struck her freedom from the record but also because when Wheatley had sought to claim such a kinship tie on her own terms, she had been denied. The dissonance of her memorialization within the white Wheatley household is even more striking when placed in relation to the circumstances of her lost years of struggle. Because at stake in the Peterses' fight in Middleton was the same question: whether John Peters had a legitimate claim to the property of his former enslavers—whether, before the law, he would be treated more like their child.

Wheatley and Peters moved from Boston to Middleton, Massachusetts, on the express extension of such a claim. Following the death of his former enslaver, John Wilkins, Peters accepted the request of Wilkins's widow, Naomi, to assist in the upkeep of her home and large agricultural estate. Peters had been enslaved on this farm, laboring for no compensation for the Wilkinses from the time of his birth until his young adulthood.[110] Since that time, however, his relationship to the Wilkins family, his status, and his prospects for returning to their farm had changed. As a free man, he had renegotiated his relationship with Naomi Wilkins, proving himself an adroit farm manager, caretaker, and confidant. With a disabled daughter (also named Naomi) but no living sons of their own, the Wilkinses had come to rely on Peters as something *like* one. Or, indeed, as one—for as Waldstreicher notes, there are some indications that Peters may have been a blood relation to his enslavers.[111] Whatever their submerged connections, the senior Naomi Wilkins created a new formal connection by deeding Peters the Wilkins home and over a hundred acres of its surrounding land on the basis that Peters would maintain the farm and her comfort.[112]

Accepting Wilkins's agreement propelled John Peters and Phillis Wheatley Peters into new roles: as the Wilkins's legitimate legatees, as black propertied members of the white Middleton community, and as heads of a growing household. For as Dayton relates, Wheatley likely gave birth to a child immediately before, or just after, their arrival in Middleton. Joining Naomi Wilkins, her daughter, and her enslaved servant, Dinah Cubber, in the Wilkins home were John, Phillis, their infant, and a nurse hired to attend to Phillis and her newborn.[113] This unusual assembly was unsettling to Naomi Wilkins's extended relatives and community, who legally protested the widow's decision. It also quickly became dissatisfactory to Wilkins herself, who sought to reestablish order and regain her prior status. Wilkins had lost a great deal of status in her agreement with Peters. She had formerly enjoyed her role as a prominent landowner's wife who could command the labor of those whom she enslaved. Now she was a widow who depended, for her comfort and care, on the favor of a man she had formerly enslaved. John and Phillis, by contrast, had ascended from being children enslaved within white homes to being the heads of a white estate where they placed *their* free black child at the household's center. Cubber's status seemed to remain stagnant yet was changed too. In his will, John Wilkins had promised that the family would afford her lifetime support if she remained to care for his daughter and wife.[114] When conflict emerged between Naomi Wilkins and Peters—and it did almost immediately—Cubber aligned herself with the old order's promises and against the new.

While the details of the Wilkins-Peters conflict remain somewhat opaque, Phillis's role—as both writer and mother—was central. It was Wilkins and Cubber's desire that Wheatley Peters contribute more time to the household's labor—and presumably less to her child and her writing—that caused initial and corrosive bitterness.[115] In August 1780, Naomi Wilkins began court proceedings to eject the Peterses from her former home and land, alleging John Peters's ill treatment of her, her and Cubber's overwork, and his mismanagement of the farm.[116] White landowners united their interest behind Wilkins. In a list of signatures as fateful as that which prefaced *Poems*, fifty-nine white freeholders signed an attestation against John Peters's character.[117] He was not, in the view of Wilkins or the Middleton townspeople, like a son but an interloper and now an adversary. Though they struggled to maintain their hold on the Wilkins farm, the Peterses lost their claim and eventually retreated to Boston in 1783, landless and in debt.[118]

As Dayton points out, they lost far more than money and status in the process, as one or both of the infants Wheatley gave birth to in Middleton died there.[119] The deaths of these children were not necessarily connected to the struggle that raged in their household. But it is without a doubt that one child's life was almost destroyed in it. In June 1782, John Peters brought a claim against Dinah Cubber before the Essex County Court "for assaulting the infant child of the said John Peters, & with force and Arms Attempting to distroy the Life of said child"[120] (figure 1.1). There is no further record to render the violent act Peters referred to, what led to it, or who stopped its completion. Neither is there a clear record of the child who suffered Cubber's harm. We do not know this child's name or age or whether the harm they suffered contributed to their subsequent death. Yet even without context or explanation, this fragment is a shocking and extraordinary record.

It is also, on some level, ordinary. For when black children appear in early American archives, it is most often through acts of violence—in their traffic and sale or in the compounded violence that records their deaths as losses of property.[121] Yet if this record reinscribes the archival link between black children and harm done to them, it also intervenes in it. Because unlike most black children in archives of early America, this child appears in the act of their parent's legal redress of that harm. In bringing his suit against Cubber and before the court, Peters—likely acting with Wheatley—asserted the wrongfulness of Cubber's violence and the *right* of his child to protection. At once, Peters's suit called his child's welfare, and his parental right to defend it, into existence. The Peterses did not take further recorded action against Cubber, who it seems never faced any penalty.[122] Yet even as an unfulfilled legal censure, the Peterses outrage before the court registered their extraordinary demand that, in 1782, black children should be free and protected under American law.

John Peters and Phillis Wheatley Peters's claim required an audacious assertion of free black family in direct refusal of the American Grammar. And yet for all the power behind this act, we only have one sentence from which to retell it (for now). Moreover, even as the extensive court documents

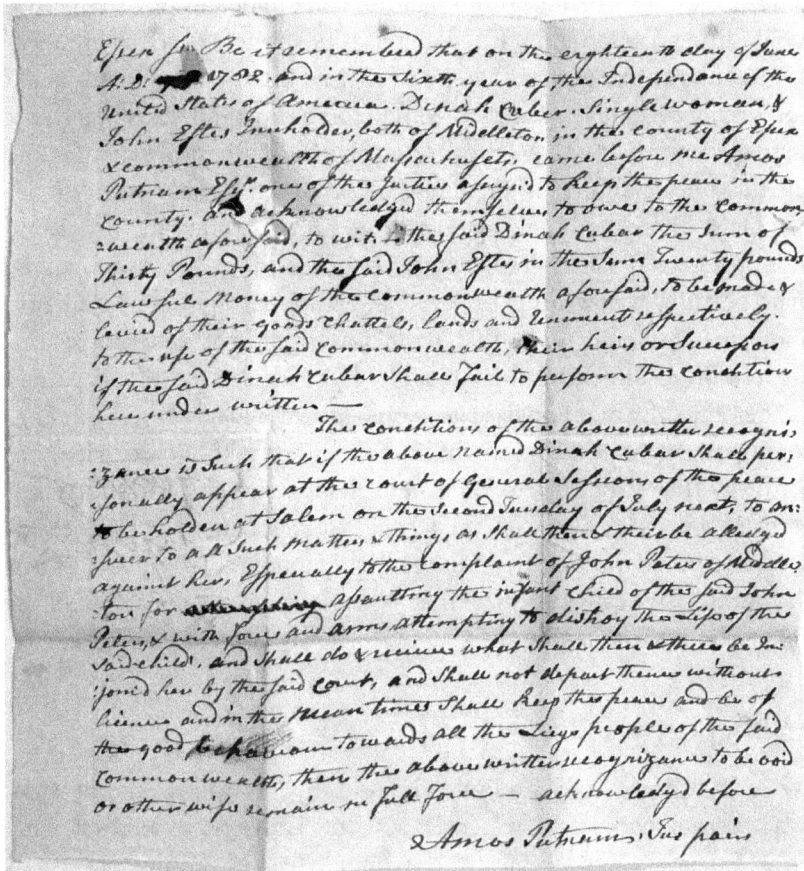

Figure 1.1. [Record of the Peterses' Complaint against Dinah Cubber]. Court of General Sessions of the Peace, Essex County, files, Dinah Cober's recognizance, July 1782. JU-SJC/GEN.ES/series 003. Massachusetts Supreme Judicial Court Archives, Massachusetts Archives, Boston, Massachusetts.

pertaining to the Wilkins-Peters dispute give wider context to the drama surrounding this act, they do so while entirely marginalizing Wheatley as an actor in the drama, leaving her unnamed or referencing her only as "wife."[123] If we had more letters that Wheatley wrote during this period, we might gain a deeper knowledge of what transpired, of how she felt amid such strife, and of her personal role in her children's care and protection. And if we had her manuscript, we might understand more.

Wheatley's lost manuscript might not contain details of, or reference to, her time in Middleton. If the manuscript she advertised in 1784 was the exact same manuscript that she advertised in 1779, its contents would necessarily predate the Peterses' Middleton period and, most likely, the births of any children. Moreover, regardless of when or whether she amended her manuscript, she might never have given comment on her free black family's struggle against white property and power, because her readers were largely representatives of the same. Yet if we imagine that Wheatley was writing, or revising, within her besieged Middleton home, the possibility forms that her manuscript might have subtly commented on or alluded to her struggle. Her elegies might have gained further empathy or emphasis based on her own maternal grief. And her commentaries on freedom might have expanded with the experience of her own. The list of titles to Wheatley's manuscript gives no suggestion of this. Yet if we consider the unlikely place of her lament on black childhood in a poem merely titled "To the Right Honourable William, Earl of Dartmouth," we can appreciate that Wheatley's given subject of address did not limit the meaning she sought to convey.

An Elegy to Philandra

When Wheatley wrote "To Philandra an Elegy," to whom, and of what, was she speaking? Not addressed as "Mrs." or "Lady" but by her first name alone, Philandra was a subject with whom Wheatley presumably shared intimate familiarity. Philandra was not an entirely unheard-of name, as birth and death records from the period occasionally present Philandra and a variant, Philanda.[124] But it was not a common name. Nor was it a name of an exact classical reference. Combining the Greek *phil* and *andra*, it seemed to convey the meaning "to love man" while also conjuring the mythic Cassandra, the priestess who told the truth but was never believed.[125] Or the name might have referenced *Philander*, a 1758 play by Charlotte Lenox; or *Philandre*, a sixteenth-century French novel; or a character named Philandra from a 1692 English novel, *The Female Gallant*.[126] Perhaps Philandra's meaning or identity is somewhere in between these. Or possibly it was the name of a friend—an enslaved woman or another free black woman, like Wheatley herself.[127] Roberts's recent discovery of a likely Wheatley poem addressed to an enslaved woman named Rose makes this possibility all the more expectant.[128] Or perhaps Philandra—beginning with the same "Phil" as "Phillis" was a name she gave to a child.

Even if Philandra's identity remains unresolved, the name's present-yet-unknown place in Wheatley's known-yet-absent manuscript returns us to the American Grammar—and to the meaning it has allowed and suppressed over time. Philandra seems an apt name to add to Spillers's list of black women's "confounded identities" in the "American Grammar Book": "'Peaches' and 'Brown Sugar,' 'Sapphire' and 'Earth Mother,' 'Aunty,' 'Granny,' God's 'Holy Fool,' a 'Miss Ebony First,' or 'Black Woman at the Podium.'"[129] Phillis is another such name often called up to perform certain affective or pedagogical functions within white American imaginations across the nineteenth century. She would be the "sooty prodigy" around whom white family sentiments and "silken bands" cohered and the "literary curiosity" with whom white women and girls practiced their literacy. Later, this version of Phillis would become the example of good character selected by Northern whites for the primers they put before black freedpeople upon Emancipation.[130] In each of these instances was a confirmation of Spillers's contention that "if I were not here, I would have to be invented."[131]

Yet if we can deconstruct the American Grammar by way of the primers that installed it, we can also break down the "attenuated meanings" long sedimented over Wheatley's name to "speak a truer word" concerning her.[132] Even acknowledging the limits and gaps in Wheatley's archive, the poet's own words offer evidence of insightful, inventive authorship: of possibilities for claiming kinship, of concern extended toward black children as well as white, and of the recognition that freedom rested, necessarily, on an interdependent footing. In Wheatley's verse, the deaths of white children were occasions for their parents not to cry out in grief but to listen to their children's heavenly lessons. Overt anguish was reserved for black children's bondage and, in that anguish, the foment of black freedom's meaning. As many possibilities as Wheatley delivered into American literary culture, she also wrote and claimed possibilities for herself. *She* was the "babe belov'd" for whom grief had poured, the child deserving of her enslaver's concern, and later, the free black mother who demanded her child's legal protection. These were "marvels of [her] own inventiveness," and by recognizing them, we better perceive the insurgent author and the imprint she left.[133]

Wheatley's version of the American child—precious, full of celestial knowledge, held free, black, and belov'd—had its own immediate legacy in the care and protection of black children that the end of slavery in Massachusetts made more possible, if still very precarious, at the time of her death.[134] Yet while histories of black childhood in the antebellum North illuminate cultural, educational, and legal efforts that resonate with Wheatley's own, her American child nevertheless *also* deserves its own elegy.[135] For the possibility of this American child's future significantly faded beneath the dominant culture of sentiment and slavery that followed. Antebellum slavery's further invasion of black kinship by property relations, the law's focalization of white children's "best interests" within white family sanctity, and the cultural deformation of black children as dangerous, not endangered, formed a more secure and interlocking edifice for the American social grammar after Wheatley's death. While abolitionists followed Wheatley in highlighting the plight of enslaved children, nineteenth-century white writers and readers devoted their overwhelming attention and sentiment to the suffering white child alone.

Yet black children's apparent exclusion from this culture again concealed extraction. White Americans would invest *more* material, affective, and imaginative resources in keeping black children within their domestic order across the antebellum period and after it. Giving support to the deepening contradictions of the American social order, sentimental culture strengthened the affective common sense of its "golden links" and "silken bands." Yet neither that sense nor its cover of tenderness would hold indefinitely. After Wheatley, black children and adults who had been forcibly written into the "child's place" would struggle, write, play, and perform routes out of it. For though many of Wheatley's radical interventions were written over, the opening created by her poetry was never closed.

2

"Wilt Thou Bring My Baby Home?"

Tom Wiggins and the Unending Antebellum Family

Wilt thou bring my baby home?
Now he is satisfied
Yes he will be brought to you
And I will see him aft'ra while
—Tom Wiggins, "Wilt Thou Bring My Baby Home?" (1881)

Sometime in 1853 and somewhere near Columbus, Georgia, a four-year-old black child stole himself into the parlor of his enslavers. It was late into the night. Seating himself at the piano—so often presided over by the white women of the family—the child proceeded to play selections of their music from his memory. Drawn by his playing, the "young ladies" descended upon the parlor, and before long, their entire household had "gathered around him to witness and wonder" at the child's "marvelously strange" performance. They invited him to play on.[1]

This is where the career of Tom Wiggins—or "Blind Tom, the Marvelous Musical Prodigy"—was said to begin. At least, this was the origin story supplied by Wiggins's enslavers, the Bethunes, who maintained an enormously profitable scheme to direct Wiggins's performance career while keeping him enslaved between the 1850s and his death in 1908. In 1850, James Bethune purchased an infant Tom, his elder siblings, and his parents, Charity and Mingo Wiggins, from a neighboring enslaver.[2] In doing so, Bethune incorporated the Wiggins family as an asset of his estate and as its labor force in intended perpetuity. Yet when he discovered Tom's unusual talent of playing and composing for piano, Bethune disaggregated Tom as a separate asset and recalibrated the kind of labor and scope of profits he intended to reap from him. Creating elaborate instrumental and vocal repertoires for Tom and eventually setting him on national and transatlantic tours, Bethune's machinations, combined with Wiggins's talent, made "Blind Tom" one of the most widely known American performers of the nineteenth century.[3] Delivering classical arrangements with agility, performing stunts like facing away from the piano while playing, and amazing white audiences simply by the concomitant fact of his virtuosity, blackness, blindness, and supposed "imbecility," Wiggins captured enduring and widespread fascination.[4] With such renown came great returns: across his career, Wiggins would amass at least $500,000—and likely far more—for the Bethunes.[5]

The vignette of young Wiggins in the parlor—where it is he who makes the Bethunes captives, as his audience—was, if a plainly specious cover story, also an integral component of the Bethunes' system for maintaining Wiggins's enslavement and for maintaining slavery itself. It was this mode of storytelling, printed in his souvenir songbook—*Songs, Sketch of the Life of Blind Tom, the Marvelous Musical Prodigy* (1868)—and repeated in other pamphlets, newspapers, and later, before the law that allowed the Bethunes' scheme to endure after slavery's legal end. What James Bethune claimed, and what audiences and the judiciary accepted, was that Wiggins's career was a family business.

As this chapter relates, nineteenth-century legal developments in the definition and protection of family, children, custody, and contract not only accommodated the Bethune family's hold on Wiggins but extended that hold after Emancipation. Indeed, in 1865, when Wiggins came before the court as a minor, the rights of his parents, the sanctity of freely entered contracts, and the law's protection of children's "best interests" each informed the court's judgment, yet that *informed* judgment nevertheless left Wiggins in slavery after slavery's end.[6] As I elaborate in this chapter, it was not the failure of such legal constructs—freedom, family, contract, or childhood—to apply to or include Wiggins but rather how they applied to him that decided his ongoing captivity. I unravel the problem of the law's application by tracing antebellum and postbellum continuities of white family that necessitated, according to both custom and the courts, their continuous dependence on black families. These ongoing dependencies took manifold economic and legal forms. For the Bethunes, it was first an 1865 contract of indenture that rebound Wiggins to James Bethune and, later, the legal determination of Wiggins's "unsound mind" and "childlike" status that extended this effect.[7] Yet if these legal frameworks supported Wiggins's captivity, it was the

Bethunes' consistent recourse to story and family sentiment that more broadly facilitated it. According to Bethune, Wiggins *was* a Bethune, he belonged at the center of the Bethune family, and his place there was, like Odell's Wheatley, bound by "links" of affection.[8] As narratives of Wiggins's captivity underscore, where black subjects could be imagined in a white family's embrace, black family became soluble.

The white embrace of Wiggins was a skillful variation on sentimental culture's dominant conventions. For readers of nineteenth-century sentimental fiction would have known then, as scholars confer now, that the figure meant to reside in the center of the bourgeois parlor—the figure who commanded the heart and hearth of sentimental culture—was not a black child but a white one.[9] As "the angel of the house," the white child had come to form the cultural center of the American family across the antebellum period, ascending to most beatific form in Stowe's 1852 literary invention of Eva and in the innumerable theatrical, commercial, and illustrated iterations that followed in her wake.[10] The conception of innocence expressed through Eva and her counterparts can be traced, in part, to the poetics of childhood innocence that Wheatley had shaped in her elegies and to the feminized cultural sphere that surrounded the children whom she elegized. Yet nineteenth-century authors narrowed the expanse of Wheatley's imagination of innocence. Where Wheatley routed dynamic political messages and directed a range of emotions from her readers, nineteenth-century authors consolidated childhood's affective economy in the depiction of children's suffering and in the evocation of reader sympathy, and tears, for that suffering.[11] Moreover, where Wheatley had demanded the recognition of black children's plight in her verse, whiteness dominated both the representation of the nineteenth-century suffering child and the extension of sympathy to them. During the antebellum period, antislavery representations of enslaved children's suffering competed against their representational antagonists: the alternately "vacant," incorrigible, or "wicked" picaninny figures whose attributes crystallized into Topsy's "goblin-like" form.[12]

As a child whose performance career began in the mid-1850s, Wiggins's cultural stature emerged in close relation to Eva and Topsy's opposing dyad. Yet the stories told about Wiggins, the repertoire he performed, and the material exploitation underlying his career give away the profound enmeshment beneath Eva and Topsy's representational opposition. Indeed, in the same songbook in which Wiggins appears at the piano to the delight of his enslavers, Bethune interspersed other stories where Wiggins was made "strange," physically imposing, and a "violent" threat to other children.[13] These stories imbued him with the familiar menace of the picaninny and concealed the conditions of violence that Wiggins himself suffered.[14] Reading across Wiggins's promotional texts and public criticism, both kinds of stories—those that sensationally malign or sentimentally embrace Wiggins—fold together; that is, neither kind appears an aberration. Moreover, in reading responses to Wiggins's performances, it seems clear that audience enjoyment of Wiggins's repertoire hinged in large part on the exchange of affects, and childhoods, that could be alchemized through him. Audiences commented on the "wonder" of his "striking" physicality and blackness, yet they remarked, too, on the "simple sweetness and pathos" with which he sang a sentimental song of a white child longing for their mother.[15] The dance of antisympathy and innocence, and of black childhood and white, that occurred across Wiggins's repertoire reverberates as a disturbance to the binary optics of childhood, indicating a constant negotiation—and cohabitation—of childhood's black-and-whiteness not only in Wiggins but in the cultural imaginary in which he performed. Indeed, reading the stories in which Wiggins was conscripted—on stage, in sentimental narrative, and before the law—produces a fact otherwise obscured: that the cultural center of the American family was doubly occupied. The black prodigy was, all along, the other angel of the house.

If Wiggins's repertoire illuminates the relationship of white and black childhood in their agonist, rather than antagonist, relationship, the profitability of his repertoire makes clear that the crucible of black and white childhood was not only culturally valuable but materially so. When Bethune purchased Wiggins as a disabled infant, he claimed to see him as a financial "incumbrance."[16] Wiggins's career is a refutation of this idea not only because of the vast wealth he generated for Bethune but also because the Bethunes' efforts to capture Wiggins's value—in cultural form, in the press, before the courts—index a wider, more ordinary set of strategies by which many Americans sought to incorporate black children's labor and value across the antebellum and postbellum periods. Black children were immensely valuable to those who enslaved them, for even if they were purchased and sold "cheaply," the entire system of hereditary slavery rested in them. And black children were valuable beyond slavery—as indicated by the many whites, South and North, who sought to indenture black children upon Emancipation.[17] They were valuable, too, to all who produced and enjoyed American childhood's culture—in its suffering, monstrosity, sentiment, and innocence. The Bethune family labored to keep Wiggins's value circulating in each arena. They found authority to do so through family law and through the fictions of family that were allowed to support the law as evidence.

Against the Bethunes' successful incorporation of Wiggins into their family story, there is no narrative body of evidence to contest it on the same terms. For indeed, Wiggins never produced an autobiography to refute the *Sketch* of his life, nor did he write a coming-of-age story to discredit the claim that he was, as his obituary reads, "A child all his life."[18] Yet writing Wiggins into their family was never a completed task, because the Wiggins family refused to dissolve into the Bethunes'. Seeking to free her son from bondage in the 1880s, Charity Wiggins entered court petitions for Wiggins's deliverance. Her efforts resulted in the exposure of Wiggins's captivity but not in his freedom, as Wiggins was delivered from one Bethune only to be placed in the custody of another.[19] Yet if Charity's plea failed as a decisive ending of her son's captivity, it was Wiggins himself who left the most resounding record of events. In his music, Wiggins supplied not a final note but rather a repeating chorus that still asks and replays a version of Charity's question: "Wilt Thou Bring My Baby Home?" (1881).

"Wilt Thou Bring My Baby Home?" is among a handful of Wiggins-authored vocal compositions whose text is extant yet whose reading as evidence of anything other than his "peculiar idiosyncrasies" has been undermined by their labeling as "beautiful music, words without sense."[20] As the title of this song conveys, however, Wiggins's personal history gives sense to his lyrics, even where his nonnormative syntax and discordant arrangement challenge easy interpretation. Calling up a mother's "home" to which Wiggins was never returned, the lyrics of this and other songs remap the master's household where he was held. Through song, Wiggins supplies an unsentimental reprise to the parlor story, where we find him not a child absorbed in the piano's keys and embraced by white family but rather a listening witness to that family, not playing their music by rote, but recording their discord.

"Mother Dear Mother"

As one critic wrote upon witnessing twelve-year-old Wiggins perform in 1861, his audiences were "crowds of wondering people who [would] leave the hall still wondering, and only to go again."[21] They did go again in swelling numbers across the 1860s, filling concert halls across the US, Great Britain, and France and only slowing in the late 1880s. Before his death in 1908, Wiggins had performed across hundreds of stages, entertaining thousands of Americans and Europeans.[22] His place within the popular imaginary was so prominent that US president James Buchanan brought him to perform at the White House while enslaved and that writers Mark Twain and Willa Cather wrote him, in crude caricature, into their own canonical legacies.[23]

Whether playing works of Beethoven, Chopin, Wagner, Verdi, or Mendelssohn with sensitivity and force; or producing vocal imitations of a church organ, banjo, or harp; or playing different melodies with each hand at once, Wiggins demonstrated his vast kinesthetic and sonic knowledge. When he performed his own compositions, he introduced audiences to experiments beyond their period's sonic lexicon, playing rumbling cluster chords and capturing the sounds of industry, agriculture, and war that surrounded him in his "Battle of Manassas," "Sewing Song," "Cyclone Gallop," and "Rainstorm."[24] Believing, however, that his musical faculties were impossible products of what audiences perceived as his compounded "idiocy" and "unadulterated" African origin, they transformed the singular virtuosity they witnessed in Wiggins into "wonders," "marvels," and "incomprehensible facts" that could only be made sense of in the natural accident of the "prodigy."[25] Prodigy, in its adjacency to childhood, might not have endured as the container for Wiggins's lifelong career. Yet Wiggins's tenure as a "marvelous musical prodigy" was made elastic because his childhood was (figure 2.1).[26] Indeed, where his early sheet music describes Wiggins's chronological age as "only ten years old"—marking his prodigious talent as out of proportion to his childhood—later descriptions of Wiggins emphasized that it was his childhood that was out of proportion: he was a "child in middle age as at seven."[27] This juvenile extension of Wiggins's cultural categorization and social status was facilitated by the nullification of his legal adulthood. For when Wiggins reached the age of majority in 1870, he

Figure 2.1. Sheet music for "Oliver Gallop" and "Virginia Polka," 1860, National Museum of African American History and Culture, Digital Collections.

received neither the rights of personhood nor the franchise of citizenship newly entailed to him and to other black men. This was because, in 1865, he did not receive his freedom.

To live in the suspension of childhood as Wiggins did was in a very real sense to inhabit slavery's sanctioned afterlife. And if the latter four decades of Wiggins's career give material manifestation to slavery's failure to end, the judgment that sanctioned this extension reveals the specific interests and undercurrents of antebellum law that interdicted

Wiggins's freedom upon Emancipation as well as the freedom of many other black minors at that moment. It was the antebellum period's emerging body of family law—drawn on by those who sought Wiggins's deliverance from Bethune—that, in the end, certified his ongoing captivity.

Throughout the Civil War, Bethune skillfully kept Wiggins from Emancipation's encroachment while hiring him out to perform across the Confederacy and for its benefit.[28] At the war's end, however, a black man named Tabbs Gross attempted to emancipate Wiggins by a writ of *habeas corpus* filed first in an Indiana court and then in Ohio.[29] Gross had previously sought to contract with Bethune for a share in Wiggins's management, and he took legal action with a dual purpose: to release Wiggins from Bethune and to capture Wiggins's profits for himself.[30] His initial writ was denied. Yet Gross immediately renewed his appeals, this time testing two nascent and fragile premises: that US law would unequivocally disallow slavery's continuation and that it would extend its stated concern for white minors and white families to Tom and his family.

Despite his nebulous standing in relation to Tom and his family, Gross's case leveraged questions of immediate legal salience: the sanctity of a parent's custody over their child on the one hand and the best interests of that child on the other. Efforts to bring these two concerns into alignment had become the hallmark of a distinctly American body of rulings that spread North and South between the 1820s and Wiggins's case in 1865. Across the antebellum period, a "deepening concern for the welfare of the child" and the rising primacy of children's "best interests" had produced new powers for the state to intervene in the family while altering the balance of power within it.[31] By the midcentury, judges routinely acted in *parens patriae*, assuming temporary guardianship over minors whose custody was in dispute until their "best interests" had been determined.[32] In struggles between white mothers and fathers for sole guardianship of their children (usually following divorce proceedings where abuse or adultery had been proven), courts increasingly recognized a child's "tender years" as a deciding factor in assigning custody. A subjective rather than chronological marker of early childhood, "tender years" marshaled the ascending cultural force of children's innocence, mother-child bonds, and the court's power to justify the placement of young children with their mothers, contravening the law's general deference to patriarchal authority.[33]

If jurists moderated paternal and maternal standing by their actions in antebellum cases, they did so on the uncontroversial basis of custody itself or the belief that "the basic right of the child [was] not to liberty but to custody."[34] Though commonly held by the nineteenth century, this premise was itself novel, having emerged with the modern construction of childhood and helping define its most fundamental premises. The notion that white children naturally belonged to their parents above all other parties—lords and masters on the one hand or themselves on the other—was, like *Partus*, an innovation of the late seventeenth century and inextricable from its social-juridical grammar. Child custody's legal coherence in Anglo-America followed from a landmark 1660 piece of legislation in England that gave new standing to the father, irrespective of his class status, over his child. It was this formulation of custody, ratified in the Tenures Abolition Act, combined with the ascendance of marital coverture, that shaped early America's founding family belief that white men should "enjoy rights to their own wives and children" both.[35] And indeed, it was the confluence of this formulation within the context of slavery that enlarged the husband-father's authority, producing what Brewer names the "tripartite array of master/husband/father" as the arbiter of all private relations.[36] Early Americans sought to secure and protect this composite figure's authority both by their general adherence to English common law and in their innovations upon it. Nineteenth-century jurists, too, were engaged in protecting this grammar of American family and this construct of custody, forming a "cement of domestic bonds" to enclose the private sphere and the child's place at its center.[37]

While American family law was written to secure white family interests, free black families made use of its premises and extensions in their own attempts to legally protect their families, as the Peterses had. It was by invoking parental rights and mother-child bonds that Sojourner Truth successfully sued for her son's freedom in 1828.[38] And it was free African Americans' wider understanding of children's legal standing that led them to legal activism on behalf of free black children in 1840s Boston and Philadelphia, as Kabria Baumgartner and Crystal Webster document.[39] Yet for the majority of black people who remained enslaved during this period, legal constructs of childhood and family were not only out of reach but actively adversarial to their exercise. Under the statutory laws of Georgia in which the Wiggins family was held in bondage, the "condition of the [enslaved] mother" precluded any judicial "tenderness" toward black mother-child bonds; moreover, the notion that "chattels personal" were held "in the hands of their respective owners or possessors" asserted custody of a different kind.[40] After Emancipation, these solvents to black family developed new means in the form of contracts. It would be the mere claim of a freely entered contract that would decide Wiggins's ongoing enslavement. Because, like many other enslavers in the immediate post-Emancipation period, Bethune combined the legality of children's indenture and the heretofore unintelligible legal status of black families to build a case for Wiggins's ongoing enslavement. Maintaining before the court that Charity and Mingo Wiggins had freely agreed to a contract of indenture that allotted 90 percent of their son's profits to Bethune, Bethune successfully recast Wiggins's exploitation as a labor arrangement established on, rather than against, Charity and Mingo's parental rights.[41] There were issues in the credibility of this claim as evident in the asymmetry of its financial arrangement as in its very status as a contract. For even had he proposed such an arrangement, Charity and Mingo did not, in fact, have the freedom to consent to it. Alleged by Bethune to have entered freely into this contract in Georgia—a state not yet readmitted to the Union, a state yet to renounce slavery, and a state that therefore *did not yet recognize their right to contract*—Charity and Mingo were nevertheless held responsible to the never-produced, impossible contract's terms.[42]

The judge who decided Wiggins's case in Ohio acknowledged the contract's suspect standing. He upheld it, however, on the basis that "no one ha[d] the right to intervene . . . between the parents and Bethune."[43] What lay primarily between "the parents and Bethune" was the institution of slavery and, secondarily, Bethune's contracts with other white men. There was Perry Oliver, whom Bethune had previously contracted as Wiggins's manager, and also Joseph Eubanks, W. P. Howard, Joseph Poznanski, and James Bethune's son, John Bethune, who were joined in the corporation variously called the "Blind Tom Combination" or "Blind Tom Company."[44] It was these men to whom Bethune was contractually bound, yet by imagining the fictive indenture contract as the bond in need of legal protection, the judge determined it valid. The accord between the Ohio court and an enslaver from Georgia was both an early compromise of reunification and a foreshadowing of the court's wider role in abetting former slaveholders who sought to recapture black children under similar terms. The child whom the court protected was not Wiggins but an abstraction invoked and then dispensed with. Indeed, while claiming that the welfare of minors was the "polar star" guiding his judicial action, the judge in Wiggins's case demurred from his authority to decide Wiggins's best interests. He instead gave Wiggins, a minor, the burden to choose between two exploiters—Gross and Bethune—to the best of his "comfort" and "happiness."[45]

Both the court and the press recorded that Wiggins chose to remain with Bethune. Yet "choice" itself fails to express anything of the legal, social, and cultural conditions in which Wiggins was said to make his. Neither the "choice" of the free adult nor the "best interests" of the child serve as adequate guidance for understanding the situation in which Wiggins found himself: a nominally free yet materially unfree black and disabled sixteen-year-old who stood before an Ohio court while his family remained in Georgia and who, moreover, was told that his family had been spoken for by his, and their, enslaver. The difficulty of situating Wiggins before the law and in its terms was not the result of his unusually close bond to Bethune, as the press claimed, nor the result of his exceptional status as a marvelous and strange prodigy, for indeed, the indenture that resulted from the case was common. Instead, the difficulty of narrating Wiggins's "choice" in the law's terms results from the long-standing tangle created between the juridical structures of slavery and family, which had confounded the categories of welfare, custody, and freedom that might have pertained to Wiggins in this moment, securing instead an abstraction of childhood that served others' best interests.

If the outcome of the court case proves inarticulate as a decision, the tour that Bethune set Wiggins on immediately following the case provides a summation of what the court had secured for Bethune, for the grammar of American family, and for the public. Launching Wiggins on a rapid tour of the northeastern US, England, Scotland, and France, Bethune tested the desire of white audiences to see and hear more of Wiggins and found that, if anything, their appetite had expanded. Moreover, the success of the tour, and the popular commentary it generated, confirms that what the public wanted to hear, feel, and imagine from Wiggins was not a radically new repertoire to usher in a new era but a sentimental reprise to call up the old. In fact, they received both, for during this tour, Wiggins was made to sing a new song made of familiar sentiments: "Mother Dear Mother, I Still Think of Thee" (figure 2.2). Written by W. P. Howard and Captain Burgess and sung by Wiggins on his 1865 and 1866 tours, "Mother Dear Mother" was saturated in family feeling yet estranged in relation to its singer:

> Mother, dear mother, how sad is my plight;
> So far from thy care—away from thy sight;
> No lov'd ones are near, no loved ones so dear,
> To bid me a welcome, a fond welcome here;
> My soul has grown weary; it findeth no rest
> Away from the idols that rise in my breast;
> But mother, dear mother, weep not for me—
> Mother, dear mother, I still think of thee![46]

This song would eventually be bound as sheet music, where Wiggins appears on the cover standing over a tufted chair, a plush carpet, and a Kirkman piano, each communicating the bourgeois domestic space where purchasers might imaginatively place Wiggins and play the song for themselves.[47] Yet even in the depiction of Wiggins alone in the parlor, the cause of Wiggins's aloneness—or the forced separation of Wiggins from his *own* mother—was made to appear unrelated to the suffering and longing that "Mother Dear Mother" exclaimed. For while the song impressed audiences with its feeling, it did not prompt written reflections on Wiggins's recent ordeal or his ongoing plight. Though they did remark on the song's affecting "sweetness" and even attributed the song's lyrics to Wiggins (incorrectly), audiences left no further comment on "Mother Dear Mother" as an expression of Wiggins's exploited, estranged, and enslaved position.[48] This was likely because they knew better. Wiggins was not the song's suffering child and Charity not the "Dear Mother" the song's supplicant longed for. Audiences had only to turn through *Songs, Sketch of the Life of Blind Tom* to confirm this. Reprinted among other songs and sketches, "Mother Dear Mother" appeared after accounts of Wiggins—who "pinch[ed]" and "bit . . . younger

Figure 2.2. "Mother Dear Mother, I Still Think of Thee," sheet music (London: Hopwood and Crew, ca. 1870), Harvard Theatre Collection.

children to make them cry."⁴⁹ And also among stories of Charity, who "whipped children of the plantation," who believed her son to possess "no sense," and whose "neglect" as a mother to Tom was only remedied by the Bethunes' embrace of him.⁵⁰ Placing the whip in Charity's hand while removing it from Bethune's, these stories delivered the plantation's violence, conditions of endangerment, and structure of abuse in inverse. And rendering Wiggins himself as a chief aggressor, these accounts summoned the suffering of other—always unnamed—children, in so doing voiding the possibility of his own suffering. These stories of Wiggins's violence and the broader cultural distortion of black childhood in which they fit worked to dissolve the material and affective circumstances of his subjected black childhood and to distribute them through another. Sung into these imaginative and epistemic conditions, "Mother Dear Mother" made Wiggins its vessel, not its speaker.

Why this song entered Wiggins's repertoire at the moment of his nonemancipation, of his legal reattachment to his enslaver, and upon his farthest journeys away from his own mother is a question that can only be answered obliquely. At its base, "Mother Dear Mother" was merely a sentimental tune among Wiggins's many prosaic songs and "parlor selections," its lyrical content neither referential nor antireferential to Wiggins.⁵¹ Yet in the confluence of slavery's end, Wiggins's reenslavement, and his widening popularity, "Mother Dear Mother" performed the sonic dissimulation of slavery in general and the obfuscation of his enslavement in particular. Sung by Wiggins, "Mother Dear Mother" allowed those before him to witness and sublimate his plight, to see, hear, and feel Wiggins still bound in the Bethune family fiction while imagining that it was of someone else's sorrow he sang.

The Rescued Child

The feat of affective alchemy that white audiences accomplished through Wiggins—muting his suffering and hearing another's—did not depend, alone, on the violent mischaracterization of Wiggins or that of his mother. It depended, too, on the clarity with which white audiences could hear the voice, and feel the pain, of the proper suffering child through him. As "the epitome of sentimental expression," the figure of the suffering child was ubiquitous by the time of Wiggins's late 1860s tour, recognizable across literary and visual representation by their innocence, by the plots of misfortune that ensnared them, and by their essential deservedness of maternal care. Whether drawn as white "ragamuffins," lamented in songs about factory children, or imagined in stories of poor orphans, each suffering child formed an opportunity for inciting empathy, for eliciting tears, and in some cases, for advancing social prescriptions and political reforms, teaching readers how to *"feel right,"* as Stowe put it.[52]

In its orphan's lament for lost "loved ones" and its wistful longing for "childhood's sunny home," "Mother Dear Mother" broadly reiterated suffering childhood's structure of feeling, though it left its political emphasis unfulfilled.[53] Indeed, if the suffering child's attributes were recognizable in the lyrics of Wiggins's song, they bore an ambiguous relationship to Wiggins's political situation as an enslaved performer. This was not because enslaved youths were unthinkable as "suffering children" in song, in literature, or in other cultural performances—Frederick Douglass had depicted his own enslaved, suffering childhood with emphasis in each of his successive narratives and had underscored the separation of black children from their mothers as one of slavery's core tragedies.[54] Other black authors such as Harriet Jacobs, contributors to and editors of the *Christian Recorder* and *Colored American*, and white antislavery authors such as Lydia Maria Child and Charles Whipple brought poignant literary descriptions to the suffering of enslaved children for whom they sought freedom.[55] Penning a treatise on "The Family Relation as Affected by Slavery" (1858), Whipple declared the "daughters and sons of slavery" to be "utterly helpless," susceptible to being "carried off" at any given moment by the caprices of enslavers, their debts, or their speculative pursuits.[56] While such a carrying off had facilitated Wiggins's career—making him perhaps the most famous captive child of the 1850s and 1860s—he did not ever become an antislavery cause célèbre or a target of rescue.[57]

The question of which children could—by daring abolitionist strategy and public outcry—be rescued from slavery was underwritten by two other questions of public debate during the antebellum period: which children were, in fact, true slaves and which children truly needed deliverance from slavery. These questions exposed ongoing instabilities of slavery and freedom and black and white childhood that had purportedly been settled centuries before: the issue of "whose child could be enslaved."[58] Though white children had been defined as unenslaveable in the early American period, during the antebellum period, a notion of a white slave child nevertheless captured public concern, troubling slavery's definition and explicitly competing for sympathy with enslaved black children. Originating in American and English labor organizing of the 1830s, the specter of the white slave child became an emblem for exposing the rampant abuses of free labor by contrast, rather than similarity, to chattel slavery.[59] Calling up images of white children deformed, brutalized, or dying in factories, propagandists depicted enslaved black children and adults as well cared for by distinction, opening themselves—often intentionally—to appropriation for slavery's cause (figure 2.3).[60] Proslavery writers such as William Harper would caustically ask why abolitionists of chattel slavery could not spare empathy for the slaves of their own race.[61] And as the English author of "The Factory Girl" related in verse, abolitionists' "tender hearts" might have been "sighing" as "negro wrongs were told," yet it was "the white slave" who "was dying" all the while.[62]

As the compound "white slave" indexes, the term's political and cultural force arose from readers' knowledge of "slavery" as an abject and violable condition. Yet the terror of white slavery was more in the attachment of whiteness and white childhood to slavery and less in the acknowledgment of slavery's wrongs. White slavery's later meaning—as a reference to sex work—operated by a similar logic.[63] Both were frightful conjunctions that defied the ideal reproductive order and its supposed protection of white families from despotic bondage. As one author wrote, "If this is not slavery, it is something worse."[64] Worse, in part, because abolition could not end it but also worse because its sufferers were white.

White antislavery propagandists would challenge this claim, sometimes by overt rebuttal but at other times by strategic racial concession. As Mary Niall Mitchell has detailed, antislavery advocates conceded to raise their own figure of the white slave child—not the white "factory girl" but the enslaved child who could pass for white and whose enslavement, for that reason, might incite the concern of whites otherwise unmoved.[65] Child pursued a related version of this logic in her story "Mary French and Susan Easton," where a white girl's wrongful enslavement

Figure 2.3. "I'm not to blame for being white, sir!" [Satire of Charles Sumner] (Boston: G. W. Cottrell, ca. 1862), Library Company of Philadelphia, Digital Collections.

with a black girl is the story's central dilemma and the driver of its emotional force.[66] No one, of course, accomplished a more effective transposition of black suffering for white than Stowe herself, making Eva the figure who suffers demonstrably and fatally from slavery, not Topsy, who is enslaved by Eva's family. In both antislavery and proslavery construction, the white slave figure accomplished a feat of feeling and imagination: it asked readers, audiences, and witnesses to feel black children's pain but to deny its location *in* them, to sympathize with the suffering caused by slavery but to deliver that sympathy to suffering childhood's proper, whiter, subject. Both in Harper's cruel claim that "children of negro slaves" were "the most vacant human beings" and in Wiggins's critics' claims that he was "a vacant receptacle" were resonances of this operation at work and its repeating effect. For though black children were never in any sense empty of feeling, thought, or value, they were relentlessly *emptied*—their feeling, thought, labor, and value siphoned as resources, leaving the appearance of lack in their place.[67] The ease with which listeners of "Mother Dear Mother" dissociated the song from the singer and the difficulty Wiggins faced in voicing his own claims in the dominant culture's terms were related to this apparent lack and the violent vacuum that created it.[68]

The credibility of Wiggins's "choice" to remain with his enslaver in 1865 erodes further once understood in this context, especially given the easy ventriloquism it implies. Yet if his indenture was staked on hollow ground, no records suggest that anyone mounted further legal challenges to it across the late 1860s or early 1870s. There was no popular outcry that Wiggins was unjustly held, held in danger, or in need of rescue. Indeed, this lack of concern was part of a larger pattern. While formerly enslaved black children were being made captive to schemes of indenture across the South and others being sent to apprenticed labor in the North, the concern that white antislavery advocates had once expressed for the suffering of black children was rapidly receding.[69] It was concern for white children's suffering that would endure, supplying a cause—or "polar star"—around which white antislavery and proslavery cultures could reunite.

An 1868 title from the American Tract Society (ATS), *The Rescued Child*, diagrams this realignment in stark relief. For though the ATS had declared itself an antislavery advocate by the outset of the Civil War,

The Rescued Child exposed its principle allegiances to whiteness after slavery's end. A story of a wealthy white baby girl named Pearl who is held hostage by a wicked "negress," Molly, *The Rescued Child* highlights the contortions of social reality that authors often employed to situate sentimental fiction's "angel" in her cradle. Indeed, in these contortions, the story fits amid a genealogy of fiction writing that made recourse to misfortunate circumstances while obscuring misfortune's structural conditions—it is this genealogy that would produce *Little Lord Fauntleroy* two decades later.[70] Yet the kind of misfortune that befalls Pearl—abduction by a black woman who seeks to use her for extortion—bears significantly upon slavery's immediate end. Its timeliness is signaled by the arrival of the white police officer, who admits, "I confess, I would like to rescue that suffering child," and it is located equally in the squalor he seeks to deliver her from: Molly's "vile den," where Pearl appears a "perfect picture of infantile loveliness" and where Molly's children are nowhere mentioned or seen[71] (figure 2.4).

At one level, the absence of Molly's children in this story simply reflects the disinterest of the author, Mrs. J. W. Schenk, in writing about them. Yet in another, the absence of Molly's children is the condition by which Pearl appears and, more specifically, the condition by which she appears as a "suffering child" in need of rescue.[72] Pearl's plight—stolen from her parents and kept for monetary gain—accomplishes the striking use and erasure of black children's endemic enslaved condition and its extension. It was Molly's unimagined children, more likely than Pearl, who would be held in such treachery, separated from their mother by their past sale as chattel or, perhaps more recently, by indenture.

By inverting the available and immediate context of its historical moment, *The Rescued Child* narratively blots out racial slavery's not-yet-ended violence toward black children. And delivering a "thrill of genuine satisfaction" to the police officer who rescues Pearl and to the readers who witness Pearl's salvation from a "horrible future" with Molly, *The Rescued Child* leaves no doubt about who is imperiled and who is dangerous.[73] Reflected against Pearl's "pure white[ness]" and standing between Pearl and her story of white family reunification, Molly is "a fiend in human shape," a disturbing embodiment of free blackness who reinscribes white childhood's innocence by posing a danger to it and who necessitates, for that reason, the heroic entrance of law enforcement.[74]

Figure 2.4. [Illustration of Molly, Pearl, and Police] *The Rescued Child* by Mrs. J. W. Schenck (New York: American Tract Society, 1868), the Baldwin Library of Historical Children's Literature, Special and Area Studies Collections, George A. Smathers Libraries, University of Florida.

In its hypervilification of Molly and its hyperbolic construction of white childhood, *The Rescued Child* diagrams a set of tropes and tools by which white cultural producers responded to—and recoiled from—black freedom and, moreover, how they integrated the policing of black freedpeople into, and as, white children's protection from suffering. In fact, the fantasy that black women (or girls cast as women) harmed the white children they were employed to care for became a justification for the policing, incarceration, and lynching of black women in slavery's afterlife.[75] Yet if *The Rescued Child* ushered in a new era through its fiendish depiction of Molly, it more accurately called upon and expanded earlier caricatures, like those of callous and neglectful Charity and of Tom and his appetite for children's pain.[76]

In promotional material, press coverage, and the songbook *Songs, Sketch of the Life of Blind Tom*, the Bethunes repeatedly claimed that Wiggins posed a danger to children; that he had, since a young age, relished the sound of their cries; and that, if left unrestrained, he would enjoy doing harm to children. Sounds of children suffering were described as a source of such "exquisite pleasure" to Wiggins that he had supposedly been found "burn[ing] an infant sister," "chok[ing] his brother nearly to death," and later, even strangling a white child.[77] Critics at Wiggins's shows would repeat similar claims: they noted the "considerable delight" that children's crying "seemed to afford him" during an 1866 performance in London, that he "revel[ed] in the suffering of his fellow creatures," and that pain was his lifelong "amusement."[78] These often-repeated suppositions about what Wiggins purportedly felt are most efficiently dispensed with as crude fictions and racist fantasies insinuated upon him. And yet, what if Wiggins *did* enjoy the sound of children crying? Or, at the very least, what if the sound of children crying brought about a response in him—if not enjoyment, then some other expression of his acute sensitivity?

Allowing such possibilities would not locate anything aberrant in Wiggins but would instead serve to locate Wiggins *in context*, within a cultural economy driven by children's pain. For if Wiggins enjoyed the sound of children crying, he did so within a culture that prized the production of tears, that made children's suffering the center of cultural power, and that arose out of the conditions, social relations, and violence of slavery. If the ecological and industrial attention of Wiggins's musical compositions demonstrates, as Daphne Brooks argues, Wiggins's capacity to serve as a recorder or "instrument of modernity," his demonstrable responses to pain might be understood similarly: as audibly playing what more quietly thrummed through sentimental culture and the cult of the child.[79] And if Wiggins was playing a record of harm back, his audiences were more likely than him to be the participants in the harm's original making.

For as much as arbiters of nineteenth-century culture and law declared the protection, rescue, and welfare of white children from suffering as their guiding commitment, they were also the cause of white children's suffering and its concealment. Even as the white slave child facilitated a negation of black children's plight, they nevertheless arose to indict the dire conditions that poor working white children *did*, in fact, face—conditions structured by, and supportive of, white elites and the middle class.[80] And while the free wage market that enriched sentimental literature's bourgeois readers endangered the poor children they shed tears for, the middle-class household held its own dangers for children.

The prevailing notion of bourgeois childhood produced by nineteenth-century law and culture inscribed the white child firmly within the family and dependency on family firmly within the child. While these double installations appeared to reflect, and protect, the child's natural status, they did far more to produce and naturalize that status. Guaranteed custody but not liberty, middle-class white children lost legal traction and independence outside of the home during this period, making their lives increasingly private except in special cases of legal intervention. Legal intervention, moreover, came to signal the breakdown of family order—reifying the unbroken relations of the family as the child's best interests above all. If the child appeared more protected from violence by these legal innovations, it was the family's relations—governed by fatherly authority and tended by motherly care—that were strengthened. Such relations were given additional privacy, and so were the abuses within them.

And while breaking down the walls of the bourgeois family reveals white children's precarity within them, entering the plantation household—where white family teetered even more closely atop black subjection—exposes the violence of the American family for white children more starkly. As work by Nell Painter, Stephanie McCurry, and Elizabeth Fox-Genovese has outlined, while plantation violence was disproportionately and pervasively enacted upon the enslaved, it was not reserved for them alone.[81] Abuse descended down the plantation's racial, gendered, and age-based hierarchies, not only from enslaver to enslaved. And just as the "array of master/husband/father" blurred Man's fatherly authority with his masterly supremacy, the simile of black childlikeness blurred the position of his most vulnerable subordinates: if enslaved people were like children, what did that mean for white children's status?[82]

When abolitionists such as Whipple condemned slavery's power to "annihilate" the "blessed relations" of family among the enslaved and to "deteriorate it" among masters, perhaps he sought to highlight the deformation caused by this comparison—the way that violence directed at enslaved people might bleed into the treatment of the white children to whom they were compared. Yet in upholding the ideal of the family's "blessed relations," Whipple declined to interrogate how those relations—between white fathers, mothers, and their children—ensnared and endangered both those who were free and those who were enslaved.[83] As Painter explains, and as proslavery writers exploited, there was "nothing at all contradictory between family feeling and hierarchy, between attachment and the conviction that some people absolutely must obey others."[84] Both within and far beyond the plantation household, the family's "blessed relations" seeded and concealed abuse.[85]

The predicament of vulnerability that emerged with white children's fortification in the family did not, however, endanger them most of all. For though white children were made vulnerable by their legal dependency under familial authority, they remained marginally protected by the recognition of their childhood. And by the fact that, for them, childhood would end. White children, and especially nondisabled white male children, ascended toward legal independence before the law and the prospect of exercising manhood's authority over others. For black children, however, this arc of childhood could neither begin in earnest nor end with finality. The grammatical estrangement of black children from childhood's protections and cultural recognition was a state one could not naturally age out of. And for those who were commonly affiliated with children—black adults and disabled people—their lawful likeness to children would put them in predicaments of grave danger and lesser resolution. Wiggins's legal commitment in 1870—and the ongoing enslavement it supported—reveals that the racial and ableist implications of childlikeness could survive, and even strengthen, beyond the antebellum household's order, grammar, and similes.

"Links That Bound Tom"

The antebellum household that surrounded Wiggins proved abstractly and legally flexible in the post-Emancipation era and geographically moveable. For in 1869, Bethune established a second property, "Elway," in Warrenton, Virginia, where he drew new fortifications around Wiggins. Bethune described Elway as a place of respite for Wiggins between tours.[86] In reality, Elway was the site of concealment, where Bethune kept Wiggins from any further entreaties for his freedom and hundreds of miles from his family in Georgia. And if Elway was where Bethune guarded his access to Wiggins's labor, Elway itself required the labor of many more black workers—for the management of its 545 acres, the tilling of its crops, the raising of its livestock, and the ordering of its household.[87] Though Elway plainly depended on black labor for its productivity and for its purchase (with wealth derived from Wiggins), Bethune nevertheless made his Virginia property into the setting of a new story about Wiggins's dependence on him. Upon establishing Wiggins's perennial residence at Elway, Bethune brought this formulation before the law, marshaling claims of Wiggins's "idiocy" to construct a new and indefinite custodial status for him.

In 1870, Bethune petitioned a Fauquier, Virginia, judge to deem Wiggins insane and, further, to grant his son, John Bethune, permanent status as Wiggins's "committee."[88] In seeking Wiggins's commitment, Bethune blatantly inverted the prior claim that as a minor, Wiggins had possessed sufficient judgment to decide his own custody. Though Wiggins had just reached the age of majority in 1870, the court forestalled Wiggins's potential claim to independence from Bethune by rendering him a perpetual, indefinite dependent. Equally insidious, the court effectively suspended Wiggins's future labor as contractless, recasting him as a burdensome charge, not a lucrative earner. Under this new legal guise, the Bethunes secured Wiggins's labor as a de facto inheritance that could pass from father to son without interruption.

Bethune's claim rested on a set of nineteenth-century legal developments that, like family law, centered custody and dependence yet pertained to relations of lesser clarity and produced more indefinite outcomes. By the 1870s, persons accused of insanity, lunacy, idiocy, or incompetence were routinely brought before probate courts, leading to their commitment to asylums, workhouses, prisons, or, like Wiggins, private conservatorships. Disabled white people, disabled black people, and many nondisabled black people were subject to commitment on the basis of such claims, as court judgments relied for evidence on little more than testimony regarding troublesome or unproductive behavior.[89] While commitment decisions developed their own protoeugenic lexicon and drew upon the English common law status of *non compos mentis* (of unsound mind), these judgments relied, too, on the child as the measure of irrationality and as the figure who rationalized custody, not liberty. To be judged incompetent or insane was, as Kim Nielsen describes, to be "reverted to the legal standing of a child."[90]

First enslaved, then apprenticed, then committed—all to Bethune—Wiggins's place in the Bethune family after 1870 reflected Bethune's perceptive manipulation of the law as well as the law's permission for manipulation as it pertained to black and disabled people. For while the child gained greater legal coherence across this period, the legal affiliation of black and disabled people with the child remained an effective tool for the suspension of coherent personhood. That suspension of coherence, moreover, empowered white men as the uniquely dependable parties who could manage, discipline, or speak for figures of such supposed dependency. In Wiggins's case, the aligned authority of the Fauquier County judge, James Bethune, and John Bethune legitimized conditions of captivity that were—despite all improbability—more indefinite than the condition of hereditary slavery into which Wiggins had been born.

If Elway served as an effective setting for the extension of Wiggins's captivity, it also became the site for the narrative resuscitation of the antebellum family in fiction. In 1945, thirty-seven years after Wiggins's death, a grandson of James Bethune, Norborne T. N. Robinson, published his personal recollections of Wiggins at the Virginia property, recalling Elway during the 1870s and 1880s as a site of languid holidays. In his picaresque account, Robinson plays boyhood companion to adult Wiggins, the pair sharing "summer vacations" on the Bethune farm.[91] The duo—who bear a striking resemblance to Twain's Huck Finn and Jim—run about the Bethune property with "absolute leisure," absconding for fishing expeditions, singing duets, and establishing "links that bound Tom and [Robinson] together" in perpetuity.[92]

"How did he happen?" Robinson asks at the outset of his recollections. As an answer, he supplies the same origin story that had long framed Wiggins.[93] Setting his tale at supper, not midnight, Robinson's story nevertheless culminates in the family's wonder at, and embrace of, Tom. Following Aunt Mary's "beckon[ing]" to the parlor, all seven of the Bethune children and their mother and father are "stopped dead in utter amazement" by what they see and hear: "Seated at the piano was a three-year-old Negro boy, his fat legs dangling from the piano stool, his upturned face wearing a look of utter rapture, his chubby fingers wandering unerringly over the keys. At that hour a great concert pianist was born."[94]

Returning to this white family fable as the site of Wiggins's musical "birth," Robinson repeats other essential pillars of Wiggins's story: the ventriloquized disinterest of Charity in Wiggins ("He jes' ain't got no sense. You can't learn him nothin'") and—most dramatically—the threat of Wiggins's violence.[95] Dramatizing Wiggins as poised to "hurl" a kitten against a kitchen wall, Robinson describes himself rescuing the animal by reprimanding Wiggins. And when Wiggins "suddenly and silently" wraps his hands around the neck of Robinson's seven-year-old cousin, the measured words "I wouldn't do that Tom" diffuse the scene and save the white child. Contemplating "what Tom might have done," Robinson exhumes the monstrous, but always forestalled, possibility of a white child suffering by Wiggins's hand.[96] Resettling Wiggins within the bounds of white family authority after this narrative climax, Robinson continues his scenes of roving mischief and pleasure, delivering a timeless, and almost endless, story.

Buried in a brief two sentences, however, Robinson acknowledges that life at Elway did not roll on endlessly—that, in fact, the "links" of Wiggins's captivity in the Bethune household broke apart. Mentioning the successful suit of John Bethune's widow, Eliza Bethune, for Wiggins's custody but offering no further detail, Robinson papers over what had been a multiyear, multiply appealed legal battle of the mid-1880s, with his family, and Wiggins, at the center. If Robinson chose to leave off with little mention of these events, it was likely because they exposed subordinate defiance where he narrated an even-keeled patriarchal order. Indeed, the case that Eliza Bethune brought against James Bethune for custody of Wiggins leveraged her savviness of family law, her exploitation of her rights as a wife, and her strategic willingness to form—or perform—an unlikely alliance: between herself and Charity Wiggins.

Ironically, it was James Bethune who set the terms by which he lost custody of Wiggins. For when he named his son John as Wiggins's custodian in 1870, he had not foreseen that John would die before him, in 1884.[97] Though James Bethune resumed custody of Wiggins upon his son's death, Eliza Bethune had seen an opening. In 1885, she began a two-year legal struggle to wrest custodial powers over Wiggins, claiming that John's responsibilities descended to her.[98] In an attempt to fortify her claim, Eliza called on Charity Wiggins to join in filing a second writ of *habeas corpus* for Wiggins's release.

Charity and Eliza's claims to Wiggins were strangely paired and strange in themselves. Eliza's stake in Wiggins was, at its base, one of a widow's inheritance, enunciating the fact that she, too, believed Wiggins to be heritable, whereas Charity's claims were staked upon her maligned and long-dispossessed maternal rights—rights she could only invoke indirectly as *prochein ami*, or "next friend to the infant," rather than as mother to son.[99] Despite the discordant and competing concerns presented by Eliza and Charity and flouting the press's favor for Bethune, Eliza and Charity eventually won their case.[100] Wiggins, however, did not win his freedom. Instead, he received a new guardian, and not his mother. In 1887, Wiggins was placed in Eliza Bethune's custody and sent to New York, where he labored for her profit until his death. And while Charity initially settled with her son, she left New York in 1888 under obscure circumstances—or perhaps under circumstances that were made obscure by Eliza.[101] If the case failed to produce a victory for Wiggins's freedom or the reconstitution of Wiggins's family, it did produce something in the law. Early twentieth-century law textbooks came to cite Wiggins's case as a precedent establishing "the relationship of curator and insane person" as "similar to that of next friend and infant."[102]

Made instructional for the child's ongoing use as a measure of black and disabled dependency, Wiggins's *habeas* suit is instructive, too, about the social changes that underlay it. The struggle between James and Eliza not only marred Bethune's genteel family portrait; it also exposed how, within white households, white women were gaining degrees of traction and dexterity in navigating the laws that regulated and legitimized their families. Yet Eliza's status as the case's victor underlines the fact that white women did not extend their gains beyond themselves; her custody of Wiggins was ultimately an extension, not a break, in the Bethunes' transfer of Wiggins as property. Though Wiggins's extended exploitation was the case's outcome, the case effectively laid bare the exploitation that came before it. Tom's status upon his release from Bethune—possessing only ten dollars' worth of clothing and one silver flute—gutted the fantasy that his indenture had ever been compensated.[103]

Moreover, though Charity Wiggins's claim to her son was not fulfilled in earnest by the court's decision, the fact of her claim was itself disruptive, challenging Bethune's assertion that she had "acquiesce[d]" to her son's prior captivity.[104] While the case's outcome seems to confirm that Charity was induced to come forward for Eliza's benefit, Charity's own potential for strategy and her own ulterior motives are equal possibilities. For if the attachment of Charity's petition to Eliza's positions her claim as ancillary, it is worth remembering that it would have been extremely difficult for Charity to have made her claims independently, or earlier, given the judiciary's wide disregard for black women's claims against white property owners, the distance Bethune maintained between Charity and her son, and Bethune's long-standing misrepresentation of her. Understood in the context of these exigencies, Charity's 1885 claim appears less belated and more considered. The crisis created by John's death was certainly an opening that Eliza sought to exploit. But it might also have been an opening that Charity recognized, a rare opportunity to breach the Bethune family's well-guarded boundaries. Cast in the press as an acquisitive "aunty" who played pawn to Eliza—a "hard featured, coarse, aggressive looking woman"—the pair serve, in retrospective narrative, as antiheroes subverting a long-standing sentimental story.[105]

To frame their case as a vindication of subordinate solidarity or as a bid for Tom's freedom, however, misrepresents what was, in effect, only an insubstantial alliance, a minor modulation in Wiggins's captivity, and another suspension of his will. As in the prior case, the press reported that Wiggins expressed a desire to remain with James Bethune in 1885.[106] Yet unlike in the prior case, this expression of will decided nothing. The disregard of Wiggins's alleged choice seems to assert a change in the law's interpretation of his legal status; however, it more so clarifies that Wiggins's will had decided neither case. Though the 1865 decision claimed to speak in his voice, the case was a resolution affirmed between Bethune's interests, his contracts, and the law. Bethune's loss in the court in 1887 reflected, on the one hand, an erosion of the absolute white patriarchal entitlement he had earlier enjoyed. Yet on the other, it merely reflected that the law respected the standing, marriage contract, and inheritance of another white man—his son.

While the legal cases in which Wiggins was made to appear fail to produce a coherent statement of Wiggins's will, the void of such agential expression does not point toward Wiggins's deficiency. It points instead toward the deficient frameworks—of personhood, will, and independent capacity—that rendered Wiggins's black disabled subjectivity unintelligible; that declared dependence and freedom to be incongruous; and that narrowed the scope of his best interests to a series of exploitative arrangements. In these conditions, Wiggins's lack of power to assert agency reads not as the absence of his will but rather as its categorical capture and suspension—in the breach of minority and majority, child and family, and freedom and property. This breach is a difficult place to close the story of his enslavement and an impossible place to begin a story of his freedom. Yet there nevertheless remains something other than closure to consider.

"Wilt Thou Bring My Baby Home?"

Bound as "the true results of the mind of this extraordinary being" to be "regarded with interest," Wiggins's self-authored compositions for voice and piano were copyrighted in the late 1860s and 1880s by various white men affiliated with the Blind Tom Company.[107] Lyrically and musically notated by them, these *Specimens of Blind Tom's Vocal Compositions* were printed for their profits: to be sold as tokens of Wiggins that audiences could take home and replay. Given their production and circulation within the economy of Wiggins's exploitation, these songs cannot be taken as unadulterated "Words and Music by Blind Tom" as advertised, nor can they be used to construct a point of view for Wiggins entirely outside of, or in opposition to, his captors.[108] Yet placing such a burden—of autobiographical personhood and independent, resistant motivation—on Wiggins's compositions is not necessary to understand the irresolution they introduce not against but into the midst of an otherwise closed story.

In fact, the framing that his managers placed around Wiggins's compositions only highlights the instability of meaning that they identified within them. Describing Wiggins's "Specimens" as "the true results of [Wiggins's] mind" and as "beautiful music, words without sense," Wiggins's managers reiterated the long-standing claim that Wiggins was himself without sense, encouraging those who played or listened to his sheet music to suspend their search for it.[109] Yet elsewhere in Wiggins's *Vocal Compositions*, they raised curiosity about the sense they denied, claiming that "the thoughts expressed in these Songs were suggested to the Author by actual occurrences."[110] Rather than resolve these contrary assessments of what meaning might be found in Wiggins's songs, we might instead draw meaning from their contradiction: that Wiggins's songs may truly convey his thoughts about "actual occurrences" in his world without conforming to the sense, or grammar, of that world—indeed, that his meaning might be hard to make sense of and be *true* at the same time.

SPECIMENS OF BLIND TOM'S VOCAL COMPOSITIONS (1880)
The Man Who Got the Cinder in His Eye
The Man Who Snatched the Cornet out of His Hands
The Boy with the Axles in His Hands

VOCAL COMPOSITIONS (1881)
Wilt Thou Bring My Baby Home?
The Man Who Mashed His Hand
Mother Wilt Thou Come and Cure Me?
I Wish Dear Jodie Would Come Home
The Man Who Sprained His Knee

If true expressions of "actual occurrences," the titles and lyrics of Wiggins's compositions deliver scenes of suffering, pain, accident, wishing, and longing across a cast of men, a boy, a baby, and a mother. While none of these figures can be positively identified and only one—Jodie—is named, the cinder that flies from fire into eyes, the axels that burden a boy, and the accidental "mashing" of a man's hand are nevertheless identificatory in themselves, suggesting a plantation, like Elway, as the setting where such misfortunes might occur.¹¹¹ Moreover, Wiggins's repeating question, "Wilt Thou?" uttered by a child pleading—"Mother Wilt Thou Come and Cure Me?"—and by a mother pleading not *with* her baby but with someone *for* her baby underline the plantation as the imaginative and/or "actual" source of Wiggins's varied forms of lament.

Placed within Wiggins's wider repertoire, these dyadic mother-child compositions must be situated, too, within sentimental culture. Indeed, they might even be taken as reiterations of the mother-child longing that Wiggins had been made to sing of in "Mother Dear Mother." Yet closely reading and listening to "Wilt Thou Bring My Baby Home?" offers a set of relations and an array of feelings that significantly disturb the sentimental mode. If "Mother Dear Mother" represented a key strain in the cultural sublimation of Wiggins's suffering, "Wilt Thou Bring My Baby Home?" (1881) performs the former song's rejoinder:

> Wilt thou bring my baby home?
> Now he is satisfied,
> Yes he will be brought to you
> And I will see him aft'ra awhile.
>
> I thought I heard my mother singing
> And sitting there on the steps.
> I think I see her with her sister
> Awaiting for the hack* to come.
>
> Wilt thou bring my baby home?
> Now he is satisfied,
> Yes he will be brought to you
> And I will see him aft'ra awhile.
>
> Now the roses are in bloom,
> And in the garden safe,
> Bring the can along
> And there it will be safe

---

* "Hack" refers to "a driver of a hackney carriage" or "a horse used for hire." See *Oxford English Dictionary*, s.v. "hack, n.2," http://oed.com.

> Go and ask my mother if she is ready
> To go and take a walk with me
> Tell me what time you will all be back
> We will be back at six o'clock
>
> Wilt thou bring my baby home?
> Now he is satisfied.
> Yes he will be brought to you
> And I will see him aft'ra awhile.[112]

Interpreting the lyrics of this song as a single supplicant's cry, the sense here might be lost—and Wiggins's unintelligibility affirmed. Yet to read these lyrics as the jumbled words of a single speaker would be to avoid recognizing their coherence, not as a soliloquy, but as undifferentiated dialogue comprising at least three tangled voices addressing the title question: *Wilt thou bring my baby home?* Given the custodial struggle that ensued a few years after this song's 1881 composition, "Wilt Thou Bring My Baby Home?" seems to anticipate Charity's 1885 claim for her son's custody. Yet rather than read this song as a prophecy, I would suggest this song as a sonic and lyrical record of earlier, unrecorded claims made by Wiggins's mother.

If this song documents Charity's prior journey to visit her son in Virginia, *Wilt thou bring my baby home?* was, arguably, the plea she traveled there to make. In which case, the song's lyrics also record Bethune, who answered, "Yes he will be brought to you"—conceding to a visit but ultimately concluding it "aft'ra awhile." Hearing from Charity and Bethune in the chorus, we can understand it to be Wiggins himself who "thought [he] heard his mother singing" and who sought to "take a walk with [her]."[113] And if it is Wiggins here, then it is Bethune who again responds to impose constraint, prompting Wiggins to acknowledge his master's watchful measure of his time, whereabouts, and company.

Sung over "broken chords," layers of syncopation, and a time shift to twelve-eight meter, the lyrics and music of "Wilt Thou Bring My Baby Home?" deny resolution, allowing Wiggins's unsentimental portrait of the Bethune plantation order to hang open.[114] While the song neither reveals itself as an interior view of Wiggins nor "affirm[s] and legitimize[s] [his] psychological autonomy" as an autobiographical narrative might, it does provide a strikingly different account of Wiggins's postbellum life, of his bondage to Bethune, of his filial bonds to Charity, and of the tension between them.[115] Indeed, it supplies another "tripartite array"—the mother/child/master in place of the master/husband/father.[116] Suspended in relation to both figures, Wiggins primarily appears throughout the song as spoken of and spoken for, yet not entirely so, for he emerges in critical spells of his own thinking, aural recognition, and sight. Indeed, exceeding but not entirely eschewing first-person coherence, "Wilt Thou Bring My Baby Home?" puts forth interdependence as both its central problematic and its interpretive key. If the puzzle of the song is in deciphering where one subject takes leave and another begins, its solution may be that such boundaries are ultimately illusory. Recognizing the song's social critique at the level of the lyric, we can duly appreciate Wiggins as a sonic and poetic commentator of slavery's sentimental cover, of its supposed end, and of the independent subjecthood on which freedom was premised and denied to him.

Indeed, by attuning ourselves to his sonic and lyrical work, we can begin to understand Wiggins as a measurer of slavery's failure to end, not only as a figure marked by the tragedy of that failure. To read Wiggins's "words without sense" for their critical import is not to dismiss Wiggins's cognitive divergence nor to reinstate the normativity of his sense. Rather, it serves to underscore the continuity of his critical perception and disabilities, clarifying that his divergence was in itself insightful and, moreover, that Wiggins's insights actively audit the captive conditions in which he existed as a disabled black person born under slavery and living in the simultaneous breakdown and renewal of its order.

The fact that neither the voices, positions, nor relations between Bethune, Wiggins, and Charity are clarified by "Wilt Thou?" bears on the counternarratives and conclusions that can be drawn from it. For if a critical understanding of nineteenth-century sentiment, childhood, and suffering loosens the fictive links drawn between Wiggins and Bethune, Wiggins's song does not supply a neat replacement story nor Charity's full reinstatement in it. The discord, dissonance, and vocal entanglement of Wiggins's song caution against writing a story of mother-son longing over their estrangement and into the void of their legal claims to each other. Rather than crafting a sentimental black family story over

Bethune's white family fiction, reprising the lament of "Mother Dear Mother" but in black voices, Wiggins's song instead leaves its listener adrift in other possibilities: of unreconciled estrangement and of tenuous connection, of provisional allegiance and of relative comfort, and above all, of constrained choices—all the internal discord and submerged strife that the American family privately housed.

An unsentimental record of the American family as perceived by Wiggins, the song locates Wiggins as both interred within its bounds and a witness to its faltering. For even as Wiggins's unending enslavement testifies to white patriarchal power's endurance, Wiggins's song and the legal struggle that subtends it reveal the vulnerability of the American family's structure of domination and the dependence it concealed as independence. Wiggins's cultural, material, and affective importance to the Bethune family and to the American popular imaginary reveals that the antebellum family structure—its master/husband/father placed at its top and its white child at its center—could be unsteadied by the figure it held captive and monstrous. Not only does this revelation again upend the fallacy that Man's freedom arose from his independence; it suggests that the efforts to keep Wiggins and other black children enslaved after freedom's due were central, not subsidiary, to the post-Emancipation reassembly of white power.

For even as Wiggins remained enslaved in what appeared to be a continuous regime of white patriarchal power and its sentimental cover, he lived through a time of power's significant revision, wherein the family no longer held as the site of Man's absolute power and where the law no longer aligned as power's absolute exercise. Bethune's loss of Wiggins's custody to Eliza heralds that both inside and beyond the plantation, the power of men like Bethune was subject to challenge and, moreover, that white women were mobilizing their own power behind the titles of wife and mother. As the next chapter discusses, the maintenance of Man's supremacy in the aftermath of black Emancipation would require different strategies of power, the recruitment of subordinates like Eliza, and new stories—told in a newly scientific grammar.

Composing both the sounds of postbellum modernity and the ongoing resonance of the antebellum, Wiggins, it seems, uniquely understood how the old could remain inside the new. He knew the incompleteness of freedom and the hollowness of societal concern for the "best interests" of those deemed like children. Despite the tragedy evident in his unending enslavement, however, Wiggins's archive of lyrical irresolution reminds us that neither rescue from captivity, nor manumission, nor family reunification might have truly meant his freedom. Indeed, Wiggins's songs provide anticlimactic interventions in legal freedom, intimating how Emancipation did not mean leaving behind antebellum arrangements for all. Yet without accomplishing a flight to free black personhood, he did pursue a subversive if not straightforward fugitive route: not out of the household but into its structure, where he listened, performed, and recorded its decay.

3

The Anatomy of Sammy Tubbs

Black Emancipation and the Human's Reconstruction

As Sammy Tubbs "glanced thoughtfully over his whole body" and "passed his hands over his chest and stomach," he exclaimed, "What a curious piece of machinery this is!"[1] A twelve-year-old black boy, born enslaved but growing up free, Sammy was coming to know the inner workings of his emancipated human body, and it delighted him. Filled with this irrepressible wonder, Sammy proceeded to give a detailed description of oxygenated blood moving through his arteries, of his organs metabolizing energy, and of his lymphatic and neural workings—or the "digestive, nutritive, respiratory, [and] vegetative nervous" systems of human physiology as understood by American science in the 1870s. Sammy had acquired this knowledge by listening closely to the white doctor for whom he worked, by reading medical journals, and by observing the illnesses and injuries that befell his pet monkey, Sponsie.[2]

We can imagine that each lesson Sammy learned—through reading, bodily experiences, and his comparative knowledge of Sponsie—lent Sammy a sense of affiliation with the scientific model of the human, his outward displays of pride at his knowledge matched internally by a sense of perfect coherence within the order of nature. For though he referred to his "machinery," he knew its biological particularities—and better than most. Understanding the systematic relationship of his breath, his blood, and his muscular movement, Sammy must have felt his humanness acutely and viscerally. Sammy's lessons were not, however, undertaken for his own self-regard; they were meant for the instruction of others. As a fictional character, Sammy's acquisition of knowledge did not edify him but instead edified the white child readers of *Science in Story: Sammy Tubbs, the Boy Doctor, and "Sponsie," the Troublesome Monkey*, authored by Dr. Edward Bliss Foote and published in 1874.

Sammy—or "our prodigy," as Dr. Foote described him—was there to ensure that readers would "keep up" and guard against "let[ting] a little black boy do better than [them]"[3] (figure 3.1).

Sammy Tubbs, a fictive freed black child laborer in New York City, was the pedagogical tool that Dr. Foote believed was key to, yet missing from, anatomical instruction for white children. By the 1870s, Foote was a prosperous medical provider and the widely read author of *Medical*

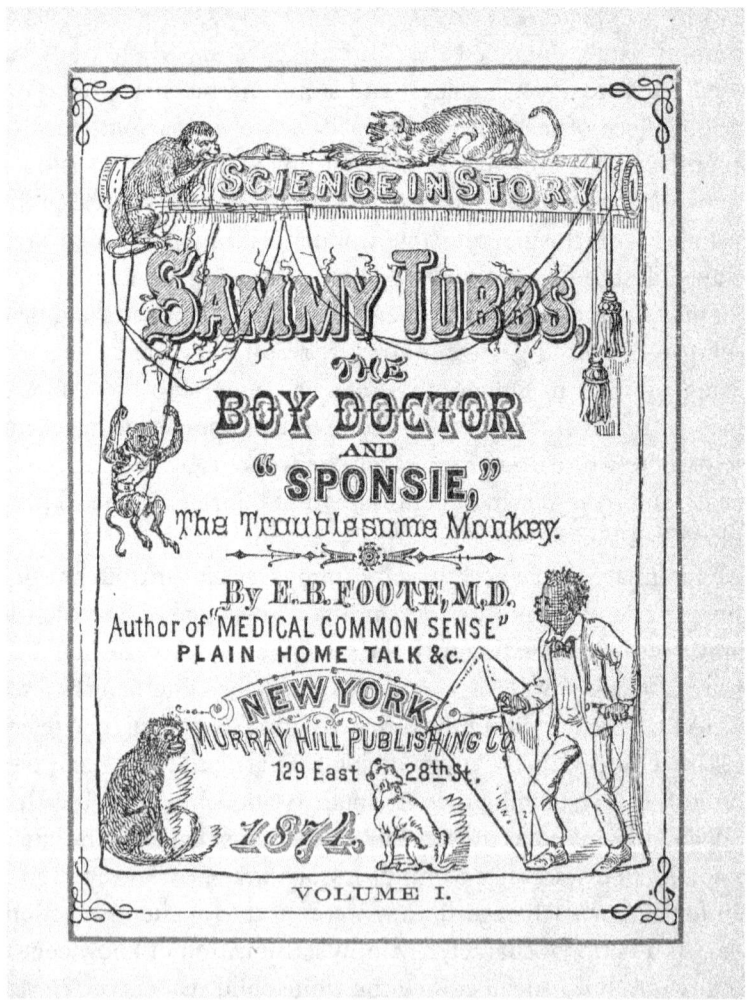

Figure 3.1. Edward Bliss Foote, *Science in Story: Sammy Tubbs, the Boy Doctor, and "Sponsie," the Troublesome Monkey*, vol. 1 (New York: Murray Hill, 1874), front matter.

Common Sense (1858) and *Plain Home Talk* (1870).[4] Despite his considerable medical authority in many American homes, Foote believed that reaching the children in those homes would require him to employ a special—and necessarily *black*—conduit. Fearing that anatomy and physiology made for "dry reading," the doctor created Sammy with the hope that, much as "pill-venders coat their nauseous drugs with an envelope of sugar," his "desired object"—of teaching white children about their human bodies—might be "ingeniously concealed in [the] acceptable garb" of Sammy, his sweetener.[5]

Spanning over a thousand pages across five illustrated volumes, *Science in Story* wove extensive lessons of anatomy, physiology, and hygiene together with equally extensive episodes of Sammy Tubbs, Sponsie, and Dr. Hubbs, a successful white physician practicing out of his Manhattan townhouse. Each volume integrated its lessons in human science with morality tales and grotesque hijinks, the former that shaped Sammy's character and the latter that subjected Sponsie to illness, violence, and eventual death. Though Sponsie's narrative tends toward destruction across the series, Sammy's arc progresses upward, from his initial position as Dr. Hubbs's door boy, to student, then to erstwhile medical practitioner himself.

Science in Story's tale of Sammy's uplift tracks with Dr. Foote's stated support of black education and black-white integration and with his antislavery roots.[6] Yet the series betrays a more extractive than emancipatory investment in blackness—indicated by Foote's statements on Sammy's utility to white children and in the link between Sammy and troublesome Sponsie. Indeed, playing both foil and "partner" to him, Sponsie tugs Sammy from his human splendor, tethering him instead to the conceit of black-primate kinship.[7] Moreover, though Foote rhymes the surnames of the black child and white doctor—Tubbs and Hubbs—their assonant relationship does not necessarily temper Sponsie's effect, for Hubbs was a double not to Sammy but to the author himself. A wealthy, progressive white physician in New York City, Dr. Hubbs served as Dr. Foote's envoy within the story.

Sponsie's doubling of Sammy, and the fictional Dr. Hubbs's mirroring of the real Dr. Foote, raises the question of Sammy's resemblance. There is, however, no evidence to suggest an original, living Sammy behind Foote's fictional one. Foote never trained black children in science or medicine as he imagined his counterpart, Dr. Hubbs, to have done; nor is there any record of his engagement with the world of free black New Yorkers that surrounds Sammy in the story. Why, then, would Dr. Foote have imagined a black child—and a prodigy—to tell his story and teach his lessons? We can begin to locate an answer to this question in Morrison's identification of white Americans' persistent dependence on an "Africanist presence" for "informing, stabilizing," and occasioning "critical moments of discovery" across American literary history.[8] And we can get closer still by returning to the explanatory power of Spillers's utterance, "If I were not here, I would have to be invented," as it illuminates Sammy's fictional invention—and Wheatley's previous fictionalization.[9] Not finding a freed black boy prodigy doctor with a pet monkey in his surround but intuiting this configuration as instructive, Dr. Foote drafted Sammy into prodigy's pattern and an American tradition. Yet if pattern and tradition supply the cultural context for Sammy, his specific location—in an anatomy textbook for white children—announces his more precise function, further underlined in the textbook's title, *Science in Story*, and timestamped by its 1870s publication. Conceived alongside the advance of Darwinism and in the aftermath of black Emancipation, Sammy was a finely tuned instrument for remodeling the human atop a shifting order.

This chapter takes Sammy's story as a guide to the nineteenth century's biocentric reconception of the human and Dr. Foote's biography as a personal account of Man's role in it. Educated and credentialed to inform, diagnose, and prescribe to the masses, Foote's career tracks the increasing power that scientific knowledge lent to the white men who wielded it across the nineteenth century and the increasing public acceptance of biological knowledge as authority in and of itself.[10] This transition—or, what Wynter describes as the turn from Man_1 to Man_2—constituted a shift in how white men organized knowledge of themselves and power over others, increasingly manifest in the regulation and purification of national populations.[11] The rule of white men over those subjected within the US national population—black and Indigenous people—was also rearticulated during this period: as the onus of the "optimally economic" and "naturally selected" to extract value from and cull those whom Wynter identifies as the "dysselected" and unproductive.[12]

It was amid these epochal and evolutionary revisions that Foote sought to deliver "knowledge of [them]selves" to white children, who by pedagogy, discipline, and the incorporation of knowledge would achieve Man's modern remaking.[13] Indeed, by its explicit pedagogical investments and textbook form, *Science in Story* makes visible the mediating place of the child between Man_1 and Man_2. As pupils learning to understand their bodies, social positions, and power in biological terms, white children were the living agents, drivers, and models of humanism's biocentric shift. As this chapter argues, instructing white children in human anatomy did not complement or follow from Man_2's ascent but constituted it. Yet if white children were key to the human's remodeling, Sammy indexes the role that blackness would play in what changed and in what remained, or the sublation of old in new.[14] For in narrating anatomy lessons for white children through his black child protégé, Dr. Foote confirmed that in this new scientific era, the authority that white men claimed to hold naturally remained fixated upon black children. And while Sammy was ultimately a fiction, he was also a figment of something more material: the relentless extraction of human knowledge from black people.

Extracting knowledge from black people's bodies—living and dead—has been core to the production of human-biological knowledge since the advent of medical science in the US. While this practice was rooted deeply in the past and extends into the present, the procedures of such extraction were systematized in the nineteenth century: in the routine theft of black cadavers for medical school training, in J. Marion Sims's now infamous gynecological experiments on enslaved women, and in the wider performance of surgical demonstrations on black patients.[15] It bears underscoring in this context that Dr. Foote's deployment of a black anatomy instructor was undertaken in logical if perverse relation to the field of human anatomy that was already instructed through black people and, moreover, that this reliance was itself a perversion, given the scientific questioning of black humanness during this period.

While inextricable from the nefarious practices of extraction in which he was trained, Dr. Foote's invention of Sammy was equally the product of the progressivism for which he is remembered. For when Dr. Edward Bliss Foote is recalled in the present, it is not as a figure of antiblack medical abuse but as the founder of the Free Speech League and a daring advocate of birth control. Foote has been anthologized in the last fifty years as a radical and democratic supplier of reproductive health information and contraceptive devices to patients across the US and, for this reason, as a target of Anthony Comstock's federal crusade against birth control as "obscenity."[16] Understood as a "feminist [in a time] when men rarely spoke in favor of women's rights," Foote has been cast as a minor but crucial character in the major story told about twentieth-century feminism's roots so often narrated around the fulcrum of white women's reproductive choice.[17] Sammy's adjacency to the *ur*-story of American feminist body politics highlights the entanglement of white progressive knowledge projects like Foote's with the (now) denounced knowledge projects emblematized by Sims or the shared black extraction beneath political projects distinguished as reactionary versus progressive.

Dr. Foote self-consciously emphasized this distinction in his time. Establishing his position on the side of white women's reproductive autonomy through a corpus of literature and organizing, he sought, in *Science in Story*, to place himself on the side of black freedom, writing Dr. Hubbs as a tolerant challenger to white supremacy.[18] *Science in Story*'s limited picture of black freedom, however, suggests that the author drafted his story of black freedom not from the expansive desires of black people but from the literature of black Emancipation—drafted by "friends of the Negro" like himself.[19] Indeed, Sammy's suitability to instruct white reader's in the "kindlier feelings of humanity" indexed his derivation from white-authored lessons, dictums, and disciplines addressed to the newly freed in the form of primers, readers, and advice manuals.[20]

Variegated in the antiblack and antislavery political strains running through it, *Science in Story* was also doubly bound in relation to its pedagogical form. For though Sammy appears a vision of black freedom lifted from the *Freedman's Spelling Book* or *Third Reader*, he descended, too, from a different set of lessons in print.[21] Sammy's vocation as an instructor to white children was an extension of children's literature's long reliance upon pedagogies instilled in black. For indeed, the close and extractive relationship between white childhood and black was not just sentimentally affective, as the last chapter detailed, but also instructive, as this chapter illustrates. Placing "our prodigy" into a literary lineage of black lessons for white children reveals that the figurative use of blackness in story and the material abuse of black people in science were not coincidences of a racist culture but integrated lessons in humanism's evolving episteme.

Lesson 1

DEVELOPMENT

Rare among white-authored black characters of the nineteenth century, Sammy Tubbs appears to grow up across *Science in Story*'s first four volumes. Foote introduces Sammy with a new status on the first page of each. When readers meet Sammy at the beginning of volume 2, he has ascended from "Boy Tubbs" to "Student Tubbs"; by the start of volume 3, to "Practitioner Tubbs"; and by volume 4, to "Lecturer Tubbs." Readers witness the progression of Sammy's education and maturation from their first encounter with Sammy playing in his mother's washtub to scenes of him lecturing to large audiences. Indeed, when Sammy delivers a lecture on the brain and nervous system at volume 4's conclusion, the event provides a culmination to Sammy's arc, enacting a transition in which Sammy's work on himself has ended and his work for the good of others has begun. Standing before a packed crowd in a neatly tailored suit, Sammy is an image of poise, equanimity, and rationality.

Anticipating Sammy's lecture with great interest, "people of all shades of color, from the lightest blonde to the blackest Ethiopian," fill the seats and aisles of an aptly named Lincoln Hall.[22] "Gracefully" taking the stage—Dr. Hubbs behind him—Sammy is greeted "by such a clapping of hands and stamping of feet as [i]s almost deafening."[23] By this time, Sammy is known among black patrons of his dispensary as a gentle practitioner and among Dr. Hubbs's white circle as a charming "encyclopedia," "literary curiosity," and even a "Ben Franklin" in "jet enamel and ivory trimmings."[24] Given this audience endearment, the scene of Sammy's performance is not a tense examination of his knowledge but an assured demonstration of it.[25] Discussing details of the "brain [and] cerebro-spinal system" to the "vegetative, cranial, and pneumogastric" nerves, Sammy proceeds to instruct his audience in sophisticated but plain language, describing how "what we call electricity . . . is doubtless the stimulus which our brain employs in performing, under the direction of our will," all "our voluntary motions" and "involuntary" actions.[26] Identifying himself with the "we" of his audience and describing "our brain" and "our will," Sammy advances the notion of common human anatomy and consciousness among those described as the "lightest" and the "blackest" and all in between.[27]

After much applause, Sammy returns at the end of volume 4 to his medical practice, serving the community of freedpeople to whom his family belonged. This is not the end of the story, as there is a fifth volume of *Science and Story* "for private reading," but Foote nevertheless narrates volume 4's end as a coda. As narrator, Foote admits that "it [has been] my desire, from time to time, to call your attention to Sammy's growth."[28] By the time of Sammy's lecture, Foote assures readers that Sammy's character has "been gradually changing" for the better, as Sammy has "seized the brush of knowledge and the easel of opportunity," has "studied hard," and has "cultivated the kindlier feelings of humanity."[29] Though Dr. Foote instructs readers that Sammy is only a doctor "to the extent of being a practitioner of medicine among his own people," the fictional Dr. Hubbs exclaims of his former "door-tender," "My boy is not only an anatomist, but a philosopher, economist, and philanthropist."[30] Once a child delighted at knowledge of his own body, now a young man equipped for the biocentric age, Sammy completes a precocious arc of "industry" before he is twenty years old.[31]

If a straightforward coming-of-age story, Sammy's trajectory measures something less internal to his character and more indicative of his relationship to white patriarchal power. When we first meet Sammy in volume 1, he is described as "a little slave baby . . . owned by a white man in the State of Tennessee." He does not "belong to any white man now," however, "because the good Mr. Lincoln . . . set all the slaves free."[32] After receiving their freedom and "permi[ssion] to go where they had a mind to," the Tubbs family moves to "the great city of New York," where Mother Tubbs works as a washerwoman and Father Tubbs as a whitewasher. Described and illustrated as playing in his mother's "tubs," the joke of Sammy's surname becomes clear: his family are not newly self-styled "Freemans"; instead they have taken (or been given) a humbler namesake—of the wash buckets over which they labor.[33] Beneath this joke lays a more malignant one: Sammy might just have sprung from a washtub as from his mother.

Flown from his enslaver's grip by the grace of the "good Mr. Lincoln," Sammy's ascent to an acolyte of the "good doctor" is less a liberation from white patriarchal authority than its reinstatement in new terms.[34] Indeed, even as Sammy's arc fantastically departs from the exigent and restricted realities faced by most freedpeople, Sammy nevertheless represents the illusory promise offered to freedpeople with the contraction and deferral of their freedom. Nominally freed from slavery but not from its structure of domination or its geography, freedpeople were met with the imposition of responsibilities for which they were perpetually in debt and lessons for which they could never be enough prepared. As Hartman has written, black freedom was "nothing if not burdened, responsible, and obligated."[35] Emancipation's strictures, responsibilities, and lessons were enforced through black codes, economic entrapment, and escalating policing across the latter 1860s and 1870s.[36] Yet they were written, in gentler tones, by white "Friends of the Negro" who sought to direct black freedom even before it was won. In *Advice to Freedmen* (1864), *Plain Counsels for Freedmen* (1866) and *The Freedman's Spelling Book* (1865), the newly freed found instruction in the self-limitation of freedom embedded at the syllable level of their literacy lessons:

> Lesson 171. The great-est vic-to-ry is a vic-to-ry o-ver our-selves, pro-duc-ing pu-ri-ty and rec-ti-tude of char-ac-ter. Free-dom from wrong is the high-est free-dom.
> Lesson 185. The ab-o-li-tion of slave-ry has made an al-ter-a-tion in the con-di-tion of the freed-men, and laid up-on them cor-res-pond-ing du-ties.[37]

Despite his role as instructor, Sammy remains a perpetual pupil of these lessons. Across *Science in Story*, his unending tutelage is manifest in his ongoing need of Dr. Hubbs's advising, in his unfulfilled medical credentials, and in illustrations that bend Sammy toward his books and instructor, like the *Freedman's Third Reader*'s prostrated students (figures 3.2–3.3). Bearing both a visual and an allegorical resemblance to the *Speller* and *Reader*'s pictured pupil, Sammy stands in deeper relation to the *Reader*'s paragon of purity and rectitude: Phillis Wheatley. Employed as evidence that Christian virtue could "raise one from the lowest position to the notice and esteem of the wise and good," the *Reader* offered Odell's memoir of Wheatley to the newly freed, not as a guide in black freedom's expansive imagination, but as a worthy recipient of benevolence: she was "more like a child than a slave" to "the wise and good" people who had enslaved her.[38]

Figure 3.2. Front matter, *The Freedman's Third Reader* (Boston: American Tract Society, 1865–66).

Figure 3.3. Sammy Tubbs and Dr. Hubbs, *Science in Story: Sammy Tubbs, the Boy Doctor, and "Sponsie," the Troublesome Monkey*, vol. 4 (New York: Murray Hill, 1874), 16.

Odell's Wheatley registers near the spine of Sammy's character arc—in Foote's incongruous description of his medical trainee as a "literary curiosity" and in his placement of Sammy among the Hubbs household—as servant, tutee, and "one of the family."[39] Sammy's relation to Wheatley via the literature of black Emancipation, moreover, underscores the significance of Wheatley's antebellum imprint in writing the white imagination of black freedom. Yet if Odell's Wheatley supplies the frame to usher "our prodigy" back into the white patriarch's household after freedom's brief interlude, something else trails him in. When Dr. Hubbs takes Sammy into his home in *Science in Story*'s first volume, he lets in his shadowy partner, too, pledging to "ma[k]e a good man of Sammy and a—well, tolerably good monkey of Sponsie."[40]

Sponsie's unruliness exceeds Dr. Hubbs's disciplinary intent, however, and while readers watch Sammy develop across the series, they see Sponsie split and multiply. Over a cascade of unlikely accidents and convolution, Sponsie gets hopelessly lost. However, in the interim created by his disappearance, a nearly identical monkey takes Sponsie's place only to become captive to the usurped Sponsie upon his return. When these multiple deceptions unravel, both monkeys—Sponsie 1 and Sponsie 2—are retained as equally beloved fixtures of the Hubbs household, though always poised to incite more chaos. Serving as comic relief, the Sponsies underscore Sammy's manly development in distinction to their behavior, which is explicitly referred to as "childlike."[41] Yet the Sponsies are attached to Sammy by a deeply etched fulcrum secured both by old caricatures of black-primate kinship and by the period's supposed scientific confirmation of it. Even before readers meet Sammy and Sponsie, the series' front matter depicts them together—both before an open book—in the medallion image above the text copyright.[42] And when Sammy first receives Sponsie in the series' first volume, the monkey joins him in the "firm of S. and S." When Sponsie 2 lays captive beneath the floorboards in volume 3, his howling seems a part of Sammy's dreams.[43] And when Sammy takes the stage for his capstone lecture at volume 4's end, he does so over Sponsie 1's dissected brain.[44] As much as the lecture acts as a summit for Sammy's development, it also serves as a violent rebuke of the Sponsies' unruly, monkeyed blackness.

Providing a cadaver for Sammy's virtuosic anatomy lecture, Sponsie 1's death also supplies another lesson about black manhood routed through Civil War caricature. Wearing monkey-sized military uniforms and holding unloaded guns, Sponsie 1 and Sponsie 2 spend the eve before Sammy's lecture staging playful skirmishes across the streets of lower Manhattan. The fun ends, however, when the guns are accidentally loaded, leading to Sponsie 1's death and Sponsie 2's fugitive flight. Reviving cartoons of black soldier buffoonery that circulated throughout the Civil War—of hapless "colored *infant*-ry," and ape-ish "intelligent contraband"—Sponsie's death measures the gulf between freedmen and men, instructing readers about the severe consequences of playing at duties beyond one's capacity[45] (figures 3.4–3.5). It is not Sponsie 1's death, however, but Sammy's pragmatic decision to "make good use of [it]" that concludes the racial utility of Sponsie 1 to the story.[46] Indeed, the fact that Sammy's elegant lecture occurs over the dead body of his pet provides a chilling confirmation of Sammy and Sponsie's relational utility. In the killing of Sponsie, Foote violently severs Sammy's nascent manliness from the shadow of unruly Caliban blackness that has tailed him. Moreover, able to perceive the medical opportunity of Sponsie 1's death, this exquisitely disciplined version of Sammy is now ready to discipline others, acting as the "young missionary" of the "good doctor."[47]

Figure 3.4. "Raising Colored Infantry," pen and ink with watercolor and albumen, circa 1863, Library Company of Philadelphia, Digital Collections.

Sammy swiftly takes up this task, carrying out Dr. Hubbs's program for remediating the ills of poor urban life by establishing order in a social world increasingly unsettled by black people moving, working, and thinking "as they had a mind to."[48]

A champion of Hubbs's new order, Sammy serves as an intermediary between bourgeois white authority and black freedpeople. Yet as Dr. Foote makes clear, Sammy's purpose was circumscribed by his effect

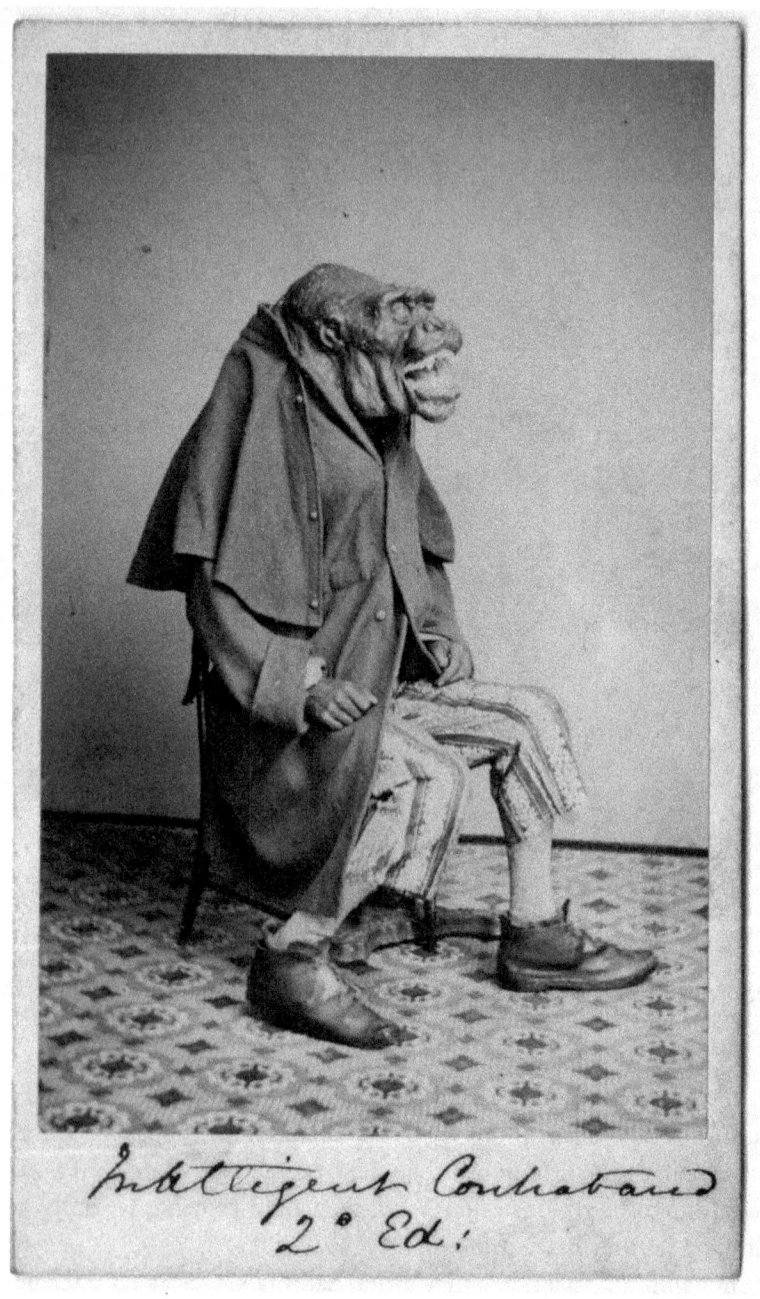

Figure 3.5. "Intelligent Contraband," photograph, albumen on carte-de-visite mount, circa 1863, Library Company of Philadelphia, Digital Collections.

not on the fictional world altered by black freedom but on the real one. Foote repeatedly reminds readers that "our prodigy" is there to serve their progress. Periodically interrupting the story to address readers directly, Foote expresses his wish that "when my young readers who have had so much better home instruction [than Sammy], see how ready Sammy was to learn everything useful... they will not be less interested in studies of so much importance to their health and happiness."[49] Below this statement, Foote's intended audience is illustrated: a bespectacled and cherubic white child, drawn as if peering into the book.[50]

And if Sammy's development of knowledge and "kindlier feelings" were some of Dr. Foote's teaching tools, Sammy's value lay equally in his endlessly renewable need for development. This developmental elasticity is apparent in what remains unfinished in Sammy's medical training and manhood at volume 4's end, and it looms, too, in Sponsie 2's unspent potential to return with more crude than kindly lessons in the final volume. As Sponsie 2's specter over Sammy's lecture confirms, the link between Sammy and liminal, fungible blackness remained unbroken. Though clad in Emancipation's aspirations and schooled in science, Sammy, in the end, represented something old and unfree for Dr. Foote and his readers.

Dr. Foote likely understood the need to balance new and old when he drafted Sammy, for he was a shrewd surveyor of the American literary imagination and its market. In his successful works for adult readers, from *Medical Common Sense* and *Plain Home Talk*, to his "Health Monthly" newsletter, to many more texts published by his Murray Hill Publishing Company, Foote demonstrated an attunement to his audience and an ability to communicate with modulated sensitivity and sensationalism.[51] Perhaps his crafting of Sammy came from writerly market research, from the letters he received from children and adults seeking his health advice, or from the counsel of his wife, a former schoolteacher who would have known children's reading habits well.[52] He may also have drafted Sammy from his own reading. Born in 1829 to a "prosperous and esteemed" merchant family in Cleveland, Ohio, Foote likely grew up with access to the period's popular stories and their instructive black parts.[53] Whether Foote relied on personal knowledge or publishing acumen, Sammy's role bears a distinct relationship to the array of pedagogies in black offered to white child readers of the middle nineteenth century: lessons in refining their humanity told in blackened consequences.

Lesson 2

THE DISCIPLINE OF INK

If it was often the task of sentimental literature to teach readers how they should feel toward children, literature *for* children had long been structured by a related didactic purpose: teaching young readers how they should behave, or act, *as* children. Indeed, English and Anglo-American authors of children's stories had inculcated readers in the behavior, appearance, and divergent fates of good and bad children since the eighteenth century at least, from the catechisms of the *New England Primer*, to stories of Goody Two-Shoes, Sally Bark, and Jem Preston, who acted as reflections in which "the GOOD themselves will see; The Naughty, what they ought to be."[54] Yet by the mid-nineteenth century, the consolidation of innocence in white child figures like Eva and the vacating of innocence from black child figures like Topsy provided authors of conduct literature a new and vivid coding.[55] The mirror that such stories held up to children was no longer a metaphor for internal reflection. It had become a more practical looking glass, in which a child's moral standing could be confirmed by racial appearance.

In 1848, English publishers began to print two 1845 works by German author Heinrich Hoffmann: *Slovenly Peter*, translated from *Struwwelpeter*, and *The Inky Boys*, translated from *Die Geschichte von den Schwarzen Buben*. By 1851, American publishers began to print Hoffmann's works as well in both faithful and broad adaptations.[56] Like a century of conduct-centered children's literature before them, Hoffmann's *Slovenly Peter* and *The Inky Boys* instructed readers in moral conduct and discipline, conveying their lessons by illustrating the terrible consequences of improper, profane, and lazy behavior. Given their familiar resonance within past conduct-centered stories for children, neither text was entirely novel. Yet what would define these stories and their impact on American children's literature was their use of blackness and racialized deformity as the embodied consequence of white children's misbehavior.

In both its original and adapted forms, *Slovenly Peter* tells the story of a child who suffers disfiguring consequences after rejecting bodily discipline. Refusing to wash, comb his hair, or cut his nails, Peter's body undergoes a transformation outsize to his level of neglect and excess in racial meaning (figure 3.6). His hair extends into a coarse and wild "shock," his fingernails grow long and "black as soot," and in most illustrations, a wash of color darkens his face. The racial coding of *Slovenly Peter* is vivid yet not entirely clear, for though Peter's wildness certainly evokes a transatlantic imaginary of black and brown savagery, it also alludes to a white figure interpolated into that imaginary. Hoffmann may have drafted his "Peter" from an eighteenth-century disabled German child known as "Peter the Wild Boy," who, after being found living ferally in the woods of Hamelin in the 1720s, was made to perform as a prodigy for the British court.[57] However much *Slovenly Peter* revived

Figure 3.6. Illustration of "Slovenly Peter" in *A Laughter Book for Little Folks: With a Profusion of Humorous Engravings* (Philadelphia: Davis Porter, ca. 1865–66), Harvard University Libraries.

the history of Peter "the Wild"—and the already racialized inscription of prodigy that captured him—*Slovenly Peter*'s explicit connotations of blackness and brownness would have been as salient by its publication in the 1840s in Germany as it was in the US in the 1850s.

Rejecting self-mastery, Slovenly Peter's transformation presents a frightful trajectory away from the child's intended vector toward manhood—suggesting that failure to understand one's place at the top of the human hierarchy could reduce one to the bottom of it. Moreover, if *Slovenly Peter* shows the fall from Man's stature to be swift, it also shows it to be permanent, for Peter does not recover himself at the story's end; he is left an abject figure of mockery.[58] Presenting both a frightful vulnerability to transformation and the still worse possibility of permanence, *Slovenly Peter* played with the instability of race as a mutable and imprecise category yet also as a category clarified through the violent consequences of being black. The alignment of *Slovenly Peter*'s US debut with the enforcement of the 1850 Fugitive Slave Act underscores the salience of blackness to *Slovenly Peter*'s schema of racial consequences. An 1850 English adaptation captures the immediate danger of blackening in this context, presenting a version where Tom, the slovenly child in question, is mistakenly "sold [as] a Negro Slave" and by one descending panel of text and illustration, becomes subject to an overseer's lash (figure 3.7). This version performs a punitive recasting of the white slave not as an innocent suffering child but as a child who deserved, for becoming so black, to suffer. No level of contrition can save this blackened child. For him, "tis too late!"[59]

If *Slovenly Peter* and its feminized companion, *Slovenly Kate*, used blackening to enforce white children's bodily discipline, *The Inky Boys* wielded the same threat differently, ostensibly to instill racial tolerance. *The Inky Boys* tells the story of three white boys who tease a "black-a-moor" for his black skin and are then punished by St. Nicholas for their indiscretion. Following their acts of harassment, St. Nicholas dips each child into an inkwell "till they are black, as black can be."[60] Early illustrations of *The Inky Boys* emphasize the inkiness of their resulting blackness more than its racial meaning. In these versions, the boys become flat, gray-black silhouettes that appear mechanical and toylike; they do not truly come to resemble the "black-a-moor" (figure 3.8). By becoming blacker and *less* human than the "poor" and "harmless" black man, the Inky Boys are taught a lesson about the inhumanity of their racist attacks. Yet whether read more or less

Figure 3.7. "The Boy Who Was Frightened at Soap and Water," in *The Young Ragamuffins* (London: David Bogue, 1850), Osborne Collection of Early Children's Books, Toronto Public Library.

generously, the basis of this fable remains clear: blackness is either a pitiable condition or a punishment. The lesson of *The Inky Boys* is not to respect black people but rather to civilly contain one's disrespect.

This lesson about racial civility is not the only lesson that *The Inky Boys* circulated, however. In a McLoughlin Brothers 1867 edition of *The Inky Boys*, the uncivil children undergo a transformation that blackens them physiognomically, altering the crux of the story (figures 3.9–10). In this version, the rowdy white children harass the "black-a-moor" while waving a "Union" flag above their heads. The flag both locates the story and gives it a greater political edge, identifying the children's behavior in historical, geographical, and classed terms that previous versions lack. The "black-a-moor," who in this case strolls the streets of a Northern city, comes under the attack of children who support the Union but are unabashed in their racism. Ragged and urchin-like, these Inky Boys caricature children of the white working class, perhaps even referencing the white mobs whose racist violence surged in Civil War draft riots.[61] The blackened transformation of these Inky Boys also signals something about the class of their whiteness.

Figure 3.8. Illustration from "The Inky Boys," in *A Laughter Book for Very Little People* (Philadelphia: W. P. Hazard, 1851), Harvard University Libraries.

Figures 3.9–3.10. Illustrations from *The Inky Boys* (New York: McLoughlin Brothers, 1867), American Antiquarian Society.

Predictably, the physiognomic transformation that St. Nicholas's ink produces—curled hair, larger lips, and curved noses—is more citational of black caricatures than of black people's appearances. The boys' blackness is still permanent and inky, but it is also corked, drawing on features of blackface minstrelsy in the enunciation of their eye whites and in the outline of the third child's lips. The moral of this edition of *The Inky Boys* elaborates on previous versions to critical distinction. Again, readers learn that overt racism is condemnable. But they also learn who is to blame for this overly expressive form of racism: poor whites, identifiable by their rowdiness and penchant for minstrelsy. When understood within the class politics of children's literature itself—as a consumer good primarily enjoyed by bourgeois children and their families—the moral resounds further. Rather than providing a mirror in which "the GOOD themselves will see; The Naughty, what they ought to be," this version presents middle-class children with a story of who they are not and whom they should never emulate.

Both *Slovenly Peter* and *The Inky Boys* enjoyed wide popularity, appearing in US print from the 1850s far into the twentieth century.[62] The impact of these stories extends beyond their many imprints, however. The use of "inking" as the consequence of white children's misbehavior would appear in stories that stretched outside of Hoffmann's conceit, as in the tale of "Miss Mopsa," in which a white girl recklessly spills ink over her books, leading to her own ink-blackening and eventual hanging.[63] The significance of racial deformation and inking is visible, too, in the inky materiality of late nineteenth-century children's stories. Highly saturated chromolithography was a hallmark of McLoughlin Brothers picture books, which featured a range of racial lessons as unsubtle as their mode of color printing.[64] In one of their more disturbing series—*Nine Little Niggers* and *Ten Little Niggers*—the illustrations are so highly saturated that they appear as if ready to bleed onto the readers' fingers. In one surviving copy, the blue-black ink of the caricatures has indeed bled, staining the entire book in caricatured, instructive blackness.[65]

Vivid across these works, the permeation of inky blackness can be viewed in another way: in the formation of individual reader consciousness. A mid-nineteenth-century copy of Arnaud Berquin's *The Looking-Glass for the Mind* bears the mark of a reader who found their storybook wanting of ink's instructive racial pedagogy. Though this edition was printed in 1845, *The Looking-Glass* comprised a set of Berquin's eighteenth-century stories that predated—and likely influenced—Hoffmann's nineteenth-century stories, including "Crazy Samuel," which presents a scenario so like *The Inky Boys* as to suggest Hoffmann's direct reference to it. In the story, three white boys harass Samuel, a white elder. Samuel defends himself by throwing dirt and rocks at his attackers, who attempt to flee the chaos they have incited. The reader of this copy of *The Looking-Glass* must have recognized the resonance between Hoffmann's story and Berquin's, for they decided to hand-color the faces of the troublesome boys with dark brown ink. It is not possible to know when this reader marked their copy of *The Looking-Glass* nor what passed through their mind as they did so. Yet their inking of Berquin's troublemakers suggests that the reader had internalized Hoffmann's story and, identifying not with its child characters but with its discipline, turned Samuel's retaliatory dirt into their own punishing ink[66] (figure 3.11).

Figure 3.11. [Hand-colored] illustration from "Crazy Samuel," in M. Arnaud Berquin, *The Looking-Glass for the Mind*, 20th ed. (New York: D. Appleton, 1845), 49. American Antiquarian Society.

Slovenly Peter and *The Inky Boys* instilled a resonant lesson in American children's literature: good children were white; bad children were (turned) black. Across Hoffmann's two stories and their American adaptations, readers learned that children who did not control their bodies, impulses, or uncouth racism would be liable to trade their precious white childhoods for the conditions of black children, their progression toward human perfection for perpetual black childlikeness. White children would have understood this threat viscerally, not least because black children were the established targets of their own violence. As Bernstein shows, through doll play, nursery rhymes, jokes, and a proliferation of caricatures, white children learned that within the bounds of their imaginations, homes, and schoolyards, antiblack violence was a sanctioned form of play. Moreover, as Wynter and McKittrick contend, this "play" was more than children's rehearsal of white supremacy as politics, or even a performance of it; it was the practice of internally reinforcing the "collective . . . biocentric belief system wherein" the "dysselection of blackness," was "reflexively experienced" and embodied as "common sense."[67] The infamous exclamation that Frantz Fanon described as his "hailing" by white children—"Look! A Negro!"—reappears through this analysis and children's literature's blackened archive both as a reflexive utterance and as a *knowing* one: the hurling of blackness at another, as delivered by a white child well-read in *The Inky Boys*'s plot, if missing its lesson in civility.[68]

Sequestering his black character from a rowdy street address by drawing him into the middle-class townhouse, Foote arranged *Science in Story* to ensure that readers did *not* miss this last lesson. Because, for Dr. Foote, the knowledge that he sought to cultivate among children could not be communicated chromatically or anatomically alone; it required teaching the "kindlier feelings" that animated the skin color and sinews of humanness.[69] Yet if he kindly offers his protagonist domestic comfort, a place for quiet study, interracial friendship, and a path of rectitude rather than abuse, Dr. Foote nevertheless seeks to extract from Sammy: it is by consuming Sammy's story that readers achieve their knowledge. For them, he is less a mirror in which readers might see themselves and more a facilitator of their self-conception, like the inky characters of previous stories. In fact, he is inked too. Describing Sammy as a "Ben Franklin" in "jet enamel and ivory trimmings," Foote discloses that Sammy is, after all, blackened.⁷⁰ And though this comparison seems to place "our prodigy" on par with Franklin, readers literate in the racial alchemies of children's literature would know that jet enamel was a transformative substance, not an embellishment.

Science in Story is an archive of the amalgamated substances—of science *and* story, whiteness and blackness, animal and human, and child and Man—incorporated to transform the common sense and specialist knowledge of the human across the nineteenth century. Indeed, even as it consolidates an ideal human anatomy, the story draws out the "impossible purity" of such a human, displaying the many degraded "parts" involved—not cast out—in its making.⁷¹ It is Sponsie's remains that produce Sammy's knowledge and Sammy who supplies white children with "knowledge of themselves." What this series of incorporations intimates is the connection and dependence running through human hierarchies, even in a period where they were articulated sharply and enforced with violence. Indeed, if Foote's story depends on this apparent contradiction, it is because his knowledge did. Despite training in medicine in a period of outright accusation against black humanity, it was black people themselves who were made to explicate the human's inner anatomy.

Lesson 3

THE HUMAN, DISSECTED

Dr. Foote's credibility as a source of medical knowledge ascended with the field of American medicine as it became the increasingly disciplined, institutionalized, and exclusionary purview of elite white men. Recognized and self-described as an "eclectic" physician, Foote combined the empirical approach of allopathic medicine with a broader array of homeopathic methods that remained viable approaches to healing across much of the nineteenth century. Yet by the time of his authorship in the 1870s, it was his allopathic approach—and his possession of a medical degree—that most clearly pronounced his authority, locating him within medicine as a specialized discipline and elevated profession.⁷²

Few American medical practitioners of the early nineteenth century had possessed medical school credentials, deriving their practices more from experience and tradition than from a programmatic study of the human body and organ pathology. But by the 1840s, leaders of

American medicine began to train a new generation of doctors with standardized anatomical, physiological, and clinical knowledge. Founding the American Medical Association in 1847, physicians demarcated medicine as a hallowed profession, reserved almost exclusively for educated white men.[73] When Foote began his medical training in 1858 in Philadelphia—the geographic center of American medicine—he entered a racially segregated pedagogical environment bent on elevating medicine's empirical basis, rigor, and public standing.[74]

Attending Penn Medical University, Foote studied within an institution self-consciously invested in championing a particular notion of medical progress. Established in 1853 by obstetrician Joseph S. Longshore, Penn Medical University provided what Longshore described as a "beautifully progressive" program.[75] Requiring coursework of greater length and breadth than many peer institutions, Penn offered extensive opportunities for anatomical learning with the school's "natural preparations" in addition to courses in medical history, philosophy, and jurisprudence. And Penn proclaimed itself progressive in another way: it was one of the first medical schools to admit both men and women. The white men and white women who attended Penn Medical University during the 1850s—for there is no record of any nonwhite pupils—joined Longshore in his vision to intervene in what ailed the social body: poverty, contagion, and vice. Preparing students for this "exalted mission," Penn Medical University saw the physician as an "arm of science" extended toward the suffering, ignorant, and poor. White women doctors were to play a crucial part in Penn's crusade, as a "comfort and solace to a suffering world."[76]

Longshore believed that white women were both untapped resources to medicine and underserved recipients of medical care. Requiring Penn's medical students to take courses in obstetrics and gynecology, Longshore intended to dislodge taboos surrounding women's reproductive health and to broaden physicians' general knowledge of it. "Obstetrical Anatomy, Physiology, and Pathology" were taught, like Penn's courses in "Practical Anatomy," "Surgical Anatomy," and "Pathology," through the study of "specimens," "natural preparations," and "postmortem examinations"—in other words, by students' dissection of human cadavers and by the examination of preserved human remains.[77] How those human bodies and parts were procured, and to whom they belonged, was of subsidiary importance to ensuring their availability to Penn's medical educators and students.

Though there are no discrete records of Penn Medical University's supply of cadavers, the school could not have functioned without participating in Philadelphia's extensive trade in black people's bodies. Long after Dr. Foote's studies, Pennsylvania established its 1883 Anatomy Act, deeming the bodies of deceased persons not claimed by the living legally transferrable to medical institutions.[78] Prior to this, there were few legal channels for the acquisition of cadavers. Yet students of Penn Medical University, and of Philadelphia's many other medical schools, were educated over "abundant" human remains.[79] Records of black grave theft, outcries of nineteenth-century black Philadelphians, and the remains of black persons still held by Philadelphia institutions confirm that through a network of doctors, city officials, and grave robbers, black people's bodies were cultivated as the foundation of Philadelphia's "beautifully progressive" offerings in medical education.

Philadelphia's extensive, systematic theft of black people's bodies was not unique; rather, it was part of a "domestic cadaver trade" that targeted black people as especially vulnerable and already commodified sources for knowledge extraction.[80] As work by Todd Savitt, Michael Sappol, Kenneth Nystrom, Deirdre Cooper Owens, and Daina Ramey Berry has uncovered, the bodies of deceased black people, enslaved and free, were the foundation of American medical education and experimentation from Pennsylvania and New York to South Carolina, Georgia, and Louisiana.[81] The fate of black people's bodies subjected to medical expropriation were varied; some were carelessly disposed of after their abuse, while others became part of university collections, used for decades and longer in medical students' education. Yet the extraction of knowledge from black people's bodies was not limited to their physical use within institutional settings. Knowledge of the human body derived from black people, in the form of studies, theories, and practices, circulated as the epistemic basis for human anatomy in America.

Repeatedly representing the human in both "normal" and "pathological" states through encounters with bodies that were more often black than white, medical educators refined their idea of the biological human through knowledge of black people's anatomies. Put another way, the composite human model that emerged from American medical education was, in aggregate, black. Black human anatomies were, of course, as diverse in their human composition as any, their physiological blackness signaling their status as targets for medical violation and little else. Yet in their numerical overrepresentation, black people's stolen bodies fundamentally marked the creation of the nineteenth century's medical knowledge of being human.[82] Unearthed, traded, and violated in a manner that white physicians found unthinkable for the bodies of other whites, with the exception of white sex workers and convicts, black people were forced into a surrogacy with, and as, the human. This human surrogacy was a status conferred belatedly after death. But it was also a role that many black people were forced to live through—brought near to death for the purposes of testing human receptivity to medical intervention. Like the cadavers over which Dr. Longshore and his students worked, living black people were made to suffer for, and as, the human anatomy that Foote was meant to master.

When, for instance, Dr. Longshore taught obstetrics and gynecology to Edward Bliss Foote in the late 1850s, he likely did so with knowledge derived from enslaved women subjected to Sims's experiments. By the time Foote began his training at Penn, Sims's gynecological findings had spread widely. These findings had come, as Deirdre Cooper Owens, Nicole Ivy, and C. Riley Snorton have detailed, from the bodies of Anarcha, Betsey, Lucy, and at least nine other enslaved women who were subjected to unanesthetized experimental surgeries on a plantation outside of Montgomery, Alabama, between 1844 and 1849.[83] As Sims himself asserted, he conducted these experiments with the express goal of entering his name in medical history.[84] Sims took what he gained from these women to establish a career in the north as an expert in gynecology and a champion of women's health. In 1852, Sims published his study "On the Treatment of Vesico-Vaginal Fistula," a paper derived from these experiments.[85] Moving to Philadelphia and then New York, Sims founded the New York Woman's Hospital in 1855, hailed as the first women's hospital in the nation.[86] Beginning in 1854 and spanning the next several decades, Sims lectured before growing crowds of prominent obstetricians and other physicians on his repair of vesicovaginal fistulae and the use of silver sutures.

Whether Longshore ever attended Sims's presentations or read his articles, I cannot prove. Given Longshore's interest in the progress of obstetrics and gynecology, however, and his proximity to Sims's circuit, it is likely. Even if Longshore never encountered Sims directly, by the time of Foote's matriculation at Penn, Sims's name and practices—his surgical techniques and his famed "clamp suture"—had certainly made their way into Longshore's intellectual surround, if not his teaching. The career that Dr. Foote built upon graduating from Penn, staked upon his progressive approach to women's reproductive health, cannot be divorced from Sims as an intellectual antecedent, nor from Anarcha, Betsey, and Lucy as the uncredited sources of Sims's knowledge. Indeed, Sims's experiments and Foote's progressivism were interlocking pieces in the repro-focalization of white womanhood, or the Woman's part in Man's biocentric revision. White women's reproductive knowledge of themselves came to animate a major sector of feminist struggle. It also served as the vector on which white women would claim parity with white men and their partnership in the endeavor of human improvement.

Sammy appears more aligned than adjacent to Foote's feminist legacy when understood within the genealogies of antiblack medical abuse that flowed into Foote's knowledge of the human in general and into the sex-differentiated category of Woman. Subjected blackness—and black people—were the defining anatomical and epistemic foundations of both. This shared and essential dependence on blackness was made to disappear, however, by the biological circumspection of black humanness that ran alongside it. Indeed, the centrality of black human surrogacy to American medical history has been well hidden in part because of concurrent scientific developments: the inscription of race as biological difference. While white physicians of the mid-nineteenth century were using black people's stolen bodies as laboratories in which to model and teach the human's anatomy in universal terms, many were equally involved in an overlapping project: locating anatomical evidence to split, or speciate, blackness from the human.

Darwin's theory of shared origins ushered blackness back into humanness, if in dysselected status, after 1859. Yet the protoevolutionary theories popularized by scientists in the decade prior rendered this an especially tenuous reinstatement. During the 1850s, prominent naturalists such as Louis Agassiz put forth the theory of polygenesis as a viable alternative to shared human origins, proposing that black, Native American, Asian, and Caucasian people were separate species to which separate principles, rules, and natural fates applied.[87] A theory based in biblical readings as much as in empirical claims and rooted in seventeenth- and eighteenth-century racial frameworks, polygenesis aptly marked the epochal transition it extended across, its confounding number of contradictions signaling a breakdown of old explanations and the need for new.[88]

It would be a mistake, however, to view polygenesis as an insubstantial theory destined to be overturned. For if polygenesis reveals obvious inconsistencies—in the racial categories it constructed and in its categorical slippage between "species" and "race"—these irregularities are more revealing of strategic pliancy than illogic. On one level, the imprecise usage of species and race merely reflects that the two were, as Jackson argues, coevolving classifications whose meanings were produced through each other, not discrete and discoverable truths of nature.[89] On another level, the broader vagaries of polygenesis reflect the necessary flexibility of any theory to capture all that whiteness demanded of race as a technology and of blackness as its ever-expendable resource. Polygenesis—like any theory of the human's hierarchy—needed to serve less as a coherent school of thought than as a platform on which multiple strains of subjection could be articulated.[90]

Natural selection's eventual toppling of polygenesis appears more a modulation than a break where the status of black people is concerned. And indeed, the continuity between the two theories in regard to blackness becomes evident when viewed through the principle of recapitulation that survived their rupture. A theory that emerged from entwined genealogies of natural history, zoology, medicine, and *Naturalphilosophie* and French Transcendentalism in the nineteenth century's first decades, recapitulation proposed that a species' evolutionary development could be viewed synecdochically through the development of an individual organism from embryo to maturity, or that the life of a species ran in parallel to the life of any given member of the species.[91] Distilled in the 1860s by Ernst Haeckel as "ontogeny recapitulates phylogeny," the theory maintained its status as both common sense and observable fact into the twentieth century.[92] Recapitulation was not a theory exclusive to human evolution—indeed, Agassiz himself studied the principle in fish fossils, not in human anatomies.[93] But Agassiz and others would put the theory to human use, asserting that the parallel he perceived between black adults and white children was the expression of evolutionary inheritance.[94] If recapitulation's usefulness to such claims was immediate and intuitive, it was because, despite its status as a unifying theory of all life-forms, the theory arose from a humanist story: that of blackness and the human child.

At its base, recapitulation depended on the linear, predictable, and progressive vector of humanism's child toward its preconceived fulfillment, or the child's telos toward manhood as its ontological end. Yet the child's centrality to the theory was as much in its measure of underdevelopment as in its potential. Reinforcing childhood as a natural state of lack, recapitulation seamlessly retooled the claim of black childlikeness—a simile embedded within slavery's regime and suited to its violence—into an evolutionary law that no decree of Emancipation, or federal amendment, or anticolonial struggle could wholly circumvent. By remapping race's already developmental axis onto newly bio-evolutionary horizons, recapitulation stabilized racial power in the face of its nominal breakdown. It also set the stage, and delivered the terms, for Man$_2$'s signature project, toward which all his other biocentric refinements tended: eugenics.

Eugenics was the conclusion to recapitulation's history, both by indirect implication and by the specific genocidal programs that the theory's proponents—most famously, Haeckel—underwrote. For indeed, Haeckel became a foundational thought leader of German National Socialism.[95] Scaffolding the typology of heritable traits put forth by Francis Galton in *Hereditary Genius* (1869) and flowing easily into Herbert Spencer's gauntlet of racial survival, recapitulation's premise, wherein the relative underdevelopment or refinement of an individual body stood in for the evolutionary progress of its race, gave Man's anti-black and anti-Indigenous violence a new and globally scaled mandate: to direct natural selection and dysselection by pronatalism and sterilization.[96] In this way, the struggle to maintain dominance over the human established its new front, fought less around whether black people belonged to the human family and more around whether they belonged to the human future.

The prescription to recapitulation's parallelism, eugenics was also the concluding lesson of Dr. Foote's *Science in Story*. For though announcing his friendliness to the Negro, it was "promot[ing] the physical perfection of his race" that was, in the end, Foote's most central project.[97] Indeed, when Dr. Foote died in 1906, his obituary named "race improvement through rational control of marriage and parentage" as his "favorite theme."[98] The retrospective abridgment of Foote's legacy to that of "birth control advocate" in the late twentieth century repeats the well-known excision of eugenics from white feminism's historiography. But the selfsameness of Foote's feminism and his project of racial purification reveals more than the centrality of eugenics to white women's ascendant biopolitical power. Sammy's place inside these projects charts the vital presence of blackness within Foote's imagination of the human and yet the problem that black imagination, now free, posed to Foote's control over the human's future. Foote's desire to extract human knowledge from Sammy, to make him the tutee of white authority, and to limit his development of an independent storyline suggests Foote's attempt to curtail the possibility that Sammy and those whom he represented might shape the human on their own terms. Though Dr. Hubbs offered Sammy his friendship, his knowledge, and his dictums on freedom in *Science in Story*, it was Sammy's emergent freedom and *his* knowledge of the human that Foote feared, desired, and sought to control.

For if black people were subjected as the resource for the human's remodeling and refinement, they were also the agitating force that pressed upon the human, threatening to move, shift, and alter its boundaries. Black Emancipation—and the delivery of Manhood rights to black men—might have formed a radical challenge to Man, a potential rewriting, or an overturning of his epoch. Yet the legal interdiction of black freedom, as well as the longer empirical transition in Man's power, narrates a more protracted struggle over the human: one that did not begin or end with Emancipation, and one that was driven by more (and minor) actors. Foote responded not to black people's "permi[ssion] to go where they had a mind to" after 1865 (indeed, there was no such permission given) but instead to black people's emergent and unceasing insistence to go where they had a mind to. Reading Foote's final volume of *Science in Story*—and the eugenic project into which it conscripts Sammy—extends this point, sketching the new terrain of the human's struggle that whites attempted to hold and that black people "go[ing] as [they] please[d]" threatened.[99] It was this threat that progressives and reactionaries—the Negro's "friends" and foes—attempted to contain through eugenic control, the project upon which white women's power would rise, and the specter that necessitated an end to Sammy's story.

Lesson 4

"PRIVATE READING"

Science in Story's fifth volume conveys its lessons in racial reproduction through radical provocation followed by rational retraction, offering a vision of black masculinity and interracial romance first to be celebrated, then made suspect, and then condemned. Foote opens this instructive arc with the augmentation of Sammy's body, modeling his lessons in human reproduction through Sammy's newly acquired musculature and "fine proportions" and with his shift in title—from Lecturer Tubbs to Gymnast Tubbs.[100] Volume 5's central setting—in a gymnasium where Sammy acts as proprietor—not only stymies Sammy's ascent to Dr. Tubbs but also provides the physical regimen that readies Sammy to model Foote's last lessons. Masculinized by his gymnastic practice, Sammy's body becomes the site for knowledge of sex and reproduction.[101] Despite this radical offering, Sammy's black manhood, sexuality, and future are ultimately suspended, left without fulfillment at the story's end: Foote's volume for "Private Reading" enters mature territory while retracting the vector of maturity previously ascribed to its protagonist.

Though the narrator proclaims that Gymnast Tubbs has become "too much of a man to be called a boy," volume 5 refers to Sammy almost exclusively by that term: deeming him "the precocious boy"; "the bright, useful boy"; and "only a boy."[102] Moreover, while Sammy is poised to enter medical college at the story's end, the future set before him lacks description, for readers never see Sammy cross medicine's institutional threshold or witness his progress therein. As if to confirm the ambivalent manhood of "our prodigy," Sammy's tie to perpetual immaturity—Sponsie 2—returns to trouble the series' end.

Sponsie returns to Sammy on the eve of another lecture—this time on reproduction and sexual hygiene. Perfectly timed to intercede upon Sammy's speech, Sponsie's return is also narratively crucial, as he ushers in the problem for which eugenic solutions must arise. Readers learn that after his accidental killing of Sponsie 1, the fugitive Sponsie 2 was kidnapped by a "menacing" Italian "beggar" and her band of four "dirty faced" and "tattered" young children.[103] As Foote's expenditure of pejoratives indicates, it is through the characterization of this devious, destitute, and overly fertile immigrant woman that he is able to initiate his argument for curbing society's "worthless fruit."[104] Bringing the supposed problem of racial degeneracy to Dr. Hubbs's parlor, Sponsie 2's mischief invites Man₂'s new regime of racial discipline.

Volume 5 does not communicate Foote's eugenic prescription through invectives lodged at the indigent Italian mother alone, however. It is through Sammy—and his audacious but futureless romance with a young white woman, Julia—that Foote finds the progressive and scientific register to deliver his manifesto on racial futurity. In one sense, Sammy and Julia's reciprocal affection announces Foote's undaunted advocacy of social integration. He lends righteousness to their coupling by making it catalyze the antiracist reform of Julia's father, and he affirms Sammy and Julia's romance by including a radical illustration: a kiss between them.[105] Yet Foote sows and reaps doubt about the sanctity of Sammy and Julia's black-white affections from the beginning. Foote imperils Sammy once by making him the black suitor of a white woman and twice by making him untrue to her. Though Julia ultimately wins Sammy's heart, Sammy pursues Julia and Dinah, a young black woman, across volume 5.[106] Soiling Sammy's previously impeccable virtue—and his suitability for Julia—Foote redeems the boy doctor strangely: by allowing Sammy to announce his own unsuitability for Julia in eugenic terms.

Though he bears affection for Julia, Sammy concludes that they shall never marry, because "the question is by no means settled that such crossings of races are favorable to the happiness of the parties immediately concerned, or to the welfare of offspring born of such a marriage."[107] Only when scientists had, by "careful investigation," removed "physiological doubts" regarding "such inter-blending" would Sammy subject any white woman to marital or sexual partnership.[108] Maintaining affection for Julia but retracting the prospect of marriage from his future, Sammy strands himself on the "verge of manhood," foreclosing his ascent to the titles of husband Tubbs and father Tubbs and the bourgeois manliness entailed therein.[109] Notably, Foote does not redirect Sammy's foreclosed desire toward a racially appropriate partner—he abandons Sammy's pursuit of Dinah as well—leaving Sammy and Julia merely "play[ing] the agreeable" and exchanging "brotherly and sisterly good-night kiss[es]" at the story's end.[110] If the Sponsies' long tether confirms Sammy's true status as the story's Caliban, Julia plays an apt Miranda to him, his only, yet denied, object of desire. And Dinah, it seems, is the necessarily absented "Caliban's Woman," her disappearance confirming that the black reproductive future she and Sammy might represent was a problem of equal concern to Foote as the miscegenated future he aborted.[111]

Sammy's relationship with Julia, and its retraction, opens the floor for Dr. Hubbs to comment more extensively on questions of interracial sex, degeneracy, and human evolutionary progress. Advancing the arguments of the real Dr. Foote, Dr. Hubbs explains that to "hasten the moral and physical redemption of the human race" and to "avoid the birth" of "unwanted fruit" and "monstrosities," it was imperative to curb "haphazard reproduction" while "promot[ing] the peopling of our planet with better specimens of humanity."[112] Dr. Hubbs establishes his argument on the dire effects of profligate reproduction and the need for intervention on new empirical evidence of unchecked reproduction's results. Citing an investigation into the "criminal" lineage of a family in upstate New York, who would soon become infamous as the "Jukes" of an 1877 eugenic study, Dr. Hubbs warns of the "swarms" of "idiots, imbeciles, drunkards, lunatics, prostitutes, and paupers!" born of one "badly organized" white woman—in this case, Margaret Juke.[113]

As Dr. Hubbs's diatribe clarifies, Dr. Foote's progressivism only went so far. Or rather, the arc of his progressivism was long but narrow, originating in his allegiance to whiteness and extending toward the endless but exclusionary progress of the human's white futurity. Though he gave Sammy a role in this arc as a health educator for the next generation, the boy doctor's beloved, trusted, and intimate placement among whites was bound to expire. Dr. Foote's vision could not admit Sammy's intimacy with whites and his growth in the same frame, forcing Sammy instead to recuse himself from the human "redemption" that Dr. Foote sought to summon. Yet while volume 5 demonstrates the limits of Dr. Foote's imagination as it pertains to his fictional black ward, it is decidedly revealing about Dr. Foote's real, not fictional, progeny. While Sammy was a figment of the author's imagination, Dr. Foote did possess a real protégé, whose name did not rhyme with but extended his own. This was

Dr. Edward Bond Foote Jr.—a very literal Man$_2$—the son to whom he would entrust his progressive vision and eugenic project (figure 3.12).

Between his writing of *Science in Story* in the early 1870s and his 1906 death, the elder Dr. Foote and the younger prescribed, wrote, and advocated for birth control and race improvement extensively, creating a shared archive in the form of many E. B. Foote–authored publications from their Murray Hill Publishing Company. In 1886, with his father as

DR. E. B. FOOTE, JR.

DR. E. B. FOOTE, SR.

Figure 3.12. Portraits of Dr. Edward Bond Foote Jr. and Dr. Edward Bliss Foote in *Pioneers of Birth Control in England and America* by Victor Robinson (New York: Voluntary Parenthood League, 1919), National Library of Medicine Digital Collections.

consultant, Foote Jr. published *The Radical Remedy in Social Sciences, or Borning Better Babies through Regulating Reproduction by Controlling Conception*, which decried "go-as-you-please" reproduction and "the hydra-headed monsters, [of] crime, pauperism and disease" that resulted from it.[114] Advertising *Science in Story* as a "highly instructive" and "really laughable" narrative in the pamphlet's back pages, *Radical Remedy* also referenced the series in its interior text, where Dr. Hubbs's eugenic speech was restated with critical amplifications.[115] Repeating the use of the Juke family as a cautionary tale, *Radical Remedy* gave blackened color to the Juke's notoriety, writing that "there descended" hundreds of criminals "of the dangerous class" of "paupers," "undesirables," and "prostitutes"—all from "one woman called Margaret, who, like Topsey [sic] merely 'growed' without pedigree."[116] Taking a bad white woman and turning her black, Foote Jr. telegraphed a half century of cultural repertoires and racial pedagogies to his readers, making shrewd use of Topsy as a tool of racial refinement.

How Dr. Foote Jr. came to pen this allusion to Topsy—much like the question of *why* Dr. Foote Sr. invented Sammy Tubbs—entails both plain and complex answers. Because, by the 1880s, to "grow like Topsy" had become a common American idiom, a reference to unchecked growth—that is, growth that defied an authority's intended design. The fact that a black child character was the figure who gave ungoverned, anxiety-producing growth its measure became increasingly obscured over the course of this idiom's twentieth- and twenty-first-century use.[117] For Foote Jr., however, the original meaning of the phrase was not obscure but urgent. In likening Margaret to Topsy on the basis that she, like the enslaved child, had just "growed," he specified Margaret's unknown, or sui generis, origins as a central and foreboding fault. For the problem of such uncertain origins was—understood within eugenics—that they did not *stay* in the past, that they impinged upon the future. This problem was itself an inheritance from slavery, like Topsy. Because those whom slavery purported to make "kinless" by law and violence very often found other means, beyond the white patriarchal family, to become, as Brigitte Fielder puts it, "kinful."[118]

It was Margaret's infamous "kinfulness" that incited Foote Jr.'s metaphorical blackening. For indeed, not only did Margaret defy the legitimate structure of family; she also gave birth to generations of mixed-raced children. The blackening Foote applied to her, then, was only a reiteration of a stain already upon her, the result of a failed bodily discipline far graver than that of Slovenly Peter or the Inky Boys. And indeed, if *Radical Remedy* conveys the loss of racial status that follows from interracial sex by its comparison of Margaret to Topsy, placing *Radical Remedy* back in the context of its authors' biographies, legacies, and their other literary works reveals that controlling the likes of Margaret Juke, protecting the likes of fictional Julia, and supporting the work of figures like Margaret Sanger were parts of the same project for the Footes.[119]

The Footes aligned themselves with white women who shared in the fight against "go-as-you-please" reproduction and who imagined reproductive choice as the prerogative of some to decide the future, not the prerogative of all to live it "as they had a mind to." Put differently, it was their eugenics that made the Footes recognizably feminist. Understanding eugenics as the meeting ground between powerful, enfranchised, credentialed white men and white women holding relatively less power elucidates how the reproductive self-knowledge white women developed across this period formed as a compatible corollary, rather than a challenge, to Man_2's authority. Just as it clarifies the consolidation of white power running through white progressive and white feminist histories, it also reconnects these histories to their reactionary counterparts. Both were fixated on the white child's future and on vanquishing "monstrosities" from that future before they could be born.

Naming his "hydra-headed monsters" as "crime, pauperism and disease," Foote Jr. depersonalized these figures as problems of the social body as a whole, not as particular racialized members of it. Yet as *Science in Story*'s cordoning-off of its black milieu underscores, the Footes located these problems as unfurling from, and exacerbated by, black freedom. The monsters for which Foote Sr. and Jr. sought social-scientific study and eugenic intervention were the same "vampire[s]" and "incubus[es]" that white reactionaries conjured and slayed by mob violence and campaigns of lynching terror across southern states.[120] The Footes and their reactionary counterparts would both make white women and their reproductive sanctity the cause of their campaigns while engaging in a broader project to curb and contain black life to the same land, labor, and order that slavery had formerly secured. For while articulating reproductive degeneracy as the specter on the horizon, Foote Jr.'s language of "going as you please" telegraphed that the human's future was threatened not only by black reproductive autonomy but equally by the more varied forms of generation and regeneration that black people were undertaking—moving freely, creating new social worlds, gaining literacy, creating their own curricula, and reshaping the human by their own self-understanding.[121]

Deserting Sammy's adulthood for his investment in "race improvement," Dr. Foote ends his series by avoiding details of Sammy's life and the shape it might have taken. As readers prepare to see Sammy off to medical school, Foote's agent of mischief intervenes to provide a spectacular and violent diversion. It is not Sammy's graceful leave-taking but Sponsie 2's "frightful," "bleeding," and "gasping" departure that concludes the story's action.[122] Again dressed in his soldier's uniform, Sponsie 2 entangles himself in the gymnasium's whirring machinery, going tail-first toward a horrific, fatal disembowelment. Finding Sponsie 2's mangled body, Sammy repeats the disturbing calculus occasioned by the first monkey's death. Sammy dissects Sponsie 2 and this time makes a scientific model from Sponsie's skin and head. Though saddened by Sponsie's demise, Foote notes that Sammy had "outgrown his companion of former years as many a boy had outgrown his pictorial primer or toy drum."[123] Sammy spends the story's end cleaning up the mess of his outmoded double's remains.

Science in Story's conclusion suggests that much as Sammy has outgrown his surrogate monkeys, readers should be ready to shed Sammy—their primer in black "garb"—at the series' end. "The author hopes," Foote writes in the last pages, "that at the conclusion of this series, you have obtained a pretty good knowledge of yourselves."[124] Having "ke[pt] up with Sammy" and learned all they could from him—of their skeletons, muscles, nerves, nutrition, excretion, and sexual organs—readers should be sufficiently knowledgeable of their own humanness to dispose of Sammy's. By his summation of his lessons in humanness and by the racial pedagogies that trail behind them, Foote confirms the central role of science and story for accomplishing the human's revision and for securing Man$_2$'s dominance after and over black freedom.

Foote's declaration of pedagogical accomplishment, however, also connotes the ongoing anxiety of this dominance, pointing toward a new and major area of intellectual inquiry: less about what white children could be taught and more about *how* they learned. The impressionable, changing, and growing minds of white children would become a central object of scientific inquiry in the last decades of the nineteenth century, producing child study as a new empirical front for American social reproduction—taking its theoretical framing from recapitulation and its purpose from eugenics. Alongside white children's minds, the contents, knowledge, and inner workings of black children's minds, too, became sites of white power's concern yet were disparately addressed. Foote telegraphed this problem—of black children living and thinking as they "had a mind to"—when he concluded his fictional black prodigy's story with the assertion, or omen, that Sammy "lives to speak for himself."[125]

4

"Oscar Moore Can Tell You"

Unbinding Brightness in the Archive of a Wonderful Boy

Dear Doctor:
This will admit you to the Central Music Hall, Corner Randolph and State Streets, Wednesday, December 5th, 1888 at 10:30 O-Clock A.M.

Dr. Clevenger wishes to exhibit to the physicians of Chicago a case of extraordinary memory development in a three-year-old mulatto child, who is congenitally blind, but not idiotic, as such anomalies usually are. There has been but one similar instance recorded, so far known. The Doctor will be indebted for any reference to kindred *lusu naturae* to be found in medical literature.

Please bring this card with you. * NOT TRANSFERABLE.[1] (figure 4.1)

On the morning of December 5, 1888, a small, blind, black child stood before the scrutiny of white physicians, newspaper reporters, and other onlookers crowded within Chicago's Central Music Hall. This audience had gathered to behold something about the child: what they would come to call his "brightness," or his mind's expansive capacity to absorb, retain, and transmit information in measures beyond what they believed a child's mind—or any human mind—to be capable of.[2]

This child, who confounded common sense and thus commanded white attention, was Oscar Moore. He was just three years old. He had been born to formerly enslaved parents, Fanny and Henry Moore, near Waco, Texas, in 1885. In the brief years and months since that time, Moore had been swept by a current of white speculation in his brightness toward repeated scenes of spectacle, leading to this one in Chicago. Well practiced in his repertoire, Moore knew what to do. He was to demonstrate his brightness by feats of lengthy recitation and calculation at the prompting of the white man beside him, Hans Peter Neilsen Gammel, who questioned him from a small pamphlet, *Hand-Book of the*

> Chicago, December 3, 1888.
>
> Dear Doctor:
>
> This will admit you to the
>
> ## CENTRAL * MUSIC * HALL
>
> Corner Randolph and State Streets, Wednesday, December 5th, 1888,
>
> . . . AT 10.30 O'CLOCK, A. M. . . .
>
> Dr. Clevenger wishes to exhibit to the physicians of Chicago a case of extraordinary memory development in a three-year-old mulatto child, who is congenitally blind, but not idiotic, as such anomalies usually are.
>
> There has been but one similar instance recorded, so far as known. The Doctor will be indebted for any reference to kindred *lusu naturæ* to be found in medical literature.
>
> *Please bring this card with you.*   *   NOT TRANSFERABLE.

Figure 4.1. [Ticket 1], Central Music Hall Physicians' Exhibition, Chicago, Illinois, December 5, 1888, Shobal Vail Clevenger Papers, 1864–1924, US National Library of Medicine.

Wonderful Boy, a Few Things of What the Little Blind Two Year Old Boy, Prof. Oscar Moore, Can Tell You. The physicians were then to examine Moore's brightness, invited to this "Physician's Exhibition" by Dr. Clevenger and admitted by the tickets with which he had solicited their attendance. Around the doctors, the wider white assembly was to enjoy Moore's brightness, primed by their familiarity with the pleasures to be drawn from prodigious black children.

Moore delivered his performance and endured the examination, the medical men analyzed what they observed in him, and the audience members did, it seems, enjoy themselves. In the aftermath of the "Physician's Exhibition" in Chicago, Moore's renown as "Bright" Oscar expanded across the US, as did the value he generated for men like Gammel, who propelled Moore from the Midwest to the Northeast in wider performance circuits and toward larger financial schemes. Well before he reached the age of ten, Moore had demonstrated his brightness across many stages, in dime museums, at newspaper offices, and in elite parlors. He had endured more scrutiny and more spectacle, and he had experienced the transfer, traffic, and litigation of his brightness by the white men who vied to profit from him. Despite all that Moore's brightness generated for these white showmen, managers, scientific inquirers, and popular audiences across the nineteenth century's last dozen years, however, almost nothing about Moore's brightness would be recounted in popular cultural circuits of the twentieth century. Moreover, nearly nothing of it might be reconstructed from the perspective of the twenty-first.

Moore's brightness—that which had filled the Central Music Hall and produced white wonder, that which white men had converted into both capital and scientific currency—might only be glimpsed, and guessed about, through the single extant photograph that keeps his image, name, and brightness in the same frame (figure I.1, discussed in this book's introduction). If deciphering the photograph's visible props and hidden scaffolding has served to open this book's inquiry into the larger story of black prodigy, however, the photograph also delivers more immediate facts about its subject: that within a few weeks of Moore's exhibition in Chicago, Moore had been taken to New York City, that his managers paid David H. Anderson to take his portrait there, and that they began selling the image to audiences in the plural form of cabinet cards, each printed with the label "Bright."[3] In its present singularity, moreover, the photograph suggests something else: that the historical process that orphaned this photograph is in itself a crucial part of the story of Oscar Moore.

Indeed, the process that stranded the photograph from its context, and that which relegated the story of Oscar Moore near to obscurity, was not affected merely by the unthought erosion of cultural knowledge over time. It was also brought about by a deliberate revision written over the past. In the early twentieth century, the man who had assembled Moore's *Hand-Book* and made use of it in Chicago wrote a different kind of story. Penning his personal memoirs—not as a showman but as the bookseller and businessman he became—H. P. N. Gammel claimed that his investment in Moore's brightness delivered no returns, that in the end, Moore amounted to "nothing."[4] Abetted by Moore's disappearance from the stage at the turn of the century and, relatedly, by the wider decline in popular knowledge of him, Gammel's "nothing" might have dissolved the scene at the Central Music Hall, casting doubt on what had been worth witnessing and suggesting, perhaps, that there had been nothing to witness at all.

This chapter approaches the story of Oscar Moore over the impasse of nothingness to reinstate the circumstances of his story and to map the shifting cultural ground beneath it. Reopening the "Physician's Exhibition" in trespass of the explicit, exclusive dictate of Clevenger's tickets and infringing upon the *Hand-Book*'s bound set of questions, I do so to examine what conditioned white men to gather in wonder, greed, speculation, and fear around three-year-old Oscar Moore and, importantly, not to reexamine Moore or his brightness. Locating brightness primarily in archival remains of Moore's performance of it, I eschew an empirical interest in deciding what Moore *really* knew, how, or why. Brightness was something whites attempted to behold, to categorize, and to fix in place, yet equally—and against their efforts— it was something beyond their comprehension and control. In recognition of this, the method of "unbinding" that this chapter applies to the *Hand-Book* and other sources is not undertaken as a reparative act of freeing Moore or his brightness from their enclosure. As I argue, in many ways, Moore already exceeded and evaded those confines.

To "unbind," then, is to query what the gaps in Moore's archive and the formal "looseness" of Moore's *Hand-Book*, tickets, and other ephemera have to do with one another. Such ephemeral, flimsy, and cheap print materials can, as Meredith McGill notes, tell us different stories about "formal knowledge" and "social authority" in the past and about the archives that hold them in the present.[5] Identifying this as a methodological opening also makes visible a methodological limit, however: that this monograph is itself an act of rebinding, placing Moore within, and on the cover of, my work. Yet releasing any claim to produce Moore's complete story and questioning his photograph as a transparent view of him, I heed Hartman and Édouard Glissant in reckoning with this archive as both woefully fragmented and rightfully opaque.[6] Without certainty, I nevertheless assert what I do know: that "nothing" was not the end.

Reconstructing what led to the scene in Chicago, what took place there, and what followed from it reveals Moore's importance not only to Gammel and Clevenger but to his period's patterned dependence on the work and worth of black children. While contesting Moore's erasure, however, I identify greater import in tracing the arc of Moore's story *and* its redaction, in charting the ledger of brightness as its value ascended and then as its currency degraded, and in following the uncertain fate of

Moore's career of prodigy as it crossed into "the century of the child."[7] Placing Moore's story in the context of white Americans' new projections and measurements of childhood's value, Moore's disappearance marks a beginning as much as an ending.

For if what set the stage for the white enjoyment of Moore's brightness in 1888 was the desire of white Americans to retain access to black children as generators and conveyors of humanism's lessons, the precipitous end of Moore's career by the turn of the century marks the resetting of that stage and critical revisions to those lessons. Popularly described as "the second coming of Blind Tom" and performing in the cultural space that Wiggins still occupied, Moore performed his repertoire in elliptical relation to the order Wiggins was made to replay.[8] While appearing to renew Wiggins's role for another generation, however, Moore's career of prodigy began in tension with the new eugenic paradigms that Sammy Tubbs was intended to inculcate.

The interrelation of Moore's memory, knowledge, intelligence, and blindness and his black juvenile embodiment—all that "Bright" condensed in shorthand—was a problem for the eugenic consolidation of the human. Witnesses to his deviation and seeking to reconcile it, the doctors who examined Moore worked to delimit the bounds of his exception and to contain its implications within their taxonomies. Yet following the "Physicians' Exhibition," Dr. Clevenger would equivocate over Moore's categorical location, rationalizing brightness as the inherited effect of partial white ancestry on the one hand while, on the other, classifying Moore as a *lusus naturae*—a freak or sport of nature.[9] Spectacularizing Moore as such an "anomaly," Clevenger and his colleagues notably declined to study Moore within the category of perhaps the greatest salience and availability: as a child.[10]

For though the contents of Moore's mind presented a problem for the dominant understanding of human heredity, the new sciences of child psychology and pedagogy and the emerging movement of child study might have supplied a way of reintegrating the divergent black child into the dominant white order's terms.[11] In the years immediately preceding Moore's popular ascent, white psychologist G. Stanley Hall opened the field of child study with the specific aim of enumerating what children knew and how they learned.[12] Giving finer calculus to the blank slate's inscription, Hall admitted and even celebrated the mutability of children's development—yet his field ultimately aligned its work with the determinism of eugenics. As the previous chapter demonstrated, the strength of the latter's lie was to be found in the former's evidence. Child study, child psychology, and pedagogy were the means by which Dr. Foote's science of "borning better babies" could be advanced and vindicated—in the measurement of "gifted" children.

By the early twentieth century, the invention of "intelligence quotient" testing and a range of other rubrics made the measurement of children against statistical and psychological standards into a common practice.[13] The figure of the "gifted" child emerged in this context, defined by their vertical distance from those deemed "moronic," "imbecilic," or "feeble," and by the special resources of "gifted education," newly allocated to them.[14] If supposedly measurable by testing, however, giftedness would come to encompass a broad and vague set of children's cognitive, social, and physical qualities; it was in many ways as overladen and ill defined as Moore's brightness. Unlike brightness, however, giftedness was not to be trafficked across sideshow stages. Giftedness was the profit of excellent child-rearing in middle-class homes and the pride of white parents. Embodied in white children, it was the coin by which the century—and the future—was to become theirs.

Indeed, in the rising economy of giftedness, Dr. Foote's admonition to white children—*not to let a little colored child do better than them*—resounds more seriously. Yet if competing with Moore's vast stores of knowledge was a challenge, it was ultimately Moore's immeasurability that posed a graver problem. For the expansive contents and unknown workings of Moore's mind represented the failures of dominant empiricisms of race and childhood *to* measure, threatening the legitimacy of the human model that their measures upheld. And worse than destabilizing the present order, Moore portended a different future, one in which his brightness potentially grew, or "*just grew*," in directions not only unpredicted by dominant rubrics but disruptive to them. Though Moore's vanishing from the stage cannot be narrated as a deliberate act to avert this future, both his disappearance and the claim that he amounted to "nothing" indicate that the very conditions that led to his exploited career eventually became hostile—and even dangerous—to its continuation.

Pieced together across fragmentary archival sources, the successive acts of white men to exploit, enjoy, dissect, and later disappear Moore's brightness map these changing conditions or the individual acts and historical shifts that made "nothing" of the vital story that Oscar Moore can tell us. Yet as valuable as assembling this story is for charting the relation between childhood's measure and the power held by men, in its disassembled state, Moore's story is revealing too: of gaps left open between questions and answers and of all the possibilities that exist where "nothing" is known.

The Pursuit of Brightness

Oscar Moore was born on August 19, 1885, in Waco, Texas. Or near there. Sometime before his second birthday, the cognitive capacity later called his brightness was noticed by his mother, Fanny. Or it was discovered by H. P. N. Gammel. Or by Gammel's children, or by someone else entirely. After this discovery, Moore was adopted by Gammel. Or he was apprenticed to a man named William Thaison.[15] The details of Moore's early life, like those of his later years, are shot through with indeterminacy. "Or" splits multiple claims about and to Moore, suggesting competing possibilities for how his spectacular career began. Even the only catalog record of Moore—attached to his photograph—inscribes this uncertainty, describing him as a prodigy of "memory or mathematics" and mistakenly suggesting that he was photographed in Anderson, New York, in the 1870s rather than *by* Anderson, the New York City photographer, in 1889.[16]

Beginning my archival inquiries from this photograph's locus of disorientation, my reconstruction of Moore's life has necessarily attended to multiple levels of ambiguity. Yet there is more than uncertainty structuring the story of Moore's beginning. Beneath the surface of archival disorientation, there is another surface: the origin story laid by Gammel to cover his and others' speculative calculations. Around the outset of Moore's first tour in the middle of 1888, Gammel began to spin a tale that highlighted the unlikely accident of Moore's brightness while hiding the deliberate negotiations that produced his career and leased Gammel control of it. Neither this story nor the exploits it covered were original; rather, they were supported by the ground they retread. Placing Moore within a narrative of white family stewardship and sentiment, Gammel mined both the cultural pattern of prodigy and the specific precedent of Tom Wiggins's captive career. Though Gammel attempted to secure his narrative at the same time that James Bethune lost control of his, the dueling family fictions aired by James and Eliza Bethune in Wiggins's custody case were likely not a deterrent but potentially a blueprint—offering Gammel multiple legal and narrative conceits on which to scaffold his investment.

Gammel explained to newspaper reporters that he assumed his place beside Moore through a neighborly coincidence, because his own children caught sight of Moore in his home as they traveled to and from school. One outlet reported how "the first indication of the baby's wonderful memory was discovered by his [Gammel's] children," who were "astonished to hear the little fellow lisp their names the second time he touched them."[17] In a separate account, Gammel's children "took such a fancy in him" that they "begged" their father to take Moore home, certain that he too would be charmed by the child's precocity.[18] Collapsing the hundred-mile distance and racial lines between the Moores in Waco and the Gammels in Austin, Gammel made his stage pairing with Moore close and near familial, tying the white innocence of his children to the nefarious claim that Moore was "[his] little black boy."[19]

A one-sentence entry printed on March 6, 1888, in the *Fort Worth Daily Gazette* offers an intervention into this claim, however: describing a "transfer" of "the wonderful blind negro boy, Oscar Moore," from an "H. W. Warren" to a "Wm. Thaysen of Austin," Texas, "for a healthy sum."[20] Indicating the involvement of at least two other men—and nowhere mentioning Gammel—the news item forms an evidentiary puncture in Gammel's account. Moreover, describing a monetary exchange between white men for a black child, the notice strips the sentimental trappings of Gammel's story while asserting the ongoing salience of enslaved exchange in the postbellum era. If the figure in question is never enumerated, the reader of this notice was to understand that, by the same logic that a sum of money could be humanized as "healthy," a "blind negro boy" could be monetized as its equivalent.

Inscribing Moore's fungibility, the "transfer" that this newspaper announced was likely that of an indenture agreement. Distinguished from bondage, the legal bind of indenture was nevertheless indistinct in both design and practice. By indenture's arrangement, Warren and then Thaison would have been licensed to reap the value of Moore's labor under the unchecked pretense that they were responsible for his care and education.[21] Whereas Gammel alleged to have adopted Moore, the likelihood that Warren and Thaison acted as Moore's successive apprentice-masters recasts Gammel's role as subcontractual, clarifying that it was other white men, not his children, who tied Gammel and Moore together. However much this news entry reframes Gammel's claims, it does little to explain how Moore became the pecuniary interest of these men, nor on what terms they took him from his parents. Whatever the Moores' consent or resistance may have been, the widespread coercion involved in black apprenticeship (and the specific precedent of Wiggins's indenture) suggests that neither Fanny's nor Henry's claims to their son nor their articulation of his best interests would have held weight against the interests of Warren or Thaison once a contract had been drawn or even imagined.[22]

References to Henry Moore's presence at Oscar's performances suggest that Oscar's removal from his family was neither complete nor permanent, however, and perhaps, too, that Oscar's career may have even aligned with the interests of his family. Given the extreme exigencies faced by black agricultural laborers in the post-Reconstruction south, it is plausible that the Moores strategically sought their son's apprenticeship, recognizing the value of his brightness as a path out of poverty, debt, and white supremacist terror. Lacking records left by Henry or Fanny, however, neither their motives nor their agency in contracting Oscar's labor can be decided. Rather than providing clarity to such complexity, the *Gazette*'s notice left open the sensational question of whether Moore was indeed captive property. What had been "transfer[red]," according to the notice, was the speculative value contained in the word "wonderful" attached to "blind negro boy."

The phrase—"wonderful blind negro boy"—held forth both a promise and a problem in the time that two-year-old Moore was given its designation. When Thaison paid his "healthy sum" to Warren for Moore, he staked his investment on the knowledge that a "wonderful blind negro boy" was a proven and popular prospect for white American audiences. Casting Moore's brightness into Wiggins's shadow, Thaison likely bet on the unending white appetite for the thrill produced by a black disabled child performing feats beyond their expectation. Yet the confoundment Moore presented was untenable for the same reason that it was spectacular. Moore's brightness—his demonstration of unexplained knowledge and also his display of the normative "sense" Wiggins was said to lack—extended the implications of his performances beyond the stage. For while the entertainment value of brightness lay in its inexplicability, it nevertheless could not be left *without* explanation nor be left out of white sight.

From the outset, capturing and containing Moore's brightness—giving it form and repertoire, bracketing it, explaining it, and binding it to white people—was essential to its viability. Indeed, the removal of Moore from his family at the age of two (or earlier, in Warren's unrecorded case) represents the white interest in both claiming his value and excising it from its original social world. In binding Moore into apprenticeship, Warren and Thaison secured years of his labor while cutting off alternative possibilities of what Moore's brightness might have become if unwitnessed, unharnessed, and unanalyzed by whites, if left free among Moore's black family, kin, and community. For indeed, if the "wonderful" value of Moore's brightness proved inseparable from him, Warren, Thaison, Gammel, and later Clevenger each proved that it was not immovable: it could be drawn further from blackness and closer to whiteness by contract, by sentiments of white family, and by mythologies of blood. The term *bright* itself signified that the racial problem of Moore's cognitive capacity had a racial solution under its surface.

In 1888, when Moore began performing as "bright," the term circulated discursively as a descriptor of light, an ad word referring to clear complexions, a valence of hope, and most obviously in its application to Moore, high intelligence.[23] One might note a "bright day," suggest the promise of a "bright future," or describe "a very bright man," as did reporters writing in the volume of the Chicago *Daily Inter-ocean* that featured Moore's December 5 exhibition; or they might promote the "bright complexion" of a Pear's Soap consumer, as contemporaneous papers advertised.[24] However commonplace, these colloquial uses of *bright* occurred over a ledger of racialized commercial meaning just beneath the term's association with faultless skin.[25] As work by Walter Johnson has detailed, "bright mulatto" was one of many specific yet unstable categories used by enslavers to classify a subset of those they enslaved.[26]

Just as Moore appeared in the news as "Bright" Oscar, enslaved people half a century before him had appeared in print with their value and physiognomy also announced by "bright." In antebellum print, the invocation of "bright" beside "mulatto" appears so patterned as to render the terms nearly inseparable. Slaveholding subscribers advertised "For sale, a likely negro woman, bright mulatto, straight black hair, very intelligent and well disposed"; offered a "200 Reward" for a "Runaway . . . bright Mulatto Negro Man"; and announced a "Fourteen Hundred Dollars Reward" for a group of fugitives, including "Isaac, a bright mulatto, aged 13 years"; "Henry, a bright mulatto, aged 4 years"; "Amanda, bright mulatto, 15 years of age"; and "Milly, a bright mulatto, aged 8 years."[27] As these entries clarify, the postslavery attachment of "Bright" to Moore spoke doubly to the relations of property that encircled him and to his "proximate whiteness," or what Johnson describes as the hypervaluation of whiteness in blackness.[28]

Yet if the antebellum advertisement of "brightness" gives context to Moore's postbellum value to whites, these notices also propose something else: that brightness was not easily *held* proximate to whiteness, that it could, in fact, escape from it. The print record that names this cohort of "bright mulatto" children—Isaac, Henry, Amanda, and Milly—does so in response to their flight from slavery and its terms. Naming their brightness was an aid to the fugitives' recapture, a way of making them legible to whites accustomed to reading the features of black persons for their value: here, a reward. But these notices also expose that despite the heightened value of whiteness in blackness, those deemed bright could and did steal that value away from slaveholders to take self-possession or, in this case, collective possession: in a kinship formation of black minors.

In securing the apprenticeship of two-year-old Moore, Thaison sought to forestall the possibility of Moore's self-possession and of his belonging among his black kin. Yet the effort to bind Moore's brightness was not a feat once and for all accomplished, even if fixed in law. Moore's apprentice-masters, managers, and audiences worked on material, rhetorical, and empirical levels to maintain their hold on what, within Moore, still evaded them. Like the quotation marks typeset around "Bright," the meaning of Moore's performance was always both enclosed and displaced, made to refer to something in and beyond him, something apparent yet unapprehended. It was never enough for Moore to simply demonstrate his brightness; its reward, for white audiences and inquisitors, was to be found in capturing it.

"There Is No Predicting What May Develop Later"

When Dr. Clevenger published "An Infant Prodigy" in July of 1890, he seemed to have accomplished the capture of Moore's brightness for science and under his name. Submitting a report to the *Alienist and Neurologist* based on the findings of having "publicly exhibited [Moore] to the physicians of Chicago, at the Central Music Hall, in 1888," Clevenger established his authority as an interpreter and firsthand examiner of Moore's brightness.[29] And indeed, because the report circulated in reprintings and citations, the publication extended a long-standing line of credit to Clevenger as the singular expert in the "case" of Oscar Moore.[30] As a subject of Clevenger's analysis, Moore became a small coin in his larger accumulation of intellectual property and research, elevating Clevenger's status within medico-scientific studies of the human mind, its anatomy, and its pathologies. Though Moore's name does not rise to the surface of the doctor's professional legacy, Clevenger's eminence within Chicago's medical history, his status as a subject of medical biography, and the worthiness of his papers for preservation within the US National Library of Medicine owe an incalculable debt to Moore.[31]

Yet even as the report serves as a ledger of Clevenger's professional extractions from Moore, the report's contents—by their ambivalence and indecision—betray Clevenger's failure to extract any certain knowledge from the child. Though describing Moore's recitations and calculations, enumerating measurements from Moore's body, and supplying a detailed genealogy of his ancestors, Clevenger's report did not, in the end, answer its underlying questions: Why did this three-year-old black blind child possess such an uncommon capacity for gathering, retaining, organizing, and recalling information? From where in his body or mind did this brightness emanate? What, in the sciences of human heredity or anatomical pathology, could explain it?

Uncataloged and tucked between miscellaneous materials of his archive, the tickets that Clevenger printed as invitations to Moore's examination announce the promise of discovery that the report leaves unfulfilled. Reading them against the report's irresolution, they reanimate the double speculation—of capital and conjecture—that Clevenger made in Moore. As tickets, the cards state their value in an economy of the spectacular, and yet demarcating their exclusive address to certain

"Dear Doctor[s]," they also certify themselves as permits of scientific license. Not only did the tickets invite attendees to extract knowledge from Moore alongside Clevenger; they also suggested the rewards of bringing their own knowledge to Clevenger. Indicating a future in which "the Doctor will be indebted for any reference to kindred *lusu naturae*," the tickets established the "Physician's Exhibition" as an exchange wherein Clevenger and his colleagues were to confer around Moore as their shared interest.

Both the report and newspaper coverage confirm that the tickets fulfilled their purpose: nearly fifty doctors exchanged their tickets for the opportunity to watch as Clevenger subjected Moore to the measurement of his facial features, teeth, skull, height, sense of smell, taste, and touch over the course of two hours.[32] Indeed, the report indicates the extension of further invitations within the exhibition, like the task given to ophthalmologist Henry Gradle to examine Moore's pupils by pouring the chemical homatropine—a substance often toxically overdosed to children—into his eyes.[33] Moore might have felt his heart race, his skin flush, or his thoughts distort into hallucinations while under the drug.[34] However frightening, painful, or disorienting this and other aspects of the examination may have been for Moore, Clevenger left no record of Moore's response in his report, simply describing Moore as "very amiable."[35]

While each such description or piece of data referenced in his report reflects—and effaces—significant violence and intrusion done to Moore, they nevertheless amounted to insignificant findings for Clevenger's purpose. In the end, as one reporter noted, Moore's brightness seemed "to puzzle the doctors quite as much as it interested them."[36] In lieu of unraveling the puzzle, Clevenger's report offered split suppositions: that the "anomaly" of "Oscar's extravagant memory" was "due to pathological conditions" and yet also that it resulted from white ancestry that mixed with, and mitigated, his parents' blackness.[37] If unable to clarify the origins of brightness, neither could Clevenger foresee its future. Instead, he cast it into double-negative speculation: "It cannot be predicted that he will not develop as he now promises to do, equal and extraordinary powers of mind, even though it would be rare in one of his racial descent."[38]

Inconclusive and contradictory, Clevenger nevertheless ended his report with confidence that, irrespective of Moore's future, "in any case, science will be benefited."[39] Indeed, Clevenger predicted this outcome despite uncertainty about Moore's mortality. Declaring that Moore "appear[ed] in perfect health" in one breath, Clevenger made a contrary claim in another—that for his "strumuous [tubercular] condition," Moore might, in the end, "die young."[40] Science would benefit "in any case" because Clevenger, like Foote and the field of medicine to which both belonged, knew the essential scientific value to be captured from black life, extended or expired.[41]

"Given up as an enigma," for now, Clevenger's deferral of answers about Moore reflected both the limits of his understanding and his marked avoidance.[42] For while he conferred with colleagues, combed Moore's lineage for white ancestors, and intimated a future in which anatomical answers might be taken from him, Clevenger betrayed great disinterest in what Moore himself could have told him. Viewing Moore as a "case," an "anomaly," and a "freak," Clevenger did not register Moore as a subject who could testify in any way to his own interior thinking, corporeal being, or immaterial brightness. Scattered newspaper reports describe Moore as "lively," as posing "unexpected questions," as "always asking" for explanation, and as speaking with "a choice of select words which [was] in itself wonderful."[43] Just as the contents of Moore's questions and vocabulary fell beneath reporters' description, Clevenger, too, demonstrated a disinclination to analyzing the contents of Moore's speech, thoughts, or actions. We can expedite our understanding of his apparent oversight by recognizing the expertise and racial order that structured his view: an avid anatomist, his methodological inclination was not to conduct interviews, nor would he have been likely to consider the thoughts of black children as salient evidence, scientific or otherwise. And yet, noting that Moore possessed "the intelligence of a much older child," his report displayed an awareness—left unfulfilled—that he *could* have assessed Moore within, or against, the scientific rubrics of childhood that gained prominence around him.[44]

For during the same period that Moore's question-and-answer repertoire formed the basis of spectacle, questioning children had become a scientific method. In 1883, psychologist Hall published the findings of his study on young children, *The Contents of Children's Minds on Entering School*, inaugurating the popular American child study movement and establishing the system of child observation upon which American psychologists would calibrate their new schemas of human development. Creating an extensive survey, Hall set out to test the abstract, synthetic, and perceptive qualities of young children, not their rote recall. To Hall, children's "learning [wa]s more useful than [their] knowing."[45] Asking children to describe concepts as diverse as a beehive, the number five, and God, Hall was interested in children's correct grasp of empirical concepts but also in the processes by which they integrated different systems of knowledge.[46]

Filling in the previously rough schema of children's mental development with detailed strata and predictions of its progress, Hall helped place children's development at the center of the field of American psychology that his career anchored.[47] Yet while establishing the grounds from which scientists began to map human psychology across pedagogical, societal, and environmental matrixes, child study's underlying theories and practical application remained inexorable from the vector of racial destiny; for Hall, the early education of children was the making—or unmaking—of manhood, nation, and civilization.[48] In light of this, Clevenger's decision to approach Moore as an object of medical inquiry rather than as a subject of child study appears less as his personal failing and more as his perceptive awareness that brightness was as troublesome to new studies of childhood as it was to existing hierarchies of race—indeed, that it exposed their ongoing interdependence and their new conjuncture.

Studying black children was not a practical problem for Hall or his field but an epistemological one. The appearance of black children in Hall's early data, and then out of his major theories, tracks this. In 1883, the contents of black children's minds appeared to Hall as both worthy of note and unremarkable in distinction. For while segregating the data of "Colored" children from their "White" counterparts, Hall nevertheless reported nothing racially distinctive about black children's early patterns of thinking, learning, or understanding in *The Contents of Children's Minds*.[49] Yet as Hall advanced from his early studies toward the theories and prescriptions for which he became well known, black children disappeared, necessarily, from the child he measured in aggregate. Linking early childhood development to the fate of his race, Hall declared that the development of white manhood depended not on the refinement of white children's behavior but on the unbridling of white children's savagery.⁵⁰ Claiming that "a child repeats the history of his race," Hall ran recapitulation in reverse—articulating white childhood's ontological relationship to a phylogenetic notion of blackness in new terms.⁵¹ In Hall's schema, blackening white children was not a method of marking the bad from the good. Just as Sammy Tubbs was the raw material that formed white children's humanness, Hall made use of indeterminate savageness as the resource from which white children's optimal humanness could be evolved, through the passage of primitive play. In the individual evolutionary drama of the white male child, black children—who troubled the side-by-side equivalence of (white) children and childlike races—could not figure.⁵²

Against the use of blackness to shape, discipline, and evolve white children, Oscar Moore's brightness was value absconded. For indeed, Moore's brightness not only posed a challenge to empiricisms of child development that could not assimilate him; it was also a demonstration of a black disabled child's possession of qualities that white adults coveted and elevated for their children, and their futures, alone. In this order, evacuating brightness of its uncaptured value, clearing away its excess meaning, and suspending its implications were each necessary for the work of securing white futurity through the modern cultivation, measurement, and education of better babies and gifted children.

The spectacular anachronism, crude frameworks, and cruelty of Clevenger's exhibition of Moore diagram the suspension of Moore away from the new discourses, prescriptions, and benchmarks of childhood that burgeoned around him. Yet while this lag exposes the temporal segregation of black childhood from white childhood's turn-of-the-century schemas, it should not place black children, or the story of Oscar Moore, behind childhood's modern trajectory. Moore's subjection was enfolded into white childhood's modern reformulation, as the enclosure of Moore within Hall's work makes clear. In 1891, Hall began publishing *The Pedagogical Seminary*, a "new synthesis" of educational developments.⁵³ The first volume's contents fulfilled Hall's promise to provide an "international record of educational literature, institutions, and progress," including his own seminal work, *The Contents of Children's Minds*, among pedagogical reports from across the US and Europe.⁵⁴

Tucked into the "Foreign Miscellanies" of the journal's back pages, however, was an item less easy to synthesize: "Dr. S. V. Clevenger,

Alienist and Neurologist, July 1890, describes an infant prodigy, Oscar Moore."[55] Arranged among a series of non sequitur entries, the abridged appearance of Clevenger's report within Hall's journal identifies both a citational relation between the scientists and, more importantly, the place of Moore at the overlap of their bylines. Marking Moore as "Miscellaneous" to the synthetic aims of his work, Hall nevertheless bestowed significance on Moore in the act of locating him just so. Rather than omit his mention, Hall placed Moore as an afterthought at the edge of concern, where Moore could make no traction in the motion of scientific "synthesis" and "progress" and yet where he could still be bound inside Hall's scientific authority.

Like his place in Hall's backmatter, the ephemeral presence of Moore in Clevenger's archive marks both relegation and ongoing investment. For if he had "given [Moore] up as an enigma," the pieces of ephemera that Clevenger kept expose that the doctor held onto his investment. No longer bills of entry, the expended tickets became souvenirs for Clevenger's private collection, where they remain invitations to return to what occurred between the doctor and the child. Another souvenir kept by Clevenger—the *Hand-Book*—acts to retrieve encounters and relations beyond him. Unbound from its intended use and its value to Clevenger, the *Hand-Book* appears as a faulty container for Moore's brightness and as a compendium of evidence against "nothing."

Unbinding the *Hand-Book*

Though Clevenger's published report and private effects materialize the violence that linked him to Moore, his "Physician's Exhibition" was only a brief episode in the trajectory of Moore's captive career. Before appearing in Chicago, Moore had already spent extensive time on stages in Austin, Texas, and Cincinnati, Ohio.[56] Departing from Chicago, he traveled to Milwaukee and then to New York City, where he was made to deliver numerous performances and to endure further scientific study, this time by popular lecturer George Reed Cromwell.[57] After New York, Moore traveled to cities in Connecticut, performing for both popular audiences and Yale professors.[58] Across much of this period, the taskmaster behind Moore, and the showman visible beside him, was H. P. N. Gammel. Between them was the *Hand-Book* (figure 4.2).

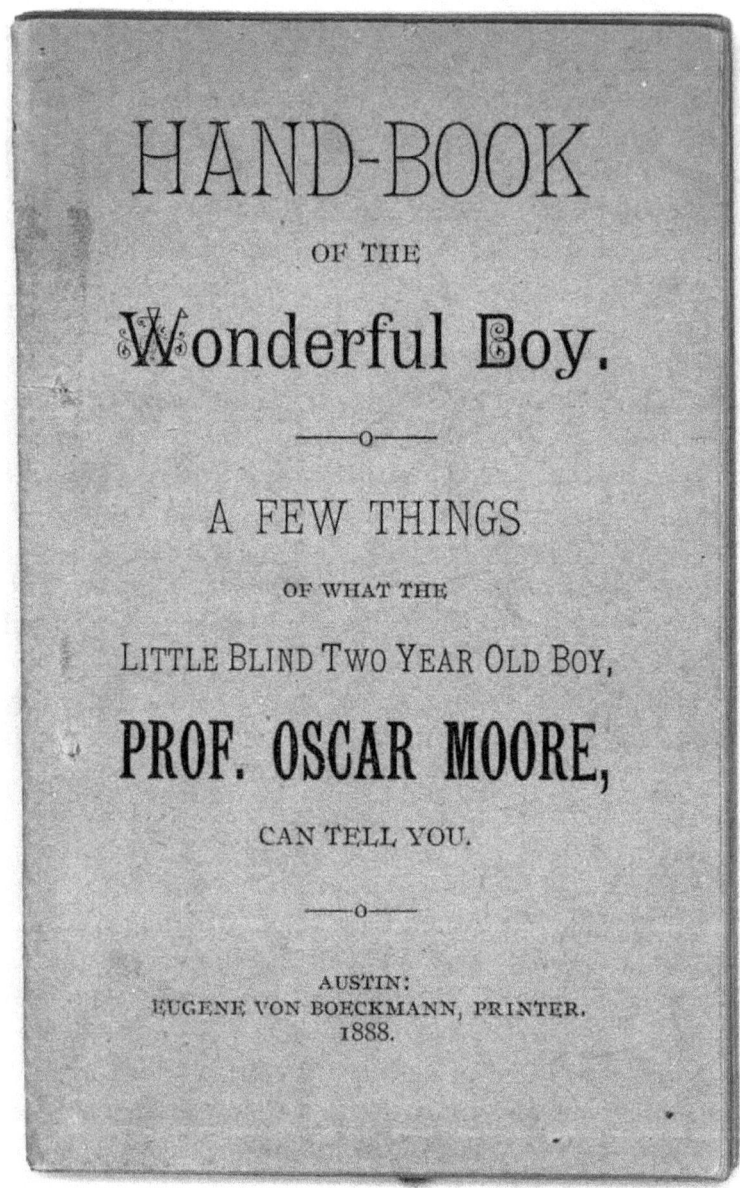

Figure 4.2. Cover and select pages from *Hand-Book of the Wonderful Boy, a Few Things of What the Little Blind Two Year Old Boy, Prof. Oscar Moore, Can Tell You* (Austin: Eugene Von Boeckmann, 1888), Shobal Vail Clevenger Papers, 1864–1924, US National Library of Medicine.

209 Ulysses S. Grant,
　　　　　　April 27, 1822
211 Rutherford B Hayes,
　　　　　　Oct. 4, 1822
213 James A Garfield,
　　　　　　Nov. 19, 1831
215 Chester A Arthur,
　　　　　　Oct. 5, 1830
217 Grover Cleveland,
　　　　　　March 18, 1837

General Questions and Answers.

218. How much does a cubic foot of copper weigh?
　　　　　　555 pounds
219. How much does a cubic foot of clay weigh?
　　　　　　135 pounds
220. How much does a cubic foot of granite weigh?
　　　　　　165 pounds
221. How much does a cubic foot of cast iron weigh?
　　　　　　450¼ pounds
222. How much does a cubic foot of wrought iron weigh?
　　　　　　486¾ pounds
223. How much does a cubic foot of lead weigh?
　　　　　　708¼ pounds
224. How much does a cubic foot of water weigh?
　　　　　　62¼ pounds
225. How much does a cubic foot of tin weigh?
　　　　　　456 pounds
226. How much does a cubic foot of gold weigh?
　　　　　　961 pounds
227. How much does a cubic foot of silver weigh?
　　　　　　654 pounds
228. How much does a barrel of flour weigh?
　　　　　　196 pounds
229. How much does a barrel of beef weigh?
　　　　　　200 pounds

Historical and Other Questions.

399 When did the first steamboat cross the Atlantic ocean?
　　　　　　In 1819
400 When was the French Revolution?
　　　　　　In 1789
401 When was the great London fire?
　　　　　　September 26, 1666
402 When were the first watches made?
　　　　　　In 1477
403 When was the German Empire re-established?
　　　　　　January 18, 1871
404 When was the French and Indian war in America?
　　　　　　In 1754
405 How far do hurricanes move in an hour?
　　　　　　80 miles
406 Where was the first settlement in America?
　　　　　　Jamestown, Va., 1607
407 Where is the highest spire in the world?
　　　　　　In Germany
408 How high is it?
　　　　　　511 feet
409 Which is the largest mountain in the world?
　　　　　　Mount Everest, in Asia
410 How high is it?
　　　　　　29,002 feet
411 How deep is the deepest place in the ocean?
　　　　　　46,236 feet
412 When was the first iron horeshoe made?
　　　　　　In 481
413 Where were the first knives made?
　　　　　　In England, 1550
414 When was the London plague?
　　　　　　1665
415 Where is the longest bridge in the world?
　　　　　　Over the St. Lawrence River

Hand-Book of the Wonderful Boy, a Few Things of What the Little Blind Two Year Old Boy, Prof. Oscar Moore, Can Tell You served multiple purposes. Printed by Gammel in Austin, the *Hand-Book*'s sixty-four pages and hundreds of questions worked both as an early outline of Moore's repertoire and as a physical facsimile of it. In Gammel's hands, the *Hand-Book* functioned as a prop for the performance while containing its script. Flipping through its pages on stage, Gammel would ask, "How much does a cubic foot of gold weigh?" and Moore would answer, "961 pounds." Gammel might then ask, "What is the population of the British Empire?" and Moore would answer, "302,356,382."[59] Gammel might next demand that Moore sing the minstrel tune "I'se Gwine Back to Dixie" or the Germanic folk song "Liebchen Hast Das Bett Gemacht?" or that he recite "The Elf-Child" by James Whitcomb Riley.[60] Moore would faithfully supply each, and his audiences would watch and wonder how.[61] Indeed, as reports of their performances relate, audience wonderment was the reliable dividend of each show, for even as Gammel varied his questions, Moore invariably demonstrated that he knew the answers.

The *Hand-Book*'s self-declaration as a book "*of*" Oscar Moore is seriously undermined once Gammel's place—on the other end of every question—is clarified. For the *Hand-Book* was, in function, a text that facilitated their relational repertoire while concealing their discrepant knowledge of it. Whereas Moore could organize the *Hand-Book*'s massive array of information in his mind and retrieve discrete pieces of it at will *without* reading it, Gammel could not recall all the questions, let alone the answers, without the textual reference. The *Hand-Book* served as a primer to Gammel in another sense, too, for its schoolroom poems, catechisms, songs, list of presidents, and geographical facts afforded him an education in Americanness as much as his relation to Moore did. And yet the *Hand-Book* was meant not to announce Gammel's limited or developing knowledge but to serve as a container for Moore's. Collating disparate forms of information and training Moore to mentally shift direction as if flipping pages, Gammel's *Hand-Book* compelled Moore to embody the comprehensive yet extraneous contents of an encyclopedia.

Indeed, acting as a codex to Moore, the *Hand-Book* supported reporters' reliance on the encyclopedia as their prevailing descriptive device, materializing Moore's brightness as a broad but mundane assemblage of facts. As one critic wrote, Moore "kn[ew] Appleton's encyclopedia by heart."[62] As another explained, though he was "but thirty inches or less in height, he [was] a storehouse of solid information" able to "lay out the average American encyclopedia."[63] Repeatedly casting him as a "walking encyclopedia," a "living arithmetic," and a "perfect little encyclopedia," critics collapsed the sentient and singular child with the didactic repertoire Gammel had designed, reducing both to the common form of a reference text.[64]

If the *Hand-Book* enclosed Moore in the encyclopedia's extensive—yet finite—contents, it did more than materialize metaphor. As a souvenir that audiences could purchase at Moore's performances, the three-by-five-inch volume acted both as a memento to be kept after the show's end and as a manual for use during it. For in the midst of questioning Moore, Gammel often invited audiences to "try him yourself."[65] Holding the *Hand-Book*—and therefore possessing a key to the answers—audience members joined the inquest, verifying Moore's brightness and commanding its demonstration.[66] Even as the *Hand-Book* suggested the encyclopedic density of Moore's brightness, this manner of its *use* insinuated that brightness was operated by external control, not directed by internal thought. Claims that Moore was a "boy phonograph" or "a human phonograph" advanced this mechanical recasting.[67] Likening Moore to a device that mimetically replayed what had been encoded into the grooves of a record, critics suggested that the contents of Moore's mind were empty except for others' inscription.

But if both the encyclopedia and the phonograph were functional containers for Moore's defiance of common sense, they operated by reaching for what *was* common sense: that children were *like* blank tablets or empty books, ready for impression, inscription, and edification, because white Americans had been understanding their own children in relation to books for well over a century.[68] A *Hand-Book*, however, was something different from the blank slates, primers, picture books, and textbooks that white Americans depended on for knowledge of their children and for their children's knowledge of themselves. If Locke's blank slate was, as Crain argues, the basis for white children's assumption of literacy and property in themselves, the *Hand-Book* expressed a different set of property relations—wherein a "blind wonderful boy" could find himself "transferred."[69]

Not only did the *Hand-Book* denote a different book-child-property correspondence; it also weighted the contents of that equation differently. In the same moment that white adults were exploring the newly recognized depths of their children's developmental dramas and imaginative lives, the *Hand-Book* interpolated Moore into a matrix of extraordinary breadth spread over remarkable shallowness. For while the recitation of poems, catechisms, and facts had featured significantly in nineteenth-century schoolrooms, performing these acts to repetitive excess did not accrue additional educational value; moreover, the *Hand-Book*'s quantity of facts could not measure against the newly qualitative methods that pedagogues were advising as new and enhanced approaches to children and their minds.[70] Indeed, the recognition of children's inward depth became so powerful as to change not only pedagogy but the broader cultural imaginary of white childhood. As psychologists developed new methods to study and schematize the matter of children's minds, a new book-child relation—iconicized by "a new creature"—emerged as a cultural representative. As Crain argues, by the turn of the twentieth century, the US's "dominant figure of childhood" had become the white child with their "head in a book" or "lost in a book."[71]

In, not *on*. Not a child depicted with his face buried in a book but rather a child likened to an encyclopedia, commanded by a *Hand-Book*, and propped—in his portrait—atop a heavy tome, Moore's relation to the various books of his ephemeral imprint diagram the distance maintained between black and white childhood as refashioned in this moment. Indeed, if the most startling feature of Moore's portrait is the rod pressed upon his right foot, the book below his left foot more quietly demands a reading. Not open before him but closed beneath him, the book acts as a reference of scale—the book is large, the child small—and as a reference to a reference book. Not standing firmly on it but held half-hovering above it by the rod, Moore's relation to the book is taut and unresolved. If the white child reading was the period's new creature, what kind of creature was Moore to represent, positioned thus? Not the "certain kind of child who naturally reads."[72] By all accounts, Moore did *not* learn to read, as he was afforded neither blind literacy education nor braille reading materials across his childhood; a decade later, in 1900, a census taker listed fourteen-year-old Moore as unable to read or write.[73]

He was not, then, the "new creature" whose imagination was a realm apart, an evolutionary theater, and a gift.

And yet even as Moore's position atop the book suspended him from the deepening social, empirical, and imaginative concerns of white adults for white children, there is another way of reading the book and Moore's estrangement from it. The white men who structured Moore's repertoire, commanded his labor, and controlled his image actively excepted him from the emerging psychological and progressive frameworks of white childhood and also from the child's deepened understanding as, and in, the contents of books. Yet Moore existed beyond these frameworks for another reason: because he exceeded them, exposed them, and illuminated their limits.

If the child's mind and the contents of a book were conceptually bound, studied, and elaborated on, brightness exposed the limits of white Americans' literacy in children. For they could not *read* Moore. This failure underscores, again, that there could be no such thing as a guide, or *Hand-Book*, to him—that indeed, the document Gammel produced to serve as such only papered over what was unknown. Nevertheless, by commanding him by the *Hand-Book*, likening him to an encyclopedia, and describing brightness as a faculty of memory "uncomplicated with many higher powers," Moore's exploiters sought to divert attention from their limited knowledge by limiting what could be seen of his.[74] A question that remains difficult to answer, but vital to ask, is whether the *Hand-Book* succeeded in its concealment or whether Moore might have, in any way, staged its failure.

If Moore was excluded from reading the *Hand-Book* as a blind child, he was nevertheless a master of its text as a performer. Without ever reading it, Moore knew the *Hand-Book* as a script of what was supposed to transpire in his performances. Yet he also likely knew the fact that such a script might "structure" a performance but nevertheless could not foreclose what Bernstein describes as performers' ability to "unleash . . . original, live variations."[75] The possibilities Moore might have unleashed went largely uncaptured in archives. Yet glimpses appear in contending ephemeral form—in newspaper coverage of Moore.

Read beside the *Hand-Book*, newspaper reports of Moore's performances confirm its use by Gammel and the audience. In lieu of adding details that could articulate differences across Moore's many performances, reports from venues of the South, Midwest, and Northeast demonstrate the consistency of reporters' enjoyment of the performance and their shared disregard for the performer.[76] Yet read closely, suggestions emerge across critics' commentaries. When, during his Chicago Music Hall performance, an audience member asked Moore a routine question, "What is the population of the Chinese empire?" Moore responded easily. But when they followed with a second query, "Where did you learn that?" a reporter noted that Moore did not respond. Instead, he said nothing. The reporter dispensed with this gap even as he noted it, writing that "[this] was a question not in the boy's catechism, and the machinery broke down."[77] Moore, it seemed, "knew not what to reply."[78] And yet Moore likely *could* have supplied an answer. He might have said that Gammel had taught him or that the answer came from the *Hand-Book*. But instead, he said nothing, creating a gap that the reporter rationalized as a malfunction. Beneath the reporter's claim of mechanical failure, however, was a breakdown of a different kind: Moore's insertion of deflection, withholding, and momentary refusal into a repertoire meant to deliver his endless responsiveness.

A few months later, in New York City, Moore performed a different kind of break. Standing atop a table at the Astor House before another large crowd, Moore kept "instant" pace with Gammel's volley of questions: "How fast does a rifle ball travel?" "Where is the largest bell in the world?" "What city has the population of 503,185?" "How many bones are in a man's body?" "Who was the thirteenth president of the United States?"[79] And on and on. Abruptly, however, Moore "grew sarcastic" and turned to ask Gammel, "*You are sure that's the right answer, are you?*" The reporter who noted this disruption did not describe Gammel's response—just that he "assured" Moore of the answer's correctness and returned quickly to his role as inquisitor. Yet the momentary reversal, wherein Moore's question rang out before the audience and pointed toward Gammel, suggests both an act of destabilization and, potentially, Moore's canny awareness behind it. Of course, the reporter may have embellished the sarcasm of Moore's delivery, and perhaps he invented the question too. And yet if even a loose record of a genuine exchange between Moore and Gammel, the reporter raised an act of Moore's subversion to a rare level of archival legibility. Posed as a double interrogatory—"You are . . . are you?"—the question punctuated Moore's easy demonstration of his own knowledge with his doubt at Gammel's. Recorded here, it leaves a mark: Moore knew that brightness was something he had over Gammel.

Placed within other critics' mention of Moore's "irrepressible" and "lively" movements, of his "piping" voice and general "nois[iness]," and especially beside his unspecified yet "unexpected questions," Moore's needling query to Gammel suggests that Moore's brightness was dynamic, kinesthetic, vocalized, and often inquisitive—indeed, that brightness was not only, nor primarily, a faculty of memory but something broader that was strategically reduced to a repertoire of memorization and that is further obscured by that repertoire's remains.[80] Filtered through the lens of his white critics and audiences, these glimpses of brightness are neither reliable nor sufficient to fill in Moore's interiority, nor are they cause to schematize brightness on any present scale or spectrum. They constitute only provisional possibilities about a child whose interests, imagination, thinking, knowing, wants, and desires remain largely opaque due both to their archival erasure and to the limits of my retrieval. However impassive he remains, these momentary breakdowns nevertheless register Moore's presence and highlight the disciplinary mechanisms through which it was constrained: the binding of the *Hand-Book*, the white man beside him, the rod at his foot. What they reveal, if only briefly, is an imprint of Moore's counterpressure.

Every act of counterpressure, defiance, or insurgency that Moore might have performed at the age of three, or four, or seven, or onward, however, was dangerous. Gammel and the other white men who surrounded him controlled not only his repertoire but also his labor; his safety; where he traveled; how much he could sleep, or eat, or play; and whether, and when, he could see his family. The winding path of Moore's career across the 1890s confirms that the actions of these men set the terms for a precarious, neglected, and isolated early childhood. Moreover, Moore's disappearance after 1900 suggests that for all he endured, he saw little material return. What had once been a rapid speculative investment in brightness became an unwieldy liability, and in turn, the same men who forced Moore into a career of prodigy abandoned him. Gammel's own exit was an early one: he left Moore in Connecticut with a new showman sometime in late 1889 or early 1890 and returned to Texas to redirect his expertise toward the "buy[ing], sell[ing], exchang[ing], and apprais[ing] of books ... of all kinds."[81] For Gammel, deserting Moore was part of his own personal ascension—as a family man, businessman, and self-styled "bookman."[82] Concealing the material and immaterial value he had extracted from Moore, Gammel framed his new identity as a separate venture entirely: in his words, "It takes a showman to show niggers and a bookman to sell books."[83] Yet just as Moore's brightness exceeded the *Hand-Book*—flashing up in an unwelcomed question—Moore's presence interrupts Gammel's attempted excision of Moore from the archive. Made to disappear and relegated to "nothing," Moore's brightness refutes Gammel's narrative authority and his incomplete accounting.

Last Returns

The end of Oscar Moore's career was slow and winding. Or it was fractious and precipitous. Newspaper notices indicate that Moore continued to perform as a prodigy until around 1901, though to declining popular note and in smaller circuits.[84] Other records expose that financial and legal conflicts began unraveling his career almost from its outset. The breakdown began atop the bid of Moore's exploiters to secure greater profit, recognition, and renown. While in New York in 1889, Gammel brought Moore before P. T. Barnum, whose capitalization of Americans' sideshow appetite had, since the beginning of his career, hinged upon the exploited labor of black disabled performers.[85] Reports of this meeting suggested Moore's recruitment into Barnum's employ. Yet these same reports deflated that prospect—concluding that Moore would "not join the circus just yet."[86] No further documents link Moore's fate to Barnum, who died in 1891. And yet it seems that some arrangement had been made. For between late 1889 and 1892, Moore labored in the custody of George A. Wells, an associate of Barnum, in Bridgeport, Connecticut.[87] While both the financial structure and content of Moore's time in Wells's custody are difficult to recover, their rupture articulates them.

In 1892, Thaison—the man in possession of Moore's bond of indenture—brought a suit for $20,000 against Wells. He claimed that Wells had "fail[ed] to properly educate" Moore, now six years old. Newspapers reported that Thaison, Wells, *and* Henry Moore held an "equal monetary interest in the development of the boy's peculiar powers."[88]

According to Thaison, Wells had squandered that interest; as Thaison put it, "[Moore] should have been on exhibition this whole time."[89] While the suit's conclusion is unclear, it coincided with Moore's rapid completion of a circuit of performances in Boston and then with his return to Texas—with his father and under Thaison's closer watch. Whatever pressure Thaison and Henry Moore placed on Oscar to renew his career, however, his performances became sporadic by the late 1890s, and by the turn of the century, they seemed to cease altogether.[90]

Census records show that in 1900, fourteen-year-old Oscar Moore was living in Memphis, Tennessee, with his older sister, Cora (Williams), and with his father, Henry, who appeared in the census as "widowed." How and when Oscar's mother, Fanny Moore, died is not clear, nor is her agreement or resistance to her youngest child's tenure as a traveling performer over the previous decade. The Moores' Memphis address in the midst of several theaters on Beale Street and Oscar's listed "occupation"—"Blind Boy"—suggest that this tenure was ongoing.[91] Yet whether Moore continued to perform across Memphis's stages, extant advertisements of his performances—again in Texas—drop off entirely after 1901.[92] No reports of Moore beyond this period conclusively detail how he carried on the rest of his life, with whom, or when he died. As such, any comment on Moore's afterlife—about the cultural legacy of his career or his presence in the archive—must open from the fact that the beginning of his afterlife, or when he died, is unknown to me.

It is possible that the end of his performance career coincided with his very young death. It is also possible that Moore's disappearance from the press simply marked the end of his stage career and the beginning of a new life, less spectacular and more difficult to trace. Without certainty, it remains plausible that Moore may have lived well into the mid-twentieth century or beyond, one of hundreds of black Oscar Moores who, across subsequent census, birth, death, and press records, form a corps of anonymity around him and from whom I have yet to disentangle him.[93]

Resting somewhere within this archival collective, the unknown remainder of Moore's life is full of unending possibility. For even as the precarious and exploited circumstances of his early life lean toward the eventuality of his early death, accepting this trajectory places unwarranted certainty where evidence is scarce and my knowledge incomplete. Writing a tragic ending for Moore would not only offer false closure; it would also return narrative authority to men like Clevenger, who conscripted Moore to "die young," and Gammel, who cast him into oblivion.[94] As Hartman proposes, to write a "counter-history" against the violence of an archive such as this demands acknowledging the "failure" of the pursuit; yet it also requires imagination, or in Hartman's more precise terms, "critical fabulation."[95] "Straining against the limits of the archive to write a cultural history of [a] captive," like Moore, requires holding open the possibility—even if unlikely—of escape.[96]

If any act, or quiet process, of his escape remains unfounded in evidence, Moore's brightness escapes archival enclosure in other forms. Written into the family lore of his showman, Gammel, the story of Moore's brightness shifted in textual form, and physical binding, across the course of the twentieth century from where it was privately kept to where it could be publicly known. Exposing the double ledger of Gammel's supposedly legitimate and illegitimate investments—and their role in securing his family's twentieth-century "good years"—Moore's place within Gammel's family archive anticipates and exposes how, even as white Americans evacuated the performance of black prodigy of its cultural currency, they still sought to incorporate that value for private use.[97]

In the early twentieth century, Gammel began writing a personal chronicle of his ascent from an indigent Danish immigrant to the prosperous business owner, "Bookman," and father of nine healthy white children that he had become. Though called his "diary," his family understood it as a book of a different kind. It contained stories "told and retold through the years" and served "partly as information, partly as soliloquy."[98] Moore was a familiar figure of enjoyment within the Gammel family's mythology, and thus, he warranted a written entry in the diary.[99]

Understood to have been "written for the family, and clearly not meant for publication," the diary—and thus, mention of Moore—was segregated from the extensive records that Gammel maintained of his business accounts, correspondence, and life among Austin's white middle class.[100] As such, when Gammel's descendants donated his papers to the University of Texas at Austin in the 1980s, neither his diary nor other evidence pertaining to Moore entered his publicly funded, publicly accessible legacy.[101] What is more, the diary's presumed destruction in a May 2000 fire effectively erased Moore from his private effects too.[102]

This would have been the end of this story's retelling if it were not for the diary's reproduction elsewhere. In 1985, Gammel's youngest daughter had transcribed passages from it as the basis of her biography *H. P. N. Gammel: Texas Bookman.*[103] Whereas Gammel had once narrated his white children as an affective link to Moore, his daughter unwittingly ensured the survival of that link long past his attempted redaction.[104] Yet like the *Hand-Book*, *Texas Bookman* is another troublesome book: it excerpts Gammel's diary without clear quotations, it uses unconventional editorial marks, and furthermore, because its coauthors have died and its publisher closed, it leaves little means of deciphering its production.

Moore's name appears neither in *Texas Bookman*'s table of contents nor in its index. Yet he is the central concern of the book's middle chapter—a nearly uninterrupted reproduction of a diary entry entitled "Not Worth Quarreling with My Sweet Wife." What Moore was worth is central to the quarrel of Gammel's account, for though he insists that his time and money were wasted on him, Gammel enumerates both the extensive value he extracted from Moore and his unresolved investment in him. Introducing Moore as "my little black boy," Gammel nevertheless exposes his ongoing discontent with what he could not possess of Moore.[105]

His account begins with a speculative vision: that he and Thaison "couldt [sic] see millions in him."[106] It then proceeds as a piecemeal array of sums invested, leased, lost, and recouped across his travels with Moore from Texas, to Illinois, to Wisconsin, to New York, to Connecticut, and back. According to Gammel, he had "wanted to make $500.00 a day on him—but failed." Sketching contracts drawn for Moore to perform in dime museums, the twenty-five-cent sale of Moore's photograph and *Hand-Book* to audiences, and his arrangement for Dr. Clevenger's "Exhibition," Gammel then interrupts his ledger with the near intervention of child welfare agents upon the conditions of Moore's laboring. Dismissing some otherwise unrecorded "trouble" with a "Humane Society" that he "got out of," Gammel indicates that the period's rising concern for white children's welfare had almost, but not quite, reached Moore.[107] Returning to the pecuniary focus of his narrative, Gammel underscores that his unconcern for Moore's welfare went unchecked: when "the boy got sick," it was $2,700 "lost," not the child, over which he worried.[108]

Declaring that he "never got anything out of him," Gammel resolves that "what [he] lost in money, [he] gained in experience."[109] And yet he gained far more. Not only did he *live* off of Moore's labor for several years; he also leveraged his career with Moore to build the foundation for another. Though in 1889 he established himself in Connecticut with Moore, Moore's father, and Wells, Gammel describes that his concern for "his wife and children" drew him back to Texas.[110] Before making his return, however, he first revisited New York City, where he used his available funds and credit to purchase a $3,000 library of books.[111] It was this large acquisition that transformed Gammel's fledgling bookstore into a reputable institution and Gammel into the Bookman.[112] His contention that showing Moore and selling books were separate and incompatible endeavors was, as this story plainly admits, a fabrication covering what was a deeply embedded, extractive relationship.

Gammel's self-making, his business, and his family's prosperity depended on Moore. His relegation of Moore to "nothing" appears all the more specious, yet also more meaningful, in light of what this ledger exposes. "Nothing" represented not a value but a voiding: Gammel's attempt to clear his debt to Moore from his name, identity, and account books. Gammel did not, or could not, erase Moore completely, however, for he concluded his entry with the following: "After he grew up, he was nothing. Memory was what he (had) over any living soul."[113] Declining to separate these divergent assessments of Moore by the preposition "but," Gammel placed his negation of Moore beside his acknowledgment of Moore's singular, precious possession. And it seems, he faltered over that possession. The parentheses that bracket "had" admit that Bohlender, as editor, had been unable to transcribe the word therein. The word Bohlender guessed at—*had*—was written illegibly by Gammel, or perhaps stumbled over by him. While his reference to Moore's "memory" encloses the expansive terrain of brightness, Gammel's scribbled admission of Moore's possession, what he *had*, enlarges brightness as the cause of some syntactical breakdown—wherein Gammel both wrote down and crossed through Moore's possession. Over his uncertain hand, his daughter's typescript placed emphasis.

Gammel's palimpsest record diagrams the specific problem of Moore's brightness as value coveted yet intractable and as a performance ultimately made untenable by the period's new discourses, models, and figures—not only of childhood exceptionality but of manhood's respectability. Yet it reflects, too, an unexceptional pattern. "They have been credited with nothing," writes Hartman of the black girls and women whose migrations, personal insurrections, collective riots, and intellectual labor fundamentally reshaped early twentieth-century American life.[114] As Hartman shows, and as Gammel's entry concedes, the activity of black children and adults thinking, moving, and being human—"as they had a mind to"—*was* the formidable force that Dr. Foote had feared in Emancipation's aftermath.[115] The crossed ledger of brightness underscores that the desire to contain this force was intermingled with the desire to possess it. For at the same time that white Americans worked to constrict the measure of the human along its eugenic model, the pattern of twentieth-century modernism and primitivism shows that extracting value, coveting, and inhabiting the social, cultural, and intellectual life that black Americans created in excess of that model formed the dominant culture's generating current.[116]

Noticing such a pattern is what prodigy, by its spectacular exceptionality, mitigates against. And indeed, the story of Oscar Moore—lacking "kindred *lusu naturae*" and cast "over any living soul"—is difficult to place in context or to decipher as part of a pattern. To unbind Moore from his captors' suspension, then, requires both disentanglement and reconnection. For this reason, the end of Moore's story is best read in its relations, even where they are tenuous. Fanny, the mother that Oscar Moore lost at an early age; Cora, the sister sometimes present; and Henry, who held some stake in his son's exploitation together constellate the fact that Moore's captors did not succeed in breaking him of his family ties even as they distorted and estranged them. Indeed, the scattered archival presence of Moore's family members indicates that though brightness was singularly held by Moore, it nevertheless facilitated the collective mobility of the Moores—and their dispersal. If these kin relations do not reconvene in any archivally traceable end, Moore's life can be situated, too, in other genealogies.

Though the comparison of Oscar Moore to Tom Wiggins arose from white Americans' limited racial imaginary, Moore and Wiggins *were* kindreds of some kind. By their overlapping succession, the two performed a living refutation of prodigy's premise—each denying the other's supposedly singular deviation from nature. The simultaneous withdrawal of white attention and investment from Moore and Wiggins should, for this reason, be read both as the result of the period's shifting cultural terrain and as their shared unsettling of it. In an era where the sciences of heredity, psychology, and pedagogy were meant to predict how and among whom intelligence, talent, and skill were to arise, Moore, a black disabled boy, and Wiggins, a black disabled man, represented the failure of those predictions as its own pattern. Yet even if the trouble they made reverberates together, neither their forms of divergence nor their interior lives can be considered closely related. Made to share in surrogacy of the same effigy, Moore and Wiggins's overlapping cultural work emerged not from any racial trait or preternatural bind but from the deliberate joining of their fates and by their disconnection from others' stories.

Indeed, during the period in which critics stretched to bind Moore, a young child, to middle-aged Wiggins, a much likelier peer to Moore was harder to perceive as such. In the same year that Moore began touring as a "wonderful blind negro boy," a young deaf and blind white girl, also from the South, began to receive nationwide attention for her own extraordinary feats of learning.[117] Helen Keller, born less than five years before Moore, became a figure of endearment and radical challenge to dominant conceptions of disabled children and their imagined futures. That Moore remains inassimilable to the history of expanding access and disabled coming of age that Keller iconicized points back to the active estrangement that Thaison, Gammel, Clevenger, Hall, and others maintained between Moore and emergent discourses of white children's care and futurity. It also reminds us that the cultural ground that Keller won was not wide; at the same time that her early life became a popular cause for wonder, white Americans were weaponizing eugenics to dispense with other disabled children's futures.[118] With this in mind, to imagine Moore and Keller as kindreds—and to interrogate the uneasiness of this pairing—is to make visible the internal violence of modern childhood's reformulation, crossed by both race and ableism.

Disability's racial history is the wedge segregating Moore from white children like Keller *and* from an emerging class of exceptionalized and celebrated black children—the orators, classical instrumentalists, and precocious scholars who began filling turn-of-the-century New Negro parlors and churches.[119] In venues meant for black audiences and protected from racial spectacle, the genre of prodigy that these children performed reflected African Americans' own remodeled conception of and investment in their children and also their incorporation of childhood's dominant white metrics.[120] For even as white supremacy founded and ruled eugenics, a subset of African Americans—largely of middle-class aspiration—began to measure, reward, and celebrate black children. They did so against eugenics' racial order but *by* the grain of its ableism. It was in this context that W. E. B. Du Bois would imagine a "talented tenth" necessary to lead the lesser black masses and the notion that hereditary "quality" was an essential part of talent's cultivation.[121] Proximate whiteness—or the racial currency of brightness—would gain value as part of this amalgam. But Moore's immeasurable, spectacular, and disabled embodiment of brightness was something outside the narrow vector of this pursuit.

Indeed, as Moore's career receded into the early twentieth century, the terrain of exceptionality that his brightness had once marked was recoded not as the site of unknown deviance but as the *knowable* location where resources, concern, and futurity for white children would be allocated and where only some black children might, against resistance, gain entry. White adults cultivated the ideal inhabitants of "the century of the child" both by freeing their evolutionary savagery and by calibrating their giftedness. The old subtended the new: Lewis Terman, who popularized the dominant measure of giftedness and the division of children by IQ, was G. Stanley Hall's student.[122] Black prodigy's palimpsest history underlaid the twentieth century's repertoire for precocious, gifted, children too. Yet more invisibly so. By the 1930s, a young black child who performed difficult feats of spelling, who possessed broad knowledge, and who delivered virtuosic piano performances would not be recognizable as the third coming of Blind Tom or the second "Bright" Oscar Moore. Instead, she would be imagined to darkly inhabit a distinctly white role, cast as "the Shirley Temple of American Negroes."[123] Hiding a history of extraction with a claim of black-white imitation, white childhood successfully reabsorbed what it had once appeared to reject.

Placed in relation, Oscar Moore's brightness prepares us to understand this extraction and what it conceals, or how black children could see the immense value of their ideas, words, questions, embodiments, and repertoires displaced, the contents of their minds discounted. Moore's story amends this false ledger, exposing how the internal relations of black and white childhood were not a circuit that flowed toward white children alone but a reserve that fueled white men's remodeling and the modernization of the human model they dominated. Yet for all that Moore's career clarifies, the end of his story refuses to hinge on this act of revelation or to close around its meaning. Just as his brightness was not selfsame with what whites understood of it, Moore's story is not selfsame with what I can tell of it. The rest of Oscar Moore's life—where he went when he left the stage, with whom he formed or re-formed kinships, and also what he thought, understood, or questioned about the shifting social order around him—remains outside of this book.

5

"This is the end of the story no it isint"

Anarranging Philippa Schuyler's Scrapbook Archive

This is the end of the story no it isint I was joust fooling you.
—Philippa Schuyler, "The Girl and Her Parents," May 18, 1936, 1935–36 Scrapbook

Writing in early 1934, Josephine Schuyler explained to her daughter, Philippa, "I intended that you should not be a child prodigy . . . but a brilliant adult and this was only the foundation."[1] At the time, Philippa was less than two and a half years old, and though these words were addressed to her, she was not likely reading them. She was reading, however, as Josephine's next entry from the following week clarifies: "You know approximately 550 words. You spell accurately 125 words. You can count up to and including 30, and many numbers above that."[2] Within a few months, Philippa was reading aloud easily from her *Wag and Puff* primer, and she was impressing her parents by correctly spelling words like *chrysanthemum* and *tuberculosis*.[3] Josephine and her husband, George, soon placed Philippa's progress before a wider audience. By the time she turned four, Philippa's achievements in literacy and geographical knowledge and her developing talent as a classical pianist and composer had gained her acclaim across New York City and then across the US.

With this attention came several overlapping designations: Philippa was a "girl prodigy," a "colored prodigy," and "the Harlem prodigy."[4] Indeed, if "prodigy" was a role that Josephine had sought for Philippa to avoid, the repertoire she directed Philippa to perform was popularly recognizable as such. For her "superior mental ability," her "expression, ease, and charm" on the piano, and her "physical fitness," Philippa fit the twentieth-century prodigy's profile of early and above-average accomplishment.[5] But Josephine was in pursuit of an adjacent designation, one with more scientific authority behind it and a "brilliant" future ahead. Taking three-year-old Philippa for IQ assessments by psychologists at Columbia and New York University, she gained numerical confirmation of what she sought: Philippa was "gifted."[6]

Gifted childhood was the "foundation" on which Philippa's mother staked her "brilliant adult[hood]" and her father, his daughter's future as a "marvelously beautiful and intelligent woman."[7] Josephine Cogdell Schuyler, a white writer from Texas, and George Schuyler, the black journalist and novelist, saw Philippa as the future fulfillment of their personal and political ideals; as Josephine put it, Philippa was "the apotheosis of [their] combined souls, hopes, bodies, future."[8] It was in Philippa's reflection of combination itself that Josephine and George placed emphasis and future hope. At the time of Philippa's birth, the Schuylers were both vocal critics of segregation as a "diabolical" system that perpetuated black exploitation and protected white supremacy.[9] As the child of their interracial union, Philippa, they believed, embodied a challenge to "the set notions of America on race."[10] Moreover, as a "gifted" child of mixed black and white ancestry, Philippa might be something more: a refutation of the eugenic doubt that race mixing was a cause of human degeneracy.[11] To unsettle the dominant science of race, the Schuylers turned to the science of the child.

The scrapbooks that Josephine kept to record Philippa's childhood developments—at monthly, weekly, and sometimes daily intervals—compose an archive of the methods and metrics that structured the science of childhood across the early twentieth century. Detailing Philippa's literacy training, her regimen of raw foods, and her growth upon a chart of "human stature," the scrapbooks constellate Josephine's conversation with fields of nutrition, physiology, pedagogy, and child psychology, and in their very form, they chart the influence and evolution of child study as a home practice.[12] Moreover, by their volume of contents and the array of intellectual strains they index, the scrapbooks belie a central claim declared by Josephine and many of those whom she cited—that "childhood is simply preparation for adulthood, it is not a state within itself."[13] Mapping the terrain of twentieth-century childhood as the site of expert debate, scientific parenting, cultural captivation, and the contest of "the century," the scrapbooks reveal how much remained staked upon the state of the child[14] (figure 5.1).

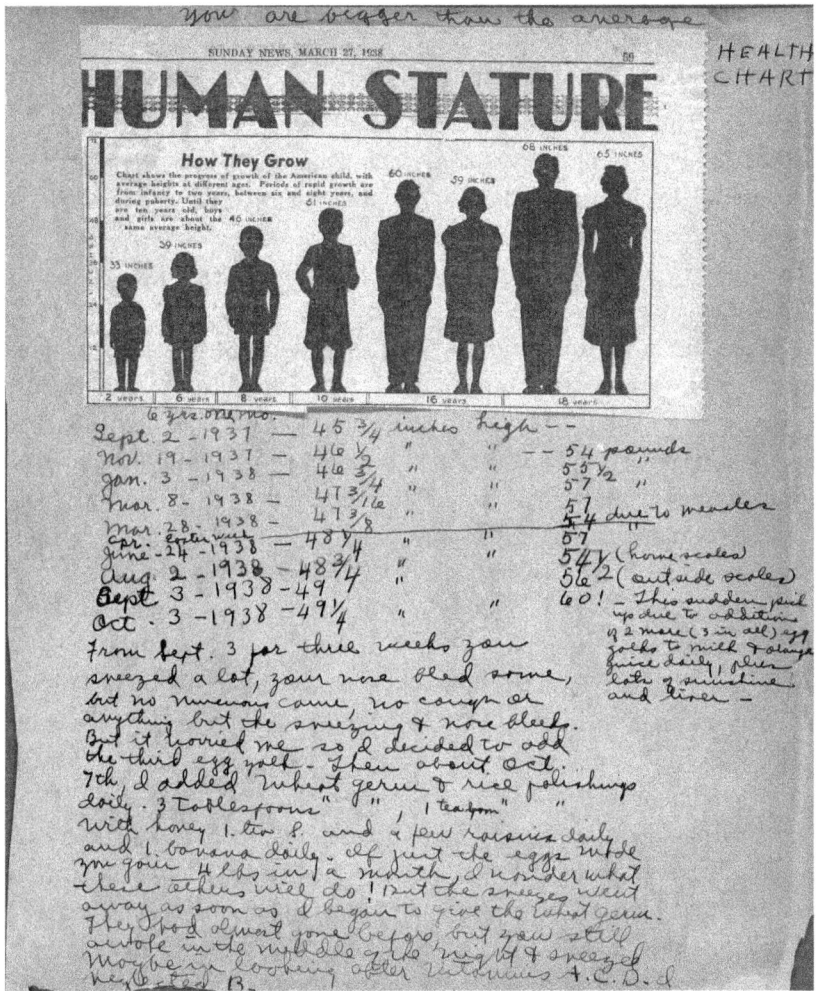

Figure 5.1. "Human Stature" [chart annotated by Josephine with Philippa's measurements], ca. September 1938, box 46, Scrapbook [Disbound], 1937–38, Schuyler Family Papers, 1915–77, Sc MG 63. Courtesy of the Schomburg Center for Research on Black Culture, New York Public Library.

Indeed, while the Schuylers' proposal for Philippa to "educate America against its set notions on race" has often been regarded as an unusual and ill-conceived "experiment," their idea was not experimental insofar as they merely redirected the dominant culture's use of children—and their measurements—to set race's notions.[15] Whether by their physical fitness, psychological development, level of literacy, or measure of IQ, children were a major source of data from which twentieth-century eugenicists established claims about the relative fitness of different racial groups and about the human future that those groups' greater or lesser reproduction portended.[16] Considering "a nation's resources of intellectual talent" to be "amongst the most precious it will ever have," Hall's student, Lewis Terman, led the field of genetic psychology in generating the popular sentiment that the study of children was "almost unequal [in] importance for human welfare."[17]

Reproduction formed the site of eugenicists' most acute and violent interventions in the state-mandated sterilization of black, Indigenous, and disabled people.[18] Yet its pronatal corrective of "borning better babies" gained meaning, and diffused power, by producing measures of *what* was better about those babies and the children they became.[19] Directing resources toward the longitudinal study of the "gifted," Terman and those who followed him cast every attribute of children—their "anthropometric measurements," their "health and physical history," their "reading interests," their "character," and their physical "beauty"—as evidence of better or worse origin and thus as the foundation of a better or baser future.[20] In tandem with this expert and institutional focus on measuring children, a more popular literacy and practice of children's measurement arose.

As Barbara Beatty, Emily Cahan, and Julia Grant have written, assessing children's development—on an individual vector toward adulthood and on a grid below or above other children—formed the dominant way of knowing the child during the first decades of the twentieth century.[21] Yet while the significance of children's measurement arose from eugenics' ascendency, children's measurements also formed the evidentiary basis for those who questioned, or altogether opposed, the eugenic principle of inheritance. Indeed, children's measurable development became the basis on which some scientists, social welfare advocates, and parents insisted on "nurture," *not* "nature," as the basis of children's better or worse outcomes and populational progress.[22] Yet whether one marshaled evidence to either side of this debate, measuring was, in itself, an aligning practice: making children knowable by their numbers and relative to averages and others. In this foregrounding of numerical knowledge, race could appear to disappear—all the while remaining embedded. For it was not by winning nature and nurture's debate but in crafting a human economy between its poles that eugenicists secured epistemic dominance.[23]

The scrapbook archive of Philippa's early life condenses the early twentieth century's dominant episteme of the measurable child. But the Schuylers' more concerted aim—to place their black child at the top of the charts—reflects, too, a counterculture that was wider than their household's iconoclasm. African Americans in the Schuylers' Harlem surround and under the wider banner of the New Negro entered the arena of reproduction, heredity, and child-rearing both by necessity and as a strategy. In the face of ongoing racial-sexual terror and against escalating state neglect and eugenic intervention, some African Americans sought not only to protect their reproductive futures but to refine them.[24] As Gregory Michael Dorr and Angela Logan document, the data of IQ and the label of "gifted" had their own currency in middle-class African American use, as did whiteness—expressed in colorist representational politics and in theories of "better breed[ing]."[25] One such theory was "hybrid vigor," or the eugenic claim that black-white mixture did not degrade, but improved, the fitness of future generations.[26] Attributed to the Schuylers as the belief that placed them at the fringes of both white and black political spheres, "hybrid vigor" more meaningfully reflects where those spheres overlapped: in the same white supremacist logic that sought whiteness as the source of "brightness" and in that logic's tacit black acceptance.[27]

Whether the Schuylers believed in hybrid vigor—or in hereditary determinism more broadly—is a difficult question to answer, not despite, but because of, the large volume of writing they left on race.[28] Yet pinpointing what they believed is neither necessary nor pertinent to understanding the future they imagined for Philippa and through her. The Schuylers' project for Philippa gains more useful reflection through another future they imagined—or speculated. In 1931, the same year that Josephine Schuyler gave birth to Philippa, George Schuyler published his speculative novel *Black No More*. Conjuring a very near future in which, by scientific intervention, black people begin to turn themselves white, the novel unfolds the comic reversals of fortune, genealogical revelations, and clandestine political negotiations that ensue. And in the ascent of the novel's down-and-out black antihero Max Disher to the position of white power broker Matthew Fisher, the novel performs the eclipsing of race's "set notions" with a new notion: that by rearranging race, rather than dismantling it, one could travel from a subjected position to the height of human stature and, from there, usurp the seat of Man's power.

Aimed at the seat of the gifted child, Philippa's ascent to the top of the IQ scale, to the center of national attention, and to the title of the American Negro's "Shirley Temple" was premised on a related method of rearrangement.[29] And indeed, Philippa's winning performances succeeded, for a time, in convincing black and white publics of her verified worth upon their scales of value. Yet to sustain her worthiness by comparative giftedness or by a comparison to Temple—the era's most beloved white child star—required Philippa's masterful effort without much material return to her or to black children like and unlike her. For the future that Philippa chased up the charts was not reachable by any black child's singular feats; nor could it be won by any amount of giftedness demonstrated or measured. It was heritable property in whiteness, not any child's given giftedness, that materially secured the century for white children—whiteness, moreover, that continued to rely on, conceal, and coin blackness. For in fact, it was not Philippa but Temple whose repertoire was born of "hybrid" origin, as Temple's lineage from both Eva and Topsy, the angelic child and the prodigious, discloses.[30]

The longer vector of Philippa's story, across her gifted childhood and into her difficult adulthood, runs in parallel to the end that *Black No More* concedes: that white power could not be meaningfully cleaved from racial logic and that, whether arranged in the dominant order or rearranged against it, hierarchizing the human served someone's subjection. Yet this was not the end of Philippa Schuyler's story, nor the sum of it. It is barely a beginning. While the scrapbooks plot Philippa's progression toward adulthood in advance, and *Black No More* supplies a parable beside them, Philippa made her own record of a different form and kind.

By reading against the linear telos of Philippa's scrapbook archive and life story, I consider Philippa's expansive occupation of her own childhood not as a temporary "state" or a "foundation" for her adulthood but as the terrain of her immeasurable value and imaginative

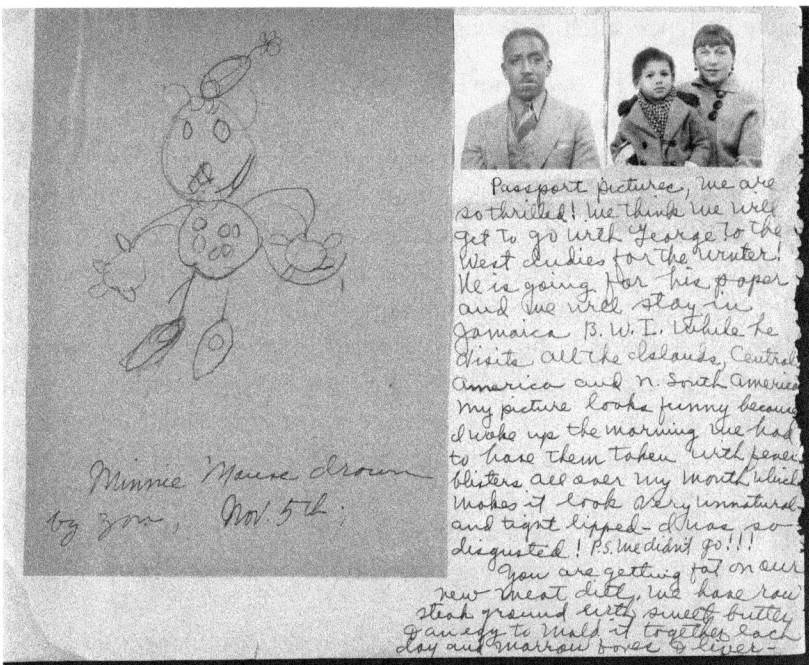

Figure 5.2. George, Philippa, and Josephine Schuyler, Passport Photographs, 1935–36 Scrapbook, Oversize 1, Philippa Schuyler Collection, Special Collections Research Center, Syracuse University Libraries.

fulfillment. In the "discords" of Philippa's musical compositions, in her anagrammatical breakdown of her literacy lessons, and in the gaze she turned upon those who studied her, Philippa enacted a practice of anarrangement that forms a radical alternative to her parents' project of rearrangement and, too, a subversive recasting of the child not as a measure but as a measurer of being human.[31] Refuting the scrapbooks' encompassing knowledge of her and interrupting their address to her, Philippa created spaces in the margins and middle of her archive from where she returned her own observations, insisting on her present value, not her future promise. In her breakdown of storytelling structures, in her practices of looking, and in her subversion of "the end" itself, Philippa's critical anarrangements of her measured, book-bound, and archived early life offer an ethic for reading black childhood in her present and in ours.

"Love Patience Intelligence and Science"

The archive of Philippa Schuyler's life originated *with* her life, because Josephine began recording observations about Philippa within days of her birth. At a few weeks old, Josephine recorded Philippa's first "accomplishments": "crawling" a precisely measured "eighteen inches" in "fifteen minutes."[32] Initiating what became a decade-spanning practice of documenting Philippa's growth and change at close intervals, Josephine also filled her early entries with photographs of Philippa, George, and herself ("Jody") and with commentaries on and vignettes of the Schuylers' home life. Later, she included news clippings, Philippa's test results, correspondences, and eventually, Philippa's own writing, visual art, musical scores, poetry, and lyrics. Exhibiting what Ellen Gruber Garvey describes as scrapbooks' characteristic function as "analog[s]" of "life itself," Josephine's scrapbooks present a diffuse log of a mother and a child's lives in relation and a meticulous log of a child's life under observation:[33]

May 25, 1933
Last night you recognized and pronounced BABY when written on your slate. You are within 7 days of being 22 months old. You can make o and I and Q on blackboard.

[November or December 1933]
Beginning the last month you had learned to read half a dozen short sentences:

"come to supper"
"go on roof"
"little girl in blue"
"I love you, Jo"

September 3, 1934
During your 37th month you evinced several of what we call, mutations. That is, you seem to be going along slowly without change, then suddenly you show marked improvement.[34]

Precise, progressive, and often numerically driven, Josephine's entries on Philippa's early life reflect the scrapbook's early twentieth-century specialization into the baby book—the companion text to the modern child. Emerging in late nineteenth-century practice and cohering into popular and commercial form by the early twentieth, the baby book arose from the era's emphasis on the child's individual progress as both measurable in itself and a measure of national, racial, and human futurity. Mediating between the "better baby" and the good mother who produced them, the baby book also invited the oversight of scientists into the home.[35] As Rima Apple has written, while baby books empowered mothers to see themselves as expert observers of their children, they also placed mothers under the dictates of childhood's professional experts—the white male psychologists, physicians, and pedagogues who decided the standards of infant care and who predicted children's normal, subnormal, or above-average progress.[36]

Josephine declared her disdain for child experts whom she called "the modernists" and instead described her approach to Philippa's care and education as the common sense of "any intelligent mother."[37] Yet by itself, her documentation of Philippa's early life admitted her observance of the period's guidance and popular practice. Josephine's intelligent motherhood, like that of other white mothers, was staked on her literacy in modern childhood's expert advice, if not total adherence to it. Her notebooks from before and during Philippa's childhood demonstrate that she read diverse works of human biology, social science, nutrition, and psychology—from Charles Alfred Tyrrell's *The Royal Road to Health* (1894), to Darwin's *The Descent of Man* (1871), to behavioralist John B. Watson's *Psychological Care of Infant and Child* (1928), to Alfred Watterson McCann's *The Science of Eating* (1918)—next to which she noted "what to eat."[38]

The regimen that Josephine developed for Philippa reflected her practical application of some theories and her experimentation with others. Closely scheduling Philippa's days with hours of homeschooling and piano practice, Josephine gave special focus to Philippa's diet and vitamin intake.[39] By four, Philippa was to consume eight to ten spoons of cod liver oil daily, a half pint of cream, tomato juice, specific quantities of raw fruits and vegetables, and small portions of meat, usually raw.[40] In addition, she was to spend certain hours of her morning sunbathing on their Harlem rooftop.[41] The rigor of Philippa's early life reflected the rigor of Josephine's practice of mothering—as she put it, she was "trying to use all of the knowledge [she had]."[42] Sending a telegram to Josephine on Mother's Day in 1936, George proclaimed his confidence in her knowledge and effort, declaring that "the miracle of [Philippa's] development" rested on Josephine's "love patience intelligence and science."[43]

In both Schuylers' views, it was by the successful harnessing of Josephine's motherly practice that Philippa's good health, brilliant future, and intelligence would rise or fall. To measure Philippa's intelligence, then, was to measure Josephine's, whether viewed through the Schuylers' belief in Josephine's efficacy or through the hereditary theories of those who began to test Philippa's intelligence a week after her third birthday at the Schuylers' behest. Guided by Terman's Stanford-Binet IQ questionnaire and variations of it, specialists of the Child Developmental Bureau at Columbia and the Clinic for the Social Adjustment of Gifted Children at NYU assessed Philippa by asking her to define words, to describe abstract concepts, to name parts of her anatomy, to describe objects in front of her or in a picture, to draw geometric shapes, to correct ungrammatical sentences, and to do mental calculations in front of them.[44] Tabulating her responses against Terman's age-based standards, both institutions numerically confirmed the Schuylers' belief that Philippa possessed "superior mental ability."[45]

At NYU, Philippa was tested by sociologist Harvey Zorbaugh, who established the clinic in 1930 to study "gifted children," defined, like Philippa, in terms of their exceptional IQ measurements.[46] Decrying the costliness of "feeble-minded" persons on the US government, Zorbaugh took the clinic's data as evidence of the "immeasurably rich return" that he projected for the "gifted."[47] As Zorbaugh's language explicates, the label of "gifted" was inextricable from its opposition to the "feeble" and also from the biopolitical order that hierarchized human worthiness for vital resources between them. Yet Philippa's high scores seemed to prove that this order was, if still a hierarchy, *not* a racial one—the IQ scores she achieved were not explicitly adjusted for her race, nor could they be taken from her on its basis; indeed, her scores afforded her access both to the label of "gifted" and to special funding and opportunities offered by Zorbaugh's clinic.[48]

Enabling Philippa to circumvent racial segregation and to secure resources, the Schuylers likely viewed IQ as a tool to safeguard Philippa from racial violence, not to subject her to it.[49] Yet IQ testing concealed a racial violence older than eugenics and more fundamental. It was the modern, mathematical recoding of a deeply rooted premise: that human value could be measured by degrees of childlikeness. Dividing a test subject's "mental age" by their "chronological age," the intelligence quotient turned childlikeness from a simile—its meaning borne from the historical relationship of childhood and blackness—to an integer seemingly unaffected by any racial variable. When Alfred Binet developed IQ in 1904, he had intended his tool not to measure race but instead to assist teachers in white children's grade-school progress.[50] Yet to even imagine childlikeness to be meaningful *as* a measure, Binet called up the social, political, and empirical salience of what being considered more or less like a child meant. Eugenicists like Terman who popularized Binet's tool made use of this latent racial meaning and its concealment in a numerical standard.

The wider acceptance of IQ's standard numerical value gave it purchase far beyond Terman's political interests. For use of the intelligence quotient did not require agreement as to either the hereditary source or racial substance of intelligence; instead, it only required an interest in obtaining evidence *of* intelligence, which might be interpreted diversely. It was IQ's apparent openness to interpretation that led to its use by behavioral psychologists who rejected Terman's genetic determinism—and its use by African Americans as a statistical means of *refuting* claims of black people's childlikeness.[51] Like the nature versus nurture debate, where "nature" proxied race, the intelligence quotient was, fundamentally, a technology of racial hierarchy. Yet it came to appear as an apt tool with which to contest it. In the Schuylers' understanding, Philippa's high IQ reflected not her mother's whiteness but her mother's effective, scientific practice of mothering. As Josephine often insisted, other children "could be the same way [as Philippa] if they had proper food and attention."[52]

When African American outlets, including the *Crisis*, the *Pittsburgh Courier*, and the *Baltimore Afro-American*, began to celebrate Philippa in their pages, they often conveyed a version of Josephine's premise: that other black children could be the same way if only they were afforded the same resources. Like the black children that the *Crisis* listed by their high IQ scores in its 1927 "Children's Number," Philippa embodied a version of what Katharine Capshaw has described as the period's "emblematic black child."[53] Set apart for her exceptional talent, Philippa's exceptionality was nevertheless leveraged toward, rather than against, the magazine's democratic vision of childhood, where black children were to receive childhood's full resources, protections, and preciousness. Indeed, across his editorship of the *Crisis*, Du Bois expressed a demand for wider societal investment in black children's care, health, and education and for their freedom from white supremacist exploitation. Within this vision, the celebration of exemplary children reflected the magazine's high regard for black children's accomplishments and its insistence that nothing should deter black children from fulfilling the potential that the healthy babies, young scholars, skilled musicians, and community leaders of its "Children's Number" represented.[54] Identifying what Capshaw describes as "the special role of the child to the movement for black social progress," Du Bois sought to carve a special space for black children to see themselves reflected and to set themselves on the path of progress.[55]

Like the annual "Children's Number," where Philippa's photograph appeared in October 1932, Du Bois and Jessie Redmon Fauset's short-lived magazine from a decade earlier, the *Brownies' Book*, sought to cultivate a similar space in a more sustained form. Brimming with stories, poems, and illustrations of, and about, black children, the *Brownies' Book* offered its readers a unique portal through which to travel into the imaginative realms reserved, in the dominant literary sphere, for white children. Readers of the *Brownies' Book* were not to lose themselves in its pages, however. Seeking black children's upright comportment, the *Brownies' Book* directed readers out of the imaginary and onto the exemplary paths of its high-achieving "Little People of the Month" and of its eminent biographical subjects, like Phillis Wheatley. Appearing in its August 1920 issue, the *Brownies' Book*'s "Story of Phillis Wheatley" largely adhered to and directly quoted from Odell's *Memoir* from 1834. Yet the author summarized Wheatley's value in contemporary terms: as "the first Negro in America to win prestige for purely intellectual attainments. And she won it, oh so well!"[56]

The *Brownies' Book*'s celebration of Wheatley's winning intellect, like the *Crisis*'s celebration of Schuyler's giftedness, was an expression of pride and admiration of young black women and girls' intellectual and creative powers. It was also a benign reflection of deeper contradictions that Du Bois courted in his recourse to black exceptionalism, in the *Crisis*'s use of IQ in "The Children's Number," and in the prescriptions and visual grammars of better breeding that appeared across the *Crisis* and in the *Brownies' Book*.[57] Linking "exemplary" behavior to a series of classed, gendered, and colorist visual attributes, Du Bois staked the future success of his race on the reproduction "of a specific kind of African American household."[58] Implicit in his magazine's representation of the elite as emblematic and explicit in his 1903 claim that "the Negro race" would be saved by a "talented tenth" of "exceptional men" lay an acceptance: that with a "talented tenth" came a "submerged" portion, and where there were "better babies," some were worse.[59]

Communicating the integration of a eugenic economy within black reproductive politics, the *Crisis*'s "repeated images of plump, happy, healthy babies" also reflected the complexity—and love—amid its political compromises. Philippa's first appearance in the *Crisis*—as a plump, happy, healthy baby atop a full page of other plump, happy, healthy babies and children—gives an overwhelming visual cue to the desire of the magazine's readers to see black children as tender angels, beloved babes, and heralds of futurity.[60] In the absence of African Americans' creative claims on such roles, these ideals remained the cultural signs and social inheritance of white children alone. Striving to make their children's preciousness legible in childhood's dominant grammar and to enumerate their value in childhood's ever-stratifying schema, twentieth-century African Americans marshaled all the "love patience intelligence and science" they had too.

Josephine understood that to make Philippa's value legible, and winning, beyond an African American audience and before a white one required more than IQ data, more than exemplary images, and more than her intelligent motherhood. It required a performance by Philippa. Philippa's performance would have to contend with that of the crowd of gifted and prodigious white children that burgeoned around her—those whom Josephine monitored in a section of her scrapbook titled the "Gifted Children Dept."[61] Clipping and annotating news stories about musical, mathematical, and literary prodigies who won citywide contests, national tournaments, and scholarships, Josephine included one performer whose arena was far wider and whose name soared above the rest: Shirley Temple. By 1935, the young Hollywood actor's amalgam of cuteness, innocence, humor, and pluck had made her something more than a gifted child and more than a prodigy; she was a transcendent combination of both: a child star. The stories that Josephine cut for her file described Temple's IQ and diet (figure 5.3).[62] Yet if Josephine kept

these clippings to inform her approach to Philippa, it was not necessarily Temple's nutrition or intelligence alone that generated her interest. It was likely, too, the seemingly ineffable set of mannerisms, affects, physical traits, and charm that drew her—attributes that gave Temple unquestionable cultural currency and that secured immense material value to her name.[63]

The *Look* magazine author who recognized Philippa as "the Shirley Temple of American Negroes" in 1939 denoted how close Philippa had

Figure 5.3.a–b [Clippings], "Shirley Bats 155 for I.Q" and "Shirley's First Essay: On Spinach," 1935 Scrapbook, box 3, Philippa Schuyler Collection, Special Collections Research Center, Syracuse University Libraries.

come to Temple's status—and how far she remained from it.[64] Brilliant, creative, witty, disciplined, and extraordinarily talented, Philippa was widely recognized in relation to Temple, yet she could neither rival her nor gain access to the levels of sustained opportunity or monetary security that Temple enjoyed. This discrepancy can be traced in part to the disparate economies of film and classical music where Temple and Schuyler made their young careers. Yet their differing cultural stature reflected more than the comparative popularity of their genres (and film's stark segregation). Schuyler's comparison to Temple signaled a limit. While Philippa could surpass Temple on the IQ scale, could master equally difficult repertoires, and could wear her hair in similar ringlets, she could not secure the value that remained bound up in Temple—in her whiteness and in what she took from blackness.

Black Leaves, Hothouse Flowers

In the world of George Schuyler's *Black No More*, a child like Philippa might have done more than rival Temple—she could have supplanted her. His 1931 novel begins from such a premise: that by assuming the phenotypical appearance of white people, black people could secure the value of whiteness for themselves. This is, at least, what Dr. Junius Crookman's patented medical procedure, Black-No-More, promises to African Americans like Max Disher, who, at the novel's outset, leaves his blackness and economic dejection behind for wealth and power as blond, blue-veined Matthew Fisher.[65] Max's transformation bears dividends quickly. He gains social mobility, money, and intellectual authority; he wins the love of a white woman who had once rejected him; and he captures major political power from the upper ranks of a white supremacist organization.

While Max succeeds in extracting the value of whiteness for himself, he learns the volatility of whiteness as a wider currency. The novel rises and falls with it. For where Max's individual vector leads upward, the mass whitening of poor black people like him leads neither to their collective security nor to the voiding of race's subjecting logic. Instead, it leaves a vacuum, exposing how dearly the American political and economic structure had depended on the exploitation of black people's labor, cultural value, psychic meaning, and social location. As Black-No-More patients push blackness toward its vanishing point, the novel's plot circles questions left in its void: What would whiteness be without its most precious yet disavowed resource? And without blackness, who would be white?

The births of mixed-raced children forestall answers. Because while phenotypical blackness has disappeared from Black-No-More patients' bodies, it reappears with the births of their children, who act as revelators of racial subterfuge and interracial sex. Max's fortune is almost toppled by the impending birth of such a child. Yet in the end, it is not Max's blackness but the blackness of the novel's self-proclaimed Caucasians that surfaces. Fearing the distant taint of blackness in her own family tree, Max's wife, and others like her, confesses the impurity of American whiteness.[66] As catalysts to such radical admissions, mixed-raced children seem at first like decisive foils to America's racial mythology—indeed, they act as corrective lessons against its "set notions." Yet they ultimately incite the creation of new racial mythologies as whites alchemize their acknowledgment of blackness in whiteness into another currency, making mixed-raced children status symbols and producing a vogue of light-brown skin.[67] This "mulatto-minded" America is decidedly not a black-imagined America, nor a racially just one. It is Black-No-More's patients—those who began the novel as poor black people—who, in the end, descend back to the bottom of the social order, debased for possessing whiteness that is *too* white. "And so on and so on," race goes.[68]

Black No More's prescience about the racial future hinges on Schuyler's grasp of race as historical fiction. Dedicated "to all Caucasians in the great republic who can trace their ancestry back ten generations and confidently assert that there are no Black leaves, twigs, limbs, or branches on their family trees," the novel proceeds to dissolve the existence of such a group, wielding satirical fiction against Caucasians' fictiveness.[69] Moreover, while ridiculing the denial of America's entangled black and white family trees, Schuyler's attention to the value of blackness in whiteness is equally grounded in history as in his present. The coincidence of the novel's publication with Philippa's birth suggests that *Black No More*'s forecast of mixed-raced value had something to do with the future Schuyler imagined, desired, or feared for her. Yet if Schuyler's personal investments are irreducible to the novel's, the vogue of mixed-raced children that Schuyler narrates is a clearer depiction not of the value ascribed to his child's ancestry but of the cultural repertoire of white childhood that she would be measured against.

By the mid-1930s, Shirley Temple's film performances had made her an icon and the seeming essence of white American childhood. With blonde ringlets, an often puckered mouth, and brown eyes remembered as blue, Temple embodied what Lori Merish describes as "cuteness as commodity fetish."[70] Across her early films, Temple exhibited childhood's expected innocence but cut it with humor, and she enlivened white girlhood's conscription of smallness, vulnerability, and delicacy with her spirited, rhythmic tap dance routines. Temple's license to modernize the script of white girlhood arose from her legitimacy within it. She was a recognized inheritor of white girlhood's repertoire; indeed, as Bernstein notes, the press declared Temple the successor to Cordelia Howard, the nineteenth-century stage's most beloved Little Eva.[71] And while citing Howard's Eva for twentieth-century audiences, Temple also made Eva her own—performing Eva's deathbed scene in the 1936 film *Dimples*. In the film, Temple embodies suffering childhood both as the title character, Dimples Appleby—a white orphaned street urchin—and as Eva St. Clare, whom Dimples plays in a production of *Uncle Tom's Cabin* opposite a blackface Topsy. Temple's multiply mediated relationship to Eva measures her modernity: where Eva was virtuous, beautiful, and innocent, Temple was known as much for her innocence as for her giftedness; for her fitness, not her frailty; and more for her high IQ than for her virtue. And where Eva and Uncle Tom had embraced in gentle "propinquity" in Americans' nineteenth-century imagination, Temple and her black male counterpart—Bill "Bojangles" Robinson—were, in the motion picture imaginary, perpetually joined in dance.[72]

As Robinson's importance to Temple's career intimates, Temple's apparent innovations on white childhood depended on black performers. And not only on those cast beside her as dance partners, across from her in blackface, and behind her in minstrel choruses.[73] As Merish details, Temple's performance of cuteness reflected her "absorption and domestication of comic styles associated with 'blackness'" and specifically "the black child performer."[74] Indeed, Temple's revival of Eva depended as much on white girlhood's scripts of innocence, virtue, and beauty articulated opposite Topsy as on her successful incorporation *of* Topsy: in the embodied and mental quickness that Topsy's character and caricatures represented and in the modern dance repertoires that Topsy performers had, across the turn of the twentieth century, inhabited, innovated, and evolved.[75]

The "racial doubling of Shirley's body" condensed a larger renegotiation of black and white childhood in the early twentieth century, where black prodigiousness mingled with and disappeared into white giftedness. And where black-and-whiteness became a pleasurable performance to absorb on screen and to enact at home, as Bernstein demonstrates through the commercial popularity of Raggedy Ann dolls and stories from the period.[76] Yet where Bernstein traces childhood's twentieth-century variegation from Eva and Topsy's nineteenth-century binary, Temple's performance of a Topsy-like Eva serves as a reminder that Eva and Topsy were always integrated, codependent figures; indeed, the angel of the house needed the prodigy not to outline her affective power but to source it. It had been Topsy's unacknowledged suffering that gave suffering white childhood its sentimental substance, and now it was Topsy's brilliance and humor that gave vigor to white childhood's more modern script. What Temple represented, then, was not a remodeling of American childhood's black and white relationship but a bolder claiming and commodification of it. Temple could come close to blackness—she could take up black dance steps, she could mimic black caricatures, and she could inhabit Topsy's prodigiousness, all without risking her whiteness; her performance was the more popular for it.

As Philippa learned across her childhood and after, America in the 1930s and 1940s was not as "enthusiastically mulatto minded" as *Black No More* projected—at least not more than it had ever been, nor in a way that shifted much social or material leverage to her and other children like her. She faced increasing discrimination as she grew, and she grew more aware of it.[77] Yet Temple's massive monetary success—as a white star who absorbed and trafficked in blackness—suggests that the value George Schuyler identified in *Black No More* was real in a different sense. Philippa's relationship to that value was mediated through Temple. As the "Shirley Temple of American Negroes," Philippa was placed at a confounding distance from the black-and-whiteness Temple profited from. For where Temple could play in blackness while maintaining her place on gifted childhood's grid and in the hearts of her audience, Philippa's success depended on performing giftedness and "Shirley Temple–ness" as forms of proximate whiteness, not as the products of blackness and black children's historical repertoires that they were.[78]

Philippa was more than successful at maintaining such a suspension; she was masterful. In an August 1940 story for the *New Yorker*, "An Evening with a Gifted Child," reporter Joseph Mitchell summarized how far nine-year-old Philippa's mastery had taken her. She had secured a weekly radio slot, playing her own compositions over national airwaves; she had won numerous piano tournaments; and she had toured the country performing difficult pieces by Bach, Debussy, and Schumann. She had composed over fifty pieces of her own, one of which she had debuted at that year's World's Fair, which dedicated a day in her honor.[79] Considering Philippa "the best example in the city of what psychologists call a gifted child," Mitchell also found her to be a "graceful child." Within minutes of meeting Philippa at the Schuylers' home, Mitchell felt his initial "feeling [of] ill at ease" dissolved by her "assurance." In Philippa's easy presence, he was "not bothered any longer by the differences in [their] ages."[80]

The potential unease felt by Philippa—a nine-year-old black girl alone in a room with a white male reporter—did not warrant his note. While this was Mitchell's oversight, it indexes Philippa's skill at managing the social relations of those above her, giving white adults like Mitchell the illusion that they were under her power and yet unthreatened by that fact. In her performance of assurance and social grace, Philippa cultivated a sense of awe—amazement at her giftedness—and also something of the "Awwwww" that white girls like Temple commanded.[81] Yet unlike Temple, she did so while embodying what whites did, in fact, fear.

Philippa's successful performance of giftedness and Temple-ness was what protected her from the ascription of Topsy-ness—that is, her relegation to the extractable value that whites desired from black children yet claimed was undesirable and menacing. Her avoidance of this evaluation was incomplete. In February 1934, the *St. Louis Globe Democrat* brought Philippa to the attention of its readers, regarding her as a racial novelty. In their estimation, "because all the other child prodigies we can remember were white children," Philippa's claim on public attention was "unusual." If Philippa was unusual, the terms by which the author classified her were familiar: "Like Topsy, [Philippa] just 'growd' as a child wonder." How "admirable it would be," the author continued, if "everybody could just grow" with such "small effort."[82] With a few words and "small effort," this reporter swept the history of black prodigies away, for in the era of Shirley Temple and the age of gifted children, they could no longer remember them. The author *could* idiomatically remember Topsy, however, and put her to use in the dismissal of Josephine and

George Schuylers' immense, well-documented, and publicized efforts as parents. Somehow, despite all evidence, this critic reconceived Philippa in the same terms as Topsy, a figure with an unnatural lack of provenance and a disturbing future of unsanctioned, undirected growth.

Josephine clipped this *Globe Democrat* story for Philippa's scrapbook, labeling it "an editorial in a big American daily concerning your accomplishments."[83] Because the paper on which she wrote has torn with age, Josephine's "your" might in fact read "our." An inconclusive annotation, it is also a brief one—giving little away about Josephine's thoughts on the article's characterization of her daughter or of her role as a mother. Yet if the Schuylers' efforts form a general rebuttal to the story's overarching claim—that Philippa "just growd"—Josephine and George also responded more specifically in the language and imagery with which they narrated their daughter's growth to each other. In a letter to Josephine in 1935, George explained his future hopes for Philippa through a striking inversion of what it meant to "just" grow: "I often speculate on what she will become and what glory she will reflect upon us. It is a wonderful thing to look forward to. I just know she is going to be a marvelously beautiful and intelligent woman. We must do everything to preserve her, like a hothouse flower, for she is of a rare and exotic breed. There are few beings like her in the world."[84]

George's reference to Philippa as "like a hothouse flower" and as a "rare and exotic breed" relates his forthright exoticization of his own child. His focus on her future "glory" objectifies her further, rendering Philippa a speculative reflection of his own, and Josephine's, value. Yet read in relation to the racial characterization of black children—common and "just grow[ing]"—George's choice of language appears, too, as an intervention upon the pernicious propagation myth ascribed to Topsy and those, like his daughter, compared to her. He likely understood that in the landscape of American race and capital, what *just grew* could be easily taken and then taken for granted. Indeed, Topsy's value continued to circulate widely in implicit and explicit extraction, yet the cultural force she created was never attributed to her, to the black children she cited, or to her disappeared black parentage. By contrast, George sought to underscore for his wife and for himself that his child deserved the investment of careful cultivation, preservation, and glorious futurity.

If George's hothouse metaphor conveys a sincere, and compromised, desire to care for and protect his daughter, it also reflected another sort of horticulture: the tending of his family tree. For while the Schuylers' documented engagement with eugenics indexes the field's twentieth-century dominance more than any unique "eugenic project" in Philippa's name, the Schuylers held their family tree, if not their racial origins, in special regard.[85] While George eviscerated white genealogical fictions in *Black No More*, he and Josephine presided over Philippa's genealogy with notable preciousness. Josephine's scrapbooks contain multiple family trees that sketch a lineage from wealthy white settlers and free blacks down to Philippa. And while Josephine retained little contact with her Texan family, Philippa's middle name—Duke—referenced them.[86] Philippa's first and last names derived from George's free black ancestor, Philip Schuyler, who, in Schuyler lore, had performed patriotically in the American Revolution like the white slaveholding colonial general of the same name. George's ancestor had taken the Schuyler name in a relation of hero to hero, not of slave to master. To give this name to his daughter was to connect her to a legacy of black American heroism and to stake an inheritance in the white patriarchal order that Philip Schuyler had helped found.[87]

Both Philippa's namesake and the broader Schuyler mythos in which it fit were anchors to George's adamant belief that in the pantheon of American manhood, he held a place. Understood in this regard, the epigraph to *Black No More* reads less as a dismissal of American heritage and more as a dare—goading any white person to locate their heritage as closely to America's roots as he could. George's confidence—that no whites could prove the pedigree of their whiteness—was matched by another confidence: that he could, through his own family, trace a truer superiority. Philippa's future glories would not just reflect upon him and Josephine; they would extend a more deeply rooted stature.

Such ideas descend squarely back into the frame of eugenics. For what was a family tree, or a hothouse flower, other than a tool and a trope made meaningful by the paradigm of better breeding? Yet to place the Schuylers solely within, or even at the fringes, of twentieth-century eugenics is to miss their orientation in a larger terrain, and a longer struggle, over Man's power. As Josephine wrote, "Genetics is a delightful game while it lasts."[88] A game in which she and George were willing to enter Philippa, but not an end in itself. For they were seeking not so much for Philippa to prove something in the arena of eugenics but for her to *take* something—social and material value—from it. This was a radical ambition, to give their black child the value, cultural investment, and futurity that remained segregated, still, for white children. It was also a politically circumscribed one: using their resources—all their love, care, scientific expertise, and political perception—not to unravel racial power but to arrange it in their service. And still, using a black child, theirs, to do it. The rightward political swing that George and Josephine Schuyler made over the course of the middle century, away from antiracism and toward the white nationalism of the John Birch Society, reads as the natural outcome of such a strategy.[89] But it was not natural; it was the repeating of a pattern where black children's value was made to serve white men's power, this time rearranged in black-and-whiteness more than in black and white.

A Coda

Philippa's story is inseparable from that of her parents because her materials remain in archives they created, because her life began under their vision and supervision, and because after she gained some independence from them, she chose to stay in their alignment.[90] In her young adulthood, Philippa expanded her tour circuit beyond the US, playing across the Caribbean, South America, West Africa, Southeast Asia, and Europe. Though witness to liberation struggles almost everywhere she went and at home, she often aligned herself with colonial elites more than with black and brown revolutionaries. To facilitate her cosmopolitan mobility, she developed an alias, Felipa Montero, who cloaked her US blackness in mythical Latin American brownness. In many ways, Philippa's cynical pragmatism about race mirrored that of her parents.[91] Yet it derived, too, from her personal resignation. She left the US weary of the "vicious barriers of prejudice" that continually thwarted her performance career.[92] By the early 1960s, she left behind performance also, reimagining her public life as a writer and journalist.

In 1967, while covering the US War in Vietnam, Philippa was involved in a fatal accident. A helicopter, carrying Philippa and several Catholic children she participated in "rescuing" from an orphanage, crashed into Da Nang Bay. Almost all the passengers survived, but Philippa and a young child—both unable to swim—drowned.[93] In her death's aftermath, Josephine devoted herself to keeping Philippa's effigy, establishing a memorial fund and penning a biography, *Philippa, the Beautiful American* (1967). Nearing the second anniversary of her daughter's death, Josephine killed herself. George lived alone until 1977, a reviled black conservative.[94]

This ending was also a beginning—of Philippa Schuyler's popular legacy and its entangled strains of tragedy and promise. Tragedy has easily fitted her story because the end of her life was calamitous, shocking, and sad. And also because, in the American cultural imaginary, the "tragic mulatta" ending is the one that makes sense of her.[95] Because expiration is always already pending for the black prodigy, whose value is coveted yet whose excess is troubling, and because, despite its place on every American family tree, mixed-raced blackness is misidentified as being without place and out of time. The tragic abridgment of her life nevertheless runs along a corollary extension of her emblematic status. Established in 1979, the Philippa Schuyler Middle School for the Gifted and Talented in Brooklyn, New York, has passed her name (and her own namesake) onto new generations of black and brown children.[96] And it has passed the promise that "gifted and talented" beginnings stake the foundation for future opportunities. Many cohorts of black children have successfully exchanged their brilliance, creativity, and giftedness for opportunities since Philippa's death. Yet in that same interval, opportunity has shown itself a flimsy structure propped against a more solid one: the property and status inherited by white children. For while giftedness is something one must give, property is something one holds outright—a structure overturned by neither nominal desegregation, nor opportunity's expansion, nor the vindication of the gifted, whether black, brown, or white. Indeed, this ongoing structural integrity marks the true achievement of eugenics: not in proving the superiority of whiteness but in establishing a system that protects it.

Philippa Schuyler's legacy, like the archive of her early life, orients toward the racial power that remains entrenched in the present, making the cultural and epistemic terrain of childhood, and the prodigy's incorporated place within it, more visible. Yet Philippa's story, archive, and especially her storytelling do more than illuminate this map. While the story of Philippa Schuyler's life aptly traces an arc of continuities between childhood, blackness, and human stature across the twentieth century, *her* stories—those she wrote, composed, and performed—confront, break, and exceed that arc as they confront, break, and exceed the arc of the scrapbook that contains them.

For Jody to Paste in My Book

In form and in structure, the scrapbooks are the wrong kind of books for apprehending Philippa as either an authorial subject or an agential actor. They are certainly records of Philippa—the baby of the baby book—and they supply knowledge about her in the observations and routines that Josephine documented. For this same reason, they are better records of Josephine, whose subjectivity, voice, and social context emerge across them. Any story of Philippa that these scrapbooks offer is circumscribed by Josephine's narrative authority and by the doubly minor status of Philippa's content as both marginalia and juvenilia. Indeed, where Philippa's handwriting, typewriting, music, and visual art appear in the scrapbooks, they make only a partial interruption and are often folded, as evidence, into the plot of her progress. Moreover, the Philippa who appears in such interruptions is not an independent, self-possessed author but a child in the process of gaining textual literacy, dependent on adults—chiefly Josephine—for access to both literacy and care. If the scrapbooks are analogs to Philippa's life, they are not analogs of her person.

By contrast, the memoir that Philippa Schuyler published in 1960, *Adventures in Black and White*, appears the appropriate text through which to reconstruct her life and self and an apt source for reevaluating Josephine's account of it. Written when Philippa was nearing thirty, the memoir offers a sequential story of her young adulthood, professional life, politics, and some personal relationships.[97] *Adventures* recounts the racial contempt she faced as a black woman performer on US stages, the remaking of her performance career and persona outside the US, and the beginning of her path as a journalist. Moreover, because it was published so near to her early death, it gains all the more completeness, and finality, as a definitive life story. On the question of her childhood, the memoir gives this summation: "I am not sorry that I was a child prodigy. There is so much to learn, and so little time in which to learn it."[98] Mirroring her mother's language from decades before, Philippa suggests that prodigy, like childhood, was not a state but the foundation beneath her adulthood. Indeed, in their agreement, Josephine's words and Philippa's reiterate the dominant measure of children—in their value to adults and in their future value as adults.

It is by a similar logic that Philippa's autobiography, but not her childhood archive, appears as the rightful source from which to tell a story about her, by her. Testifying to her successful coming of age, the memoir marks her ascension to the autopoietic legitimacy of a narrating subject. A scrapbook composed by her mother, and containing only partial and provisional views of her early learning, thinking, and experimentation as a child, fails to produce a comparable subject. Yet in its fragmentation and illegitimacy, Philippa's presence in the scrapbooks invites a different way of reading, and toward looser ends. Neither conforming to nor confirming the telos of her "gifted" childhood into her "brilliant adulthood," her scrap materials act instead as entry points into childhood as her present and to the imposition of childhood's external grid upon her internal world. In the interplay between the two and under Josephine's mediation, it is illusory if not impossible to discretely locate Philippa, the independent actor. This is less an impasse than an opening, however, to again take interdependence as an archival guide, to read her story for something other than its development, and to locate, in the absence of an ending, other arrangements of meaning.

Mediated and minor, Philippa's creative force in the scrapbook archive is still recognizable and arresting. Where they appear, entries in Philippa's spikey handwriting, her looping signature "by Philippa Duke Schuyler," and her color-saturated drawings and paintings form visual disruptions amid Josephine's dense, tidy, and copious cursive narration. But Philippa's disruptive presence emerges in her mother's narration too. What begins in the earliest scrapbooks as Josephine's careful documentation of Philippa's regimen gives way to Philippa's dynamic, responsive, and unruly interventions upon it. At "2 yrs 5 mo," Josephine listed hundreds of words in Philippa's vocabulary under categories and into columns with checks beside them—a record of her pedagogical process more than of Philippa's thinking, learning, or understanding. Eighteen months later, Philippa's grasp, expansion, and "crooked" use of her vocabulary had reconfigured Josephine's documentation of it. While she still collated Philippa's language into list form, the collated contents were no longer discrete words memorized and checked off; instead, they were novel expressions of meaning formed by Philippa's invention:[99]

1. You make up original comparisons quite your own. The other day you said: "I'm going to wash just as clean as an egg!"
2. A few days later you said: "Oh, I shall do it quicker than the beat of a metronome!" . . . Then you said, "I'll squeeze you smaller than a 32nd note!"
3. And yesterday you exclaimed: "I'm going to hug you harder than a grave stone!"
4. Another time you said: "I'm as happy as a mouse in Parmesan cheese!" "I'm as hot as electricity."
5. You told this fabulous tale to Roy Wilkins . . . "Oh, we had forty million wolves once in our bathroom! Yes, really thought so once. And do you know what happened? I threw them pieces of meat, and in the meat I stuck knives, and they ate them and committed suicide!"

Transcribed, numbered, and deemed "sayings" by Josephine, these similes, metaphors, and stories display the movement of Philippa's imagination as she turned, reworked, and gave momentum to language through her use of it. Enlivening the dull tone of the metronome and squeezing meaning from a thirty-second note, Philippa made exclamations of her own bravery, physical power, and speed from mundane and disciplinary objects. Indeed, mundane discipline was the site of her questioning and redirection. "Do mothers ever say 'go crooked to bed'?" she asked Josephine. "Why don't they if they say, 'go straight to bed'?"[100] Familiar with straightforward directives, with a musical note's fractional division, and with the metronome's faithful time-keeping, she knew, too, how to bend and warp meaning to "fabulous" disproportion—fitting forty million ravenous animals inside her apartment's bathroom and living to tell the tale to Du Bois's *Crisis* successor.

Philippa continued making, telling, and performing stories, interpolating interior and exterior ecologies of city life into vivid language, color, and sound. When she began composing music for piano at age four, the pieces she wrote were not mimetic approximations of the classical repertoire she practiced and often performed but more so sonic extensions of the stories she imagined, told, wrote, and illustrated. Philippa attuned her music both to the melodramas of tiny creatures and to the scale of the city skyline. In "Golden Fish," she wrote from the perspective of a goldfish longing to ascend "up a bright stream of water," out of his bowl—but whose "supreme flip" for "freedom" leads to his tragic death.[101] She drew pathos, too, from the vermin who survived extermination to dance in her "Cockroach Ballet." In "Rolling Home," she established a more expansive view, imagining herself roving across the city in her roller skates and looking down at the street from a towering height.[102] She looked up, in "Autumn Rain," to follow the path of a thunderstorm from her window.[103] Beginning with cracking force, the piece proceeds with scattered notes, pounds in dense minor chords, and disappears at pianissimo[104] (figure 5.4).

The scrapbooks do not, in themselves, make it possible to hear Philippa's music. To do so requires the use of different archives, instruments, and technologies—reading or playing her sheet music or finding the limited recordings that remain from her childhood. Yet the scrapbooks invite a way of engaging with Philippa's music in excess of its sonic form and in awareness of the wider imaginative practice constellated through it. In their tactility, the scrapbooks highlight the layered, haptic dimensions of Philippa's music. When she composed, she was not distilling story into song but instead creating immersive interfaces between sound, text, and image in her own unique arrangement. Listening to the scrapbooks—or extending Tina Campt's practice of "listening to images" to the scrapbooks' embedded images and text—raises the narrative substance of Philippa's music to the surface and narrative's breakdown into fragments, scraps of illustration, "first attempts," and discarded lyrics.[105] Compiling an iterative and ongoing process, the scrapbooks disallow the reduction of Philippa's music—and performance—to the profits of her disciplined training or the products of her giftedness. They displace giftedness altogether, identifying the less quantifiable, more substantial intellectual force that took the stage when Philippa did.

Yet as the signature *of* her giftedness, performing at the piano was always the site of Philippa's evaluation, where her superior status was to be confirmed, elevated, or tarnished. Whether she played in competition

Figure 5.4. [Philippa composing on her rooftop with dolls, ca. 1936], Beinecke Rare Book and Manuscript Library, Yale University. Courtesy of the Carl Van Vechten Trust.

or gave recitals alone, her audiences were primed by the label of prodigy, and by popular metrics of giftedness, to invest their listening and looking with questions and comparisons: Was she equal to other children of her age? Was she better? Had she progressed? These questions did not form impermeable foreclosures, however. For in the act of playing her original compositions, she opened imaginative space—hers—and interpolated audiences into it. In the concert auditorium and across radio waves, Philippa compelled those who listened to her also to look, feel, imagine, and notice *with* her. Even within the short duration of her early "Little Pieces"—like "Golden Fish," "Autumn Rain," "The Wolf," and "Men at Work"—Philippa carried her listeners into the dramas, fables, multiscalar perspectives, and "strange, minor" melodies of her imaginative world.[106] Indeed, echoing the unsentimental subversions that Wiggins played against the confines of nineteenth-century sentiment, Philippa delivered stormy, complex, and distinctly *un*cute affects far in excess, and in discord, of the cuteness that she was tasked to commodify.

Yet any command Philippa took of her audience was subject to negotiation: audiences' willingness to listen on her terms was contingent on her ability to win them over—with mastery, grace, and gifts, all elegantly packaged. Winning audience approval was worth more than their applause or a given title or prize; it was the coin she needed to sustain a line of opportunity ahead of her. In Josephine's perspective, "opportunity"— not just applause or approval—was the thing that Philippa must "go out and get" on the stage.[107] Both a proxy for and a promise of material security, it would "not come to [her] unsought" but required that Philippa give her giftedness in exchange.[108]

Philippa gave time, discipline, skill, and originality. The scrapbooks bear evidence both of her sustained efforts and of the opportunities that followed from them: in the form of performance programs, clipped news coverage, and awards won by Philippa and collected by Josephine. Yet in the midst of this evidence, the scrapbooks also surface moments of Philippa's refusal—breaks in which, expected to give, she instead withheld. In 1936, Josephine penned an entry about her efforts to secure a spot for Philippa on the popular radio program *Major Bowes' Amateur Hour*.[109] Performing on the show was an opportunity to reach Bowes's wide and growing National Broadcasting Company audience, but the audition, in itself, formed an opportunity: to gain favor in the entertainment and recording industry in which Bowes held a seat of power.[110] Josephine brought Philippa to the audition. The producers seated her at a piano. They stationed themselves on the opposite side of a glass partition. They waited and they watched. Philippa, however, did not begin. She was already familiar with playing before audiences and with sitting under the collective scrutinizing gaze of white men. But she did not accept this arrangement.

Josephine's entry does not capture *why* in Philippa's perspective, terms, or words. But her entry does suggest what Philippa refused and how.

It was not the setting, or the stakes, but the men's impatience to get something from her to which she responded. And the violence of their impatience. For before Philippa had settled and placed her hands at the keys, the producers decided that she had given them too little and taken too much time. The man seated directly beside Philippa "rose and picked [her] up and said: 'Play! play! Don't you understand. Play!' And he banged the piano. And he screamed." Philippa did understand—how to play, how to perform, and how to comply. But to the screaming man she simply said, "I can't play." Noting the "utterly amazed" look on Philippa's face as she received the man's abuse, Josephine's entry continues not with her intervention but with her pleading: "Please darling, they are waiting, won't you play the Soldier's March?" As a reply, Philippa played not "the Soldier's March" but instead a different piece, "very badly." In Josephine's estimation, "it was hopeless," for Philippa had "noted all these heads on the other side of the glass peering at [her]," and in return, she had "glued" her eyes "on them."[111]

Though Josephine noted the "determination" of her daughter's look, the scrapbook offers no reentry into this scene through Philippa's eyes, for there is no extant entry penned in parallel by Philippa. Limited to Josephine's recollection, this story is truncated further by her selections, occlusions, and revisions. Titling her entry "Major Bowles [sic] Is Nothing to You" and concluding it by saying, "The fact is, I did not care greatly for you to appear on the Amateur Hour," Josephine frames her account with disdain against Major Bowes and with her allegiance to Philippa. Had Josephine *not* cared for Philippa to appear, however, she would not have brought her to audition, nor would she have pleaded with Philippa to play amid the producers' abuse. Where Josephine's self-reflection bears contradiction, it also misses Philippa's reflection. For while noting the defiant stare Philippa fixed upon the men behind the glass, Josephine does not note whether, or how, Philippa looked at *her*. Without this consideration, and with the turn of a scrapbook page, this story ends.

A skilled storyteller herself, Philippa understood that an ending—whether marked in triumphant chords, played at pianissimo, or written and then revoked—could alter the meaning of the whole story that preceded it. "This is the end of the story no it isint i was joust fooling you [*sic*]," Philippa wrote in the tale she titled "The Girl and Her Parents." She deployed this coda again in a story about a fairy house, explaining, "I waxs only fooling you [*sic*] . . . I can't write any more because jody was so bad to me [*sic*]."[112] Exclaiming her mother's "bad" treatment, Philippa's story fragment loosely diagrams a scene of mother and daughter at odds: four-year-old Philippa tapping the typewriter and Josephine chastising her. Whatever the severity or content of Josephine's "bad" treatment, we can surmise that Philippa held on to the typewriter for a few more seconds—enough time to close her story: "By Philippa Duke Schuyler for Jody to paste in my book!"[113]

As both a reference to the scrapbooks and an assessment of Josephine, this sign-off forms a notable break in the dominant structure, function, and story of the scrapbooks. To the press, Josephine, George, and later Philippa each described the scrapbooks as a secret kept from Philippa during her childhood, their eventual exposure causing Philippa dismay.[114] But this exclamation—"for Jody to paste in my book"—places the scrapbooks' secrecy in question, highlighting the possibility that at some point, Philippa self-consciously contributed to the scrapbook archive, and moreover that she sought to place her evaluation of Josephine amid Josephine's endless evaluations of her. This revelation cannot overturn Josephine's outsize authority over the scrapbooks—indeed, the appearance of this exclamation itself reflects Josephine's decision to include it. Yet Philippa's ending nevertheless marks her contestation and claim *upon* the scrapbook's structure and content, not only under or within it. If unable to overturn the major story into which she was conscripted, Philippa could, and did, stage minor breakdowns.

When the Stars Are Up

She staged breakdowns, too, in the primary grammar stories of her earliest literacy. "Once upon a time," three-year-old Philippa typed, beginning a story of a "good little rabbit" and a "smart" dog who live in a house. Introducing familiar storybook animals and placing them at storytelling's most recognizable opening, Philippa seemed poised to deliver a tale in parallel to those of her *Wag and Puff* primer, with its "little brown dog" and "little white cat," in "a little brown house."[115] Instead, however, she pulled the narrative foundation beneath it (figure 5.5). Her

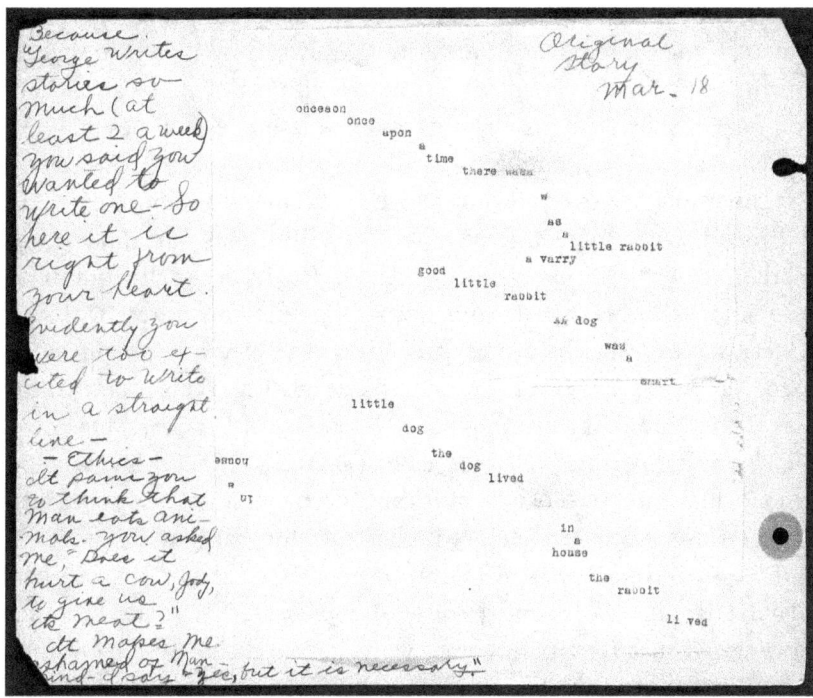

Figure 5.5. ["Little Dog, Little Rabbit" story], March 18, 1935, 1935–36 scrapbook, Oversize 7, Philippa Schuyler Collection, Special Collections Research Center, Syracuse University Libraries.

text darts diagonally down the page, decomposing individual words and dissolving the story's familiar establishment. The little dog and rabbit come apart into syllables and letters. The "house" in which they live teeters upside down over "in." If this text disorientation foremost demonstrates Philippa's typewriter dexterity, it also suggests her deliberate inversion of the stories, lessons, and disciplines offered by little dogs, rabbits, and houses to little readers like Philippa.

Like her invented phrases and trick endings, this story appears in the scrapbook as evidence both of Philippa's textual literacy and of something else: a motivation not only to make something of language and story but also to interrupt the grammar underlying them. Overturning the little house and spilling out its inhabitants, Philippa's story "mov[es] in and out of place," putting "pressure on meaning and that against which meaning is made."[116] Doing so, she anticipates what Christina

Sharpe calls "anagrammatical blackness," textually "anarranging" the literal, pedagogical template of American Grammar itself. Where we can only imagine Phillis Wheatley's encounter with her primer—and whatever poetics she made upon it—this scrapbook story establishes Philippa Schuyler, almost two hundred years later, working upon an American Grammar that had evolved and changed yet remained imposing.

Indeed, what Josephine annotated as Philippa's "original story, March 18, [1935]," is perhaps better read *not* in its originality but in its resonance with black girls' and women's poetic encounters with the American Grammar before her and after. Published in 1970 but set in 1940, Morrison's *The Bluest Eye* enacts a deeply linked anagrammatical break—not upon *Wag and Puff* but in the house of *Dick and Jane*. Morrison's novel is narrated in large part by Claudia MacTeer, who was nine in 1940, like Philippa Schuyler and Toni Morrison. It is perhaps because of Morrison's contemporaneity with her narrator that Claudia's fictional childhood and Philippa's historical one come so near to one another. Claudia lives in a world under Shirley Temple's affective spell—or in the "Awwwww" that Temple and other white girls and blue-eyed baby dolls cast on those around her. Claudia, however, is not under the spell. She is disgusted by Temple's "cu-ute[ness]," and she perceives that Temple has stolen something from her.[117] Entwined with Claudia's critical perception of her world is the more fragmentary perception of her neighbor, Pecola Breedlove. Unlike Claudia, Pecola does not hate Temple. She loves her with a passion. She does not hate but desires the blue of the baby dolls' eyes. Both Pecola's story and Claudia's narration of it are set against *Dick and Jane*, whose refrain "Mother, Father, Dick, and Jane live in the green-and-white house" extends across the chapters.[118]

Against *Dick and Jane*'s structure, a circular history of violence done to Pecola, and to her family, unspools. Pecola is orphaned by her mother's neglect and her father's sexual abuse. She exists "outdoors," a social abandonment that Claudia understands as even graver than homelessness.[119] Pecola is extremely vulnerable, and she suffers immense harm. For all that she suffers, however, she receives none of the "Awwwww" apportioned to white girls who played orphans on screen; instead, she receives only contempt for being "outdoors" and for being common. Recalling characterizations of the picaninny, one neighbor insists that Pecolas "were everywhere," variously "hanging out of windows" and "crawling over porches," "hair uncombed, dresses falling apart, shoes untied," and "star[ing]" with "great uncomprehending eyes."[120]

Without shelter or care, Pecola's story ends with what Claudia tells us at the beginning: she becomes pregnant with her father's child. Under the weight of her violation, Pecola breaks into "madness": she is seen "walking up and down, up and down, her head jerking to the beat of a drummer so distant only she could hear."[121] The violent devolution of Pecola's childhood appears to crack the foundation of the "green-and-white house" textually bound around her. Indeed, the repeating text of *Dick and Jane* contracts and becomes undifferentiated across the novel's pages, compressing its original sense into "motherfatherdickandjaneliveinthegreen-and-whitehouse," and then

*HEREISTHEFAMILYMOTHERFATHER
DICKANDHANETHEYLIVEINTHEGREE
NANDWHITEHOUSETHEYAREVERYH*[122]

Though they run beside one another, the breakdowns of Pecola, Dick, and Jane are bound in an integrated, not parallel, relation. *The Bluest Eye* exposes how the violence that places Pecola "outdoors" *is* the structure that keeps Dick and Jane inside the house. More truly still, Pecola's "outdoors" childhood—so tightly tethered to the house—forms part of its foundation. The novel ends not with the overturning of this foundation but with Pecola's perceptual flight from its reality. Pecola gets the blue eyes she desires, or she believes so, and it is this belief that signals her loss of rational subjectivity.[123] "[S]tripp[ed]" of "the child's self," as Farah Jasmine Griffin describes her, Pecola is, in Hilton Als's pronouncement, "blighted."[124] Claudia recognizes this blight in what the earth refused, that year, to grow. She knew that "no green was going to spring from our seeds" because "the damage done" was so "total."[125]

Though Pecola suffers unbearably, the totality of her loss lies not only in her but in "grown people look[ing] away" from her.[126] Yet it remains possible both to look *at* Pecola and to look with her—through her blue eyes. The novel stages this possibility. It is Pecola's altered and anarranged sense—or what she comprehends through her blue eyes—that both sets off *Dick and Jane*'s breakdown and renders it legible. As the novel makes clear, mastering the grammar of *Dick and Jane* would not have yielded the personhood or property that it entailed to white child readers to Pecola. Yet loosing herself from its sense, promise, and structure, Pecola stages an "upheaval" that breaks down both the house and the "assumption of equivalence of personhood and subjectivity" that its grammar upholds.[127] It is the force of her fragmentary subjectivity, broken from subjected personhood, that makes the primer's grammar, and its violence, visible.

Announcing a loss of sense, Pecola's blue eyes also take something back: the preciousness and value that Claudia knows to have been stolen. Claudia's hatred for Temple and Pecola's desire point to this same theft. Claudia despises Temple "because she danced with Bojangles, who was *my* friend, *my* uncle, *my* daddy, and who ought to have been soft-shoeing it and chuckling with me."[128] In the space occupied by white, wide-eyed, and twirling Temple, Claudia sees the form, shape, and movement of a black girl who should have been there instead, perhaps dancing like Topsy or "jerking to the beat" that only Pecola could hear.[129] Pecola's blue eyes are no kind of justice for the brutal abuse she suffers. Nor are they reparations for the conditions that absented black girls from their own cultural repertoire. But if you know what Claudia knows, you can see what Pecola shows us. Her blue eyes on black skin are a vivid appropriation—as garish as blackface on white, but more monstrous. In a time when Temple was cu-utely absorbing black childhood's value into whiteness, the blue eyes Morrison gives Pecola make childhood's circuit of exchange spectacular and undeniable.

A black girl with blue eyes, like a Negro Shirley Temple, was a reflection of this exchange, appearing as a novel conjunction yet revealing American childhood's deeply sedimented circuit of racial power. Related by their revelations of meaning, the real Philippa and the fictional Pecola nevertheless endured different kinds of violence. Indeed, Philippa lived in closer relation to Pecola's namesake, Peola—the beautiful mixed-raced child from the 1934 film *Imitation of Life*—than to Pecola, whose bid for proximate whiteness is reproached, not rewarded.[130] Still, the deconstructive, anarranging force of Pecola's sight, and her fragmentation of self, lights up something in Philippa's archive, refracting the fragments of Philippa that appear, disrupt, and reframe it. Indeed, Pecola's blue eyes make it possible to look into the blue eyes that stare back from Philippa's archive.

Tucked within scrapbook pages from 1935 to 1936, a penciled figure—painted over with brown hair, orange-red skin, and dense, milky blue eyes—floats on a background of cool-red brushstrokes (figure 5.5). Made when she was four, this portrait is one of Philippa's most color-saturated and detailed images, though it bears resemblance to many figures, including several self-portraits, that she drew or painted that year and later. The upward arms, loops of hair, and heart-shaped mouth repeat features of her "Lady of the Flowers" and "dolls on parade"; her use of color, pencil, and multidirectional brushstrokes form a pattern across the scrapbook's pages. They also fit within a visual pattern, or visual grammar, of "children's art," which if recognizable to most adult eyes in the present was, in 1935, the site of modernist fascination—an interest in children's image making that emerged in relation to the modernist curation of "childlike" art by "primitive" peoples.[131] It was in this cultural context—and indeed, at the fore of it—that Paul Klee made his *Angelus Novus* (1920), a monoprint figure that bears a striking, almost uncanny resemblance to Schuyler's blue-eyed figure: its body floating in space, winged arms flown up, and eyes staring back[132] (figure 5.6).

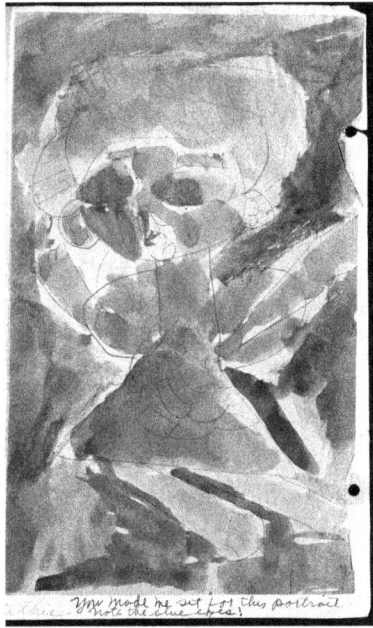

Figure 5.6. Philippa Schuyler, [Detail, "Note the Blue Eyes!"], September 1935, 1935–36 Scrapbook, Philippa Schuyler Collection, Special Collections Research Center, Syracuse University Libraries.

"This is how one pictures the angel of history"[133]—or at least how Walter Benjamin, who purchased the image from Klee, imagined his allegorical figure, whose eyes stare "fixedly" at the "one single catastrophe" of the past as it joins seamlessly into the "wreckage upon wreckage" of the present.[134] This wreckage is mistaken, by all except the angel, as "progress."[135] Yet if the angel can see history truthfully, he cannot alter it. He is blown backward into the future by progress's wrecking "storm."[136] The tempest that surrounded Benjamin's writing distinguishes his "angel" both from Klee's "Angelus" and from Schuyler's portrait. Benjamin wrote the essay in which his angel figures, "Theses on the Philosophy of History," in Nazi-occupied France in 1940.[137] Yet if differently located, Benjamin, Klee, and Schuyler were each witnesses of, and subject to, the same trajectory of human progress, viewed from different moments and locations in its eugenic project, and telegraphed as much in Philippa's depiction of blue eyes as in Benjamin's words. To understand their shared embedment in these epistemic and social conditions is to clarify the resemblance of Schuyler's and Klee's images, not as being uncanny, but as joined by history and, in turn, made sense of by Benjamin's angel, who lays that history bare. Yet the stare of Philippa's figure communicates something about her view that disallows conflation between a prodigy's view of history and an angel's or between Philippa's eyes and these blue ones.

While Philippa's blue-eyed figure resembles her self-portraits, it is not one. Beneath the painted figure is a note from Josephine: "You made me sit for this portrait. Note the blue eyes!"[138] It is Josephine who looks back from this portrait, and it was Philippa who studied and represented her. These were not blue eyes that Philippa necessarily desired to possess or to look through; they were the eyes that looked *at* her. In turn, Philippa was looking back upon them. She made Josephine "sit" for this portrait, and like the men behind the glass, perhaps Philippa "glued" her eyes upon her. Within the hundreds of pages of Josephine's observations about Philippa, this portrait performs a striking inversion of the scrapbook's purpose and form by its own purpose and form.

Indeed, giving Josephine such singular attention, this portrait shifts attention away from Philippa, relieving her as the scrapbook's subject of sustained scrutiny. One can only look *with* Philippa in the space of this portrait, seeing what she saw of her mother, how she imagined her,

Figure 5.7. Paul Klee, *Angelus Novus* (1920), © 2023 Artist Rights Society, HIP/Art Resource, New York.

and what she decided to represent of her on paper. Placing this portrait within the scrapbook's observational context, moreover, highlights the relational, intimate aspect of the staring blue eyes, which look at the painter with crossed scrutiny and closeness, their intense saturation bleeding beneath one eye into a streaky, blue-black tear. To "note the blue eyes!"—both as objects of immense value and as Josephine's way of looking—is to see this figure as unmistakably human, a participant in progress, not its angel observer. Yet if her portrait shows us what her mother cannot see about progress, Philippa's act of witnessing is neither helpless nor caught in backward flight. For even as Philippa was enlisted into her parents' story of progress, Philippa's drawing, music, and writing offer missives, and poems, from inside the storm.

Indeed, along with Josephine's caption to her portrait is another note: "This morning you announced [to us] that you were going to be a writer [and] must write. So you wrote this."[139] With "this" Josephine refers to the poem across from the portrait, made in Philippa's handwriting and signed by her (figure 5.8):

> WHEN THE
> STARS ARE UP
> WHEN THE
> STARS ARE UP
> I GO TO BED
> AND DREAM
> ABOUT WHAT
> I DO THE DAY
> BEFORE[140]

Here, Philippa presents going to bed and "dream[ing]" as striking alternatives to the scrapbook's method of logging, collating, and preserving knowledge about her. Instead of entering data about herself into the scrapbook's pages, she describes entering the quotidian contents of her days into her dreams. And delivering the command "go to bed" in the line "I go to bed," Philippa's poem subtly directs her reader, too, to consider her "crooked" approach: not to write her life down as data, nor to make her early life into the foundation of her development or legacy, but instead to consider the immediate history and value of her life, to enter the immaterial space of dreaming, and to imagine what she imagined of it.

To end a story of a life as complex and far-journeying as Philippa Schuyler's in her four-year-old dreams risks turning from the history that surrounded her and from the notion of progress in which she, too, would participate. It also risks romanticizing her childhood imagination

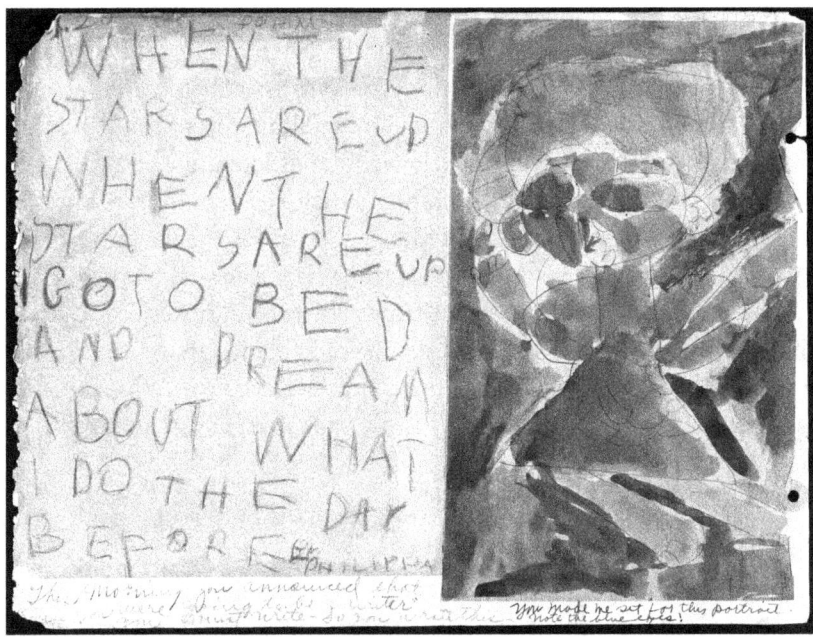

Figure 5.8. Philippa Schuyler, "When the Stars Are Up," September 1935, 1935–36 Scrapbook, Oversize 1, Philippa Schuyler Collection, Special Collections Research Center, Syracuse University Libraries.

as a refuge from history. Yet Philippa's childhood drawings, writing, music, and commentary are not a refuge from critical thinking but an incitement to it. It is by looking at Philippa's childhood image beside Klee's childlike one that we might take something new from Benjamin—that when he pictured his angel of history, he imagined a child's picturing of it too, that his imaginative figure is made possible first by children's drawing and then by Klee drawing *like* them. Staying in the imagination and immediacy of Philippa's childhood history is an invitation to consider how her small acts of perception, creation, and self-reflection might inform or shape larger ones, as indeed children's acts already have. It is also a directive to consider, again, the system of value that has made black children's dreams, thoughts, images, and imaginations seem the antithesis of grounded, serious history.

Philippa's story, like the history of black prodigy in which it fits, refutes this, revealing how often, and how dearly, black children's knowledge, imagination, and value have been put to use: for white childhood's sentimental affects and its recoded repertoires, for white patriarchal power and for white women's empowerment, for material profits, and for knowledge of the human itself. For all that has been extracted from black children, Philippa's archived act of looking back upon her mother and Pecola's sight are reminders that black children—if prodigies all—have often contested, undermined, and turned their view on the dominant social orders in which they have been embedded, even if they have not toppled them. It is possible, if we loosen what binds their archives and their endings, to both credit black children's visionary work and glimpse moments of their critical perspective. What remains is to imagine how critical acts of looking back and persistent movement might coincide.

Epilogue

"To Be Held, Free"

Prodigy is, at its essence, adaptability and persistent, positive obsession. Without persistence, what remains is an enthusiasm of the moment. Without adaptability, what remains may be channeled into destructive fanaticism. Without positive obsession, there is nothing at all.
—Octavia Butler, *Parable of the Sower*

Octavia Butler's *Parable of the Sower* opens onto an apocalyptic 2024 with this epigraph. Through the eyes of a black teenage protagonist, Lauren Olamina, the novel bears witness to the catastrophes of capitalism, state abdication, climate disaster, and endemic violence that she struggles to survive. In the beginning, Olamina's survival is premised on protection within her father's traditional family structure and under his authority. Yet after the walls of his order are breached, Olamina makes a different way, staking her survival on forms of interdependence that she builds among strangers and on the collective experiment of "Earthseed," an ethic of trust-building, resource-sharing, and nonhierarchical community order.[1]

Parable might be read as delivering the prodigy for our time: Olamina, a near-messianic figure who perceives the storm that engulfs her world with unique clarity and yet is not dragged under its tow, an agent who can turn her knowledge toward deliberate, persistent action. Yet to claim Olamina as our prodigy would be to misread the word as Butler defines it. Prodigy, here, is not a true noun describing an exceptional figure but closer to an adnoun, a way of doing, being, or performing—perhaps akin to what McKittrick and Wynter deem "being human as praxis"— something that need not, and cannot, be undertaken alone.[2] And if not embodied by a singular source, nor is Butler's prodigy directed toward a single outcome. It is "persisten[ce]" matched by "adaptability," a way of shaping change while changing.³

Suspended between "persisten[ce]" and "adaptability," "positive obsession" may be the least transparent element of Butler's prodigy, appearing at first as a potential companion to the destructive positivism that the novel warns against.⁴ It gains explanation, however, not in the novel's world but in Butler's childhood. Also the title of a personal essay in which Butler recounts her early self-conception as a reader and writer, "positive obsession" is what propels young Butler toward the "target" of becoming an author.⁵ This story begins in interdependence and adaptation too: in the act of Butler's mother pulling books from her employer's garbage to bring home to her daughter.⁶ These were "books yellow with age, books without covers, books written in, crayoned in, spilled on, cut, torn, even partly burned."⁷ In their appropriation and transfer from Butler's white employer, to her mother, to her, the contents of these irregular and refuse-bound books were re-bound into something else, turned—under the pressure of Butler's positive obsession—into the basis for her literacy, self-making, and other-world-making. Perhaps it was through Butler's orientation toward these books—of active negotiation and repair, not outright possession—that she came to understand prodigy against its prevailing meaning: not as an accident of nature but as the deliberate harnessing of difference, resources, and imagination to change the given shape of things.

The shape of things in our present looks a lot like Butler imagined. Yet many of the institutions of state, policing, capital, and family that altogether collapse in Olamina's world remain defended in ours. While the transformation of these systems is alive in the work of black, Indigenous, abolitionist, and decolonial movements, such change remains unwanted and unthinkable for many.⁸ There is no living Lauren Olamina on her way to break through this quiescence; moreover, to rely on a young black figure to teach us about our humanity—even a different praxis of it—would be not breaking our pattern but repeating it. Yet black children, in collective, *have* been telling us something urgent, both by their feats of survival and by their deaths.

The string of black children's murders that preceded and followed the February 2012 killing of seventeen-year-old Trayvon Martin, has, as Elizabeth Alexander writes, collectively acted as a "primer" impressing "fear and futility" upon young black people, deeply marking their individual psyches and coalescing into a collective shape deemed, by Alexander, "The Trayvon Generation."[9] If formative for a group of "young people who grew up in the past twenty-five years," these lessons in stolen black life have shaped everyone else too—inviting mourning, inciting action, and prompting questions like Alexander's own: If "I want my children—all of them—to thrive, to be fully alive. How do we measure what that means?"[10] For many, measuring black children's aliveness and thriving has meant using a familiar gauge: the white child, whose secure standing in American childhood starkly highlights black children's uneasy and endangered experience of it. Viewing this discrepancy, we often take up and restate Douglass's assertion—that black children *are* children and that, on such a basis, they are naturally deserving of the innocence ascribed to white children, of the protections built around them, and of the preciousness placed on their lives.[11]

Yet if we study the history of American childhood, we know that these protections were never natural—that they were built carefully, and most concertedly, around whiteness. For this reason, we also know that what and whom American childhood has best protected is whiteness. White children gain protection in their whiteness to be sure. But when the protection of children is at odds with the protection of white property, family, and patriarchy, it has not been white children's preciousness that has won out.

For though the history of childhood demonstrates children's substantial gains in legal protection, educational entitlement, and social investment across the span of the last three centuries, these gains have been characterized by contradictions, compromises, exceptions, and rollbacks.[12] White children's rising preciousness has not necessarily made them more socially respected; nor has the idealization of childhood in representation directly produced ideal conditions for their lives. And while it is unquestionable that American children possess, on the whole, more legal protections in the present than in the past, we should question why children are in need of more protection, not less, and why their protection—if elaborated to address so many kinds of threats—often fails to save them from the most basic, well-known ones: namely, the violence of adults inside and outside of their homes.

Both the recent past and present demonstrate these failures. For the Trayvon Generation is also the generation of Sandy Hook, Parkland, and

Uvalde.[13] After the latter mass killing, in which a young man murdered nineteen elementary schoolchildren and two teachers while the city's police refused rescue for fear of their own safety, Roxane Gay asked, "What is a country that will not protect its children?" Implicit in this question is the notion that it once did.[14] And while we might place pressure on the question of *whom* this country has seen as "its children," this book has disabused the idea that the only children in whom the nation has been possessively invested have been white, or that possessive investment and protection coincide.[15] The protection of men's rights and power over children's lives is an old wager. Once we recognize the frailty of American childhood to protect even the nation's chosen children—those "held free," white, and precious—can we stake black children's future here?

The cascading crises of the present reveal this contradiction and its history to us relentlessly, and the 2022 overturning of *Roe v. Wade* further compounds the question: What is a country that will not protect its children but also enforces their births? The answer is, plainly, *this* country, which has historically understood children to be of national value but not discretely priceless and that, moreover, was founded on a system of slavery that coerced children's births and endangered children's lives by design. It is untenable to posit the economically and racially complex order of the present as a neat reflection of the order of slavery that historically underlies it.[16] Yet it nevertheless remains important to return to the American Grammar as set down in *Partus*, to recognize how it shaped not only slavery's reproduction—which nominally ended—but *also* the reproduction of American freedom, which rather than being overturned has been more widely applied. The notion of freedom attached to white children by *Partus*, later expanded by birthright citizenship and further by desegregation, remains embedded within life, liberty, and property's linkage and subject to familial and other authority.[17]

A central argument of this book has been that to produce and maintain their authority, American men have sought to keep children in place. This knowledge illuminates not only present attempts at reproductive coercion and violence against children but also the escalating exertion of control over children and their books. Efforts by conservative legislators to restrict K–12 educators from teaching the history of colonization and slavery, from using any lens that might be deemed "critical race theory" or "gender inclusive," and also from reading *The*

Bluest Eye or *Parable of the Sower* with their students are not arbitrary attacks merely aimed at recognizable targets on the left, nor are these battles pitched among adults and merely *over* children.[18] Rather, they have been aimed strategically at the link between children and their books in the process of social reproduction, or in the collective autopoiesis that tells them, and us, who we are.[19] Yet if meant to guard against their arriving at different answers to that question, these efforts are already failures. Divesting American childhood of books is a nearly self-defeating task, both because childhood has depended so dearly on its mediation through books and story and because even when restricted, thrown away, written over, or burned, books remain, in one form or another, available for creative reading or alteration.

As this book has shown, neither limiting access to books nor limiting traditional literacy has effectively prevented black children or adults from reading them or from reshaping childhood through their creative and intellectual interventions. And if social reproduction has been subject to the pressures of continuous black transformation, so has the biocentric reproductive order. Though codified and violently enforced, laws governing reproduction and family have never entirely prevented black children and adults from forming different systems of kinship, caretaking, or bodily autonomy in acts of what Sophie Lewis calls "inventive kinning," through what Alexis Pauline Gumbs deems "revolutionary mothering," or in community experiments that echo in Butler's conception of "Earthseed."[20]

This knowledge is not a balm to the present, nor is it a celebration of an ingenious black past. For indeed, the structure of white supremacy that has necessitated black inventiveness has been not merely a force against which black people have propelled dialectical change but a material system meting out life and death. To measure black children's thriving and aliveness in this system is to continually confront myriad evidence that they have been afforded less life, more danger, less security, more exploitation. And yet measuring the unequal dividends of this system is not enough to see its internal parts. For if the balance sheet of childhood shows a stark dividing line between black and white, the history of American childhood shows both sides of this ledger as belonging *inside* the same closed system, where value has moved not only laterally, from black children to white, but also vertically, in service of white patriarchal power.

Indeed, the close relationship that this book traces between black and white childhood, between black children and white men's power, and between blackness and the conception of the human reveals that "inside" has encompassed more ground than previously thought—and more violence. Yet in articulating the rudiments of grammar, cultural coding, scientific knowledge, and common sense by which humanism's internal violence has proceeded, this book also identifies black children's long-standing acts of revisions at each level, the cumulative effect of which has been the human's systemic alteration, if not its wholesale transformation.

Each chapter in this book has been a lesson in the power of small parts to shape larger structures, of children delivering or contesting the power of men, of marginalia changing a dominant story, of exceptions shaping rules, and of grammatical parts shaping structural power. It is from this perspective that we might return to the American Grammar Book, not to reckon with its historical enormity, but to revise it in its smallest parts. If American children were once "held bond or free," a slight alteration in this grammar's legacy—or an experiment in the space between held and free—might spell altered conditions.

What would it mean to be held, free? To answer this question, we would need to ask more: Held by whom? And free in what sense? These answers would require thinking critically about parental rights, family belonging, and structures of care altogether different from family. Such thought, in turn, might suggest forms of caretaking and freedom tied neither to parental rights nor to property relations but to an undermining of them. If possible in grammatical abstraction, undermining or altering our historical systems of relation requires much more of us in a material sense: the recognition of children's vulnerability; their need of care, growth, and development; *and* a radical revision of what these conditions mean to, and require of, others. And also the rearticulation of freedom not as the shedding of childlike vulnerability but as something coterminous with childhood and vulnerability, materialized through the resources, care, and respect that could support all children being as Alexander wishes, "fully alive."[21] To be like children, then, would signal not a lack, a deficit, a need for growth's measured control, nor a dangerous place of subordination. It would mean being human not in progress toward Man but in a process that extends around and after him, in shapes that might make his form unrecognizable. The present offers little hope that this vision is one widely shared or deemed credible, and it is certainly not structurally supported. But history teaches us that its imagination has been patterned and its performance already begun. It teaches us, too, that it won't travel on its own.

NOTES

INTRODUCTION

1. "Bright" Oscar Moore Cabinet Card [January 1889, by David H. Anderson], Randolph Linsly Simpson Collection, James Weldon Johnson Memorial Collection, Beinecke Rare Book and Manuscript Library.
2. Because many nineteenth-century cameras required long exposure times, keeping portrait sitters still with braces or headrests was not an entirely unusual practice. What is unusual is this prop's kind, placement, and visibility. See Rudd, "Good Subjects," 195–218.
3. D. Shields, "David H. Anderson."
4. Wilson, *Mathew Brady*.
5. The "showman" in question is Hans Peter Neilsen Gammel, discussed in chapter 4. See Gammel, "Not Worth Quarreling," 37–41.
6. Burnett, *Little Lord Fauntleroy*. Burnett's novel follows the trajectory of Ceddie, a child who begins his life in relative poverty in America but learns that he is the inheritor of an earldom and estate in England. Ceddie, a boy both innocent and beneficent, travels to England, where he teaches his aristocratic family to be more kindly and responsible in their social positions. Originally published in serial format, Burnett's novel became immediately popular, leading to unauthorized theatrical stagings and followed by Burnett's own theatrical adaptation. With its mass popularity, dressing young boys in Fauntleroy suits became a middle-class and elite fad. See Gubar, *Artful Dodgers*, chap. 6; Carlson, "Little Lord Fauntleroy," 39–64; and Tortora and Eubank, *Survey of Historic Costume*, 403–4.
7. *Hand-Book*.
8. Bernard Page to the Countess of Huntingdon, Cheshunt Foundation, Westminster College, A3/5/17, as cited in Carretta, *Phillis Wheatley: Biography*, 92; "Music: Harlem Prodigy," *Time*, June 22, 1936.
9. "An Enigma to Doctors: The Wonderful Memory of a Three-Year-Old Blind Boy Put to the Test," *Louisville Courier Journal*, December 10, 1888; "An Infant Prodigy," *Wilson Advance*, January 31, 1889.
10. Foucault, "Lives of Infamous Men," 71, 82.
11. Hartman, "Venus in Two Acts," 5; Foucault, "Lives of Infamous Men," 82.
12. There are multiple scales of history "from between" that inform my approach, from transnational studies of colonial power to studies of domestic relations and family, including Foucault and Arlette Farge's *Disorderly Families* (1982). See

Foucault and Farge, *Disorderly Families*; Lowe, *Intimacies of Four Continents*; and Jenco and Chappell, "Introduction."

13 Wynter, "Ceremony Must Be Found," 22.
14 Foucault, *Order of Things*, 318; Wynter, "Unsettling the Coloniality," 290–91.
15 Wynter, "Unsettling the Coloniality," 310; Wynter, "Yours in Intellectual Struggle," 3. See also Wynter, "Ceremony Must Be Found," 34.
16 Here I invoke a broad and heterogeneous conversation, including recent and decade-spanning work by Saidiya Hartman, Katherine McKittrick, Frank Wilderson, Christina Sharpe, Denise Ferreira da Silva, Achille Mbembe, Zakiyyah Jackson, Jared Sexton, Hortense Spillers, Sylvia Wynter, David Scott, and Frantz Fanon, among others. See Hartman, *Scenes of Subjection*; McKittrick, *Dear Science*; Wynter, "Unsettling the Coloniality"; Wynter, "Ceremony Must Be Found"; Wynter, *On Being Human*; Sharpe, *In the Wake*; Wilderson, *Afropessimism*; Sexton, *Amalgamation Schemes*; D. Scott, *Conscripts of Modernity*; Jackson, *Becoming Human*; Da Silva, "Toward a Black Feminist Poethics"; and Mbembe, *Critique of Black Reason*.
17 This framing—"consent of the governed"—comes from John Locke's *Two Treatises on Government* (1689) and appears in the US Declaration of Independence (1776). Gillian Brown takes up the relationship between the two in *Consent of the Governed*.
18 Brewer, *By Birth or Consent*, 87–91.
19 Locke, *Essay concerning Human Understanding*, 104, 2.
20 Levander, *Cradle of Liberty*, 6.
21 Brewer, *By Birth or Consent*, 179–80.
22 Brewer, 1–4, 5, 28–29, 40.
23 Bloom, "Introduction," 8–10.
24 On the conflicting cultural meanings of innocence that descended from Locke, Rousseau, and other sources, see Gubar, "Innocence," 105–9; and Sánchez-Eppler, "Childhood," 38–41.
25 The full poem reads, "My heart leaps up when I behold / A rainbow in the sky: / So was it when my life began; / So is it now I am a man; / So be it when I shall grow old, / Or let me die! / The Child is father of the Man; / And I could wish my days to be / Bound each to each by natural piety." William Wordsworth, "My Heart Leaps Up" (1802).
26 McClintock, *Imperial Leather*, 45.
27 On the politics of infantilization in US proslavery thought, see Faust, introduction to *Ideology of Slavery*; and Tise, "'Positive Good' Thesis."
28 In 1851, for instance, physician Samuel Cartwright claimed to "prove the similarity of organization and physiological laws between negroes and infants" based on their supposedly "like" liver functions and blood circulation. Biologists later claimed that black people were an evolutionarily arrested race based on the theory of "recapitulation," which I discuss in chapter 3. See Cartwright, "Diseases and Peculiarities"; and S. Gould, *Ontogeny and Phylogeny*, 117.

29 McClintock, "White Family of Man"; S. Gould, *Mismeasure of Man*; Jacobson, *Barbarian Virtues*.
30 Field, *Struggle for Equal Adulthood*.
31 Work that exposes the disparate treatment of black children in the past and present is vital, even if the principle of inclusion/exclusion reified in such work demands further thought. I include among such essential works King, *Stolen Childhood*; Baumgartner, *In Pursuit of Knowledge*; Webster, *Beyond the Boundaries*; and Bernstein, *Racial Innocence*.
32 M. Morris, "Countering the Adultification," 44–48; M. Morris, *Pushout*.
33 Goff et al., "Essence of Innocence," 526–45.
34 Jackson, *Becoming Human*, 3, 20.
35 Maria Kromidas makes a persuasive argument for thinking about the child (especially in the context of contemporary teacher education) as a figure similarly overrepresented by a white "ethno-class" developmental template. She articulates the need to deconstruct this "child of Man" rather than move toward the greater inclusion of black, Indigenous, and other nonwhite children in teaching praxis shaped around the child. See Kromidas, "Towards the Human," 68.
36 Bernard Page to the Countess of Huntingdon, Cheshunt Foundation, Westminster College, A3/5/17. As cited in Carretta, *Phillis Wheatley: Biography*, 92.
37 K. Brown, *Good Wives, Nasty Wenches*.
38 J. Morgan, "*Partus sequitur ventrem*," 5.
39 Morgan, 5.
40 Emphasis in the original. See Norfolk Wills and Deeds D, August 15, 1662, 350; SAL December 1662, II, 170, cited in K. Brown, *Good Wives, Nasty Wenches*, 132–33. Though eventually known as *Partus sequitur ventrem*, Latin was not in the original Virginia law but was added in the early nineteenth century. See J. Morgan, "*Partus sequitur ventrem*," 1.
41 J. Morgan, "*Partus sequitur ventrem*," 5.
42 Spillers, "Mama's Baby, Papa's Maybe," 79.
43 In 1655, Elizabeth Keye (also spelled Key and Kay) petitioned a Northumberland, Virginia, court for her freedom based on the fact that she had completed a term of indentured service and was the child of a white man. Yet Keye was *also* the daughter of an enslaved woman. She eventually won her freedom, yet both Morgan and Brown note that she was very likely considered highly among the "doubts" that *Partus* in 1662 sought to foreclose. See J. Morgan, "*Partus sequitur ventrem*," 11–12; and K. Brown, *Good Wives, Nasty Wenches*, 132.
44 Morgan describes how mixed-raced children (like Keye) were problems of "excess, as both circulating and unregulated, and ultimately as a source of chaos." See J. Morgan, "*Partus sequitur ventrem*," 6.
45 Spillers, "Mama's Baby, Papa's Maybe," 67.
46 Spillers, 74.
47 See Norfolk Wills and Deeds D, August 15, 1662, 350; SAL December 1662, II, 170; and K. Brown, *Good Wives, Nasty Wenches*, 132–33.

48 Spillers, "Mama's Baby, Papa's Maybe," 73.
49 Forms of black social life, kinship, escape, and the general refusal of slavery's terms are documented in myriad examples across every existing slave narrative from the period and have been found in more forms of evidence—letters, legal cases, ledgers of sale, newspaper notices of fugitives, and visual and material culture—by many scholars of American slavery. See, for instance, Camp, *Closer to Freedom*; Miles, *All That She Carried*; Hunter, *Bound in Wedlock*; Penningroth, *Claims of Kinfolk*; and J. Morgan, *Reckoning with Slavery*. Quotations from J. Morgan, Reckoning with Slavery, 255.
50 Spillers, "Mama's Baby, Papa's Maybe," 80.
51 Manhood rights, the respect of womanhood, and children's protection were major demands shared by a range of black political projects and movements since the early American period and are the focus of essential work in African American political history and cultural studies. See White, *Ar'nt I a Woman?*; Higginbotham, *Righteous Discontent*; M. Mitchell, *Righteous Propagation*; and Gaines, *Uplifting the Race*.
52 Writing in 1987, Spillers names it as "our task"—the task of black feminism—to make a place for this social subject and write a "radically different text for female empowerment." Spillers, "Mama's Baby, Papa's Maybe," 80. Since Spillers writing, many scholars have explored and extended her questions regarding monstrosity and black female gender, including Christina Sharpe, Zakiyyah Jackson, and Alexander Weheliye, among others. In taking up the "baby/maybe" of her essay rather than the negated female-maternal figure, I do not move away from gender analysis but approach it from different entries across this book. See Jackson, *Becoming Human*; Sharpe, *Monstrous Intimacies*; and Weheliye, *Habeas Viscus*.
53 Work by Sarah Haley, C. Riley Snorton, and Saidiya Hartman demonstrates how black women and queer and trans black people produced forms of social life, self-presentation, and mutual care that, while highly policed and endangered, nevertheless placed pressure on the penal and extralegal enclosure of black life during slavery and especially in its aftermath. See Haley, *No Mercy Here*; Snorton, *Black on Both Sides*; and Hartman, *Wayward Lives*.
54 "An unusual or extraordinary thing or occurrence; an anomaly; something abnormal or unnatural; *spec.* a monster, a freak, from classical Latin *prōdigium* extraordinary thing or occurrence regarded as an omen, monstrous event or situation, monstrous person, freak, wonder, marvel, of disputed origin." *Oxford English Dictionary*, s.v. "prodigy, n.," http://oed.com.
55 Daston and Park, *Wonders*, 14–15.
56 White children also performed as musical, mathematical, and literary prodigies across the nineteenth century, including the famous Zerah Colburn, an early nineteenth-century prodigy of mathematical calculation. Americans met these performances with a mix of enjoyment, unease, and conversation about precocity—whether children should be on stage and whether they should demonstrate early skill. Thomas Jefferson stated an early iteration of this anxiety

when he wrote that the precocious may display "the flattering appearance of their being men while they are yet children, but" this will end "in reducing them to be children when they should be men." See Jefferson, "Query XIV," in *Notes on the State of Virginia*, 158. On Zerah Colburn, see *Memoir of Zerah Colburn*. On white child prodigies and controversies surrounding white children on stage, see Benes, "Child Performers and Prodigies"; and Gubar, "Cult of the Child." I discuss the history of "gifted childhood," its eugenic origins, and its relationship to prodigy in chapters 4 and 5.

57 William Shakespeare, "Act 1, Scene 2," *The Tempest* [1611], ed. Barbara Mowat and Paul Wernstine (Washington, DC: Folger Shakespeare Library, 2022), 335–37.
58 Curran, *Anatomy of Blackness*, 87–100.
59 Spillers, "Mama's Baby, Papa's Maybe," 74.
60 Spillers, 74.
61 Zelizer, *Pricing the Priceless Child*, 3, 6.
62 For Locke, the protection of men's property was the central import of democratic government. See Mehta, *Anxiety of Freedom*. Scholars debate whether his concept of freedom as property's protection was inherently dependent on slavery. Holly Brewer notes that Locke in fact expressed antislavery positions in his writings and political engagement. Yet regardless of his personal investments, a broader scholarship, from Edmond Morgan's *American Slavery, American Freedom* (1975) to Christopher Tomlin's *Freedom Bound* (2010) and Wendy Warren's *New England Bound* (2016), identifies the deeper structural dependencies of slavery, capitalism, American freedom, and liberalism. See Brewer, "Slavery, Sovereignty, and 'Inherited Blood,'" 1038–78; E. Morgan, *American Slavery*; and Warren, *New England Bound*.
63 The category of the freeholder—a white man who held outright legal claim to stolen land and other property became increasingly definitive of white men's power and politics in early America. Eight years after *Partus*, in 1670, Virginia passed a law restricting the franchise—political participation—to "freeholders and householders." See "Election of Burgesses by Whom" (1670), in *The Statutes at Large: Being a Collection of All the Laws of Virginia from the First Session of the Legislature in the Year 1619*, ed. William Waller Hening (New York: R. & W. & G. Bartow, 1823), 280. For more, see Kolp, *Gentlemen and Freeholders*.
64 C. Harris, "Whiteness as Property," 1707–91.
65 J. Morgan, *Reckoning with Slavery*, 18.
66 Locke, *Essay concerning Human Understanding*, 104, 2; Spillers, "Mama's Baby, Papa's Maybe," 67.
67 Lerer, *Children's Literature*, 105.
68 G. Brown, *Consent of the Governed*, 10.
69 Sánchez-Eppler, *Dependent States*; V. Watson, introduction to *Coming of Age*.
70 This is, of course, not only an American (or Anglo) literary trajectory. Franco Moretti, in *The Way of the World*, famously argued that the coming-of-age novel, or bildungsroman, was the "symbolic form of modernity" itself and that this form

was shaped under the ideological pressures of Western capitalist development. Jed Esty extends and alters this argument in *Unseasonable Youth*, which notes the bildungsroman's developmental breakdown at the edges of empire and across its colonial—"underdeveloped"—peripheries. See Moretti, *Way of the World*, 5. See also Esty, *Unseasonable Youth*.

71 Books and children have also, and often, been formed into literary metaphors. In her poem "An Author to Her Book," seventeenth-century American poet Anne Bradstreet refers to her first published volume, *The Tenth Muse*, as an "ill-form'd offspring." See Bradstreet, "Author to Her Book," 221.
72 Crain, *Reading Children*, 1.
73 Crain, 5; Weikle-Mills, *Imaginary Citizens*, 4.
74 Wynter, "Ceremony Must Be Found," 22.
75 D. Scott, "Interview with Sylvia Wynter," 119.
76 Foote Sr., *Science in Story*, 5:236.
77 Morrison, *Playing in the Dark*, 6, 13.
78 Wright, *Black Girlhood*; Fielder, "No Rights"; Webster, *Beyond the Boundaries*; Capshaw and Duane, *Who Writes for Black Children?* See also Griffin, *Read until You Understand*.
79 H. Williams, *Self-Taught*, 17–35.
80 V. Smith, *Self-Discovery and Authority*, 2.
81 Gillespie and Lynch, "Introduction," 2–3.
82 Bernstein, "Scriptive Things," in *Racial Innocence*, 69–91; Trumpener, "Modernist Picture Book," 166–82.
83 Bernstein, *Racial Innocence*, 89.
84 Benjamin, "Theses," 200; Hartman, "Venus in Two Acts," 3; D. Taylor, *Archive and the Repertoire*, 16.
85 McMillan, *Embodied Avatars*, 1; J. Brown, *Babylon Girls*, quoting from the book's subtitle, "Black Women and the Shaping of the Modern."
86 Garland-Thomson, *Extraordinary Bodies*, 8.
87 See Schalk, "Approaches to Disability Identity," 129–39. See also Schalk, *Bodyminds Reimagined*; and Kafai, *Crip Kinship*.
88 Bernstein, *Racial Innocence*, 16.
89 Bernstein, 16.
90 Stowe, *Uncle Tom's Cabin*, 159–60, 263, 268.
91 Stowe, 268.
92 Duane, *Suffering Childhood*, 1–3.
93 Bernstein, *Racial Innocence*, 19–20.
94 Bernstein, 20. See also Hochman, *Uncle Tom's Cabin and the Reading Revolution*, 210–13.
95 Bernstein, *Racial Innocence*, 20.
96 Bernstein, 8, 16.
97 Bernstein, 16.
98 Hartman, *Scenes of Subjection*, 22, 20, 35.

99 Hartman, *Scenes of Subjection*, 18, 21.
100 J. Brown, *Babylon Girls*, 57.
101 Brown, 57–58, 91.
102 Brown, 24.
103 Stowe, *Uncle Tom's Cabin*, 275, 260.
104 Stowe, 263.
105 Stowe, 263, 260, 261, 265, 273.
106 As Soderberg argues, and I follow, nineteenth-century depictions of childhood along the binary of innocence/noninnocence miss some of the other complex features and attributes that Americans assigned to children in literature and culture. Marah Gubar makes a related argument in *Artful Dodgers* that innocence was not in fact the sole representative mode through which nineteenth-century adult authors imagined white children. See Soderberg, *Vicious Infants*, 86; and Gubar, *Artful Dodgers*.
107 Wiggins, *Specimens*, 1.
108 I discuss "anarrangement"—a mode of disassembling an imposed order of things—in chapter 5, and I take the term itself from Christina Sharpe (*In the Wake*, 76) and Fred Moten (*In the Break*, 1).
109 Douglass, *My Bondage*, 39.
110 Spillers, "Mama's Baby, Papa's Maybe," 80.

1. "BABE BELOV'D"

1 Carretta, *Phillis Wheatley: Biography*, 178.
2 Carretta, 179–82.
3 Carretta and J. Mason posit that Wheatley's "To P.N.S. & Lady" is the same poem as her "To Mr. and Mrs.—on the Death of Their Infant Son," published in *Boston Magazine* in 1784 though likely written in 1778. See Carretta, *Phillis Wheatley: Complete Writings*, 188; and J. Mason, *Poems of Phillis Wheatley*, 213.
4 Wheatley, "To Mr. and Mrs.—on the Death of Their Infant Son," in Carretta, *Phillis Wheatley: Complete Writings*, 188.
5 Wheatley, "On the Death of J.C. an Infant," in *Poems*, 93.
6 Wheatley, "On the Death of a Young Lady of Five Years of Age," in *Poems*, 25–26.
7 On Wheatley's influence by Alexander Pope, see Carretta, *Phillis Wheatley: Biography*, 71, 77; and Winterer, *Mirror of Antiquity*, 31–32.
8 Gates, *Trials of Phillis Wheatley*, 5.
9 Brooks compiles compelling evidence that no such "trial" occurred. J. Brooks, "Our Phillis, Ourselves," 1–5, 8.
10 J. Shields, *Phillis Wheatley and the Romantics*, 118.
11 The phrase "ordinary road" comes from Locke, *Some Thoughts concerning Education* (1693–1706), 117, §157.
12 Wheatley, Letter to Obour Tanner, 21 March 1774.
13 Wheatley, "To the Right Honourable William, Earl of Dartmouth," in *Poems*, 74.

14 Spillers, "Mama's Baby, Papa's Maybe."
15 Dayton, "Lost Years Recovered," 309–51.
16 Jefferson, *Notes on the State of Virginia*, 144.
17 Odell, *Memoir*, 10; Wilmot Griswold, *Female Poets*, 30.
18 Odell, *Memoir*, 12.
19 Odell, 12.
20 Dayton, "Lost Years Recovered," 311.
21 Dayton, 311.
22 Odell, *Memoir*, 28.
23 Dayton, "Lost Years Recovered," 347.
24 Odell, *Memoir*, 9, 17.
25 Wheatley, "To the Right Honourable William, Earl of Dartmouth," in *Poems*, 74.
26 Notices of the sale of enslaved people trafficked on the *Phillis* appeared in the *Boston Evening Post* on July 13, 1761, and later on August 3 in the *Boston Gazette*, where they were advertised as "small negroes," "cheap for Cash." See Carretta, *Phillis Wheatley: Biography*, 12–13.
27 On early English and Anglo-American cultures of children's literature and play, see Bernstein, "Toys Are Good for Us," 458–63; Crain, *Reading Children*, 5–6; and Weikle-Mills, "Learn to Love Your Book," 35–61.
28 J. Morgan, *Reckoning with Slavery*, 19.
29 Wendy Raphael Roberts has recently discovered evidence that the Wheatleys may have exercised their power to *exchange* Wheatley as property by "loaning" her out to the Rotch family in Nantucket and New Bedford during her youth. See W. Roberts, "'On the Death of Love Rotch,'" 164.
30 Locke, *Some Thoughts concerning Education*, 117, §157.
31 Locke, 116–17.
32 Monaghan, *Learning to Read and Write*, 81.
33 Crain, *Reading Children*, 15.
34 Stories of Polly's instruction of Phillis are unsubstantiated beyond Odell's telling. As David Waldstreicher notes, other white Wheatley descendants would insist that it was Susanna herself. See Odell, *Memoir*, 10; and Waldstreicher, *Odyssey of Phillis Wheatley*, 33.
35 Congregationalist minister, politician, and slaveowner Cotton Mather promoted enslaved religious instruction. See, for example, Mather's *The Negro Christianized* (1706). Wheatley was baptized in Boston's Old South Congregationalist Church in 1771. See Carretta, *Phillis Wheatley: Biography*, 79.
36 Carretta, *Phillis Wheatley: Biography*, 41; Waldstreicher, *Odyssey of Phillis Wheatley*, 33.
37 Perlmann, Siddali, and Whitescarver, "Literacy, Schooling, and Teaching," 117–39.
38 Patricia Crain notes that "as many as six million copies of the *New England Primer* were printed between the end of the seventeenth century and the mid-nineteenth

century." See Crain, *Story of A*, 15. See also K. Roberts, "Rethinking the *New England Primer*," 489–90.
39 Monaghan, *Learning to Read and Write*, 88, 98–105.
40 *New England Primer*, 15.
41 Wakely-Mulroney, "Isaac Watts," 103–5.
42 K. Roberts, "Rethinking the *New England Primer*," 489–90.
43 Crain, *Story of A*, 43.
44 Selections from "Words of One Syllable," "Words of Two Syllables," "Words of Three Syllables," and "Words of Four Syllables," *New England Primer*, 7–9.
45 *New England Primer*, 8–9.
46 Spillers, "Mama's Baby, Papa's Maybe," 80.
47 Carretta, *Phillis Wheatley: Biography*, 91–108.
48 Carretta, 121.
49 While in London in 1773, Wheatley met Granville Sharp, a lawyer who argued several pivotal antislavery cases in England. Carretta posits that her acquaintance with Sharp and his circle gave her leverage to bargain freedom from John Wheatley. See Carretta, 118–20.
50 Wheatley, Letter to David Wooster, 18 October 1773, Ms. N-125, Massachusetts Historical Society.
51 Wheatley, Letter to Obour Tanner, 21 March 1774, Miscellaneous Bound Manuscripts, Massachusetts Historical Society.
52 Wheatley, Letter to Obour Tanner, 21 March 1774.
53 Wheatley, Letter to Obour Tanner, 21 March 1774.
54 Wheatley, Letter to Obour Tanner, 21 March 1774.
55 Wheatley, Letter to Obour Tanner, 21 March 1774.
56 Wheatley, "Letter to John Thornton, 30 October 1774," 182.
57 John Wheatley left his estate to his children Mary and Nathaniel, who died in 1778 and 1783, respectively. See "Will of John Wheatley," February 14, 1778, Ms. N-1552, Massachusetts Historical Society.
58 Separately, and on different grounds, Holly Brewer and Toby Rollo come to the conclusion that the claimed likeness of black people to children that emerged in this period was the relegation of black people to the child's *premodern*, pre-Enlightenment status. I argue differently that the elaboration of children's legal and civil disqualifications, their domestic dependence, and the intellectual capacities that developed across the eighteenth and nineteenth centuries were crucial and productive to the force and exercise of racial childlikeness as logic. Moreover, this logic itself evolved as childhood did. See Brewer, *By Birth or Consent*, 341; and Rollo, "Color of Childhood," 308.
59 Wynter, "Ceremony Must Be Found," 33–34.
60 Wynter, 35.
61 Locke, *Essay concerning Human Understanding*, 64, §27.
62 Jefferson, "Query XIV," in *Notes on the State of Virginia*, 146, 143.
63 Jefferson, 143, 142, 147.

64 Jefferson, 147, 142.
65 Jefferson, 149, 151.
66 Thomas Jefferson to Edward Bancroft, January 26, 1788, in Boyd et al., *Papers of Thomas Jefferson*, 492.
67 Jefferson, "Query XIV," in *Notes on the State of Virginia*, 151; Jefferson to Bancroft, 492; Locke, *Essay concerning Human Understanding*, 64, §27; *New England Primer*, 6–9.
68 Carretta, *Phillis Wheatley: Biography*, 45–48.
69 Wheatley, *Poems*, 74.
70 Pasulka, "Somber Pedagogy," 180.
71 Janeway [and Mather], *Token for Children*, 116.
72 Pasulka, "Somber Pedagogy," 178–80.
73 Wheatley, "A Funeral Poem on the Death of C.E. an Infant of Twelve Months," in *Poems*, 69–70.
74 Wheatley, 69.
75 Wheatley, 70.
76 Wordsworth, "Ode," 157.
77 W. Roberts, "'Slavery' and 'To Mrs. Eliot,'" 665–81.
78 As transcribed in Roberts, 676–77.
79 Roberts, 677.
80 Roberts, 676.
81 Roberts, 676.
82 Wheatley, *Poems*, 25–26.
83 Excerpts from "On the Death of a Young Lady of Five Years of Age," in *Poems*, 25–26.
84 Wheatley, 25.
85 Wheatley, 26.
86 Bernstein, *Racial Innocence*, 10–11.
87 W. Robinson, *Phillis Wheatley*, 40; Gates, *Trials of Phillis Wheatley*, 71.
88 Excerpt from "To the Right Honourable William, Earl of Dartmouth, His Majesty's Principal Secretary of State for North-America &c."
89 Wheatley, *Poems*, 74.
90 Wheatley, 26.
91 Janeway [and Mather], *Token for Children*, 116.
92 Wheatley, *Poems*, 74.
93 See Wheatley, "To the Right Honourable William, Earl of Dartmouth," in *Poems*, 74; and *New-York Journal*, vol. 3, June 1773, as printed in Carretta, *Phillis Wheatley: Complete Writings*, 130–31.
94 Wheatley, *Poems*, 74.
95 Dayton, "Lost Years Recovered," 347; Waldstreicher, *Odyssey of Phillis Wheatley*, 329.
96 Dayton, "Lost Years Recovered," 347.
97 Odell, *Memoir*, 28. Carra Glatt has verified Odell's relationship to the white Wheatleys. See Glatt, "To Perpetuate Her Name," 155.

98 Dayton, "Lost Years Recovered," 311.
99 Dayton, 311; Jeffers, *Age of Phillis*, 167–89.
100 Odell, *Memoir*, 20, 28.
101 Odell, 24.
102 Odell, 28.
103 Odell, 12.
104 Odell, 28.
105 Odell, 16.
106 Odell, 16.
107 Odell, 17.
108 May, *American Female Poets*, 39; Wilmot Griswold, *Female Poets of America*, 30.
109 Smith [Hall], *Friendship Album*. Thank you, Kabria Baumgartner, for pointing me to this source.
110 Dayton, "Lost Years Recovered," 310.
111 Waldstreicher, *Odyssey of Phillis Wheatley*, 326.
112 Dayton, "Lost Years Recovered," 311; "Naomi Wilkins to John Peters, Essex County Deeds," 138:77, via familysearch.org.
113 Dayton, "Lost Years Recovered," 332.
114 Will of John Wilkins, Essex County Probate File 29905 (1780), Americanancestors.org; Dayton, "Lost Years Recovered," 314.
115 Dayton, "Lost Years Recovered," 331–32.
116 Dayton, 330.
117 Dayton, 341.
118 Dayton, 350.
119 Dayton, 347.
120 "Record of D. Cober [sic] discharged," Essex General Sessions Peace Records, 1776–92, 93; and Recognizance, June 18, 1782. Court of General Sessions of the Peace, Essex County, files, Dinah Cober's recognizance, July 1782. JU-SJC/GEN.ES/series 003. Massachusetts Supreme Judicial Court Archives, Massachusetts Archives, Boston, Massachusetts. See also Dayton, "Lost Years Recovered," 347.
121 Hartman, "Venus in Two Acts," 1–14.
122 Dayton, "Lost Years Recovered," 347.
123 Dayton, 311.
124 Thus far available birth, death, tax, and other records for Massachusetts, Rhode Island, and Connecticut have produced several women (mostly white) named Philanda, Philinda, Philenda, or Filenda born and deceased during the period relevant to Wheatley's writing yet none that seem likely. I have also located records of an enslaved woman, "Pileander," listed as "servant" to "Mr. Brooks, Medford, Ma" (a wealthy enslaver). The relationship of Pileander to Wheatley's "Philandra" remains unproven, and indeed, Pileander may, in her case, be a misspelling of "Belinda." See "Marriages: Negroes, etc., Massachusetts, Town Clerk, Vital and Town Records, 1626–2001," FamilySearch.com.

125 Thank you, Sarah Derbew, for offering guidance both on classical references and on Greek and Latin etymology.
126 See Lennox, *Philander*; Gouttes, *Philandre* (1544); and Oldys, *Female Gallant*. As the titles, plots, and characters in these texts intimate, the name Philandra bears a linguistic relationship to the noun "philanderer" and the verb "to philander." As such, the notion of sexual license inheres in the name's meaning as much as love. See *Oxford English Dictionary*, s.v. "philanderer, n.," http://oed.com.
127 I have also considered the possibility that Philandra might be, like Phillis, the name of a ship that transported enslaved people. Based on research in the Atlantic Slave Voyages database, however, this does not seem to be so.
128 W. Roberts, "'On the Death of Love Rotch,'" 155–84.
129 Spillers, "Mama's Baby, Papa's Maybe," 65.
130 "Phillis Wheatley," in *Freedman's Third Reader*, 75–77.
131 Spillers, "Mama's Baby, Papa's Maybe," 65.
132 Spillers, 65.
133 Spillers, 65.
134 Blanck, "Seventeen Eighty-Three," 24–51.
135 Webster's work provides a vivid reminder that it was not only northern black adults but black children who carried this work forward. As she writes, "Black children themselves acted in political ways through their play, labor, and schooling—influencing prevailing ideas of race, childhood, and freedom of the time." See Webster, *Beyond the Boundaries*, 2.

2. "WILT THOU BRING MY BABY HOME?"

1 *Songs, Sketch of the Life of Blind Tom*, 6.
2 While Wiley E. Jones is typically discussed as the previous enslaver of the Wiggins family, the exact circumstances by which the Wiggins family became property of James Bethune are somewhat unclear. Indeed, earlier tax records show an M. M. Wiggins as a neighboring enslaver for whom a member of the Bethune family is listed as trustee. And Wiggins's name—often recorded as Thomas Greene Bethune—indicates another area planter. However many transactions were involved, "Slave schedules" from 1850 show James Bethune as the enslaver of nine people, the youngest thirteen months (likely Tom). See "James N. Bethune" in Schedule 2, Slave Inhabitants in the 8th District of the County Muscogee, Georgia, September 4, 1850, http://ancestry.com. See also "John Bethune" and "M. M Wiggins," Muscogee County, Georgia Property Tax Digests, 1845. http://ancestry.com.
3 Press materials demonstrate Wiggins's consistent presence on US stages between the 1850s and 1890s, often delivering multiple performances during a single day at a given venue. As one critic wrote, Wiggins "was the marvel of three generations of playgoer." See "Blind Tom Goes to Beyond," *Atlanta Constitution*, June 15, 1908.
4 The Bethune family, critics, and the courts described Wiggins as "idiotic" or "imbecilic" throughout his life. See *Songs, Sketch of the Life of Blind Tom*, 4.

5 There is no definitive archival record of Wiggins's earnings by year. However, the legal cases in which Wiggins was involved elucidate sums of money at various points in his career. In 1885, court reporters referenced that Bethune had drawn up a will for $220,000—a sum that did not include his wealth in property purchased with profits from Wiggins. Court records reported that Wiggins's longtime manager, W. P. Howard, earned $50,000 just for his share in Wiggins's profits prior to 1865. Across various periods, Wiggins's managers were earning $3,000 per month from concert proceeds, according to the 1885 case for Wiggins's custody. Given this information, it seems that the common estimate of $500,000 in earnings across his career is a low one. Some estimate that Wiggins earned far more—up to $100,000 a year (what would be close to a million dollars annually today). See Tommasini, "He Was Born into Slavery"; Southall, *Blind Tom*, 168; Riis, "Blind Tom"; "Poor Blind Tom: The Colored Prodigy Sinking Fast," *Daily American*, January 12, 1891; "Blind Tom's Return," *New York Times*, August 18, 1887; "Blind Tom Is Free," *New York Times*, July 31, 1887; "Blind Tom Insane," *Cincinnati Enquirer*, November 29, 1886; "For the Possession of Blind Tom," *Cincinnati Enquirer*, July 1, 1885; and "Law Report: Probate Court," *Cincinnati Enquirer*, July 20, 1865.
6 "The Case of Blind Tom: The Opinion of Judge Woodruff," *Cincinnati Enquirer*, July 25, 1865.
7 "Law Report: Probate Court," *Cincinnati Enquirer*, July 20, 1865; "The Blind Tom Case," *Alexandria Gazette*, July 10, 1885.
8 Though he is now referred to by the surname Wiggins (which he shared with his mother), Tom was known to the press and in court documents at different times as Thomas Greene Bethune and as Thomas Wiggins. See "Blind Tom's Legal Cognomen Is Thomas Greene Bethune," *Daily Inter-ocean*, May 5, 1869; and also "In the Matter of Thomas Wiggins, Commonly Called Blind Tom, an Idiot," New York Supreme Court, November 20, 1888, Geneva Southall Papers, series 2, box 12, Stuart A. Rose Manuscript, Archives, and Rare Book Library, Emory University.
9 Bernstein, *Racial Innocence*, 39; Calvert, *Children in the House*, 140–42.
10 Scholars including Robin Bernstein and Karen Sánchez-Eppler have demonstrated the major cultural force of innocent white girlhood in nineteenth-century culture. These representations (and analyses of them) are inextricable from a sentimental cultural emphasis on the feminized domestic sphere and the purity (and purification) of white womanhood. See Welter, "Cult of True Womanhood," 151–74; Cott, "Passionlessness," 220; Sánchez-Eppler, *Dependent States*; and Bernstein, *Racial Innocence*, 39.
11 Bernstein, *Racial Innocence*, 10–11, 113–21.
12 W. Harper, "Harper's Memoir," 55; Stowe, *Uncle Tom's Cabin*, 159–60, 263.
13 *Songs, Sketch of the Life of Blind Tom*, 5–6.
14 *Songs, Sketch of the Life of Blind Tom*, 5, 6, 8.
15 [Excerpt from] *Philadelphia Inquirer* (December 27, 1865) and *Albany Argus* (January 1866) in *Songs, Sketch of the Life of Blind Tom*, 21–22, 23; "Article 2 [Blind Tom]," *Republican Banner*, March 14, 1861.

16 See "Blind Tom in Court," *Cincinnati Enquirer*, July 21, 1865.
17 Indenture of formerly enslaved children was an arrangement quickly undertaken by enslavers and endorsed under the state "Black Codes" of 1866, which "instructed courts not only to apprentice former slave children, but also to give priority to their former masters in contracting the apprenticeship." See Zipf, "Reconstructing 'Free Woman,'" 9. As Crystal Lynn Webster details, black children in the antebellum North were also subject to indenture due to gradual emancipation and the hiring out of children by institutions. The hired indenture of black children in the North continued in the postbellum period as well. See Webster, *Beyond the Boundaries*, 65–89.
18 "Blind Tom, Pianist, Dies of a Stroke," *New York Times*, June 15, 1908. As Daphne Brooks writes, we might nevertheless consider Wiggins's music an alternative—and a challenge—to the "bondsman turned author" form of the black autobiography. I follow this consideration in my readings of Wiggins's music later in this chapter. See D. Brooks, "Puzzling the Intervals," 394.
19 Ex Parte Charity Wiggins, Chambers at Baltimore this 20th Day of August A.D. 1885. Hugh L. Bond, Cir. Judge. Geneva Southall Papers, series 2, box 3, Stuart A. Rose Manuscript, Archives, and Rare Book Library, Emory University.
20 Wiggins, *Vocal Compositions*; Wiggins, *Specimens*, 1.
21 "Blind Tom's Concert," *Augusta Register*, November 16, 1861; "Blind Tom," *Mobile Register*, March 2, 1860.
22 On Wiggins's performance for James Buchanan, see "Blind Piano Prodigy, Thomas Greene Bethune," White House History, whitehousehistory.org.
23 O'Connell, *Ballad of Blind Tom*; Twain, "Letters from Mark Twain"; Cather, *My Antonia*.
24 [Broadside] "Tom! The Blind Negro Boy—of Musical Inspiration!" [Philadelphia]: Ledger Job Printing Establishment, 1865, Library Company of Philadelphia, Digital Collections. On the modern, sonic innovations of these pieces, see D. Brooks, "Puzzling the Intervals."
25 "Blind Tom's Concert," *Augusta Register*, November 16, 1861; "Blind Tom," *Mobile Register*, March 2, 1860.
26 *Songs, Sketch of the Life of Blind Tom*.
27 [Sheet music for] "Oliver Gallop," and "Virginia Polka," circa. 1860, National Museum of African American History and Culture, Digital Collections; "Blind Tom, Pianist, Dies of a Stroke," *New York Times*, June 15, 1908.
28 Wiggins was made to perform across the South, often raising funds for the Confederacy, throughout the war. For much of this period, he was managed by Perry Oliver. See "The Sick Soldier—a Benefit," *Republican Banner*, July 24, 1861; "By Bequest," *Republican Banner*, October 10, 1861; "Blind Tom's Concert," *Augusta Register*, November 16, 1861; "Blind Tom," *Daily Dispatch*, March 4, 1862; "Musical Prodigy," *Charleston Mercury*, May 30, 1863.
29 "Law Report: Probate Court," *Cincinnati Enquirer*, July 20, 1865.
30 Prior to 1865, Gross had sought a contract with Bethune. Bethune sought a $20,000 investment from Gross to establish a contract whereby Gross would

receive half of Wiggins's profits for five years. At the war's end, the $20,000 was reduced to $10,000. After Gross paid $1,000, however, Bethune cancelled the contract, inciting Gross's legal action. See "Law Report: Probate Court," *Cincinnati Enquirer*, July 20, 1865.

31 Bardaglio, *Reconstructing the Household*, 80.
32 Grossberg, "Who Gets the Child?," 235–60 (see 242). See also Bardaglio, *Reconstructing the Household*, 79–85; and M. Mason, *From Father's Property*.
33 Between the 1830s and 1860s (North and South), jurists drew on "tender years" to justify the placement of white children, up to roughly ten years of age, with mothers. See Bardaglio, *Reconstructing the Household*, 101.
34 Grossberg, "Children's Legal Rights?," 117. Quoting Pennsylvania Supreme Court decision, Ex parte Crouse, 1838.
35 Brewer, "Transformation of Domestic Law," 310.
36 Brewer, 307.
37 Grossberg, *Governing the Hearth*, 7.
38 Recently recovered documents from the New York State archives detail Truth's successful efforts to regain custody of her son after he was sold into slavery in Alabama. The judgment in Truth's favor demanded that the "boy be delivered into the hands of his mother—having no other master, no other controller, no other conductor, but his mother." On the 1828 case, see People v. Solomon Gedney (1828), New York State Archives. New York (State). Supreme Court of Judicature (Utica). Writs of Habeas Corpus, 1807–32, J0029-82, box 3. See also Herndon, "Court Records."
39 Kabria Baumgartner discusses the activism of African American parents to gain access to schooling for their children, including a landmark discrimination case on behalf of a five-year-old black girl, Sarah Roberts, in 1840s Boston. As Webster details, black parents and adults in Philadelphia and New York were also fighting to protect, educate, and keep custody of their children and to protect them from institutional harms. See Webster, *Beyond the Boundaries*, 114–41; Baumgartner, "Black Girlhood"; and Baumgartner, "Searching for Sarah," 73–85. See also Moss, *Schooling Citizens*.
40 "Article 1: Privileges and Disabilities of Slaves," *A Codification of the Statute Law of Georgia . . . Compiled, Digested, and Arranged by William A. Hotchkiss* (1848), 802, University of Georgia Law School Digital Commons.
41 See "Local News: The Habeas Corpus Case of Blind Tom," *Cincinnati Enquirer*, July 22, 1865.
42 James Bethune filed two documents to sustain his claim. He published a belated "deed of manumission" for Tom, Charity, and Mingo, and he filed a contract with the general superintendent of the Freedmen's Bureau of Georgia. It remains unclear if Charity and Mingo were involved in the making or signing of that contract. Bethune published it in "Law Report: Probate Court," *Cincinnati Enquirer*, July 20, 1865; his letter of "Manumission" was published *after* the case's conclusion. See "Law Report: Probate Court," *Cincinnati Enquirer*, July 26, 1865.

By Georgia's preceding 1860 code, enslaved persons were forbidden to enter contracts. See "Of Slaves and Free Persons of Color," article 3 in *Code of the State of Georgia*.

43 "The Case of Blind Tom: The Opinion of Judge Woodruff," *Cincinnati Enquirer*, July 25, 1865.

44 Newspapers that refer to the "Blind Tom Company" and "Blind Tom Combination" do not specify all the men involved in this corporate entity or its exact status. Yet it seems clear that at least James Bethune, John Bethune, Joseph Eubanks (referred to as "agent" and "treasurer"), and possibly Joseph Poznanski (referred to as piano teacher and transcriber of some of Wiggins's music) were part of this entity. See "Blind Tom's Mind Unsound," *New York Tribune*, November 27, 1886. See also "His Mother Trying to Get Him Adjudged Insane," *Atlanta Constitution*, November 27, 1886.

45 "The Case of Blind Tom: The Opinion of Judge Woodruff," *Cincinnati Enquirer*, July 25, 1865.

46 "Mother Dear Mother, I Still Think of Thee," ca. 1866-67, written by W. P. Howard and Captain Burgess, in *Songs, Sketch of the Life of Blind Tom*, 14.

47 The label "Kirkman" on the piano displayed on the cover of "Mother Dear Mother" specifies this image's creation during (or in reference to) Wiggins's tour in London. The Kirkman firm was renowned for building harpsichords and fortepianos during the nineteenth century and earlier—the choice to illustrate the label underscores the luxury of the scene. See Kottick, "Jacob Kirkman," 178-82.

48 Excerpt from the *Dundee Advertiser* [Scotland], circa 1866, *Songs, Sketch of the Life of Blind Tom*, 14.

49 *Songs, Sketch of the Life of Blind Tom*, 4-6.

50 *Songs, Sketch of the Life of Blind Tom*, 4-6.

51 *Songs, Sketch of the Life of Blind Tom*, 32.

52 Perry, *Young America*, 110-37; Stowe, *Uncle Tom's Cabin*, 480.

53 Duane, *Suffering Childhood*, 3.

54 Douglass narrates his childhood with different points of emphasis across his autobiographical works, yet in each, he gives a poignant description of his mother, of separation from his mother, and of his childhood acquisition of literacy. See Douglass, *Narrative*; Douglass, *My Bondage*; and Douglass, *Life and Times*.

55 On black authors writing for black children in the antebellum US, see Weikle-Mills, "Free the Children"; Wright, "Our Hope," 22-40, 147-63; and Haywood, "Constructing Childhood," 417-28. Lydia Maria Child's antislavery works for or about children appeared in *Juvenile Miscellany*, a periodical for children that she edited, and in *An Appeal in Favor of That Class of Americans Called Africans*.

56 Whipple, *Family Relation*, 8.

57 There are no recorded instances of petitions for Wiggins's freedom or press attention to his enslavement after Gross's habeas suit and before the 1885 suit by Charity Wiggins and Eliza Bethune. However, as I discuss later in this chapter, this does not preclude the possibility of unrecorded attempts.

58 J. Morgan, "*Partus sequitur ventrem*," 5.
59 Amy Lippert writes that the white slave—both a "visual spectacle and a political weapon"—originated in the 1830s "as a call to arms for labor organizers on both sides of the Atlantic." See Lippert, "Visual Pedagogy," 7.
60 American authors often depicted English factory work as wage labor's most frightful example, republishing accounts of white slavery from England. See, for instance, Cobden, *White Slaves*.
61 W. Harper, "Harper's Memoir," 55.
62 Francis Blake, "The Factory Girl," in Cobden, *White Slaves*, 167.
63 During the late nineteenth century, "white slavery" became synonymous with sex work. See Lippert, "Visual Pedagogy," 7.
64 S. Roberts, *Tales of the Poor*, 17.
65 M. N. Mitchell, "Reading Race."
66 In one of Child's stories, a white child is forcibly blackened with ash to be sold as a slave. See Child, "Mary French and Susan Easton."
67 W. Harper, "Harper's Memoir," 55.
68 Krentz, "'Vacant Receptacle'?," 552–57.
69 In 1866 and 1867, Freedmen's Aid groups in Northern cities began recruiting "orphan" and refugee black children, some as young as eight and twelve, to work for white households in the north in formal and informal indentures. See C. Jones, *Intimate Reconstructions*, 116–17. The American Anti-slavery Society formally disbanded in 1870 after the passage of the Fifteenth Amendment; William Lloyd Garrison originally sought to disband it in 1865. See Sinha, epilogue to *Slave's Cause*, 586.
70 J. Sanders, "Spinning Sympathy," 41–61; Lindey, "Sentimental and Redemptive Girlhood," 4–27.
71 Schenk, *Rescued Child*, 18, 16. The plot of *The Rescued Child* proceeds roughly as follows: A policeman hears Pearl's cry from the street and learns that she is Molly's captive. He rescues Pearl, delivering her to a wealthy white woman who becomes her benefactor. It is revealed that Molly was the pawn of a vindictive white man who stole Pearl and placed her with Molly out of jealousy. Pearl grows up and becomes a missionary in India, returning to marry the son of her benefactor. By the story's end, she has learned of her original pedigree.
72 Schenk, 8.
73 Schenk, 8, 14.
74 Schenk, 12, 8.
75 As Crystal Feimster details, stories of "the 'Mammy' who murdered white children in her care" became the justification for black women's and girls' murder or imprisonment. Black girls as young as thirteen-year-old Mildrey Brown became victims of lynching (in South Carolina in 1892) based on such accusations. See Feimster, *Southern Horrors*, 165–66.
76 Molly—and Bethune's caricature of Charity—both belonged to what Feimster calls "the defeminizing mythology of monstrous black womanhood" that discredited black women's care for white children *and* for their own. As Sarah Haley

and Feimster detail, black women were disproportionally charged with crimes of infanticide after Emancipation, accused of committing what whites saw as the "gravest rejection of one's status as a woman." See Feimster, *Southern Horrors*, 164–65; and Haley, *No Mercy Here*, 46.

77 *Songs, Sketch of the Life of Blind Tom*, 4, 5. See also "Blind Tom," *Morning Post* (London), August 13, 1866; and N. Robinson, "Blind Tom," 336–58.

78 "Blind Tom," *Morning Post* (London), August 13, 1866; *Songs, Sketch of the Life of Blind Tom*, 4–5; N. Robinson, "Blind Tom," 352–53; "Wonderful Blind Tom: His Mother Tells What a Queer Child He Was—His Musical Abilities," *Washington Post*, November 28, 1886.

79 D. Brooks, "Puzzling the Intervals," 412. Children's pain, suffering, and vulnerability were sites not only of generalized enjoyment but also of patterned eroticism in American and English literature and culture, as James Kincaid discusses in *Child Loving*. On the masochism and sadomasochism of sentimental culture more broadly, see Noble, *Masochistic Pleasures*.

80 Though child labor was a major concern of labor activists across the nineteenth century, neither states nor the federal government implemented significant work protections for children until the early twentieth century, as can be tracked in the formation of the National Child Labor Committee in 1904, to the Children's Bureau in 1912, to the (overturned) Keating-Owen Act in 1916, and eventually to New Deal reforms. See Fliter, *Child Labor in America*; and Hindman, *Child Labor*.

81 Painter, "Soul Murder and Slavery"; McCurry, *Masters of Small Worlds*; Fox-Genovese, *Within the Plantation Household*.

82 Brewer, "Transformation of Domestic Law," 307.

83 Whipple, *Family Relation*, 12.

84 Painter, "Soul Murder and Slavery," 142.

85 On abuse within white families and the legal reforms crafted to intervene in it, see Pleck, *Domestic Tyranny*; Gordon, *Heroes*; Daniels and Kennedy, *Over the Threshold*; and Pearson, *Rights of the Defenseless*.

86 "Jas. N. Bethune," Records of Deeds, Fauquier County, Virginia, May 31, 1869, Geneva Southall Papers, series 2, box 12, Stuart A. Rose Manuscript, Archives, and Rare Book Library, Emory University; "The Story of Blind Tom: Why the Musical Prodigy Must Leave His Old Friends," *Washington Post*, August 14, 1887.

87 "Bethune, James N.," Schedule 2, Productions of Agriculture, in Center District, Fauquier County, Virginia, US Federal Census, enumerated June 12, 1880, http://ancestry.com.

88 "The Blind Tom Case," *Alexandria Gazette*, July 10, 1885.

89 Virginia—the site where the first segregated asylum for black people was established in 1869 (the Central Lunatic Asylum for the Colored Insane of Richmond)—was at the vanguard of commitment law's use in confining black people deemed troublesome. On Virginia's commitment statutes and on the broader history of commitment, see Munford, "Title 24: Insane Persons," in *Code of Virginia*, 434–44; and Appelbaum, "Evolution of Commitment Law," 343–56.

90 Nielsen, "Incompetent and Insane," 175.
91 N. Robinson, "Blind Tom," 348.
92 Robinson, 353, 350.
93 Robinson, 340.
94 Robinson, 340–41.
95 Robinson, 344.
96 Robinson, 352–53.
97 "John G. Bethune," Delaware Vital Records, 1800–1933; series number: Death Records, 13, Delaware Public Archives; Dover, Delaware, Ancestry Library Edition.
98 Before his death, John Bethune wrote Eliza out of his will based on his belief that when they married, she was still married to someone else. See "Mr. Bethune Must Pay Alimony," *Alexandria Gazette*, November 26, 1883; see also "Blind Tom's Manager's Will," *Atlanta Constitution*, June 10, 1886.
99 "Ex parte Charity Wiggins, Done at Chambers at Baltimore this 20th Day of August A.D. 1885. Hugh L. Bond, Cir. Judge," Geneva Southall Papers, series 2, box 12; "The Story of Blind Tom: Why the Musical Prodigy Must Leave His Old Friends," *Washington Post*, August 14, 1887.
100 "The Blind Tom Case," *Alexandria Gazette*, July 10, 1885; "Blind Tom's Transfer," *New York Times*, August 20, 1887; "Blind Tom: How the Wonderful Negro Idiot Conducted Himself," *Atlanta Constitution*, September 1, 1887.
101 "Blind Tom Surrendered," *Washington Post*, August 17, 1887. It seems that Charity resided with Tom and Eliza until 1888, though the cause of her departure is unclear. See "Supreme Court of New York County in the Matter of Thomas Wiggins [May 29, 1888]," Geneva Southall Papers, series 2, box 12.
102 *American Law Reports Annotated* (Rochester: Lawyer's Cooperative Publishing Company, 1927), Geneva Southall Papers, series 2, folder 12, p. 322.
103 "Blind Tom and His Mother," *New York Times*, October 12, 1886; "Blind Tom's Return," *New York Times*, August 18, 1887.
104 "Blind Tom and His Mother"; "Blind Tom Insane," *Cincinnati Enquirer*, November 29, 1886; "Blind Tom's Return," *New York Times*, August 18, 1887.
105 Quote from "The Story of Blind Tom: Why the Musical Prodigy Must Leave His Old Friends," *Washington Post*, August 14, 1887; see also "Wants to Care for 'Blind Tom,'" *New York Times*, August 12, 1887.
106 "The Blind Tom Case," *Alexandria Gazette*, July 10, 1885; "Wants to Care for 'Blind Tom,'" *New York Times*, August 12, 1887.
107 Wiggins, *Specimens*.
108 D. Brooks, "Puzzling the Intervals," 400–402.
109 Wiggins, *Specimens*.
110 Wiggins, *Vocal Compositions*.
111 One possibility for Jodie's identity is Joseph Eubanks, a long-term agent in Wiggins's performance career, and another, Joseph Poznanski, his piano instructor. Without a full, robust record of Wiggins's social and kinship networks, these

remain very thin and even unlikely speculations, however. I raise them primarily to hold open the relational complexity that Wiggins's music itself opens.
112 Wiggins, "Wilt Thou Bring My Baby Home?," in *Vocal Compositions*.
113 Wiggins.
114 Jensen-Moulton, "'Specimens' and 'Peculiar Idiosyncrasies,'" 3. Jensen-Moulton reads this piece, among others, primarily as "diagnostic indicators" (2) of Wiggins's "autism spectrum behavior" (3). While I disagree with the diagnostic emphasis of this reading, many scholars have worked to situate Wiggins in relation to autism as a way to redress violent, ableist, and sensationalist readings of him past and present. See Jensen-Moulton, "Finding Autism"; Sacks, *Anthropologist on Mars*, 188–90; and Tommasini, "He Was Born into Slavery."
115 V. Smith, *Self-Discovery and Authority*, 2.
116 Brewer, "Transformation of Domestic Law," 307.

3. THE ANATOMY OF SAMMY TUBBS
1 Foote Sr., *Science in Story*, 3:186.
2 Foote Sr., vol. 3 front matter.
3 Foote Sr., 3:1, 1:15.
4 A revised edition of *Medical Common Sense*, entitled *Plain Home Talk, Embracing Medical Common Sense*, was printed in 1867 and a third in 1896. Foote Sr., *Plain Home Talk*.
5 Foote Sr., *Science in Story*, 1:ii.
6 Before his medical training, Foote worked for antislavery-leaning publications in Ohio, Connecticut, and New York, including the *Cleveland Leader* and *Cleveland Herald*, *New Haven Journal*, *New Britain Journal*, and *Brooklyn Morning Journal*. Foote's family claimed relation to the abolitionist Beecher family. See A. Foote, *Foote Family*, 94. See also Putnam, *400 Years*, 794; and Sappol, *Traffic in Dead Bodies*, 243.
7 Foote Sr., *Science in Story*, 1:22.
8 Morrison, *Playing in the Dark*, 6, 13.
9 Spillers, "Mama's Baby, Papa's Maybe," 64–81, 65.
10 Narrating this epistemic shift, Foucault writes, "When natural history becomes biology, when the analysis of wealth becomes economics, [. . .] then, in the profound upheaval of such an archaeological mutation, man appears in his ambiguous position as an object of knowledge and as the subject that knows." See Foucault, *Order of Things*, 312.
11 Wynter, "Unsettling the Coloniality," 318.
12 Wynter, 314, 310.
13 Foote Sr., *Science in Story*, 5:236.
14 Wynter deems the transition between Man_1 and Man_2 "both discontinuous and continuous." See Wynter, "Unsettling the Coloniality," 318.
15 Revelations in 2021 about the ongoing possession and use of enslaved black and Indigenous people's bodies by institutions such as Penn, Princeton, and Harvard

reiterate this history. Moreover, the discovery that bones of Tree Africa, a black girl killed in 1985 by the police bombing of Move, a black liberation community in Philadelphia, have also been in use confirms this abuse's continuity into the present. See Schuessler, "What Should Museums Do?"; and Pilkington, "Bones of Black Children." See also Humphrey, "Dissection and Discrimination," 819–27; Savitt, *Medicine and Slavery*; Savitt, *Race and Medicine*; Sappol, *Traffic in Dead Bodies*; Washington, *Medical Apartheid*; Halperin, "Poor, the Black, and the Marginalized," 489–95; Fett, *Working Cures*; Nystrom, "Bioarchaeology of Structural Violence," 765–79; D. Owens, *Medical Bondage*; and Willoughby, *Masters of Health*.

16 Cirillo, "Edward Bliss Foote," 471–79; Sears, *Sex Radicals*; Wood, *Struggle for Free Speech*; Dennis, *Licentious Gotham*.
17 Wood, *Struggle for Free Speech*, 22. See Gerhard, *Desiring Revolution*; Rosen, *World Split Open*; and Gordon, *Moral Property*.
18 Foote inserts a racist foil to Dr. Hubbs in Sammy's prejudiced detractor, Dr. Winkles. Foote Sr., *Science in Story*, 1:133–35.
19 Like Odell's dedication to "the friends of the Africans," "friends of the Negro" was a self-designation of white abolitionists and missionaries in the US and England. See, for instance, Armistead, *Five Hundred Thousand Strokes*; and *American Freedman* 1, no. 8 (November 1866).
20 Foote Sr., *Science in Story*, 3:14–15.
21 *The Freedman's Spelling Book* and *The Freedman's Third Reader*, in *The Freedman's Spelling Book*; *The Freedman's Second Reader*; *The Freedman's Third Reader*.
22 Foote Sr., *Science in Story*, 4:15. Taking after Dr. Hubbs, Sammy becomes honorable, "high-minded," and self-restrained—traits of manliness deconstructed by Bederman in *Manliness and Civilization*.
23 Foote Sr., *Science in Story*, 4:225–26.
24 Foote Sr., 3:37, 1:113, 211.
25 Sammy is subjected to a more interrogative testing earlier by Dr. Winkles. See Foote Sr., 1:125–30, 4:21–22.
26 Foote Sr., 4:228–30.
27 Foote Sr., 4:225–26.
28 Foote Sr., 3:14–15.
29 Foote Sr., 3:14–15.
30 Foote Sr., 1:211.
31 Foote Sr., 3:22–23, 1:8, 3:14–15.
32 Foote Sr., 6–8.
33 Foote Sr., 6–8.
34 Foote Sr., 8.
35 Hartman, *Scenes of Subjection*, 125.
36 On the shifting political situation, violence, and debt-labor conditions freedpeople navigated after Emancipation, see chapters 4 and 5 in Hahn, *Nation under Our Feet*; chapters 3 and 4 in Foner, *Reconstruction*; and Saville, *Work of Reconstruction*.

37 *Freedman's Spelling Book*, 78, 85. See also Brinckerhoff's *Advice to Freedmen*; and Fisk's *Plain Counsels for Freedmen*.
38 "Phillis Wheatley," in *Freedman's Third Reader*, 75–77.
39 Foote Sr., *Science in Story*, 5:46.
40 Foote Sr., 1:23.
41 Foote Sr., 1:48.
42 Foote Sr., vol. 1 front matter.
43 Foote Sr., 1:23, 3:76–82, 3:86–93.
44 Foote Sr., 4:213.
45 "Intelligent Contraband" photograph, ca. 1863, Library Company of Philadelphia; and "Raising Colored Infantry" hand-colored cartoon, also ca. 1863, Library Company of Philadelphia. On the life of antiblack Civil War cartoons, see Burns, "Cartoons in Color."
46 Foote Sr., *Science in Story*, 4:213, 4:221–23.
47 Foote Sr., 3:54.
48 Foote Sr., 1:6.
49 Foote Sr., 1:101.
50 Foote Sr., 1:101.
51 Foote established Murray Hill Publishing Company in 1872 and would publish roughly sixty works on health from this outlet. Prior to founding his company, Foote issued the first editions of his *Medical Common Sense* (1858), *Plain Home Talk* (1870), and *Health Monthly Newsletter*. Though exact figures on his book sales are unclear, Foote—and his biographers—have estimated hundreds of thousands of sales (up to 750,000) for these works (and around 5,000 subscribers for his newsletter as of the 1880s). See Wood, *Struggle for Free Speech*, 35; and Sappol, *Traffic in Dead Bodies*, 242.
52 In the third edition of *Plain Home Talk*, Foote describes his "large correspondence with young people." See Foote Sr., *Plain Home Talk*, v. Foote's wife, Catherine Goodenough Bond, was a schoolteacher from Massachusetts. See A. Foote, *Foote Family*.
53 Dr. Foote's father, Herschel Foote, was an early white settler in Cleveland—a merchant, a justice of the peace, and the city's postmaster. See A. Foote, *Foote Family*, 257. See also Wood, *Struggle for Free Speech*, 36. In suggesting his childhood knowledge of popular stories, I reject Foote's claim (in the preface of vol. 1 of *Science in Story*) that he "had never read but one work of fiction in his life, and that one in childhood." (1:iii).
54 Newbery, *History of Little-Goody Two Shoes*; Edgeworth, *Idleness and Industry*; *Virtue in a Cottage*; and *Juvenile Story-Teller*.
55 As Barbara Hochman writes, across the second half of the nineteenth century, adaptations of *Uncle Tom's Cabin* increasingly reinforced "sharp differences between the moral and intellectual capacities" of black and white children and other characters, exemplified especially in *Young Folks Uncle Tom's Cabin* from 1901. See Hochman, *Uncle Tom's Cabin and the Reading Revolution*, 205–10.

56 Hoffmann, *Laughter Book for Very Little People*; Hoffmann, *Slovenly Peter*; Hoffmann, *Laughter Book for Little Folks: With a Profusion of Humorous Engravings*; Hoffmann, *Laughter Book for Little Folks*.
57 See Nash, "The Feral Child," in *Wild Enlightenment*, chap. 2.
58 There is at least one American adaptation in which Peter *does* redeem himself: *Slovenly Peter Reformed*. See also *Slovenly Kate*.
59 *Young Ragamuffins*.
60 Hoffmann, *Laughter Book for Little Folks: With a Profusion of Humorous Engravings*.
61 L. Harris, *In the Shadow of Slavery*, 280–92.
62 Hoffmann's *The Inky Boys* and *Slovenly Peter* reappeared in the McLoughlin Brothers catalog in 1898 and from George Routledge & Sons in 1909, Houghton Mifflin in 1919, Harper and Brothers Company in 1935, Marchbanks Press in 1935, John Winston Company in 1943, and other presses across the twentieth century.
63 See "Miss Mopsa" in *Little Miss Consequence*; and Bernstein, *Racial Innocence*, 224–25.
64 Weinstein, *Once upon a Time*, vii–ix.
65 The ink-bled copy of *Ten Little Niggers* is held at the American Antiquarian Society, where curator Laura Wasowicz showed it to me.
66 See Berquin, *Looking-Glass for the Mind*, 49.
67 McKittrick, *Dear Science*, 157–58.
68 Fanon, *Black Skin, White Masks*, 89.
69 Foote Sr., *Science in Story*, 3:14–15.
70 Foote Sr., 1:211.
71 Brody, *Impossible Purities*, 11–12.
72 "Eclecticism" gradually fell out of favor and was then gutted entirely by the influential 1910 Flexner Report, which concluded that medicine should be limited to the allopathic training of a limited number of white male practitioners. This report's influence led to many closures—which disproportionately affected black medical colleges, medical colleges that trained women, and naturopathic or homeopathic medical training. See Bailey, "Flexner Report," 209–23.
73 Facing the exclusion and antagonism of white medical institutions, African Americans opened their own medical schools across the latter nineteenth century, including Howard, Meharry, and Leonard. See Long, *Doctoring Freedom*.
74 Philadelphia and New York City were the foremost sites for American medical knowledge during the eighteenth and nineteenth centuries. See Rothstein, *American Medical Schools*.
75 Longshore, *Announcement and Catalogue*, 6, 9–12, 30–31, 7.
76 Longshore, 7.
77 Longshore, 9–10.
78 There are some "Cadaver Receiving Books" that chronicle cadaver provenance in Philadelphia after 1901 but no comprehensive records for earlier periods. Pennsylvania enacted its 1883 Anatomy Act after its 1867 act failed to intervene in the

cadaver trade. See Guerrasio, "Dissecting." See also Willoughby, *Masters of Health*; Nystrom, "Postmortem Examinations," 164–72; and Marshall, "Race, Death, and Public Health," 364–89.

79 On the "abundant" use of cadavers at Penn and other schools, see Abrahams, *Extinct Medical Schools*, 52.
80 Berry, *Price for Their Pound*, 152.
81 Kenneth Nystrom's work confirms the Newburgh Colored Burial Ground in New York; Albany (NY) Almshouse Cemetery; Charity Hospital of New Orleans; Medical College of Georgia; Eighth Street First African Baptist Church Cemetery, Philadelphia; Freedmen's Cemetery, Dallas Texas; and the Spring Street Church Presbyterian Church burial vaults in New York City as buried archaeological sites of anatomically dissected black cadavers. Archaeologists who have studied at the Medical College of Georgia found that 79 percent of the nine thousand bones found had likely belonged to black people. See Nystrom, "Postmortem Examinations," 164–72; Halperin, "Poor, the Black, and the Marginalized," 489–95; Blakely and Harrington, *Bones in the Basement*; Berry, *Price for Their Pound*; Washington, *Medical Apartheid*; Savitt, *Race and Medicine*; and Sappol, *Traffic in Dead Bodies*.
82 This overrepresentation reveals another inverted extraction beneath Man's overrepresentation of the Human described by Wynter in "Unsettling the Coloniality," 257–337.
83 D. Owens, *Medical Bondage*; Ivy, "Bodies of Work," 11–31; Snorton, *Black on Both Sides*.
84 Sims lamented that "[his] thunder had been stolen" when his procedure and technique drew attention but did not immediately lead to his fame. See Sims, *Story of My Life*, 269.
85 Sims, "On the Treatment."
86 Sims, *Story of My Life*. Cooper Owens instead names the site of Sims's experiments as the "first" women's hospital, recasting the meaning of that accolade. See D. Owens, *Medical Bondage*, 1–2.
87 Agassiz, "Diversity of Origin."
88 Europeans of the early modern period speculated in biblical terms that black people had descended from the line and curse of Ham, in distinction to whites, who descended from Japheth. This theory flowed into natural historians' taxonomies of race, which nineteenth-century ethnologists and anthropologists attempted to supply a biological basis for. See Jacobson, *Whiteness of a Different Color*, 31–34.
89 Jackson, *Becoming Human*, 12.
90 See Agassiz, "Diversity of Origin," 49, 111–13.
91 S. Gould, *Ontogeny and Phylogeny*, 33–49.
92 Ernst Haeckel, a contemporary of Darwin, popularized recapitulation as a compatible theory to evolution. His work had influence far beyond biological sciences—including modern American child psychology, discussed in the next chapter. See C. Green, "Hall's Developmental Theory," 656–65.
93 S. Gould, *Ontogeny and Phylogeny*, 63–68.

94 Of African-descended peoples, Agassiz wrote that they could "be compared to children, grown into the stature of adults, while retaining a childlike mind." Louis Agassiz to S. G. Howe, August 10, 1863, Louis Agassiz Correspondence, Houghton Library, Harvard University.
95 S. Gould, *Ontogeny and Phylogeny*, 77–78.
96 Galton, *Hereditary Genius*; Spencer, *Principles of Biology*.
97 Foote Sr., *Plain Home Talk*, v.
98 "Obituary: Dr. Edward Bliss Foote," *New York Tribune*, October 6, 1906.
99 Foote Jr., *Radical Remedy*, 35–36.
100 Foote Sr., *Science in Story*, 5:16.
101 Foote Sr., 5:16.
102 Foote Sr., 5:127, 131, 137, 141.
103 Foote Sr., 5:21–25, 29, 33, 87.
104 Foote Sr., 5:214.
105 Foote Sr., 5:203.
106 Foote Sr., 5:144.
107 Foote Sr., 5:54.
108 Foote Sr., 5:54.
109 Foote Sr., 5:235.
110 Foote Sr., 5:54–55.
111 Wynter, "Beyond Miranda's Meaning."
112 Foote Sr., *Science in Story*, 5:228, 212, 235, 232.
113 Foote Sr., 5:232, 229. When Foote referenced the Jukes in 1875, he cited the report of a physician, Elisha Harris. In 1877, a member of the Prison Association of New York, Richard Dugdale, published a larger study, leading to the Jukes's much wider notoriety in the press and in social scientific conversation. See Dugdale, *Jukes*.
114 Foote Jr., *Radical Remedy*, 35–36.
115 "[Advertisement] *Science in Story*," in Foote, backmatter.
116 Foote, 49–50.
117 All of the *Oxford English Dictionary* reference entries for "Topsy" use her name in this manner: from a Rudyard Kipling quote in 1885—"my novel *Mother Maturin* . . . Like Topsy 'it growed'"—to a 1982 *Oxford Times* quote: "The garden, like Topsy, just grow'd" (1982). See *Oxford English Dictionary*, s.v. "Topsy, n.," http://oed.com. Entering "like Topsy" into a library search engine, a newspaper database, or Google returns hundreds of results that apply this simile in *totally* different contexts. Things that can grow like Topsy, according to these results, include the State Department, a city, the home care industry, advertising sales, industry profits, a workers' strike, an orchestra, a television network, and more.
118 Fielder, *Relative Races*, 123–25.
119 After his father's death, Dr. Foote Jr. continued to direct funds through their Free Speech League to Margaret Sanger, among other birth control and feminist advocates. See Wood, *Struggle for Free Speech*, 22, 100.

120 Characterizations of black men as "incubus[es]" and "vampire[s]"—both references to the sexual threat they posed to white women—played a key role in white supremacist propaganda, especially during the 1898 elections in North Carolina. See G. Gilmore, *Gender and Jim Crow*, 85. I take "shaping the modern" from J. Brown's *Babylon Girls*.
121 Givens, *Fugitive Pedagogy*, 28–29; H. Williams, *Self-Taught*, 67–77.
122 Foote Sr., *Science in Story*, 5:190.
123 Foote Sr., 5:217.
124 Foote Sr., 5:236.
125 Foote Sr., 5:236.

4. "OSCAR MOORE CAN TELL YOU"

1 [Ticket 1], Central Music Hall Physicians' Exhibition, Chicago, Illinois, December 5, 1888. See also [Ticket 2], Central Music Hall Physicians' Exhibition, Chicago, Illinois, December 5, 1888; and [Ticket 3], Republican House Physicians' Exhibitions, Milwaukee, Wisconsin, December 7, 1888, Shobal Vail Clevenger Papers, 1864–1924, US National Library of Medicine.
2 "The Blind Child Prodigy," *Daily Inter-ocean* (Chicago, IL), December 6, 1888; "An Enigma to Doctors: The Wonderful Memory of a Three-Year-Old Blind Boy Put to the Test," *Courier Journal*, December 10, 1888; "Oscar Moore's Memory: Remarkable Mental Development of a Blind Mulatto Boy," *Washington Post*, December 23, 1888. See also [Ticket 1], Shobal Vail Clevenger Papers, 1864–1924, US National Library of Medicine; and Clevenger, "Infant Prodigy," 359–65.
3 Gammel, "Not Worth Quarreling," 37–41; Gammel's reference to the twenty-five cents for the photograph and *Hand-Book* is on p. 38.
4 Gammel, 41.
5 McGill, "Books on the Loose," 82.
6 Hartman, "Venus in Two Acts," 1–14. On opacity and its challenge to the "requirement for transparency" of post-Enlightenment epistemologies, see Glissant, *Poetics of Relation*, 190.
7 Swedish writer Ellen Key declared in 1900 that the twentieth century would be "The Century of the Child." Americans echoed and extended this call. See Key, *Century of the Child*; and Lovett, *Conceiving the Future*.
8 "Equal to Blind Tom," *Jackson City Patriot*, February 6, 1889.
9 See [Ticket 1], Shobal Vail Clevenger Papers, 1864–1924, US National Library of Medicine. Since the seventeenth century, the term *lusus naturae* has referred to "a supposed sportive action of Nature to which the origin of marked variations from the normal type (of an animal, plant, etc.) was formerly ascribed. Chiefly *concr.*, a natural production deviating markedly from the normal type, or having the appearance of being a result of sportive design; a 'freak of nature.'" See *Oxford English Dictionary*, s.v. "lusus naturae, *n*," http://oed.com.
10 Clevenger, "Infant Prodigy," 359.
11 Davidson and Benjamin, "History of the Child."

12 Hall modeled his survey (and many of his pedagogical theories) on previous studies undertaken in Germany. See G. Hall, *Contents of Children's Minds*, 3–12.
13 On the early development of Binet's IQ metric in France, see S. Gould, *Mismeasure of Man*, 176–81, 188–213.
14 See Gould, 191–92. Americans began to allocate resources to "gifted" education as early as the 1890s; however, the distinction of childhood giftedness accelerated after the development of IQ. See Jolly, *History of Gifted Education*.
15 William Thaison's surname appears elsewhere as "Thaisen" and "Thaysen."
16 The finding aid for the cabinet card begins with the following: "[Location]: Anderson, New York, circa 1875." My research has clarified that Anderson (printed on the lower left corner of the card) refers to photographer David H. Anderson, who also photographed white performers and likely photographed Moore sometime in January 1889 in New York City.
17 "A Blind Baby's Memory: Little Oscar Moore Is an Infant Encyclopedia," *Chicago Daily Tribune*, October 28, 1888.
18 "A Marvellous [sic] Child," *Daily Telegraph*, January 15, 1889.
19 "A Blind Baby's Memory: Little Oscar Moore Is an Infant Encyclopedia," *Chicago Daily Tribune*, October 28, 1888; "A Marvellous [sic] Child," *Daily Telegraph*, January 15, 1889; Gammel, "Not Worth Quarreling," 37.
20 "Waco," *Fort Worth Daily Gazette*, March 6, 1888. See also "Waco Wirelings," *Austin Daily Statesman*, March 6, 1888.
21 As an apprentice-master in Texas, Thaison was "entitled to [Moore's] services, and to all profits arising from any such services." As an apprentice, Moore was theoretically entitled to an education and to receiving a basic (and vague) standard of care, yet he was unlikely to receive either. As Karin Zipf's work on apprenticeship makes clear, it is possible that Moore was not afforded these nominal protections, especially if Moore's apprenticeship was one of the many "informal apprenticeships" that existed beyond the court's jurisdiction. See "An Act Establishing a General Apprentice Law," in Sayles and Sayles, *Revised Civil Statutes*. Also see Zipf, *Labor of Innocents*.
22 As Zipf's work shows, apprenticeship was not abolished in southern states until the passage of state-initiated child welfare acts in the 1910s. See Zipf, *Labor of Innocents*, 4.
23 The *Oxford English Dictionary* describes multiple nineteenth-century meanings for "bright" (but excludes its racial meaning), defining the word as a descriptor of shining, light-emitting, positive, hopeful, reflective, and keen things. See *Oxford English Dictionary*, s.v. "bright, adj. and n.," http://oed.com.
24 "Bright Eyes and Billiards," *Daily Inter-ocean*, December 5, 1888; "Harrison Goes Hunting: The President Elect," *Daily Inter-ocean*, December 6, 1888, ["the day was bright and cool"]; "Social Gatherings," *Daily Inter-ocean*, December 6, 1888, ["The church was bright with many lights"]. See also [Display Ad] *Pear's Soap*, September 29, 1888, *Los Angeles Times*, ["Fair White Hands. Bright Clear Complexion. Soft Healthful Skin. Pear's—The Greatest English Complexion Soap—Sold Everywhere"]. All these quotes are taken from the same issue of the *Daily Inter-ocean*

that featured Moore, with the exception of the Pear's Soap advertisement, which ran concurrently in US news syndicates.
25 McClintock, "Soft-Soaping Empire," in *Imperial Leather*, chap. 5.
26 W. Johnson, *Soul by Soul*, 139.
27 "[Classified Ad]," *Daily Picayune*, February 27, 1853; "200 Reward," *Louisville Daily Courier*, March 22, 1855; "Fourteen Hundred Dollars Reward," *Baltimore Sun*, August 19, 1852.
28 W. Johnson, *Soul by Soul*, 150.
29 Clevenger, "Infant Prodigy," 359.
30 Clevenger, 359.
31 See Stone, *Biography of Eminent American Physicians*, 90–91.
32 "An Enigma to Doctors: The Wonderful Memory of a Three-Year-Old Blind Boy Put to the Test," *Louisville Courier Journal*, December 10, 1888; "Feats of Memory by a Blind Child," *New York Tribune*, December 6, 1888.
33 Clevenger, "Infant Prodigy," 361–62.
34 Hoefnagel, "Toxic Effects," 168.
35 Clevenger, "Infant Prodigy," 359.
36 "An Enigma to Doctors: The Wonderful Memory of a Three-Year-Old Blind Boy Put to the Test," *Louisville Courier Journal*, December 10, 1888.
37 Clevenger, "Infant Prodigy," 364.
38 Clevenger, 365.
39 Clevenger, 365.
40 Clevenger, 365.
41 Clevenger studied, taught, and wrote about anatomy throughout his career. Moreover, as a biography of Clevenger from 1894 states, because he served as pathologist of the Cook County Insane Asylum (1883–85), he "enjoyed special advantages for studying insanity in the wards and its pathology in the dead house and laboratory." For context of the asylum's racial makeup, the census categorized its patients as belonging to three categories: "white," "foreign-born white," and "colored." See Stone, *Biography of Eminent American Physicians*, 90–91; and Department of the Interior, Census Office, *Report on the Defective*, 103.
42 "An Enigma to Doctors: The Wonderful Memory of a Three-Year-Old Blind Boy Put to the Test," *Louisville Courier Journal*, December 10, 1888.
43 "A Boy with a Memory: Performances of a Blind Colored Youth of about Three Years," *New York Times*, January 13, 1889; "Truly an Infant Prodigy," *Arkansas Gazette*, [from the *New York World*], May 26, 1889; "Little Oscar Moore: The Latest Addition to the Ranks of Infant Prodigies," *New York Times*, January 28, 1889.
44 Clevenger, "Infant Prodigy," 360.
45 G. Hall, "Moral Education," 87.
46 G. Hall, *Contents of Children's Minds*, 12, 18–19.
47 Hall founded the *American Journal of Psychology* in 1887, and he was the first president of the American Psychological Association, beginning in 1892. See Young, "G. Stanley Hall," 195–208.

48 Hall was "among the most prominent pedagogical experts in the nation" at the nineteenth century's end and is often credited as the founder of American psychology. See Brooks-Gunn and Johnson, "G. Stanley Hall's Contribution," 247–58.
49 G. Hall, in *The Contents of Children's Minds*, cites his belief in higher rates of color blindness among "colored and Jewish children" in his study but otherwise makes few distinctions in children's physiology or psychology based on race (33).
50 See G. Hall, "Corporal Punishments," 163–64; and Bederman, "Teaching Our Sons."
51 See G. Hall, "Corporal Punishments," 163–64.
52 Hall eventually turned his attention back to the axiomatic understanding of the "childlike" nature of the "savage." See G. Hall, *Adolescence*, 2:649.
53 "Editorial," *Pedagogical Seminary* 1, no. 1 (1891): iv.
54 "Editorial," 13–18, 139–73.
55 "Foreign Miscellanies," *Pedagogical Seminary* 1, no. 1 (1891): 300.
56 "Professor Oscar Moore," *Austin Daily Statesman*, August 16, 1888; "Vine Street Dime Museum," *Cincinnati Enquirer*, October 1, 1888.
57 "Blind Oscar the Infant Prodigy," [Handbill] Milwaukee, Wisconsin, December 7, 1888, Shobal Vail Clevenger Papers, US National Library of Medicine; "Whispers from the Wings," *New York Herald*, May 5, 1889; "A New Wonder," *New York Herald*, May 13, 1889.
58 The *New Haven Register* reported Moore's meeting with Yale Professors (unspecified) at the Tontine Hotel in New Haven. See "The Hman [sic] Phonograph," *New Haven Register*, February 19, 1892.
59 *Hand-Book*, 39.
60 The James Whitcomb Riley poem "The Elf-Child" (later known as "Little Orphan Annie") that Moore was made to recite was a commonplace feature in American classrooms. As Angela Sorby documents, reciting poems—in particular, those of popular "schoolroom poets" like Riley—was a major aspect of primary education across the late nineteenth century. Sorby, *Schoolroom Poets*, xii.
61 *Hand-Book*, 7–8.
62 *Hand-Book*, 7–8.
63 "Infant Prodigy: A Three-Year-Old Negro's Memory Sightless, but Wonderful Questions on Difficult Subjects Answered without Hesitation," *San Francisco Chronicle*, December 16, 1888.
64 "Breaking the Bonds: How the Blind Triumph," *Arizona Republican*, September 27, 1892; "Truly an Infant Prodigy," *Arkansas Gazette*, [from the *New York World*], May 26, 1889; "A Walking Encyclopedia," *Hall's Journal of Health* 36, no 2 (February 1889).
65 "A Blind Baby's Memory: Little Oscar Moore Is an Infant Encyclopedia," *Chicago Daily Tribune*, October 28, 1888.
66 "A Remarkable Boy," *Worcester Daily Spy*, January 16, 1888.
67 "The Hman [sic] Phonograph," *New Haven Register*, February 19, 1892; "A Boy Phonograph," *Charleston Courier*, February 4, 1891.

68 Crain, *Reading Children*, 2–3.
69 Crain, 5–6.
70 Sorby, *Schoolroom Poets*, xx–xxi.
71 Crain, *Reading Children*, 2.
72 Crain, 3.
73 "[Oscar Moore], 1900 U.S. Federal Census: Memphis Ward 5, Shelby, Tennessee," 1900, Ancestry Library Edition, http://ancestry.com.
74 Quote from Oliver Wendell Holmes in "[Ad] Austin and Stone's Museum," *Boston Sunday Herald*, July 21, 1892.
75 Bernstein, "Dances with Things," 69.
76 "An Infant Prodigy," *Wilson Advance*, January 31, 1889; "An Enigma to Doctors: The Wonderful Memory of a Three-Year-Old Blind Boy Put to the Test," *Louisville Courier Journal*, December 10, 1888; "The Hman [sic] Phonograph," *New Haven Register*, February 19, 1892.
77 "Oscar Moore's Memory: Remarkable Mental Development of a Blind Mulatto Boy," *Washington Post*, December 23, 1888.
78 "Oscar Moore's Memory."
79 "That Wonderful Colored Boy: Here Is a Frightful Infant Who Never Forgets What He Hears," [from the *New York Sun*], *Bismarck Daily Tribune*, March 6, 1889.
80 "That Wonderful Colored Boy"; "A Boy with a Memory: Performances of a Blind Colored Youth of about Three Years," *New York Times*, January 13, 1889.
81 [Advertisement, "Gammel's Bookstore," undated], in Bohlender and McCallum, *Texas Bookman*, 36.
82 Bohlender and McCallum, *Texas Bookman*.
83 [Gammel's Dairy Entry], 41.
84 See "A Child Wonder," *Velasco Times*, April 7, 1893; "Local News: Professor J. T. Harris," *Brenham Daily Banner*, June 22, 1894; "A Blind Prodigy," *Galveston Daily News*, April 10, 1895; "Events in Colored Circles," *Galveston Daily News*, February 23, 1896; and "Blind Oscar Moore," *Brenham Daily Banner*, September 5, 1901.
85 "Barnum Sees a Prodigy," *New York Times*, January 23, 1889; Reiss, *Showman and the Slave*.
86 "Barnum Sees a Prodigy," *New York Times*, January 23, 1889.
87 "Showman George A. Wells: Life of the Man Who Was at One Time Barnum's Partner," *New York Times*, October 9, 1892.
88 "Suit over Boy Prodigy," *New York Herald*, January 7, 1892; "It Is Claimed That He Has Not Been Properly Educated," *Heppner Weekly Gazette*, January 14, 1892; "General" [Notice of Lawsuit], *National Tribune*, January 14, 1892; "Showman George A. Wells: Life of the Man Who Was at One Time Barnum's Partner," *New York Times*, October 9, 1892.
89 "Suit over Boy Prodigy," *New York Herald*, January 7, 1892.
90 "A Blind Prodigy," *Galveston Daily News*, April 10, 1895; "Local News: Professor J. T. Harris," *Brenham Daily Banner*, June 22, 1894; "Blind Oscar Moore," *Brenham Daily Banner*, September 5, 1901.

91 "[Oscar Moore, Cora Williams, Henry Moore], 1900 U.S. Federal Census: Memphis Ward 5, Shelby, Tennessee," 1900, Ancestry Library Edition, http://ancestry.com.
92 The last performance dates I have found for Moore were in Texas in September 1901. "Blind Oscar Moore," *Brenham Daily Banner*, September 5, 1901.
93 Oscar, Cora, and Henry do not appear in the same household again, which is the central cause of the difficulty in tracking them. Cora's married (and widowed?) last name, Williams, also makes this difficult. More broadly, the family's itinerary between Texas and Tennessee (and potentially beyond) makes locating them in state- and city-specific archives and records more challenging.
94 Clevenger, "Infant Prodigy," 365.
95 Hartman, "Venus in Two Acts," 4, 10.
96 Hartman, 11.
97 Bohlender and McCallum, *Texas Bookman*, 55.
98 Bohlender and McCallum, 35, iv.
99 Bohlender and McCallum, 35.
100 Bohlender and McCallum, iv.
101 The Briscoe Center at the University of Texas at Austin houses some of Gammel's personal and miscellaneous papers from 1905 to 1940 and papers devoted specifically to Gammel's Book Store from 1891 to 1931. These papers arrived in multiple donations between the 1970s and 1986, though it is unclear exactly which of Gammel's descendants made these donations.
102 Between 2015 and 2016, I spoke and emailed with multiple Gammel descendants. They expressed their belief that the diary was lost in the Cerro Grande fire in Los Alamos, New Mexico, in 2000 (the diary was in a family member's house that was destroyed).
103 Bohlender and McCallum, *Texas Bookman*.
104 Bohlender writes in the preface to *Texas Bookman*, "This is the Bookman's book, transmitted here in tribute to his memory" (iv).
105 Gammel, "Not Worth Quarreling," 38.
106 Gammel, 38.
107 I have not been able to find additional records of this "trouble" in Chicago's or Milwaukee's Humane Society records.
108 Gammel, "Not Worth Quarreling," 38.
109 Gammel, 41, 39.
110 Gammel, 39. Gammel refers to Wells as "Barnes"—perhaps an accidental or purposeful conflation of Barnum and Wells.
111 Gammel, 40.
112 Gammel, 41.
113 Gammel, 41.
114 See Hartman, *Wayward Lives*, xv, 59.
115 Foote Sr., *Science in Story*, 1:6.
116 Phillips, "Aesthetic Primitivism," 1–25; Clifford, "On Collecting"; Mercer, introduction to *Cosmopolitan Modernisms*, 6–23.

117 See "Helen Keller's Wonderful Powers," *Chicago Tribune*, July 20, 1888; "Blind, Deaf, and Dumb: The Wonderful Doings of Little Helen Keller," *Hartford (CT) Courant*, January 18, 1889; and "Little Helen Keller: The Blind Deaf Mute," *New York Times*, September 8, 1889. See also Nielsen, *Radical Lives of Helen Keller*, 6–7.

118 Lombardo, *Century of Eugenics*; Lombardo, *Three Generations*; Bashford and Levine, *Oxford Handbook of the History of Eugenics*; Kline, *Building a Better Race*; Ladd-Taylor, *Fixing the Poor*.

119 See, for example, "A Musical Genius: A Six-Year-Old Colored Child," *Cleveland Gazette*, October 24, 1884; "Colored Juvenile Prodigy: Benny Coleman," *Louisville Courier*, August 17, 1893; "Felix Loves the Violin," *St. Louis Post-Dispatch*, April 21, 1895; and "Wonderful: Prodigy Is Claretta Avery," *Cincinnati Enquirer*, December 1, 1895.

120 M. Mitchell, *Righteous Propagation*; English, *Unnatural Selections*.

121 Du Bois, *Talented Tenth*, 1–2; Du Bois, "Black Folks and Birth Control," 166.

122 On Terman, intelligence testing, and gifted education, see Chapman, *Schools as Sorters*. See also Margolin, "Emergence of Gifted Children," 510–32; and J. Ellis, "'Inequalities of Children,'" 401–29.

123 "Philippa Schuyler, the Shirley Temple of American Negroes," *Look*, November 7, 1939.

5. "THIS IS THE END OF THE STORY NO IT ISINT"

1 "Month of January, Your 29th Month, 2 Years, 5 Months," January 1934, 1933–34 Scrapbook, Philippa Schuyler Collection, Special Collections Research Center, Syracuse University Libraries (hereafter cited as PSC, SCRC).

2 "2 yrs, 6mo," January 14, 1934, 1933–34 Scrapbook, PSC, SCRC.

3 September 3, 1934, 1933–34 Scrapbook, PSC, SCRC.

4 "The Schuylers' Secret Has Been Revealed," *Pittsburgh Courier*, January 25, 1934; "Colored Child Prodigy," *St. Louis Globe Democrat*, February 12, 1934; "Colored Girl Prodigy Spells with Ease Word of 41 Letters," *Evening Courier*, July 29, 1935; "Music: Harlem Prodigy," *Time*, June 22, 1936.

5 "Harlem's Youngest Philosopher Parades Talent on Third Birthday," *New York Herald Tribune*, August 3, 1934; "'Superior,' Claim University 'Profs,'" *Pittsburgh Courier*, August 9, 1934; "3rd broadcast" [undated, ca. November 1936], 1935–36 Scrapbook, PSC, SCRC.

6 [IQ Measurements] February–March 1936, 1935–36 Scrapbook, PSC, SCRC.

7 George Schuyler to Josephine Schuyler, October 20, 1935, Schuyler Family Papers, Schomburg Center for Research in Black Culture, New York Public Library (hereafter cited as SFP, Schomburg Center, NYPL).

8 September 3, 1934, 1933–34 Scrapbook, PSC, SCRC.

9 J. Schuyler, "Contests," September 1936, 1935–36 Scrapbook, PSC, SCRC.

10 J. Schuyler, "Contests," September 1936, 1935–36 Scrapbook, PSC, SCRC.

11 Writing in 1959, Josephine described how she and George had decided to "test" the dominant sense that "a mixture of the races would be biologically, socially,

ethically and financially disastrous" against her and George's "opinion"—that "good healthy parents, a scientific diet for mother and child, and an intelligent, pleasant home life made superior children, not their color or racial mixture." See J. Schuyler, "My Daughter Philippa," 9.

12 "Human Stature" chart, November 1938, 1937–38 Scrapbook, SFP, Schomburg Center, NYPL; Golden and Weiner, "Reading Baby Books," 675.
13 September 3, 1934, 1933–34 Scrapbook, PSC, SCRC.
14 Key, *Century of the Child*.
15 Daylanne English describes Philippa's upbringing as an "intrafamilial breeding experiment" and "eugenic project." English, *Unnatural Selections*, 23n92.
16 Lovett, *Conceiving the Future*; Currell and Cogdell, introduction to *Popular Eugenics*.
17 Terman, "Preface to the First Edition," 2.
18 Lombardo, *Three Generations*.
19 Foote Jr., *Radical Remedy*.
20 Terman, "Traits of Gifted Children," 520–22.
21 Beatty, Cahan, and Grant, introduction to *When Science Encounters the Child*, 3–4; Apple, *Perfect Motherhood*.
22 Cahan, "Toward a Socially Relevant Science," 16–17, 27.
23 Francis Galton coined the debate as the question answered by his science of eugenics. See Subramaniam, *Ghost Stories for Darwin*, 59–60. See also Schuller, *Biopolitics of Feeling*, 28.
24 M. Mitchell, *Righteous Propagation*.
25 Dorr and Logan, "Quality, Not Mere Quantity," 68–92; E. Hackley, *Colored Girl Beautiful*, 18.
26 In 1931, Harvard anthropologist Ernest Albert Hooton published *Up from the Ape*, which defined "the phenomenon known as heterosis or hybrid vigor" and described how it "often manifests itself in the first few generations of hybrid offspring in increased size and strength. This seems to be an effect of the attainment of a heterozygous condition in the individual with respect to many inherited characters." Hooton derived his theory from the research of his student, Caroline Bond Day, a black Radcliffe researcher who had conducted a study of mixed-raced black and white people. Her study, *A Study of Some Negro-White Families in the United States*, was published in 1932. Josephine Schuyler read and reviewed Hooton's work. However, neither she nor George espoused their belief in the theory. See Hooton, *Up from the Ape*, 585–90; and Hooton, *Twilight of Man*, 140–41. See also J. Schuyler, "Looks at Books."
27 I trace the concept and its overattribution to the Schuylers in "'Fine Discords.'" References to the Schuylers' belief in hybrid vigor appear in Talalay, *Composition in Black and White*; English, *Unnatural Selections*, 22; Betts, "21st-Century Introduction," 3; Kaplan, *Miss Anne in Harlem*, 156; Streeter, *Tragic No More*, 114; and the Philippa Schuyler Middle School's biography of its namesake, "Philippa Duke Schuyler," https://philippaschuyler383.org.

28 See J. Schuyler, "Looks at Books"; and "My Daughter Philippa." In her 1959 *Sepia* piece, Josephine reflected, "I had long been a student of biochemistry and I knew nature didn't concern herself with human prejudices." J. Schuyler, "My Daughter Philippa," 9.
29 "Philippa Schuyler, the Shirley Temple of American Negroes," *Look*, November 7, 1939.
30 Merish, "Cuteness and Commodity," 197.
31 "Home Life [October 1936]," 1935–36 Scrapbook, PSC, SCRC.
32 "September 4, 1931," 1931–33 Scrapbook, PSC, SCRC.
33 Garvey, *Writing with Scissors*, 11.
34 "May 25, 1933," 1933–34 Scrapbook, PSC, SCRC; [November or December 1933], 1933–34 Scrapbook, PSC, SCRC; September 3, 1934, 1933–34 Scrapbook, PSC, SCRC.
35 Golden and Weiner, "Reading Baby Books," 672.
36 Apple, *Perfect Motherhood*, 58; see also Markel and Stern, *Formative Years*, 3–4.
37 September 3, 1934, 1933–34 Scrapbook, PSC, SCRC; 1933–34 Scrapbook, PSC, SCRC.
38 1920 notebook, folder 3; and undated [ca. 1920] notebook, folder 20 in box 76: Notebooks, Diaries, 1909–67, SFP, Schomburg Center, NYPL.
39 Catherine Keyser discusses and contextualizes the Schuylers' diet in *Artificial Color*.
40 "Month of April [1935]," 1934–35 Scrapbook, PSC, SCRC.
41 "Philippa's Daily Routine [May 1935]," 1934–35 Scrapbook, PSC, SCRC.
42 "December 1934—Christmas Week," 1933–34 Scrapbook, PSC, SCRC.
43 George to Josephine Schuyler, [telegram], May 10, 1936, 1935–36 Scrapbook, SCRC.
44 Terman, *Measure of Intelligence*, 51, 121.
45 [IQ Measurements] February–March 1936, 1935–36 Scrapbook, PSC, SCRC.
46 The clinic, established by Zorbaugh in 1930 to "build up a basis of comparison, careful records, and year-by-year data on unusual children," set parameters for "giftedness" in terms of IQ. According to Zorbaugh, "All the children [. . .] studied ha[d] an Intelligence Quotient of 130 or higher, rated by [Terman's] Stanford-Binet tests," and "their mentality [. . .] f[e]ll within the top 1 percent of their generation." See "Gifted Children Studied at New York University," *New York Times*, April 20, 1930; and Dorothy Higgins, interview with Harvey Zorbaugh, "Gifted Children," *New York Herald Tribune*, January 9, 1938.
47 Zorbaugh and Boardman, "Salvaging Our Gifted Children." See also Higgins interview with Zorbaugh, "Gifted Children," *New York Herald Tribune*, January 9, 1938.
48 Harvey Zorbaugh to Josephine Schuyler, May 27, 1936, 1935–36 Scrapbook, PSC, SCRC.
49 "Children's Number," *Crisis*, October 1927, referenced in Dorr and Logan, "Quality, Not Mere Quantity," 68–92.

50 On "the original purposes of the Binet scale," see Gould, *Mismeasure of Man*, 176–81.
51 Root, "Intelligence Quotient," 267–75; "The Physical and Mental Abilities of the American Negro," *Journal of Negro Education* 3, no. 3 (July 1934): 317–18.
52 "September 3, 1934," 1933–34 Scrapbook, PSC, SCRC.
53 Capshaw, *Children's Literature*, 9.
54 Capshaw, 1, 9.
55 Capshaw, 1.
56 "The Story of Phillis Wheatley," *Brownies' Book*, August 1920, 251–53, Library of Congress. http://loc.gov.
57 Dorr and Logan, "Quality, Not Mere Quantity," 75.
58 Capshaw, *Children's Literature*, 9.
59 Du Bois, *Talented Tenth*, 1–2; Du Bois, *Philadelphia Negro*, 3.
60 Capshaw, *Children's Literature*, 9.
61 "Gifted Children Dept.," 1935 Scrapbook, PSC, SCRC.
62 "Shirley Bats 155 for I.Q.," 1935 Scrapbook, PSC, SCRC; "Shirley's First Essay: On Spinach," 1935 Scrapbook, PSC, SCRC.
63 Celebrated as "Hollywood's most profitable star" during the middle 1930s, Temple earned over $300,000 in 1938 alone. See Hatch, *Shirley Temple*, 1; and Hulbert, *Off the Charts*, 116.
64 "Philippa Schuyler, the Shirley Temple of American Negroes," *Look*, November 7, 1939.
65 G. Schuyler, *Black No More*, 23, 41.
66 Schuyler, 151–54.
67 Schuyler, 180.
68 Schuyler, 177.
69 Schuyler, v.
70 Merish, "Cuteness and Commodity," 185.
71 Bernstein, *Racial Innocence*, 121.
72 On Little Eva and Tom's "propinquity," see Bernstein, *Racial Innocence*, 6, 120. On Bill "Bojangles" Robinson's recurring roles dancing across from Temple, see Merish, "Cuteness and Commodity," 199. On the production of both interracial and intergenerational intimacy in Temple's performances with Robinson, see Osterweil, "Reconstructing Shirley," 1–40.
73 Temple performs the song "Dixie-Anna" with a large all-blackface chorus and dance ensemble in *Dimples* (1936).
74 Merish, "Cuteness and Commodity," 198.
75 See J. Brown, "Letting the Flesh Fly: Topsy, Time, Torture, and Transfiguration," in *Babylon Girls*, 67.
76 Bernstein, "The Black-and-Whiteness of Raggedy Ann," in *Racial Innocence*, 146–93.
77 P. Schuyler, "My Black and White World."
78 "Shirley Temple-ness," in Bernstein, *Racial Innocence*, 25.

79 J. Mitchell, "Evening with a Gifted Child," 29–30.
80 Mitchell, 30, 31.
81 Claudia, the narrator in Toni Morrison's *Bluest Eye* (1970), identifies "Awwwww," as the "magic" that white girls like Shirley Temple "weaved" on others around her (22–23). It is this "Awwwww" that Merish deems the affective core of cuteness as commodity. See Morrison, *Bluest Eye*, 22; and Merish, "Cuteness and Commodity," 189.
82 "Colored Child Prodigy," *St. Louis Globe Democrat*, February 12, 1934, 1933–34 Scrapbook, PSC, SCRC.
83 [February 1934], 1933–34 Scrapbook, PSC, SCRC.
84 George Schuyler to Josephine Schuyler, October 20, 1935, SFP, Schomburg Center, NYPL.
85 English, *Unnatural Selections*, 23.
86 "Cogdell Line," box 72, SFP, Schomburg Center, NYPL.
87 [Schuyler Family Tree], Louise Schuyler [George's sister] to Philippa, November 26, 1945, PSC, SCRC; see also Ferguson, *Sage of Sugar Hill*, 9.
88 J. Schuyler, "Looks at Books."
89 On the Schuylers' rightward political transformations, see O. Williams, *George S. Schuyler*, 115–49.
90 Across the 1950s and early 1960s, Philippa sometimes aligned her political views with the conservatism of her parents; at other times, she dissented from them. See Betts, "21st-Century Introduction."
91 Despite socializing with some revolutionary figures as she traveled, Philippa described her fondness and nostalgia for colonial regimes, including that of Rafael Trujillo in the Dominican Republic. Using Felipa Montero (especially in Europe), Philippa wielded her racial indeterminacy and reveled in the notion that she "[had] ten nationalities in [her] ancestry." See P. Schuyler, *Adventures in Black and White*, 222.
92 See P. Schuyler, "My Black and White World."
93 "Philippa Schuyler, Pianist, Dies in Crash of a Copter in Vietnam," *New York Times*, May 10, 1967; "NYC Says Goodby to Philippa," *New York Amsterdam News*, May 27, 1967.
94 "Josephine Schuyler, Mother of Pianist," *New York Times*, May 3, 1969; [George Schuyler Memorial Service Program, October 1977], box 1, SFP, Schomburg Center, NYPL.
95 Keyser, *Artificial Color*, 47.
96 "School for the Gifted," *New York Amsterdam News*, July 21, 1979.
97 P. Schuyler, *Adventures in Black and White*.
98 Schuyler, 299.
99 Lists of vocabulary, "Philippa's Vocabulary," 2 years, 5 months, ca. December–January 1933; SCRC, 1933–34 Scrapbook.
100 [Ca. March 1935], 1935–36 Scrapbook; June 2, 1934, 1933–34 Scrapbook, PSC, SCRC.

101 "Story of the Gold Fish," April 1936, 1935–36 Scrapbook, PSC, SCRC.
102 "Rolling Home," [illustration], March–April 1936, 1935–36 Scrapbook, PSC, SCRC.
103 P. Schuyler, "Autumn Rain," in *Three Little Pieces*.
104 P. Schuyler, "Autumn Rain," in *Three Little Pieces*.
105 Campt, *Listening to Images*.
106 P. Schuyler, *Nine Little Pieces*; "strange, minor" melodies quote from "Five Yrs. 1 Month," September 1936, 1935–36 Scrapbook, PSC, SCRC.
107 "Contests," September 1936, 1935–36 Scrapbook.
108 "Contests," September 1936, 1935–36 Scrapbook.
109 "Major Bowles [sic] Is Nothing to You," June 1936, 1935–36 Scrapbook, PSC, SCRC.
110 *Major Bowes' Amateur Hour* ran successfully from 1935 to 1945 as an NBC broadcast, eventually becoming a multimillion-dollar franchise, and serving as the blueprint for later radio and television contest programs. See Melnick, "Reality Radio," 331–47.
111 "Major Bowles [sic] Is Nothing to You," June 1936, 1935–36 Scrapbook, PSC, SCRC.
112 P. Schuyler, "The Girl and Her Parents," May 18, 1936, 1935–36 Scrapbook, PSC, SCRC; and P. Schuyler, "Once a Little Purrlpe" [Fairy House story], [April 1936], 1935–36 Scrapbook, PSC, SCRC.
113 P. Schuyler, "Once a Little Purrlpe."
114 See J. Mitchell, "Evening with a Gifted Child"; and Philippa's comments in *Adventures in Black and White*, x.
115 ["Little Dog, Little Rabbit" story], March 18, 1935, 1935–36 Scrapbook, Oversize 7, PSC, SCRC; Hardy, *Wag and Puff*.
116 Sharpe, *In the Wake*, 76.
117 Morrison, *Bluest Eye*, 22–23, 19.
118 Morrison, 3.
119 Morrison, 17.
120 Morrison, 92.
121 Morrison, 204.
122 Morrison, 3, 4, 38.
123 Morrison, 204.
124 Griffin, *Read until You Understand*, 10; Als, "Toni Morrison's Profound and Unrelenting Vision."
125 Morrison, *Bluest Eye*, 204.
126 Morrison, 204.
127 Moten, *In the Break*, 1.
128 Morrison, *Bluest Eye*, 19.
129 Morrison, 204.
130 Morrison, 67, 122.
131 Fineberg, foreword to *Discovering Child Art*; Shiff, "From Primitivist Phylogeny," 157–200.

132 Franciscona, "Paul Klee," 95–121.
133 Benjamin, "Theses on the Philosophy of History," 201.
134 Benjamin, 201.
135 Benjamin, 201.
136 Benjamin, 201.
137 Arendt, introduction to *Illuminations*, xxvi–xxvii.
138 "When the Stars Are Up," September 1935, 1935–36 Scrapbook, PSC, SCRC.
139 "When the Stars Are Up," September 1935, 1935–36 Scrapbook, PSC, SCRC.
140 "When the Stars Are Up," September 1935, 1935–36 Scrapbook, PSC, SCRC.

EPILOGUE

1 Butler, *Parable of the Sower*, 223–24.
2 Wynter, "Yours in Intellectual Struggle," 7.
3 In *Parable*, Lauren Olamina often repeats this as the refrain of Earthseed: "All that you touch, you change, all that you change, changes you, the only lasting truth is change. God is change." Butler, *Parable*, 13.
4 Butler, 11.
5 Butler, "Positive Obsession."
6 Butler, 728.
7 Butler, 727.
8 R. Gilmore, *Abolition Geography*; Ritchie and Kaba, *No More Police*; S. Lewis, *Abolish the Family*; Dixon and Samarasinha, *Beyond Survival*.
9 Alexander, *Trayvon Generation*, 68–69.
10 Alexander, 73.
11 Douglass, *My Bondage*, 39.
12 Children afforded citizenship in the US have gained major legal protections with regard to their welfare, bodily sanctity, criminal culpability, civil liability, labor, and education across the last three centuries. In the present, they are theoretically afforded the right to a K–12 education, protection from work, and rights to the basic nutrition, housing, and care that make up "welfare" broadly construed. Yet children's rights and protections remain vaguely articulated, piecemeal, and disparately supported along lines of race, gender, class, and immigration status. The recent exposure of migrant children's widespread work and the recent loosening of child labor laws in Arkansas and Iowa are points of evidence that the interests of business and the state routinely supersede the interests of children, especially poor and nonwhite children. As just one other metric of children's disparate welfare, the Annie E. Casey Foundation found in 2022 that while 17 percent of all children in the US were living in poverty, between 31 and 32 percent of African American and Native children were. If children's vulnerability is magnified by social inequality, it is also inscribed by their structural position in the law. Because many protections for children have been articulated as *prohibitions* (against harming, neglecting, exploiting, or sexually violating children), children have not been positively safeguarded from these

harms as much as given legal recourse in the aftermath of their occurrence. Indeed, the US guarantees few positive rights to children; to date, the US remains the only UN member not to ratify the United Nations Convention on the Rights of the Child. On the legal and labor histories of US children's vulnerability and protection, see Fliter, *Child Labor in America*; Pearson, *Rights of the Defenseless*; Zelizer, *Pricing the Priceless Child*; Feld, *Evolution of the Juvenile Court*; Annie E. Casey Foundation, *2022 Kids Count Data Book*, http://aefc.org, 2022; Dreier, "Alone and Exploited"; Radde, "Arkansas Gov. Sanders"; and Oladipo, "Republican Iowa Governor."

13 There have been over two hundred shootings leading to death and injury in K–12 schools since February 2012. See "K–12 School Shooting Database," https://k12ssdb.org. Gun violence is currently the leading cause of children's deaths in the US. See Gebeloff et al., "Childhood's Greatest Danger."

14 Gay, "What Is a Country?" This essay was later retitled "Don't Talk to Me about Civility. On Tuesday Morning Those Children Were Alive."

15 Gay.

16 While I have focused on the particular historical relation of black childhood to white power, any analysis of contemporary childhood in the US requires integrating black and white childhood in relation to the histories of Indigenous, Latinx, and Asian childhood and family. Some nonexhaustive points of entry include D. Adams, *Education for Extinction*; Segal and Rose, *Carlisle Indian Industrial School*; Peterson, *Indians in the Family*; Hsu, *Good Immigrants*; Choy, *Global Families*; and Brady, *Scales of Captivity*.

17 The familiar phrase "life, liberty, and the pursuit of happiness" found in the US Declaration of Independence (1776) was a rephrasing of Locke's "life, liberty, and estate" from his *Two Treatises on Government* (1689), in which he argues that government's primary role is to protect men's property. See Locke, *Two Treatises on Government*.

18 *The Bluest Eye* was one of the most banned books in US school districts during 2021–22. *Parable of the Sower* has also been frequently banned. See Pen.org, "10 Most Banned Books"; Kirby, "D.C.'s Library Foundation"; and Alter, "Book Bans Rising."

19 Mazzei and Hartocollis, "Florida Rejects."

20 Describing multiple queer and nonheteronormative practices of "kinning" and referencing Donna Haraway's concept of "oddkin," Laura Kessler's "transgressive care," and black, queer, and lesbian experiments in mutuality and surrogacy, Sophie Lewis writes that such forms of "inventive kinning ha[ve] taken place in every corner of the planet ever since the institution of marriage started being forcibly imposed on poor, indigenous, and colonized people." See S. Lewis, *Full Surrogacy Now*, 147–49. Alexis Pauline Gumbs, China Martins, and Mai'a Williams describe "revolutionary mothering" as part of a thread of black feminist and queer politics of motherhood theorized by Audre Lorde and June Jordan during the late twentieth century. Alongside this genealogy of revolutionary mothering,

I also place the history of black mother's antilynching activism and public demonstrations of black mother's mourning, from the turn-of-the-twentieth-century writings of Ida B. Wells, to the public grief of Mamie Till Mobley, to the invocation of black maternal loss in the present mourning of slain black children. On these various threads, see Gumbs, Martens, and Williams, *Revolutionary Mothering*.

21 Alexander, *Trayvon Generation*, 73.

BIBLIOGRAPHY

ARCHIVES
American Antiquarian Society
   Children's Literature Collection
   Graphic Arts Collection
Beinecke Rare Book and Manuscript Library, Yale University
   Betsy Beinecke Shirley Collection of American Children's Literature
   James Weldon Johnson Memorial Collection
Dolph Briscoe Center for American History, University of Texas at Austin
   Gammel's Book Store Records
John Hay Library, Brown University
   Lownes History of Science Collection
Houghton Library, Harvard University
   Harvard Theatre Collection
Massachusetts Historical Society
   Manuscript Collections
Harry Ransom Center, University of Texas Austin
   Minstrel Show Collection
Billy Rose Performing Arts Division, New York Public Library
   Circus and Magic Posters and Scrapbooks Collection
Stuart A. Rose Manuscript, Archive, and Rare Book Library, Emory University
   Geneva H. Southall Papers
Schomburg Center for Research in Black Culture, New York Public Library
   Schuyler Family Papers
Special Collections Research Center, Syracuse University Libraries
   Philippa Schuyler Collection
US National Library of Medicine, National Institutes of Health
   Shobal Vail Clevenger Papers
Waco-McLennan County Clerk, Waco, Texas
   Official Public Records

NEWSPAPER CLIPPINGS (BY PERIODICAL, WITHOUT AUTHOR ATTRIBUTION)
Alexandria Gazette. "The Blind Tom Case." July 10, 1885. Virginia Chronicle, Library of Virginia.
———. "Mr. Bethune Must Pay Alimony." November 26, 1883. Virginia Chronicle.

Appeal, The (St. Paul, MN). "Cincinnati." October 22, 1892. Library of Congress: Historic American Newspapers Online.

Arizona Republican (1890–1922). "Breaking the Bonds: How the Blind Triumph Over Their Physical Misfortune. A Sightless Lad from the South Who Has a Wonderful Memory—Great Success of a Farmer—a Typewriter of Value." September 27, 1892. ProQuest.

Arkansas Gazette [from the *New York World*]. "Truly an Infant Prodigy." May 26, 1889. Readex.

Atchison (KS) Globe. "A Wonderful Memory." December 28, 1888. Gale Cengage.

Atlanta Constitution. "Blind Tom at Home." July 2, 1888. ProQuest.

———. "Blind Tom Goes to Beyond." June 15, 1908. ProQuest.

———. "Blind Tom: How the Wonderful Negro Idiot Conducted Himself." September 1, 1887. ProQuest.

———. "Blind Tom's Manager's Will." June 10, 1886. ProQuest.

———. "Blind Tom's Transfer." From the *New York Sun*. July 2, 1888. ProQuest.

———. "His Mother Trying to Get Him Adjudged Insane." November 27, 1886. ProQuest.

Atlanta Daily World. "Diet Is Given Credit for Philippa Schuyler's Art." March 8, 1942. ProQuest.

Augusta Register. "Blind Tom's Concert." November 16, 1861. Readex.

Austin Daily Statesman. "A Prodigy: A Marvel in the World of the Marvelous, a Wonderfully Endowed Boy, over Whom There Is a Wrangle." March 1, 1888. ProQuest.

———. "Waco Wirelings." March 6, 1888. ProQuest.

Austin Weekly Statesman. "Professor Oscar Moore." August 16, 1888. Vol. 17, No. 38 edition. Portal to Texas History Online.

Baltimore Afro-American. "A Day with Little Philippa Schuyler, Famous Child Piano Prodigy—and What a Busy Day!" August 24, 1940. ProQuest.

———. "Philippa Schuyler Day at the Fair, June 19." June 15, 1940. ProQuest.

———. "Philippa Schuyler Fetes Orphans on Her Birthday." August 9, 1941. ProQuest.

———. "Philippa Schuyler Spells, Draws on Third Birthday." August 11, 1934. ProQuest.

———. "$3,600 Piano Is Birthday Gift to Five-Year-Old Girl." August 1, 1936. ProQuest.

Baltimore Sun. "Fourteen Hundred Dollars Reward." August 19, 1852. ProQuest.

Bismarck Daily Tribune [from the *New York Sun*]. "That Wonderful Colored Boy: Here Is a Frightful Infant Who Never Forgets What He Hears." March 6, 1889. Readex.

Boston Globe. "Amusement Announcements." July 21, 1892. ProQuest.

———. "Brooklyn's Child Prodigy Grows Up." August 12, 1930. ProQuest.

———. "His Memory a Wonder: Blind Oscar Moore, a Six-Year-Old Colored Boy from Texas, Who Seems Unable to Forget What He Once Has Heard." July 17, 1892. ProQuest.

Boston Herald. "Amusements: Now Open at the Washington Garden." August 23, 1848. ProQuest.

———. "Austin and Stone's." August 9, 1892. Readex.

———. "[Ad] He Is the Most Remarkable Child on Earth." July 20, 1892. Readex.

Boston Sunday Herald. "[Ad] Austin and Stone's Museum." July 21, 1892. Readex.
Brenham (TX) Daily Banner, The. "Blind Oscar Moore." September 5, 1901. Vol. 26, No. 209 edition. Portal to Texas History Online.
———. "Blind Oscar Moore: The Wonder of the Century Tonight at Lusk's Hall." September 4, 1901. Vol. 26, No. 208 edition. Portal to Texas History Online.
———. "Local News: Professor J. T. Harris." June 22, 1894. Vol. 19, No. 144 edition. Portal to Texas History Online.
Caledonian Mercury. "Blind Tom." December 11, 1866. Gale Cengage.
Charleston Courier. "A Boy Phonograph." February 4, 1891. Readex.
Charleston Mercury. "Musical Prodigy." May 6, 1863. ProQuest.
———. "Musical Prodigy." May 30, 1863. ProQuest.
Chicago Defender. "Pianist and Composer: Philippa Schuyler." March 11, 1939. ProQuest.
Chicago Tribune. "A Blind Baby's Memory: Little Oscar Moore Is an Infant Encyclopedia." October 28, 1888. ProQuest.
———. "For an Ex-Confederate Monument." November 28, 1888. ProQuest.
———. "Helen Keller's Wonderful Powers." July 20, 1888. ProQuest.
———. "A Negro Prodigy in Court." July 22, 1865. ProQuest.
———. "To Superintend the Insane." March 9, 1893. ProQuest.
Cincinnati Enquirer. "Amusements." March 6, 1866. ProQuest.
———. "Blind Tom in Court." July 21, 1865. ProQuest.
———. "Blind Tom Insane." November 29, 1886. ProQuest.
———. "The Case of Blind Tom: The Opinion of Judge Woodruff." July 25, 1865. ProQuest.
———. "For the Possession of Blind Tom." July 1, 1885. ProQuest.
———. "Law Report: Probate Court." July 20, 1865. ProQuest.
———. "Law Report: Probate Court." July 26, 1865. ProQuest.
———. "Local News: The Habeas Corpus Case of Blind Tom." July 22, 1865. ProQuest.
———. "Louis Hawkins . . . Who Promised to Be Second Blind Tom." February 8, 1902. ProQuest.
———. "State of Affairs in the South: Free Labor a Failure, and Why." September 14, 1865. ProQuest.
———. "Vine Street Dime Museum." October 1, 1888. ProQuest.
———. "Wonderful: Prodigy Is Claretta Avery." December 1, 1895. Readex.
Cleveland Gazette. "A Musical Genius: A Six-Year-Old Colored Child." October 24, 1884. Readex.
Courier Journal (Louisville, Kentucky). "An Enigma to Doctors: The Wonderful Memory of a Three-Year-Old Blind Boy Put to the Test." December 10, 1888. ProQuest.
———. "Questions and Answers: [Is Blind Tom Alive?]." April 14, 1901. ProQuest.
Daily American. "Poor Blind Tom: The Colored Prodigy Sinking Fast." January 12, 1891. ProQuest.
Daily Dispatch (Richmond, Virginia). "Blind Tom." March 4, 1862. ProQuest.
Daily Inter-ocean (Chicago, Illinois). "The Blind Child Prodigy." December 6, 1888. Gale Cengage.

———. "Blind Tom's Legal Cognomen Is Thomas Greene Bethune." May 5, 1869. Readex.
———. "Bright Eyes and Billiards." December 5, 1888. Readex.
———. "The City in Brief." October 28, 1888. Gale Cengage.
———. "Harrison Goes Hunting: The President Elect." December 6, 1888. Readex.
———. "The Last Slave." August 16, 1887. Readex.
———. "Social Gatherings." December 6, 1888. Readex.
Daily Nebraska State Journal. "Prodigy of Memory: A Three Year Old Child Who Answers a Thousand Questions." October 14, 1888. Readex.
Daily Picayune. "City Intelligence." February 7, 1849. ProQuest.
———. "[Classified Ad]." February 27, 1853. ProQuest.
Daily Telegraph (Napier, New Zealand). "A Marvellous [sic] Child." January 15, 1889. Issue 5425. Papers Past.
Detroit Free Press. "Blind Tom: A Sketch of the Musical Prodigy Who Has for Years Puzzled the Public." July 25, 1889. ProQuest.
———. "Infant Prodigies." January 14, 1850. ProQuest.
———. "Oscar Moore, of Texas: An Infant Colored Prodigy." September 2, 1888. ProQuest.
El Paso (TX) International Daily Times. "How the Blind Triumph over Their Physical Misfortune." September 8, 1892. Vol. 12, No. 209 edition. Portal to Texas History Online.
Evening Courier (Camden, NJ). "Colored Girl Prodigy Spells with Ease Word of 41 Letters." July 29, 1935. ProQuest.
Fort Worth Daily Gazette. "A Boy's Wonderful Memory." February 4, 1889. Vol. 13, No. 216 edition. Portal to Texas History Online.
———. "Waco." March 6, 1888. Vol. 13, No. 217 edition. Portal to Texas History Online.
Gainesville (TX) Daily Hesperian. "Waco." March 7, 1888. Vol. 9, No. 86 edition. Portal to Texas History Online.
Galveston Daily News (Galveston, TX). "A Blind Prodigy." April 10, 1895. Gale Cengage.
———. "Events in Colored Circles." February 23, 1896. Gale Cengage.
———. "Truly an Infant Prodigy." June 11, 1889. Gale Cengage.
Hartford (CT) Courant. "Blind, Deaf, and Dumb: The Wonderful Doings of Little Helen Keller." January 18, 1889. ProQuest.
———. "Classified Ad: J. Morris New York Concert and Olio Exhibition." July 31, 1841. ProQuest.
Heppner (OR) Weekly Gazette. "It Is Claimed That He Has Not Been Properly Educated." January 14, 1892. Historical Oregon Newspapers.
Homer (LA) Guardian. "A Wonderful Prodigy." January 25, 1889. Library of Congress: Historic American Newspapers.
Jackson City Patriot. "Equal to Blind Tom." February 6, 1889. Readex.
Kansas City Star. "The Last Slave." August 20, 1887. Readex.
Liberator. "Letter: The Little Slaves to the Sabbath School Children of New England." March 27, 1832.

Look. "Philippa Schuyler, the Shirley Temple of American Negroes." November 7, 1939.
Los Angeles Times. "Child Prodigy at the Piano." January 7, 1934. ProQuest.
Louisville Courier. "Colored Juvenile Prodigy: Benny Coleman." August 17, 1893. Readex.
Louisville Daily Courier. "200 Reward." March 22, 1855. ProQuest.
Louisville Daily Journal. "Amusements: Welch, Delevan, and Nathan's National Circus." September 25, 1850. ProQuest.
Manchester Guardian. "Theatre Royal—Blind Tom." September 26, 1866. ProQuest.
Michigan Farmer. "Prodigy of Memory: A Three-Year-Old Child Who Answers All Sorts of Questions." November 17, 1888. ProQuest.
Milwaukee Daily Sentinel. "Amusement Notes." December 12, 1888. Gale Cengage.
———. "Musical and Dramatic Notes." December 6, 1888. Gale Cengage.
Minneapolis Tribune. "Blind Tom's Only Rival, the Marvel of the Plains." January 8, 1888. ProQuest.
Mobile Register. "Blind Tom." March 2, 1860. Readex.
Morning Herald. "Review: Chatham Theatre—the Infant Prodigy." June 6, 1840. ProQuest.
Morning Post (London). "Blind Tom." August 13, 1866. Gale Cengage.
Nashville Republican and Gazette. "A Prodigy." April 10, 1834. ProQuest.
National Tribune (Washington, DC). "General [Notice of Lawsuit]." January 14, 1892. Library of Congress: Historic American Newspapers.
New Haven Register. "The Hman [sic] Phonograph." February 19, 1892. Readex.
———. "Is a Human Phonograph." February 17, 1892. Readex.
———. "[Ad] Oscar Moore." March 3, 1892. Readex.
New Journal and Guide. "Philippa Schuyler Wins Seventh Philharmonic Award." April 25, 1942. ProQuest.
New York Amsterdam News. "NYC Says Goodby to Philippa." May 27, 1967. ProQuest.
———. "School for the Gifted." July 21, 1979. ProQuest.
New York Herald. "A New Wonder." May 13, 1889. Readex.
———. "Suit over Boy Prodigy." January 7, 1892. Readex.
———. "Whispers from the Wings." May 5, 1889. Readex.
New York Herald Tribune. "Completes Her First Orchestral Composition at Thirteen." August 2, 1944. ProQuest.
———. "Girl Prodigy, 8, Writes Her Own Birthday Music." August 1, 1939. ProQuest.
———. "Harlem's Youngest Philosopher Parades Talent on Third Birthday." August 3, 1934. ProQuest.
———. "Negro Girl, 4, Is Star of Piano Play Tourney." June 7, 1936. ProQuest.
———. "Philippa Schuyler Breaks New Record." June 24, 1939. ProQuest.
New York Times. "Barnum Sees a Prodigy." January 23, 1889. ProQuest.
———. "A Boy with a Memory: Performances of a Blind Colored Youth of about Three Years." January 13, 1889. ProQuest.
———. "Blind Tom and His Mother." October 12, 1886. ProQuest.
———. "Blind Tom Is Free." July 31, 1887. ProQuest.

———. "The Blind Tom Mystery." June 18, 1908. ProQuest.
———. "Blind Tom, Pianist, Dies of a Stroke." June 15, 1908. ProQuest.
———. "Blind Tom's Return." August 18, 1887. ProQuest.
———. "Blind Tom's Transfer." August 20, 1887. ProQuest.
———. "Gifted Children Studied at New York University." April 20, 1930. ProQuest.
———. "Henry Ward Beecher on the Situation." February 21, 1866. ProQuest.
———. "Josephine Schuyler, Mother of Pianist." May 3, 1969. ProQuest.
———. "Little Helen Keller: The Blind Deaf Mute." September 8, 1889. ProQuest.
———. "Little Oscar Moore: The Latest Addition to the Ranks of Infant Prodigies." January 28, 1889. ProQuest.
———. "Menuhin's Sister Delights Audience." November 27, 1934. 1935 Scrapbook. Box 3. PSC, SCRC.
———. "Philippa Schuyler, Pianist, Dies in Crash of a Copter in Vietnam." May 10, 1967. ProQuest.
———. "Review: Studies in Race Mixture by Edward Byron Reuter." April 12, 1931. ProQuest.
———. "Showman George A. Wells: Life of the Man Who Was at One Time Barnum's Partner." October 9, 1892. ProQuest.
———. "Wants to Care for 'Blind Tom.'" August 12, 1887. ProQuest.
New York Tribune. "Barnum Sees a Prodigy: But Oscar Moore Will Not Join the Circus Just Yet." January 23, 1889. ProQuest.
———. "Blind Tom's Mind Unsound." November 27, 1886. ProQuest.
———. "Cincinnati Centennial." July 5, 1888. Readex.
———. "Feats of Memory by a Blind Child." December 6, 1888. Readex.
———. "The Last Slave." October 7, 1885. ProQuest.
———. "A Musical Miracle." July 31, 1904. ProQuest.
———. "Obituary: Dr. Edward Bliss Foote." October 6, 1906. ProQuest.
Pedagogical Seminary. "Editorial." 1, no. 1 (1891): iv.
———. "Foreign Miscellanies." 1, no. 1 (1891): 300.
Philadelphia Inquirer. "Most Wondrous Phenomenon." January 14, 1889. Readex.
Philadelphia Tribune. "Philippa Schuyler Heard at the Shore." June 27, 1940. ProQuest.
Pittsburgh Courier. "1500 Miles [Birth Announcement]." September 26, 1931.
———. "Philippa Schuyler Writes about Mexico for Magazine." March 17, 1945. ProQuest.
———. "Philippa Will Broadcast on August 1, Then Celebrate." July 31, 1937. ProQuest.
———. "The Schuylers' Secret Has Been Revealed: 29-Month Old Prodigy." January 25, 1934. ProQuest.
———. "'Superior,' Claim University 'Profs.'" August 9, 1934.
Republican Banner (Nashville, Tennessee). "Article 2 [Blind Tom]." March 14, 1861. ProQuest.
———. "By Bequest." October 10, 1861. ProQuest.
———. "The Sick Soldier—a Benefit." July 24, 1861. ProQuest.
San Francisco Chronicle. "[Francis Evans] Colored Lad Who Is a Criminal Prodigy." October 14, 1900. ProQuest.

———. "Helen Keller: What a Blind Deaf Mute Has Accomplished." October 13, 1889. ProQuest.

———. "Infant Prodigy: A Three-Year-Old Negro's Memory Sightless, but Wonderful Questions on Difficult Subjects Answered without Hesitation." December 16, 1888. ProQuest.

San Marcos (TX) Free Press. "A Texas Prodigy." December 27, 1888. Vol. 15, No. 52 edition. Portal to Texas History Online.

South China Morning Post. "The Evolution of a Superior Race: An Interesting Theory." November 24, 1917. ProQuest.

St. Louis Globe Democrat. "Colored Child Prodigy." February 12, 1934. 1933–34 Scrapbook. Oversize 7. PSC, SCRC.

St. Louis Post-Dispatch. "Felix Loves the Violin." April 21, 1895. ProQuest.

Time Magazine. "Music: Harlem Prodigy." June 22, 1936. [Clipping] Philippa Schuyler Collection. Special Collections Research Center, Syracuse University Libraries.

Velasco (TX) Times. "A Child Wonder." April 7, 1893. Vol. 2, No. 32 edition. Portal to Texas History Online.

———. "Church Services." April 14, 1893. Vol. 2, No. 33 edition. Portal to Texas History Online.

Washington Post. "Blind Tom Not Dead." June 10, 1889. ProQuest.

———. "Blind Tom Surrendered." August 17, 1887. ProQuest.

———. "A Mathematical Prodigy." December 30, 1888. ProQuest.

———. "Oscar Moore's Memory: Remarkable Mental Development of a Blind Mulatto Boy." December 23, 1888. ProQuest.

———. "Plays, Writes Own Music at Age of Five: Philippa Schuyler Wins National Award for Pianists." September 13, 1936. ProQuest.

———. "The Story of Blind Tom: Why the Musical Prodigy Must Leave His Old Friends." August 14, 1887. ProQuest.

———. "Wonderful Blind Tom: His Mother Tells What a Queer Child He Was—His Musical Abilities." November 28, 1886. ProQuest.

Weekly Ohio State Journal. "An Intellectual Prodigy." October 22, 1845. ProQuest.

Wilson (NC) Advance. "An Infant Prodigy." January 31, 1889. North Carolina Newspapers.

———. "Professor Oscar Moore: A Three-Year-Old-Pickaninny." January 31, 1889. North Carolina Newspapers.

Worcester Daily Spy. "A Remarkable Boy." January 16, 1888. Readex.

SOURCES

Abbot, Ann Wales. "Friendless and Homeless Children." In *The Child's Friend*, 97–101. Philadelphia: Lindsay & Blakiston, 1857.

Abdur-Rahman, Aliyyah. "A Tenuous Hold." *Black Scholar* 49, no. 2 (Spring 2019): 38–43.

Abrahams, Harold J. *Extinct Medical Schools of Nineteenth Century Philadelphia.* Vols. 30–32. Philadelphia: From the Transactions and Studies of the College of Physicians of Philadelphia, 1962–64.

Adams, David Wallace. *Education for Extinction: American Indians and the Boarding School Experience, 1875–1928.* Lawrence: University Press of Kansas, 1995.

Adams, John Stowell. "I Am Going There, or, The Death of Little Eva." Sheet music. Boston: Oliver Ditson, 1852. Gale Cengage.

Agamben, Giorgio. *Homo Sacer: Sovereign Power and Bare Life.* Translated by Daniel Heller-Roazen. 1995. Stanford: Stanford University Press, 1998.

Agassiz, Louis. "The Diversity of Origin of the Human Races." *Christian Examiner*, July 1850.

Alcott, William. *The House I Live In, or, The Human Body, for the Use of Families and Schools.* Boston: Light and Stearns, 1837. National Library of Medicine.

Alexander, Elizabeth. *The Black Interior.* St. Paul, MN: Graywolf Press, 2004.

———. *The Trayvon Generation.* New York: Grand Central, 2022.

Alexander, James W. *Maria Cheeseman, or, The Candy-Girl.* Philadelphia: American Sunday-School Union, 1855. Library of Congress Digital Collections.

Als, Hilton. "Toni Morrison's Profound and Unrelenting Vision." *New Yorker*, January 27, 2020.

Alter, Alexandra. "Book Bans Rising Rapidly in the U.S., Free Speech Groups Find." *New York Times*, April 20, 2023. http://newyorktimes.com.

Appelbaum, Paul. "The Evolution of Commitment Law in the Nineteenth Century." *Law and Human Behavior* 6 (1982): 343–56.

Apple, Rima. *Perfect Motherhood: Science and Childrearing in America.* New Brunswick: Rutgers University Press, 2006.

Arendt, Hannah. Introduction to *Illuminations: Essays and Reflections*, vii–lxiii. 1968. Edited by Hannah Arendt. Boston: Mariner Books, 2019.

Ariés, Philip. *Centuries of Childhood: A Social History of Family Life.* New York: Vintage, 1962.

Armistead, Wilson. *Five Hundred Thousand Strokes for Freedom: A Series of Anti-Slavery Tracts of Which Half a Million Are Now First Issued by the Friends of the Negro.* London: W. & F. Cash, 1853. Gale Cengage.

Aubrey, James. "Revising the Monstrous: Du Plessis' Short History of Prodigies and London Culture in 1730." *Studies in Eighteenth-Century Culture* 23 (1994): 75–91.

Avery, Gillian. *Behold the Child: American Children and Their Books.* Baltimore: Johns Hopkins University Press, 1994.

Backscheider, Paula R. *Eighteenth-Century Women Poets and Their Poetry: Inventing Agency, Inventing Genre.* Baltimore: Johns Hopkins University Press, 2005.

Bailey, Moya. "The Flexner Report: Standardizing Medical Students through Region-, Gender-, and Race-Based Hierarchies." *American Journal of Law & Medicine* 43 (2017): 209–23.

Bardaglio, Peter. *Reconstructing the Household: Families, Sex, and the Law in the Nineteenth-Century South.* Chapel Hill: University of North Carolina Press, 1995.

Barker, Clare. *Postcolonial Fiction and Disability: Exceptional Children, Metaphor and Materiality.* New York: Palgrave, 2011.

Bashford, Alison, and Philippa Levine, eds. *The Oxford Handbook of the History of Eugenics*. New York: Oxford University Press, 2010.

Baskervill, William Malone, Atticus Greene Haygood, and James Biddle Eustis. *Shall the Negro Be Educated or Suppressed? A Symposium on Dr. Haygood's Reply to Senator Eustis's Paper on Race Antagonism*. New York: Printed for the Open Letter Club, 1889. Gale Cengage.

Baumgartner, Kabria. "Black Girlhood and Equal School Rights." In Baumgartner, *In Pursuit of Knowledge*, chap. 5.

———. *In Pursuit of Knowledge: Black Women and Educational Activism in Antebellum America*. New York: New York University Press, 2019.

———. "Searching for Sarah: Black Girlhood, Education, and the Archive." *History of Education Quarterly* 60, no. 1 (February 2020): 73–85.

Bay, Mia, Farah J. Griffith, Martha S. Jones, and Barbara Savage, eds. *Toward an Intellectual History of Black Women*. Chapel Hill: University of North Carolina Press, 2015.

Beatty, Barbara, Emily D. Cahan, and Julia Grant, eds. *When Science Encounters the Child: Education, Parenting, and Child Welfare in 20th-Century America*. New York: Teachers College Press, 2006.

Beatty, Barbara. *Preschool Education in America: The Culture of Young Children from the Colonial Era to the Present*. New Haven: Yale University Press, 1997.

Bederman, Gail. *Manliness and Civilization: A Cultural History of Gender and Race in the United States, 1880–1917*. Chicago: University of Chicago Press, 1990.

———. "'Teaching Our Sons to Do What We Have Been Teaching the Savages to Avoid': G. Stanley Hall, Racial Recapitulation, and the Neurasthenic Paradox." In Bederman, *Manliness and Civilization*, chap. 5.

Bell, Chris. "Introducing White Disability Studies: A Modest Proposal." In *Disability Studies Reader*, 2nd ed., edited by Lennard Davis, 275–82. New York: Routledge, 2006.

Bendixen, Alfred, and Stephen Burt, eds. *The Cambridge History of American Poetry*. New York: Cambridge University Press, 2015.

Benes, Peter. "Child Performers and Prodigies in New England, 1795–1830." In *The Worlds of Children, 1620–1920, Dublin Seminar for New England Folklife Annual Proceedings*, 197–208. Boston: Boston University Press, 2002.

Benjamin, Walter. *Illuminations: Essays and Reflections*. 1968. Edited by Hannah Arendt. Boston: Mariner Books, 2019.

———. "Theses on the Philosophy of History." In Arendt, *Illuminations*, 196–209.

Berg, Allison. *Mothering the Race: Women's Narratives on Reproduction, 1890–1930*. Urbana: University of Illinois Press, 2002.

Berne, Patty. "Skin, Tooth, and Bone—the Basis of Our Movement Is People: A Disability Justice Primer." *Reproductive Health Matters* 25, no. 50 (May 2017): 149–50.

Bernstein, Robin. "Dances with Things: Material Culture and the Performance of Race." *Social Text* 27, no. 4 (Winter 2009): 67–94.

———. *Racial Innocence: Performing American Childhood from Slavery to Civil Rights*. New York: New York University Press, 2011.

———. "Signposts on the Road Less Taken: John Newton Hyde's Anti-racist Illustrations of African American Children." *J19: Journal of Nineteenth-Century Americanists* 1, no. 1 (2013): 97–119.

———. "Toys Are Good for Us: Why We Should Embrace the Integrated History of Children's Literature, Material Culture, and Play." *Children's Literature Association Quarterly* 38, no. 4 (2013): 458–63.

Berquin, M. Arnaud. *The Looking-Glass for the Mind, or, Intellectual Mirror: Being an Elegant Collection of the Most Delightful Little Stories and Interesting Tales; Chiefly translated from that much admired work L'ami des enfans, by M. Arnaud Berquin.* New York: D. Appleton, 1845. [Original English trans. ca. 1787]. American Antiquarian Society.

Berry, Daina Ramey. *The Price for Their Pound of Flesh: The Value of the Enslaved, from Womb to Grave, in the Building of a Nation.* Boston: Beacon Press, 2017.

Best, Stephen. *The Fugitive's Properties: Law and the Poetics of Possession.* Chicago: University of Chicago Press, 2004.

Betts, John Rickards. "P. T. Barnum and the Popularization of Natural History." *Journal of the History of Ideas* 20, no. 3 (1959): 353–68.

Betts, Tara. "A 21st-Century Introduction to Philippa Duke Schuyler's Adventures in Black and White." In *Adventures in Black and White*, by Philippa Duke Schuyler, edited with an introduction by Tara Betts, 1–8. New York: 2Leaf Press, 2018.

Blakely, Robert L, and Judith M. Harrington, eds. *Bones in the Basement: Postmortem Racism in Nineteenth-Century Medical Training.* Washington, DC: Smithsonian Institution Press, 1997.

Blanck, Emily. "Seventeen Eighty-Three: The Turning Point in the Law of Slavery and Freedom in Massachusetts." *New England Quarterly* 75, no. 1 (March 2022): 24–51.

Blight, David W. *Race and Reunion: The Civil War in American Memory.* Cambridge, MA: Harvard University Press, 2001.

Bloom, Allan. *Emile, or On Education, by Jean Jacques Rousseau.* New York: Basic Books, 1979.

Boas, George. *The Cult of Childhood.* London: Warburg Institute, 1966.

Bogdan, Robert. *Freak Show: Presenting Human Oddities for Amusement and Profit.* Chicago: University of Chicago Press. 1988.

Bohlender, Dorothy Gammel, and Frances Tarlton McCallum. *H. P. N. Gammel: Texas Bookman.* Waco: Texian Press, 1985.

Boster, Dea H. *African American Slavery and Disability: Bodies, Property, and Power in the Antebellum South.* New York: Routledge, 2013.

Bowditch, William. *White Slavery in the United States.* New York: American Tract Society, 1855. Hein Online.

Boyd, Julian P., et al. *The Papers of Thomas Jefferson*, vol. 14. Princeton, NJ: Princeton University Press, 1958.

Bradstreet, Anne. "An Author to Her Book." In *The Works of Anne Bradstreet*, edited by Jeannine Hensley, 221. Cambridge, MA: Belknap Press, 1967.

Brady, Mary Pat. *Scales of Captivity: Racial Capitalism and the Latinx Child*. Durham: Duke University Press, 2022.
Braudy, Leo. *The Frenzy of Renown: Fame and Its History*. New York: Oxford University Press, 1986.
Braun, Lundy. *Breathing Race into the Machine: The Surprising Career of the Spirometer from Plantation to Genetics*. Minneapolis: University of Minnesota Press, 2014.
Bremner, Robert. *Children and Youth in America: A Documentary History 1600–1865*. 3 vols. Cambridge, MA: Harvard University Press, 1970–74.
Brewer, Holly. *By Birth or Consent: Children, Law, and the Anglo-American Revolution in Authority*. Chapel Hill: University of North Carolina Press, 2007.
———. "Slavery, Sovereignty, and 'Inherited Blood': Reconsidering John Locke and the Origins of American Slavery." *American Historical Review* 122, no. 4 (2017): 1038–78.
———. "The Transformation of Domestic Law." In *Cambridge History of Law in America*. Vol. 1, *Early America*, edited by Michael Grossberg, 288–323. New York: Cambridge University Press, 2007.
Brinckerhoff, Isaac. *Advice to Freedmen*. New York: American Tract Society, 1864.
Broderick, Dorothy M. *The Image of the Black in Children's Fiction*. New York: R. R. Bowker, 1973.
Brodhead, Richard. "Sparing the Rod: Discipline and Fiction in Antebellum America." *Representations*, no. 21 (Winter 1988): 67–96.
Brodie, Janet. *Contraception and Abortion in Nineteenth Century America*. Ithaca: Cornell University Press, 1994.
Brody, Jennifer. *Impossible Purities: Blackness Femininity and Victorian Culture*. Durham: Duke University Press, 1998.
Brooks, Daphne. *Bodies in Dissent: Spectacular Performances of Race and Freedom, 1850–1910*. Durham: Duke University Press, 2006.
———. "Fraudulent Bodies / Fraught Methodologies." *Legacy* 24, no. 2 (2007): 306–14.
———. "Puzzling the Intervals: Blind Tom and the Poetics of the Sonic Slave Narrative." In *The Oxford Handbook of the African American Slave Narrative*, edited by John Ernest, 391–414. Oxford: Oxford University Press, 2014.
Brooks, Joanna. "Our Phillis, Ourselves." *American Literature* 82, no. 1 (March 2010): 1–28.
Brooks-Gunn, Jeanne, and Anna Duncan Johnson. "G. Stanley Hall's Contribution to Science, Practice, and Policy: The Child Study, Parent Education, and Child Welfare Movements." *History of Psychology* 9, no. 3 (2006): 247–58.
Brown, Eli F. *The House I Live In; or, An Elementary Physiology for Children in the Public Schools*. 1887. New York: Vann Antwerp, 1888. National Library of Medicine.
Brown, Gillian. *The Consent of the Governed: The Lockean Legacy in Early American Culture*. Cambridge, MA: Harvard University Press, 2001.
Brown, Jayna. *Babylon Girls: Black Women Performers and the Shaping of the Modern*. Durham: Duke University Press, 2008.
———. *Black Utopias: Speculative Life and the Music of Other Worlds*. Durham: Duke University Press, 2021.

———. "The Human Project: Utopia, Dystopia, and the Black Heroine in Children of Men and 28 Days Later." *Transition, an International Review* 110 (2012): 121–35.

Brown, Kathleen. *Good Wives, Nasty Wenches, and Anxious Patriarchs: Gender, Race, and Power in Colonial Virginia.* Chapel Hill: Published for Institute of Early American History and Culture by the University of North Carolina Press, 1996.

Brown, Ricardo. *Until Darwin: Science, Human Variety and the Origins of Race.* London: Pickering & Chatto, 2010.

Burnett, Frances Hodgson. *Little Lord Fauntleroy.* New York: Scribner's, 1886.

Burns, Sara. "Cartoons in Color: David Gilmour Blythe's Very Uncivil War." In *Seeing High and Low: Representing Social Conflict in American Visual Culture,* edited by Patricia Johnston, chap. 3. Berkeley: University of California Press, 2006.

Burstein, Andrew. *Sentimental Democracy: The Evolution of America's Romantic Self-Image.* New York: Hill and Wang, 1999.

Butchart, Ronald. *Schooling the Freed People: Teaching, Learning, and the Struggle for Black Freedom, 1861–1876.* Chapel Hill: University of North Carolina Press, 2010.

Butler, Octavia. *Parable of the Sower.* New York: Seven Stories Press, 1993.

———. "Positive Obsession." In *Octavia E. Butler: Kindred, Fledgling, Collected Stories.* New York: Library of America, 2021. [Originally published as "Birth of a Writer," *Essence Magazine,* 1989.]

Cahan, Emily. "Toward a Socially Relevant Science: Notes on the History of Child Development Research." In *When Science Encounters the Child: Education, Parenting, and Child Welfare in 20th-Century America,* 16–34. New York: Columbia Teachers College Press, 2006.

Calvert, Karin Lee Fishbeck. *Children in the House: The Material Culture of Early Childhood, 1600–1900.* Boston: Northeastern University Press, 1992.

Camp, Stephanie. *Closer to Freedom: Enslaved Women, and Everyday Resistance in the Plantation South.* Chapel Hill: University of North Carolina Press, 2004.

Campt, Tina. *Listening to Images.* Durham: Duke University Press, 2017.

Capshaw, Katharine, and Anna Mae Duane, eds. *Who Writes for Black Children? African American Children's Literature before 1900.* Minneapolis: University of Minnesota Press, 2017.

Capshaw, Katharine. "Childhood, the Body, and Race Performance: Early 20th-Century Etiquette Books for Black Children." *African American Review* 40, no. 4 (Winter 2006): 795–811.

———. *Children's Literature of the Harlem Renaissance.* Bloomington: Indiana University Press, 2004.

Carey, Roderick L. "A Cultural Analysis of the Achievement Gap Discourse: Challenging the Language and Labels Used in the Work of School Reform." *Urban Education* 49, no. 4 (2014): 440–68.

Carlson, Katherine L. "Little Lord Fauntleroy and the Evolution of American Boyhood." *Journal of the History of Childhood and Youth* 3, no. 1 (2010): 39–64.

Carretta, Vincent. *Phillis Wheatley: Biography of a Genius in Bondage*. Athens: University of Georgia Press, 2011.

———. *Phillis Wheatley: Complete Writings*. New York: Penguin, 2001.

Cartwright, Samuel. "Diseases and Peculiarities of the Negro." *New Orleans Medical and Surgical Journal*, May 1851, 691–716.

Cather, Willa. *My Antonia*. New York: Harcourt Mifflin, 1918.

Cavitch, Max. *American Elegy: The Poetry of Mourning from the Puritans to Whitman*. Minneapolis: University of Minnesota Press, 2007.

Cervenak, Sarah Jane. *Wandering: Philosophical Performances of Racial and Sexual Freedom*. Durham: Duke University Press, 2014.

Chambers, Terah T. Venzant, and Daniel D. Spikes. "'Tracking [Is] for Black People': A Structural Critique of Deficit Perspectives of Achievement Disparities." *Educational Foundations* 29, nos. 1–4 (Fall/Winter 2016): 1–13.

Chapman, Paul Davis. *Schools as Sorters: Lewis M. Terman, Applied Psychology, and the Intelligence Testing Movement*. New York: New York University Press, 1988.

Chatelain, Marcia. *South Side Girls: Growing Up in the Great Migration*. Durham: Duke University Press, 2015.

Child, Lydia Maria. *Antislavery Catechism*. Newburyport, MA: Charles Whipple, 1836.

———. *An Appeal in Favor of That Class of Americans Called Africans*. New York, 1836.

———. *The Freedman's Book*. Boston: Ticknor and Field, 1865.

———. "Mary French and Susan Easton." *Juvenile Miscellany* 6, no. 2 (May/June 1834). American Antiquarian Society, Historical Periodicals Collection, Readex.

Choy, Catherine Ceniza. *Global Families: A History of Asian International Adoption in America*. New York: New York University Press, 2013.

Cirillo, Vincent J. "Edward Bliss Foote: Pioneer American Advocate of Birth Control." *Bulletin of the History of Medicine* 47, no. 5. (September 1973): 471–79.

Clevenger, Shobal Vail. *The Evolution of Man and His Mind: A History and Discussion of the Evolution and Relation of the Mind and Body of Man and Animals*. Chicago: Evolution, 1903.

———. "An Infant Prodigy." *Alienist and Neurologist* 11, no. 2 (July 1890): 359–65.

Clifford, James. "On Collecting Art and Culture." In *The Predicament of Culture*, 215–52. Cambridge MA: Harvard University Press, 1988.

Clifton, Lucille. "i am accused of tending to the past." In *The Collected Poems of Lucille Clifton 1965–2010*, edited by Kevin Young, 327. Rochester, NY: BOA Editions, 2012.

Cobb, Jasmine Nichole. *Picture Freedom: Remaking Black Visuality in the Early Nineteenth Century America*. New York: New York University Press, 2015.

Cobden, John C. *The White Slaves of England*. Buffalo, NY: Derby, Orton and Mulligan, 1853.

The Code of the State of Georgia. Prepared by R. H. Clark, T. R. R. Cobb, and D. Irwin. Atlanta: John H. Seals, 1861.

Cohen, Cathy. "Deviance as Resistance: A New Research Agenda for the Study of Black Politics." *Du Bois Review: Social Science Research on Race* 1, no. 1 (2004): 27–45.

———. "Punks, Bulldaggers and Welfare Queens: The Radical Potential of Queer Politics?" *GLQ* 3, no. 4 (1996): 437–65.
Collins, Patricia Hill. "It's All in the Family: Intersections of Gender, Race, and Nation." *Hypatia* 13, no. 3 (Summer 1998): 62–82.
Cott, Nancy. "Passionlessness: An Interpretation of Victorian Sexual Ideology, 1790–1850." *Signs* 4, no. 2 (1978): 219–36.
Cox, Aimee Meredith. *Shapeshifters: Black Girls and the Choreography of Citizenship*. Durham: Duke University Press, 2015.
Crain, Patricia. *Reading Children: Literacy, Property, and the Dilemmas of Childhood in Nineteenth-Century America*. Philadelphia: University of Pennsylvania Press, 2016.
———. *The Story of A: The Alphabetization of America from the New England Primer to the Scarlet Letter*. Stanford: Stanford University Press, 2000.
Crenshaw, Kimberlé. *Black Girls Matter: Pushed Out, Overpoliced, and Underprotected*. New York: African American Policy Forum and Center for Intersectionality and Social Policy Studies, Columbia Law School, 2015.
———. "From Private Violence to Mass Incarceration: Thinking Intersectionally about Women, Race, and Social Control." *UCLA Law Review* 59, no. 6 (August 2012): 1418–73.
Crenshaw, Kimberlé W., Andrea J. Ritchie, Rachel Anspach, Rachel Gilmer, and Luke Harris. *Say Her Name: Resisting Police Brutality against Black Women*. New York: African American Policy Forum, Center for Intersectionality and Social Policy Studies, Columbia Law School, 2015.
Curran, Andrew. *Anatomy of Blackness: Science and Slavery in an Age of Enlightenment*. Baltimore: Johns Hopkins University Press, 2011.
Currell, Susan, and Christina Cogdell, eds. *Popular Eugenics: National Efficiency and American Mass Culture in the 1930s*. Athens: Ohio University Press, 2006.
Daniels, Christine, and Michael V. Kennedy, eds. *Over the Threshold: Intimate Violence in Early America*. New York: Routledge, 1999.
Da Silva, Denise Ferreira. "Toward a Black Feminist Poethics: The Question of Blackness toward the End of the World." *Black Scholar* 44, no. 2 (2014): 81–97.
Daston, Lorraine, and Katherine Park. *Wonder and the Order of Nature, 1150–1750*. New York: Zone Books, 1998.
Davidson, E. S., and L. T. Benjamin, Jr. "A History of the Child Study Movement in America." In *Historical Foundations of Educational Psychology*, edited by J. A. Glover and R. R. Ronning, 41–60. New York: Plenum Press, 1987.
Davidson, Jenny. *Breeding: A Partial History of the Eighteenth Century*. New York: Columbia University Press, 2009.
Davis, David Brion. *The Problem of Slavery in the Age of Revolution, 1770–1823*. Ithaca: Cornell University Press, 1975.
———. *The Problem of Slavery in Western Culture*. Ithaca: Cornell University Press, 1966.
Davis, Elizabeth Lindsay, ed. *Lifting as They Climb*. Washington, DC: National Association of Colored Women, 1933. ProQuest.

Davis, John, and M. Grace Baron. "A Celebrated Slave Pianist Coping with Stress." In *Stress and Coping with Autism*, edited by M. Grace Baron, L. P. Lipsitt, J. Groden, and G. Groden, chap. 5. New York: Oxford University Press, 2006.

Davis, Lennard. *Enforcing Normalcy: Disability, Deafness, and the Body*. New York: Verso, 1995.

Davis, Rebecca Harding. "Blind Tom." *Atlantic Monthly*, November 1862, 580–85.

Day, Caroline Bond. *A Study of Some Negro-White Families in the United States*. Cambridge, MA: Peabody Museum of Harvard University, 1932.

Dayton, Cornelia. "Lost Years Recovered: John Peters and Phillis Wheatley Peters in Middleton." *New England Quarterly* 94, no. 3 (September 2021): 309–51.

Dennett, Andrea Stulman. *Weird and Wonderful: The Dime Museum in America*. New York: New York University Press, 1997.

Dennis, Donna. *Licentious Gotham: Erotic Publishing and Its Prosecution in Nineteenth-Century New York*. Cambridge, MA: Harvard University Press, 2009.

Department of Education. Civil Rights Data Collection. *2013–2014 Gifted and Talented Enrollment Estimations*. http://ed.gov.

Department of the Interior, Census Office. *Report on the Defective, Dependent, and Delinquent Classes of the Population of the United States, as Returned at the Tenth Census* (June 1, 1880), by Frederick Howard Wines. Washington, DC: Government Printing Office, 1888.

De Rosa, Deborah C. *Domestic Abolitionism and Juvenile Literature, 1830–1865*. Albany: SUNY Press, 2003.

Deutsch, Helen, and Felicity Nussbaum, eds. *Defects: Engendering the Modern Body*. Ann Arbor: University of Michigan Press, 2000.

Dew, Thomas Roderick. "Abolition of Negro Slavery." *American Quarterly Review* 12 (1832): 189–265. Reprinted in *The Ideology of Slavery: Proslavery Thought in the Antebellum South, 1830–1860*, edited by Drew Gilpin Faust, 21–77. Baton Rouge: Louisiana State University Press, 1981.

Dickey, Bronwen. "She Was Killed by the Police. Why Were Her Bones in a Museum?" *New York Times*, October 19, 2022.

Dillon, Elizabeth Maddock. *The Gender of Freedom: Fictions of Liberalism and the Literary Public Sphere*. Stanford: Stanford University Press, 2004.

Dippold, Steffi. "The Wampanoag Word: John Eliot's Indian Grammar, the Vernacular Rebellion, and the Elegancies of Native Speech." *Early American Literature* 48, no. 3 (2013): 543–75.

Dixon, Ejeris, and Leah Lakshmi Piepzna Samarasinha. *Beyond Survival: Strategies and Stories from the Transformative Justice Movement*. Chico, CA: AK Press, 2020.

Dorey, Annette K. Vance. *Better Baby Contests: The Scientific Quest for Perfect Childhood Health in the Early Twentieth-Century*. Jefferson, NC: McFarland, 1999.

Dorr, Gregory Michael, and Angela Logan. "'Quality, Not Mere Quantity, Counts': Black Eugenics and the NAACP Baby Contests." In *A Century of Eugenics in America: From the Indiana Experiment to the Human Genome Era*, edited by Paul A. Lombardo, 68–92. Bloomington: Indiana University Press, 2011.

Douglass, Frederick. *The Life and Times of Frederick Douglass*. Hartford, CT: Park, 1882.
———. *My Bondage and My Freedom*. New York: Miller, Orton and Mulligan, 1855.
———. *Narrative in the Life of Frederick Douglass, An American Slave, Written by Himself*. Boston: Published at the Anti-slavery Office, 1845.
Douthwaite, Julia V. *The Wild Girl, Natural Man, and the Monster: Dangerous Experiments in the Age of Enlightenment*. Chicago: University of Chicago Press, 2002.
Dreier, Hannah. "Alone and Exploited, Migrant Children Work Brutal Jobs across the U.S." *New York Times*, February 28, 2023.
Duane, Anna Mae. *Suffering Childhood in Early America: Violence, Race, and the Making of the Child Victim*. Athens: University of Georgia Press, 2010.
Du Bois, W. E. B. "Black Folks and Birth Control." *Birth Control Review*, June 1932, 166–67.
———. "Black Mother." *Crisis* 5, no. 2 (December 1912): 78.
———. *Black Reconstruction in America, 1860–1880*. 1935. New York: Free Press, 1998.
———. "The Conservation of Races." In *Oxford W. E. B. Du Bois Reader*, edited by Eric J. Sundquist, 38–47. 1896. New York: Oxford University Press, 1996.
———. "A Negro Student at Harvard at the End of the 19th Century." *Massachusetts Review* 1, no. 3 (Spring 1960): 439–58.
———. *The Philadelphia Negro: A Social Study*. Philadelphia: Published for the University of Pennsylvania, 1899.
———. *The Souls of Black Folks*. Chicago: A. C. McClurg, 1903.
———. *The Talented Tenth: Excerpt from "The Negro Problem."* New York: James Pott, 1903.
Dugatkin, Lee Alan. *Mr. Jefferson and the Giant Moose: Natural History in Early America*. Chicago: University of Chicago Press, 2009.
Dugdale, Richard Louis. *The Jukes: A Study in Crime, Pauperism, Disease and Heredity*. 1877. New York: G. P. Putnam's Sons, 1910. Gale Cengage.
Edelman, Lee. "The Future Is Kid Stuff: Queer Theory, Disidentification, and the Death Drive." *Narrative* 6, no. 1 (1998): 18–30.
Edgeworth, Maria. *Idleness and Industry Exemplified in the History of James Preston and Lazy Lawrence*. Philadelphia: J. Johnson, 1802.
Edwards, Laura. *Gendered Strife and Confusion: The Political Culture of Reconstruction*. Urbana: University of Illinois Press, 1997.
———. "'The Marriage Covenant Is at the Foundation of All Our Rights': The Politics of Slave Marriages in North Carolina after Emancipation." *Law and History Review* 14, no. 1 (Spring 1996): 81–124.
Edwards, R. A. R. *Words Made Flesh: Nineteenth-Century Deaf Education and the Growth of Deaf Culture*. New York: New York University Press, 2012.
Ehrenreich, Barbara, and Deirdre English. *For Her Own Good: 150 Years of the Experts' Advice to Women*. Garden City, NY: Doubleday, 1979.
Elam, Harry Justin, and David Krasner, eds. *African-American Performance and Theater History: A Critical Reader*. New York: Oxford University Press, 2001.

Ellis, Cristin. *Antebellum Posthuman: Race and Materiality in the Mid-nineteenth Century*. New York: Fordham University Press, 2018.
Ellis, Jason. "'Inequalities of Children in Original Endowment': How Intelligence Testing Transformed Early Special Education in a North American City School System." *History of Education* 53 no. 4 (November 2013): 401–29.
English, Daylanne. *Unnatural Selections: Eugenics in American Modernism and the Harlem Renaissance*. Chapel Hill: University of North Carolina Press, 2004.
Esty, Jed. *Unseasonable Youth: Modernism, Colonialism, and the Fiction of Development*. New York: Oxford University Press, 2012.
Fabian, Ann. *The Skull Collectors: Race, Science, and America's Unburied Dead*. Chicago: University of Chicago Press, 2010.
Fairer, David, and Christine Gerard, eds. *Eighteenth Century Poetry: An Annotated Anthology*. 3rd ed. Chichester: Wiley Blackwell, 2015.
Fallace, Thomas. "The Savage Origins of Child-Centered Pedagogy, 1873–1913." *American Educational Research Journal* 52, no. 1 (February 2015): 73–103.
Fanon, Frantz. *Black Skin, White Masks*. Translated by Richard Philcox. New York: Grove Books, 2008.
Faust, Drew Gilpin, ed. *The Ideology of Slavery: Proslavery Thought in the Antebellum South, 1830–1860*. Baton Rouge: Louisiana State University Press, 1981.
Federici, Sylvia. *Caliban and the Witch: Women, the Body, and Primitive Accumulation*. New York: Autonomedia, 2004.
Feimster, Crystal. *Southern Horrors: Women and the Politics of Rape and Lynching*. Cambridge, MA: Harvard University Press, 2009.
Feld, Barry C. *The Evolution of the Juvenile Court: Race, Politics, and the Criminalizing of Juvenile Justice*. New York: New York University Press, 2017.
Feldstein, Ruth. *Motherhood in Black and White*. Ithaca: Cornell University Press, 2000.
Ferguson, Jeffrey. "The Newest Negro: George Schuyler's Intellectual Quest in the 1920s and Beyond." PhD diss., Harvard University, 1998.
———. *The Sage of Sugar Hill: George S. Schuyler and the Harlem Renaissance*. New Haven: Yale University Press, 2005.
Fett, Sharla. *Working Cures: Healing, Health, and Power on Southern Slave Plantations*. Chapel Hill: University of North Carolina Press, 2002.
Field, Corinne. *The Struggle for Equal Adulthood: Gender, Race, Age, and the Fight for Citizenship in Antebellum America*. Chapel Hill: University of North Carolina Press, 2014.
Fielder, Brigitte. "No Rights That Any Body Is Bound to Respect: Pets, Race, and African American Child Readers." In *Who Writes for Black Children? African American Children's Literature before 1900*, edited by Katharine Capshaw and Anna Mae Duane, 164–81. Minneapolis: University of Minnesota Press, 2017.
———. "'A Queer Semblance of a Baby': Alice Dunbar Nelson's Queer Futurity." *Legacy* 37, no. 1 (2020): 83–108.
———. *Relative Races: Genealogies of Interracial Kinship in Nineteenth-Century America*. Durham: Duke University Press, 2020.

Fineberg, Jonathan, ed. *Discovering Child Art: Essays on Childhood, Primitivism, and Modernism*. Princeton, NJ: Princeton University Press, 1998.

Fisk, Clinton Bowen. *Plain Counsels for Freedmen*. Boston: American Tract Society, 1866.

Fleetwood, Nicole R. *On Racial Icons: Blackness and the Public Imagination*. New Brunswick: Rutgers University Press, 2015.

———. *Troubling Vision: Performance, Visuality, and Blackness*. Chicago: University of Chicago Press, 2011.

Fliegelman, Jay. *Prodigals and Pilgrims: The American Revolution against Patriarchal Authority*. Cambridge: Cambridge University Press, 1982.

Fliter, John A. *Child Labor in America: The Epic Legal Struggle to Protect Children*. Lawrence: University Press of Kansas, 2018.

Foner, Eric. *Reconstruction: America's Unfinished Revolution, 1863–1877*. 1988. New York: Harper and Row, 2014.

Foote, Abram William. *The Foote Family: Comprising the Genealogy and History of Nathaniel Foote of Wethersfield, Connecticut*. Rutland, VT: Marble City Press-Tuttle, 1907. Ancestry Library Edition.

Foote, Edward Bliss, Sr. *Dr. Foote's Health Monthly*. New York: Murray Hill, 1876–96.

———. *Fable of the Spider and the Bees Verified by the Facts and Press and Pulpit Comments Which Should Command the Serious Attention of Every American Citizen*. New York: [New York National Defense Association], 1879. Harvard University.

———. *Home Cyclopaedia*. New York: Murray Hill, 1902.

———. *Medical Common Sense: Applied to the Causes, Prevention and Cure of Chronic Diseases and Unhappiness in Marriage*. Boston: Wentworth Hughes, 1858.

———. *Plain Home Talk: About the Human System—the Habits of Men and Women—the Prevention of Disease—Our Sexual Relations and Social Natures*. New York: Murray Hill, 1871.

———. *Science in Story: Sammy Tubbs, the Boy Doctor, and "Sponsie," the Troublesome Monkey*. 5 vols. New York: Murray Hill, 1874–75. American Antiquarian Society.

———. "To the Editor: In Reply to A. Comstock's Attack." *New York Times*, April 14, 1876. ProQuest.

Foote, Edward Bond, Jr. *Human Wonders, Freaks, and Diseases*. New York: Murray Hill, 1892.

———. *The Radical Remedy in Social Sciences, or Borning Better Babies through Regulating Reproduction by Controlling Conception*. New York: Murray Hill, 1886. National Library of Medicine Digital Collections.

———. *Tips on the Human Race: How to Win in the Lottery of Life*. New York: Murray Hill, 1894.

Ford, Donna Y., Brian L. Wright, Christopher J. P. Sewell, Gilman W. Whiting, and James L. Moore III. "The Nouveau Talented Tenth: Envisioning W. E. B. Du Bois in the Context of Contemporary Gifted and Talented Education." *Journal of Negro Education* 87, no. 3 (Summer 2018): 294–310.

Foucault, Michel. "The Lives of Infamous Men." 1977. In *Archives of Infamy*, edited by Elizabeth Wingrove, 67–84. Minneapolis: University of Minnesota Press, 2019.

———. *The Order of Things: An Archaeology of the Human Sciences*. 1970. New York: Vintage, 1994.
Foucault, Michel, and Arlette Farge. *Disorderly Families: Infamous Letters from the Bastille Archives*. 1982. Minneapolis: University of Minnesota Press, 2016.
Fox-Genovese, Elizabeth. *Within the Plantation Household: Black and White Women of the Old South*. Chapel Hill: University of North Carolina Press, 1988.
Franciscona, Marcel. "Paul Klee and Children's Art." In *Discovering Child Art: Essays on Childhood, Primitivism, and Modernism*. Princeton, NJ: Princeton University Press, 1998. 95–121.
Fraser, Nancy, and Linda Gordon. "A Genealogy of Dependency: Tracing a Keyword of the U.S. Welfare State." *Signs* 19 (1994): 309–36.
The Freedman's Spelling Book; The Freedman's Second Reader; The Freedman's Third Reader. Boston: American Tract Society, 1865–66. Facsimile of the first edition. New York: AMS Press, 1980.
French, Anna. "Raising Christian Children in Early Modern England: Salvation, Education, and the Family." *Theology* 116, no. 2 (2013): 93–102.
Fried, Stephen. *Rush: Revolution, Madness, and the Visionary Doctor Who Became a Founding Father*. New York: Crown, 2018.
Frost, Linda. *Never One Nation: Freaks, Savages, and Whiteness in U.S. Popular Culture, 1850–1877*. Minneapolis: University of Minnesota Press, 2005.
Frow, John, Melissa Hardy, and Vanessa Smith. "The Bildungsroman: Form and Transformations." *Textual Practice* 34, no. 12 (Fall 2020): 1905–10.
Fuentes, Annette. "Birth Control: From Womb Veils to Lysol." *New York Times*, July 12, 2001. ProQuest.
Fuss, Diana, ed. *Human, All Too Human*. New York: Routledge, 1996.
Gaines, Kevin. *Uplifting the Race: Black Leadership, Politics, and Culture in the Twentieth Century*. Chapel Hill: University of North Carolina Press, 1996.
Galton, Francis. *Hereditary Genius: An Inquiry into Its Laws and Consequences*. London: Macmillan, 1869.
Gammel, Hans Peter Neilsen. [Diary entry, undated]. Appears in "Not Worth Quarreling with My Sweet Wife." In Bohlender and McCallum, *H. P. N. Gammel*, 37–41. Waco: Texian Press, 1985.
———, ed. *Laws of Texas, 1822–1897*. Austin: Gammel, 1898.
Garland-Thomson, Rosemarie. *Extraordinary Bodies: Figuring Physical Disability in American Culture and Literature*. New York: Columbia University Press, 1996.
———. "Feminist Disability Studies." *Signs* 30, no. 2 (2005): 1557–87.
———. *Freakery: Cultural Spectacles of the Extraordinary Body*. New York: New York University Press, 1996.
Garvey, Ellen Gruber. *Writing with Scissors: American Scrapbooks from the Civil War to the Harlem Renaissance*. New York: Oxford University Press, 2013.
Gates, Henry Louis, Jr. *The Trials of Phillis Wheatley*. New York: Basic Books, 2003.
Gay, Roxane. "What Is a Country That Will Not Protect Its Children?" *New York Times*, May 25, 2022.

Gebeloff, Robert, Danielle Ivory, Bill Marsh, Allison McCann, and Albert Sun. "Childhood's Greatest Danger: The Data on Kids and Gun Violence." *New York Times*, December 14, 2022.

Generett, Gretchen Givens, and Amy M. Olson. "The Stories We Tell: How Merit Narratives Undermine Success for Urban Youth." *Urban Education* 55, no. 3 (2020): 394–423.

Gerhard, Jane. *Desiring Revolution: Second Wave Feminism and the Re-writing of American Sexual Thought, 1920–1982*. New York: Columbia University Press, 2002.

Gillespie, Alexandra, and Deidre Lynch. Introduction to *The Unfinished Book: Oxford Twenty-First Century Approaches to Literature*, edited by Alexandra Gillespie and Deidre Lynch, 1–15. New York: Oxford University Press, 2021.

Gilmore, Glenda. *Gender and Jim Crow: Women and the Politics of White Supremacy in North Carolina, 1896–1920*. Chapel Hill: University of North Carolina Press, 1996.

Gilmore, Ruth Wilson. *Abolition Geography: Essays toward Liberation*. New York: Verso, 2023.

Ginsberg, Lesley. "Of Babies, Beasts, and Bondage: Slavery and the Question of Citizenship in Antebellum Children's Literature." In *The American Child: A Cultural Studies Anthology*, edited by Caroline F. Levander and Carol J. Singley, 85–105. New Brunswick: Rutgers University Press, 2003.

Givens, Jarvis. *Fugitive Pedagogy: Carter G. Woodson and the Art of Black Teaching*. Cambridge, MA: Harvard University Press, 2021.

Glatt, Carra. "'To Perpetuate Her Name:' Appropriation and Autobiography in Margaretta Matilda Odell's Memoir of Phillis Wheatley." *Early American Literature* 55, no. 1 (2020): 145–76.

Glick, Megan. *Infrahumanisms: Culture, Science, and the Making of Modern Non/Personhood*. Durham: Duke University Press, 2018.

Glissant, Édouard. *Poetics of Relation*. Translated by Betsy Wing. Ann Arbor: University of Michigan Press, 1997.

Glymph, Thavolia. *Out of the House of Bondage: The Transformation of the Plantation Household*. New York: Cambridge University Press, 2003.

Goff, Phillip Atiba, Mathew Christian Jackson, Brook Di Leone, Carmen Marie Culotta, and Natalie DiTomasso. "The Essence of Innocence: Consequences of Dehumanizing Black Children." *Journal of Personality and Social Psychology* 106, no. 4 (2014): 526–45.

Golden, Janet, and Lynn Weiner. "Reading Baby Books: Medicine, Marketing, Money and the Lives of American Infants." *Journal of Social History* 44, no. 3 (Spring 2011): 667–87.

Goldsby, Jacqueline. *A Spectacular Secret: Lynching in American Life and Literature*. Chicago: University of Chicago Press, 2006.

Gordon, Linda. *Heroes of Their Own Lives: The Politics and History of Family Violence: Boston, 1880–1960*. New York: Viking Press, 1988.

———. *The Moral Property of Women: A History of Birth Control Politics in America*. Urbana: University of Illinois Press, 2002.

———. *Woman's Body, Woman's Right: A Social History of Birth Control in America.* New York: Grossman, 1976.

Gould, George M. *Anomalies and Curiosities of Medicine: Being an encyclopedic collection of rare and extraordinary cases, and of the most striking instances of abnormality in all branches of medicine and surgery, derived from an exhaustive research of medical literature from its origin to the present day.* Philadelphia: W. B. Saunders, 1897, 1898, 1900. Medical Heritage Library Online.

Gould, Stephen J. *The Mismeasure of Man.* New York: W. W. Norton, 1981.

———. *Ontogeny and Phylogeny.* Cambridge, MA: Belknap Press of Harvard University Press, 1977.

Gouttes, Jean des. *Philandre.* 1544. Edited by Pascale Mounier. Paris: Classiques Garnier, 2015.

Grant, Julia. *Raising Baby by the Book: The Education of American Mothers.* New Haven: Yale University Press, 1998.

Grant, Ruth, and Nathan Tarcov. "Some Thoughts concerning Education" and "Of the Conduct of Understanding." 1693, 1706. By John Locke. Edited by Ruth W. Grant and Nathan Tarcov. Cambridge: Hackett, 1996.

Green, Christopher D. "Hall's Developmental Theory and Haeckel's Recapitulationism." *European Journal of Developmental Psychology* 12, no. 6 (2015): 655–56.

Green, Hilary. *Educational Reconstruction: African American Schools in the Urban South, 1865–1890.* New York: Fordham University Press, 2016.

Greenberg, Cheryl Lynn, Jacqueline M. Moore, and Nina Mjagkij. *To Ask for an Equal Chance: African Americans in the Great Depression.* Lanham, MD: Rowman & Littlefield, 2009.

Greenblatt, Stephen. *Marvelous Possessions: The Wonder of the New World.* Chicago: University of Chicago Press, 1991.

Griffin, Farah Jasmine. *Read until You Understand: The Profound Wisdom of Black Life and Literature.* New York: W. W. Norton, 2021.

Grossberg, Michael. "Children's Legal Rights? A Historical Look at a Legal Paradox." In *Children at Risk in America: History, Concepts, and Public Policy*, edited by Roberta Wollons, 111–40. Albany: SUNY Press, 1993.

———. *Governing the Hearth: Law and the Family in Nineteenth-Century America.* Chapel Hill: University of North Carolina Press, 1985.

———. *A Judgment for Solomon: The d'Hauteville Case and Legal Experience in Antebellum America.* New York: Cambridge University Press, 1996.

———. "Who Gets the Child? Custody, Guardianship, and the Rise of a Judicial Patriarchy in Nineteenth-Century America." *Feminist Studies* 9, no. 2 (Summer 1983): 235–60.

Gubar, Marah. *Artful Dodgers: Reconceiving the Golden Age of Children's Literature.* New York: Oxford University Press, 2009.

———. "The Cult of the Child and the Controversy over Child Actors." In *Artful Dodgers: Reconceiving the Golden Age of Children's Literature*, chap. 5. New York: Oxford University Press, 2009.

———. "Entertaining Children of All Ages: Nineteenth-Century Popular Theater as Children's Theater." *American Quarterly* 66, no. 1 (2014): 1–34.

———. "Innocence." In *Keywords for Children's Literature*, 2nd ed., edited by Nina Christensen and Philip Nel, 105–9. New York: New York University Press, 2021.

———. "Risky Business: Talking about Children in Children's Literary Criticism." *Children's Literature Association Quarterly* 38, no. 4 (Winter 2013): 450–57.

———. "Who Watched *The Children's Pinafore*? Age Transvestism on the Nineteenth-Century Stage." *Victorian Studies* 54, no. 3 (2012): 410–26.

Guerrasio, Venetia M. "Dissecting the Pennsylvania Anatomy Act: Laws, Bodies, and Science, 1880–1960." PhD diss., University of New Hampshire, 2007.

Gumbs, Alexis Pauline, China Martens, and Mai'a Williams, eds. *Revolutionary Mothering: Love on the Front Lines*. Oakland: PM Press, 2016.

Hackley, E. Azalia. *The Colored Girl Beautiful*. Kansas City, MO: Burton, 1916.

Hadden, Sally E. "The Fragmented Laws of Slavery in the Colonial and Revolutionary Eras." In *Cambridge History of Law in America*. Vol. 1, *Early America*, edited by Michael Grossberg, 253–87. New York: Cambridge University Press, 2007.

Hahn, Steven. *A Nation under Our Feet: Black Political Struggles in the Rural South from Slavery to the Great Migration*. Cambridge, MA: Belknap Press of Harvard University Press, 2003.

Haley, Sarah. *No Mercy Here: Gender, Punishment, and the Making of Jim Crow Modernity*. Chapel Hill: University of North Carolina Press, 2016.

Hall, Catherine. "Gendering Property, Racing Capital." *History Workshop* 78, no. 1 (2014): 28–29.

Hall, G. Stanley. *Adolescence: Its Psychology and Its Relations to Physiology, Anthropology, Sociology, Sex, Crime, Religion, and Education*. 2 vols. New York: Appleton, 1904.

———. *The Contents of Children's Minds on Entering School*. 1883. New York: E. L. Kellogg, 1893.

———. "Corporal Punishments." *New York Education* 3 (November 1899): 163–65.

———. "Editorial" and "Foreign Miscellanies." *The Pedagogical Seminary: An International Record of Educational Literature, Institutions, and Progress* 1, no. 1 (1891).

———. "Moral Education and Will-Training." *Pedagogical Seminary* 2, no. 1 (1892): 72–89.

———. "Universities and the Training of Professors." *Forum* 17 (May 1894): 297–309.

Hall's Journal of Health. "A Walking Encyclopedia." 36, no. 2 (February 1889). Gale Artemis.

Halperin, Edward C. "The Poor, the Black, and the Marginalized as the Source of Cadavers in United States Anatomical Education." *Clinical Anatomy* 20 (2007): 489–95.

Hammond, James Henry. "Hammond's Letters on Slavery." In *The Pro-slavery Argument: As Maintained by the Most Distinguished Writers of the Southern States*, 99–174. Charleston: Walker, Richards, 1852.

Hand-Book of the Wonderful Boy, a Few Things of What the Little Blind Two Year Old Boy, Prof. Oscar Moore, Can Tell You. Austin: Eugene Von Boeckmann, 1888. Shobal Vail Clevenger Papers, 1864–1924. US National Library of Medicine.

Hanke, Lewis. *All Mankind Is One: A Study of the Disputation between Bartolomé de Las Casas and Juan Ginés de Sepúlveda in 1550 on the Intellectual and Religious Capacity of the American Indians.* DeKalb: Northern Illinois University Press, 1974.

Hardy, Marjorie. *Wag and Puff.* Chicago: Wheeler, 1934.

Harley, Sharon. "For the Good of Family and Race: Gender, Work, and Domestic Roles in the Black Community, 1880–1930." *Signs* 15, no. 2 (Winter 1990): 336–49.

Harper, Frances Ellen Watkins. "Enlightened Motherhood." Speech before the Brooklyn Literary Society, 1892.

Harper, William. "Harper's Memoir." In *The Pro-slavery Argument: As Maintained by the Most Distinguished Writers of the Southern States.* Charleston: Walker, Richards, 1852.

———. "Memoir on Slavery, Read before the Society for the Advancement of Learning of South Carolina at Its Annual Meeting at Columbia, 1837." Charleston: James S. Burges, 1838. Reprinted in *The Ideology of Slavery: Proslavery Thought in the Antebellum South, 1830–1860*, edited by Drew Gilpin Faust, 78–135. Baton Rouge: Louisiana State University Press, 1981.

Harris, Cheryl. "Whiteness as Property." *Harvard Law Review* 106, no. 8 (June 1993): 1707–91.

Harris, Leslie M. *In the Shadow of Slavery: African Americans in New York City, 1626–1863.* Chicago: University of Chicago Press, 2003.

Hartman, Saidiya. *Scenes of Subjection: Terror, Slavery, and Self-Making in Nineteenth Century America.* New York: Oxford University Press, 1997.

———. "Venus in Two Acts." *Small Axe* 26 (June 2008): 1–14.

———. *Wayward Lives, Beautiful Experiments: Intimate Histories of Social Upheaval.* New York: W. W. Norton, 2019.

Hatch, Kristen. *Shirley Temple and the Performance of Girlhood.* Newark, NJ: Rutgers University Press, 2015.

Hayes, Kevin. *A Colonial Woman's Bookshelf.* Knoxville: University of Tennessee Press, 1996.

Haywood, Chanta. "Constructing Childhood: The Christian Recorder and Literature for Black Children, 1854–1865." *African American Review* 36, no. 3 (2002): 417–28.

Herndon, Lisa. "Court Records from Sojourner Truth's 1828 Legal Battle to Free Her Son from Enslavement Part of 1-Day Display at Schomburg Center." September 29, 2022, New York Public Library. http://nypl.org.

Hicks, Cheryl. *Talk with You like a Woman: African American Women, Justice, and Reform in New York, 1890–1935.* Chapel Hill: University of North Carolina Press, 2010.

Higginbotham, Evelyn Brooks. *Righteous Discontent: The Women's Movement in the Black Baptist Church.* Cambridge, MA: Harvard University Press, 1993.

Higgins, Dorothy. [Interview with Dr. Harvey Zorbaugh.] "Gifted Children." *New York Herald Tribune*, January 9, 1938. ProQuest.

Higonnet, Anne. *Pictures of Innocence: The History and Crisis of Ideal Childhood.* London: Thames and Hudson, 1998.

Hillard, George S., and Loomis Joseph Campbell. *The Primer, or, First Reader.* New York: William Ware, 1864. Gale Cengage.

Hilton, Leon J. "Avante's Law: Autism, Wandering, and the Racial Surveillance of Neurological Difference." *African American Review* 50, no. 2 (Summer 2017): 221–35.
Hindman, Hugh D. *Child Labor: An American History.* Armonk, NY: M. E. Sharpe, 2002.
Hochman, Barbara. *Uncle Tom's Cabin and the Reading Revolution: Race, Literacy, Childhood, and Fiction, 1851–1911.* Amherst: University of Massachusetts Press, 2011.
Hodgson, Lucia. "Infant Muse: Phillis Wheatley and the Revolutionary Rhetoric of Childhood." *Early American Literature* 49, no. 3 (2014): 663–82.
Hoefnagel, Richard. "Toxic Effects of Atropine and Homatropine Eye-Drops in Children." *New England Journal of Medicine* 264, no. 4 (1961): 168–71.
Hoffmann, Heinrich. *The English Struwwelpeter, or, Pretty Stories and Funny Pictures.* London: Routledge & K. Paul, 1909.
———. *The English Struwwelpeter: Slovenly Peter.* Leipsic: Friedrich Volckmar, 1848.
———. *The Inky Boys. Peter Prim's Series.* New York: McLoughlin Brothers, 1867. American Antiquarian Society.
———. *Laughter Book for Little Folks.* New York: James Miller, ca. 1870. American Antiquarian Society.
———. *A Laughter Book for Little Folks: With a Profusion of Humorous Engravings.* Philadelphia: Davis Porter, ca. 1865–66. American Antiquarian Society.
———. *A Laughter Book for Very Little People.* Philadelphia: W. P. Hazard, 1851. Harvard University Digitized Collections.
———. *Lustige Geschichten und drollige Bilder: Mit 15 schön kolorirten Taflen für Kinder von 3–6 Jahren.* Frankfurt: Literarische Anstalt, J. Rütten, 1845.
———. *Slovenly Peter, or, Pleasant Stories and Funny Pictures.* Philadelphia: W. P. Hazard, 1851. Harvard University Digitized Collections.
———. *Slovenly Peter Reformed: Showing How He Became a Neat Scholar.* Philadelphia: Willis P. Hazard, 1853. Beinecke Rare Book and Manuscript Library.
———. *Strewel Peter: A Picture Book for Boys and Girls.* New York: McLoughlin Brothers, 1898. Gale Cengage.
Hogan, John D. "G. Stanley Hall and the Journal of Genetic Psychology: A Note." *Journal of Genetic Psychology* 177, no. 6 (October 2016): 191–94.
Hogarth, Rana. *Medicalizing Blackness: Making Racial Difference in the Atlantic World, 1780–1840.* Chapel Hill: University of North Carolina Press, 2015.
Hole, Robert. "Incest, Consanguinity and a Monstrous Birth in Rural England, January 1600." *Social History* 25, no. 2 (2000): 183–99.
Holland, Charlie. *Strange Feats and Clever Turns: Remarkable Specialty Acts in Variety, Vaudeville and Sideshows at the Turn of the Twentieth Century as Seen by Their Contemporaries.* London: Holland and Palmer, 1998.
Hollingworth, Leta S. *Gifted Children: Their Nature and Nurture.* New York: Macmillan, 1926.
Hooton, Ernest Albert. *Apes, Men, and Morons.* New York: G. P. Putnam's Sons, 1937.
———. *Twilight of Man.* New York: Putnam's Sons, 1939.
———. *Up from the Ape.* New York: Macmillan, 1931.

Horwitz, Morton J. *The Transformation of American Law, 1780–1860*. Cambridge, MA: Harvard University Press, 1977.

[Howard, William P.] *Mother Dear Mother, I Still Think of Thee: Sung by Blind Tom at His Popular Concerts with Greatest Success*. London: Hopwood and Crew, 1867. Harvard Theatre Collection.

Hsu, Madeline Y. *Good Immigrants: How Yellow Peril Became the Model Minority*. Princeton, NJ: Princeton University Press, 2017.

Hughey, Matthew W. "Backstage Discourse and the Reproduction of White Masculinities." *Sociological Quarterly* 52, no. 1 (Winter 2011): 132–53.

Hulbert, Ann. *Off the Charts: The Hidden Lives and Lessons of American Child Prodigies*. New York: Knopf, 2018.

"Human Wonders: The Blind Baby, Oscar Moore." *Buchanan's Journal of Man* 3, no. 1 (February 1889): 24–27.

Humphrey, David C. "Dissection and Discrimination: The Social Origins of Cadavers in America, 1760–1915." *Bulletin of the New York Academy of Medicine* 49, no. 9 (1973): 819–27.

Hunter, Tera. *Bound in Wedlock: Slave and Free Black Marriage in the Nineteenth Century*. Cambridge, MA: Belknap Press of Harvard University Press, 2017.

———. *To 'Joy My Freedom: Southern Black Women's Lives and Labors after the Civil War*. Cambridge, MA: Harvard University Press, 1997.

Hunt-Kennedy, Stefanie. *Between Fitness and Death: Disability and Slavery in the Caribbean*. Urbana: University of Illinois Press, 2020.

Hyde, James Nevins. *Early Medical Chicago: An Historical Sketch of the First Practitioners of Medicine: With the Present Faculties, and Graduates since Their Organization, of the Medical Colleges of Chicago*. Chicago: Fergus Printing Company, 1879. National Library of Medicine, Digital Collections.

Ibrahim, Habiba. *Black Age: Oceanic Lifespans and the Time of Black Life*. New York: New York University Press, 2021.

Illinois Board of State Commissioners of Public Charities. *Special Report of an Investigation of the Management of the Cook County Hospital for the Insane by the State Commissioners of Public Charities*. Springfield, IL: H. W. Rokker, State Printer and Binder, 1886.

Irving, Kathryn. "'Happy and Useful': Educating Children with Disabilities in Nineteenth-Century America." PhD diss., Yale University, 2016.

Isani, Mukhtar Ali. "Contemporaneous Reception of Phillis Wheatley: Newspaper and Magazine Notices during the Years of Fame, 1765–1774." *Journal of Negro History* 8 (Autumn 2000): 260–73.

Ivy, Nicole. "Bodies of Work: A Meditation on Medical Imaginaries and Enslaved Women." *Souls* 18, no. 1 (January–March 2016): 11–31.

Jackson, Zakiyyah Iman. *Becoming Human: Matter and Meaning in an Antiblack World*. New York: New York University Press, 2020.

Jacobson, Matthew Frye. *Barbarian Virtues: The United States Encounters Foreign Peoples at Home and Abroad, 1876–1917*. New York: Hill and Wang, 2000.

———. *Whiteness of a Different Color: European Immigrants and the Alchemy of Race.* Cambridge, MA: Harvard University Press, 1998.

James, Erica Moiah. "Every Nigger Is a Star: Reimagining Blackness from Post–Civil Rights America to the Postindependence Caribbean." *Black Camera* 8, no. 1 (Fall 2016): 55–83.

Janeway, James [and Cotton Mather]. *A Token for Children: Being an exact account of the conversion, holy and exemplary lives and joyful death of several young children. By James Janeway, Minister of the Gospel. To which is added, A token for the children of New-England.* Printed and sold by Z. Fowle, in Back-Street, near the Mill-Bridge, 1771. Gale Eighteenth Century Collections Online.

Jarvis, Edward. *Primary Physiology for Schools.* Philadelphia: Thomas, Cowperthwait, 1850. National Library of Medicine Digital Collections.

Jeffers, Honorée Fanonne. *The Age of Phillis.* Middleton, CT: Wesleyan University Press, 2020.

Jefferson, Thomas. *Notes on the State of Virginia; with the appendixes—complete. To which is subjoined, a sublime and argumentative dissertation on Mr. Jefferson's religious principles.* 1780. Baltimore: Printed by W. Pechin, Corner of Water & Gay-Streets, 1800. Gale Eighteenth Century Collections Online.

Jenco, Leigh K., and Jonathan Chappell. "Introduction: History from between and the Global Circulations of the Past in Asia and Europe, 1600–1950." *Historical Journal* 64, no. 1 (2021): 1–16.

Jensen-Moulton, Stephanie. "Finding Autism in the Compositions of a 19th-Century Prodigy: Reconsidering 'Blind Tom' Wiggins." In *Sounding off: Theorizing Disability in Music*, edited by Neil Lerner and Joseph N. Straus, 199–215. New York: Routledge, 2006.

———. "'Specimens' and 'Peculiar Idiosyncrasies': Songs of 'Blind Tom' Wiggins." *American Music Review* 40, no 2 (Spring 2011): 1–5.

Johnson, Lillian. "I Met Philippa Schuyler and Was Immediately Conquered!" *Baltimore Afro-American*, June 8, 1940. ProQuest.

Johnson, Walter. *Soul by Soul: Life in the Antebellum Slave Market.* Cambridge, MA: Harvard University Press, 1999.

Jolly, Jennifer L. *A History of Gifted Education.* New York: Routledge, 2018.

Jones, Catherine. *Intimate Reconstructions: Children in Postemancipation Virginia.* Charlottesville: University of Virginia Press, 2015.

———. "Ties That Bind, Bonds That Break: Children in the Reorganization of Households in Postemancipation Virginia." *Journal of Southern History* 76, no. 1 (February 2010): 71–106.

Jones, Jacqueline. *Labor of Love, Labor of Sorrow: Black Women, Work, and the Family, from Slavery to the Present.* New York: Basic Books, 1985.

Jones, Jean Yarvis, and Jan Fowler. *Child Abuse: History, Legislation and Issues, Congressional Report, 79–257 ED.* Washington, DC: Library of Congress, 1980.

Jones, Martha S. *All Bound up Together: The Woman Question in African American Public Culture, 1830–1900.* Chapel Hill: University of North Carolina Press, 2007.

———. *Birthright Citizens: A History of Race and Rights in Antebellum America.* New York: Cambridge University Press, 2018.
Jordan, June. "The Difficult Miracle of Black Poetry in America." In *Some of Us Did Not Die: New and Selected Essays by June Jordan.* New York: Basic/Civitas, 2002.
———. *Technical Difficulties: African American Notes on the State of the Union.* New York: Pantheon, 1992.
Journal of Negro Education. "The Physical and Mental Abilities of the American Negro." 3, no. 3 (July 1934): 317–18.
Juang, Linda P. "Deconstructing the Myth of the 'Tiger Mother': An Introduction to the Special Issue on Tiger Parenting, Asian-Heritage Families, and Child/Adolescent Well-Being." *Asian American Journal of Psychology* 4, no. 1 (2013): 1–6.
The Juvenile Story-Teller, a Collection of Moral Tales: Adorned with Cuts. New Haven: John Babcock and Son, 1819. Readex, Early American Imprints.
Kafai, Shaydah. *Crip Kinship: The Disability Justice and Art Activism of Sins Invalid.* Vancouver: Arsenal Pulp Press, 2021.
Kant, Immanuel. "What Is Enlightenment?" In *Foundations of the Metaphysics of Morals: And, What Is Enlightenment?* Translated by Lewis White Beck. 1784. Upper Saddle River, NJ: Prentice Hall, 1997.
Kaplan, Carla. *Miss Anne in Harlem: The White Women of the Harlem Renaissance.* New York: Harper Collins, 2013.
Keller, Helen. *The Story of My Life.* New York: Doubleday, Page, 1903.
Kelley, Mary. *Learning to Stand and Speak: Women, Education, and Public Life in America's Republic.* Chapel Hill: University of North Carolina Press, 2006.
Kerber, Linda. "The Republican Mother: Women and the Enlightenment—an American Perspective." *American Quarterly* 28 (1976): 187–205.
———. *Women of the Republic: Intellect and Ideology in Revolutionary America.* Chapel Hill: University of North Carolina Press, 1980.
Key, Ellen. *The Century of the Child.* 1900. New York: G. P. Putnam and Sons, 1909.
Keyser, Catherine. *Artificial Color: Modern Food and Racial Fictions.* New York: Oxford University Press, 2018.
Kincaid, James. *Child Loving: The Erotic Child and Victorian Culture.* New York: Routledge, 1992.
King, Wilma. *Stolen Childhood: Slave Youth in Nineteenth Century America.* 2nd ed. Bloomington: Indiana University Press, 2011.
Kirby, Kristen Page. "D.C.'s Library Foundation Is Hiding Provocative Books around the City. It's Up to You to Find Them." *Washington Post,* August 31, 2017. http://washingtonpost.com.
Kline, Wendy. *Building a Better Race: Gender, Sexuality, and Eugenics from the Turn of the Century to the Baby Boom.* Berkeley: University of California Press, 2001.
Kohli, Rita, Marcos Pizarro, and Arturo Nevárez. "The 'New Racism' of K–12 Schools: Centering Critical Research on Racism." *Review of Research in Education* 41 (March 2017): 182–202.

Kolp, John. *Gentlemen and Freeholders: Electoral Politics in Colonial Virginia*. Baltimore: Johns Hopkins University Press, 1998.
Kottick, Edward L. "Jacob Kirkman: Harpsichord Maker to Her Majesty." *Early Keyboard Journal* 31 (2014): 178–82.
Krentz, Christopher. "A 'Vacant Receptacle'? Blind Tom, Cognitive Difference, and Pedagogy." *PMLA* 120, no. 2 (2005): 552–57.
Kromidas, Maria. "'Agent of Revolutionary Thought': Bambara and Black Girlhood for a Poetics of Being and Becoming Human." *Jeunesse, Jeunesse: Young People, Texts, Cultures* 11, no. 1 (Summer 2019): 19–37.
———. "Towards the Human, after the Child of Man: Seeing the Child Differently in Teacher Education." *Curriculum Inquiry* 49, no. 1 (2019): 65–89.
La Courreye Blecki, Catherine, and Karin Wulf. *Milcah Martha Moore's Book: A Commonplace Book from Revolutionary America*. University Park: Pennsylvania State University Press, 1997.
Ladd-Taylor, Molly. *Fixing the Poor: Eugenic Sterilization and Child Welfare in the Twentieth Century*. Baltimore: Johns Hopkins University Press, 2015.
Largent, Mark A., and Georgina M. Montgomery, eds. *A Companion to the History of American Science*. Chichester: John Wiley & Sons, 2016.
Leeb, Rebecca T., Leonard J. Paulozzi, Cindi Melanson, Thomas R. Simon, and Ileana Arias. *Child Maltreatment Surveillance: Uniform Definitions for Public Health and Recommended Data Elements, Version 1*. Atlanta: Center for Disease Control and Prevention, National Center for Injury Prevention and Control, 2008.
Lennox, Charlotte. *Philander: A Dramatic Pastoral*. London: Printed for A. Millar, in the Strand, 1758.
Lerer, Seth. *Children's Literature: A Reader's History from Aesop to Harry Potter*. Chicago: University of Chicago Press, 2008.
Lesnik-Oberstein, Karín. "Introduction: Voice, Agency and the Child." In *Children in Culture, Revisited*, edited by Karín Lesnik-Oberstein, 1–17. New York: Palgrave Macmillan, 2011.
Levander, Caroline. *Cradle of Liberty: Race, the Child, and National Belonging from Thomas Jefferson to W. E. B. Du Bois*. Durham: Duke University Press, 2006.
Lewis, Robert. *From Traveling Show to Vaudeville: Theatrical Spectacle in America, 1830–1910*. Baltimore: Johns Hopkins University Press, 2003.
Lewis, Sophie. *Abolish the Family: A Manifesto for Care and Liberation*. London: Verso, 2022.
———. *Full Surrogacy Now: Feminism against Family*. New York: Verso, 2019.
Lindey, Sara. "Sentimental and Redemptive Girlhood in the Abolitionist Adaptation of Maria Susanna Cummins's *The Lamplighter*." *Children's Literature Association Quarterly* 47, no. 1 (Spring 2018): 4–27.
Lippert, Amy. "The Visual Pedagogy of Reform: White Slavery in America." *Journal of Urban History* 46, no. 4 (March 2019): 854–88.
Little Miss Consequence. New York: McLoughlin Brothers, ca. 1859–62.

Locke, John. *An Essay concerning Human Understanding*. 1690. Edited with an introduction by Peter H. Nidditch. New York: Oxford University Press, 1975.
———. *Some Thoughts concerning Education and of the Conduct of the Understanding*. 1693–1706. Edited with an introduction by Ruth W. Grant and Nathan Tarcov. Cambridge: Hackett, 1996.
———. "*Two Treatises on Government*" and "*A Letter Concerning Toleration*." 1689. Edited by Ian Shapiro. New Haven: Yale University Press, 2003.
Lombardo, Paul, ed. *A Century of Eugenics in America: From the Indiana Experiment to the Human Genome Era*. Bloomington: Indiana University Press, 2011.
———. *Three Generations, No Imbeciles: Eugenics, the Supreme Court, and Buck v. Bell*. Baltimore: Johns Hopkins University Press, 2008.
Long, Margaret Geneva. *Doctoring Freedom: The Politics of African American Medical Care in Slavery and Emancipation*. Chapel Hill: University of North Carolina Press, 2012.
Longmore, Paul K., and Lauri Umansky, eds. *The New Disability History: American Perspectives*. New York: New York University Press, 2001.
Longshore, Joseph Skelton. *Announcement and catalogue of the Penn Medical University of Philadelphia, male and female departments, for 1857–58: With the valedictory address to the graduating classes, delivered at the public commencement, held in the Musical Fund Hall, May 30th, 1857*. Philadelphia: Printed by M. P. Williams, 1857. National Library of Medicine Digitized Collections.
Lott, Eric. *Love and Theft: Blackface Minstrelsy and the American Working Class*. New York: Oxford University Press, 1993.
Loveland, Jeff. "Georges-Louis Leclerc de Buffon's *Histoire Naturelle* in English, 1775–1815." *Archives of Natural History* 31, no. 2 (2004): 214–35.
Lovett, Laura L. *Conceiving the Future: Pronatalism, Reproduction, and the Family in the U.S., 1890–1938*. Chapel Hill: University of North Carolina Press, 2007.
Lowe, Lisa. *The Intimacies of Four Continents*. Durham: Duke University Press, 2015.
Luczak, Ewa. *Breeding and Eugenics in the American Literary Imagination: Heredity Rules in the Twentieth Century*. New York: Palgrave Macmillan, 2015.
MacCann, Donnarae. *White Supremacy in Children's Literature: Characterizations of African Americans, 1830–1900*. New York: Garland Publishers, 1998.
Mackey, Nathaniel. "Other: From Noun to Verb." *Representations* 39 (Summer 1992): 51–70.
Mallipeddi, Ramesh. *Spectacular Suffering: Witnessing Slavery in the Eighteenth-Century British Atlantic*. Charlottesville: University of Virginia Press, 2016.
Mansfield, Katherine Cumings. "Giftedness as Property: Troubling Whiteness, Wealth, and Gifted Education in the United States." *International Journal of Multicultural Education* 17, no. 1 (2015): 1–18.
Margolin, Leslie. "The Emergence of Gifted Children." *Social Problems* 40, no. 4 (November 1993): 510–32.
Markel, Howard, and Alexandra Minna Stern, *Formative Years: Children's Health in the United States, 1880–2000*. Ann Arbor: University of Michigan Press, 2002.

Marshall, Jubilee. "Race, Death, and Public Health in Early Philadelphia, 1750–1793." *Pennsylvania History* 87, no. 2 (2020): 364–89.

Marten, James, ed. *Children in Colonial America*. New York: New York University Press, 2006.

Mason, Julian. *The Poems of Phillis Wheatley*. Edited and with an introduction by Julian D. Mason Jr. Chapel Hill: University of North Carolina Press, 1988.

Mason, Mary Ann. *From Father's Property to Children's Rights: The History of Child Custody in the United States*. New York: Columbia University Press, 1994.

Mather, Cotton. *The Negro Christianized: An Essay to Excite and Assist the Good Work, the Instruction of Negro-Servants in Christianity*. Boston: Printed by B. Green, 1706. Gale Eighteenth Century Collections Online.

May, Caroline. *The American Female Poets: With Biographical and Critical Notices*. Philadelphia: Lindsay and Blakiston, 1859.

Mayes, Keith. *The Unteachables: Disability Rights and the Invention of Black Special Education*. Minneapolis: University of Minnesota Press, 2022.

Mazzei, Patricia, and Anemona Hartocollis. "Florida Rejects AP African American Studies Class." *New York Times*, January 19, 2023.

Mbembe, Achille. *Critique of Black Reason*. Durham: Duke University Press, 2017.

McArthur, Benjamin. "'Forbid Them Not': Child Actor Labor Laws and Political Activism in the Theatre." *Theatre Survey* 36 (1996): 63–80.

McCann, Alfred Watterson. *The Science of Eating: How to Ensure Stamina, Endurance, Vigor, Strength, and Health in Infancy, Youth and Age*. New York: George H. Doran Company, 1918.

McClintock, Anne. *Imperial Leather: Race, Gender, and Sexuality in the Colonial Contest*. New York: Routledge, 1995.

———. "The White Family of Man." In McClintock, *Imperial Leather*, chap. 6.

McCurry, Stephanie. *Masters of Small Worlds: Yeoman Households, Gender Relations, and the Political Culture of the Antebellum South Carolina Low Country*. New York: Oxford University Press, 1995.

McDougald, Elise Johnson. "The Task of Negro Womanhood." In *The New Negro: An Interpretation*, edited by Alain Locke, 369–84. New York: A. and C. Boni, 1925.

McGill, Meredith. "Books on the Loose." In Gillespie and Lynch, *Unfinished Book*, 79–93. New York: Oxford University Press, 2021.

McKittrick, Katherine. *Dear Science: And Other Stories*. Durham: Duke University Press, 2021.

———. *Demonic Grounds: Black Women and Cartographies of Struggle*. Minneapolis: University of Minnesota Press, 2006.

———. "Science Quarrels Sculpture: The Politics of Reading Sarah Baartman." *Mosaic* 43, no. 2 (June 2010): 113–30.

McMillan, Uri. *Embodied Avatars: Genealogies of Black Feminist Art and Performance*. New York: New York University Press, 2015.

McRuer, Robert. *Crip Theory: Cultural Signs of Queerness and Disability*. New York: New York University Press, 2006.

Meckel, Richard A. *Save the Babies: American Public Health Reform and the Prevention of Infant Mortality, 1850–1929*. Baltimore: Johns Hopkins University Press, 1990.

Mehta, Uday Singh. *The Anxiety of Freedom: Imagination and Individuality in Locke's Political Thought*. Ithaca: Cornell University Press, 1992.

Melnick, Ross. "Reality Radio: Remediating the Radio Contest Genre in Major Bowes' Amateur Hour Films." *Film History: An International Journal* 23, no. 3 (2011): 331–47.

A Memoir of Zerah Colburn. Springfield, MA: G. and C. Merriam, 1833. American Antiquarian Society.

Mercer, Kobena. *Cosmopolitan Modernisms*. Cambridge, MA: MIT Press, 2005.

Merish, Lori. "Cuteness and Commodity Aesthetics: Tom Thumb and Shirley Temple." In *Freakery: Cultural Spectacles of the Extraordinary Body*, edited by Rosemarie Garland-Thomson, 185–206. New York: New York University Press, 1996.

———. *Sentimental Materialism: Gender, Commodity Culture, and Nineteenth-Century American Literature*. Durham: Duke University Press, 2000.

Miles, Tiya. *All That She Carried: The Journey of Ashley's Sack, a Black Family's Keepsake*. New York: Random House, 2021.

Mintz, Steven. *Huck's Raft: A History of American Childhood*. Cambridge, MA: Belknap Press of Harvard University Press, 2004.

Mitchell, Joseph. "An Evening with a Gifted Child." *New Yorker*, August 30, 1940.

Mitchell, Mary Niall. "Reading Race: Rosebloom and Pure White, or So It Seemed." In *Raising Freedom's Child: Black Children and Visions of the Future after Slavery*, chap. 2. New York: New York University Press, 2008.

Mitchell, Michele. *Righteous Propagation: African Americans and the Politics of Racial Destiny after Reconstruction*. Chapel Hill: University of North Carolina Press, 2004.

Monaghan, Jennifer. *Learning to Read and Write in Colonial America: Literacy Instruction and Acquisition in Cultural Context*. Amherst: University of Massachusetts Press, 2005.

A Monstrous Birth: or, A True Relation of Three Strange and Prodigious Things like Young Cats, All Speckled, Which Came from a Woman Dwelling at Wetwan in Yorkshire: And How the Devil Kept Her Company. London: For Livewel Chapman, at the Crown in Popes-head-alley, 1657. Early English Books Online.

Moretti, Franco. *The Way of the World: The Bildungsroman in European Culture*. 1987. New York: Verso, 2000.

Morgan, Edmund. *American Slavery, American Freedom*. New York: W. W. Norton, 1975.

Morgan, Jennifer. *Laboring Women: Reproduction and Gender in New World Slavery*. Philadelphia: University of Pennsylvania Press, 2004.

———. "*Partus sequitur ventrem*: Law, Race, and Reproduction in Colonial Slavery." *Small Axe* 22, no. 55 (March 2018): 1–17.

———. *Reckoning with Slavery: Gender, Kinship, and Capitalism in the Early Black Atlantic*. Durham: Duke University Press, 2021.

Morris, Monique W. "Countering the Adultification of Black Girls." *Educational Leadership* 76, no. 7 (April 2019): 44–48.

———. *Pushout: The Criminalization of Black Girls in Schools.* New York: New Press, 2016.
Morris, Richard C. *Reading, 'Riting, Reconstruction: The Education of Freedmen in the South, 1861–1870.* Chicago: University of Chicago Press, 1981.
Morrison, Toni. *The Bluest Eye.* 1970. New York: Alfred A. Knopf, 2000.
———. *Playing in the Dark: Whiteness and the Literary Imagination.* New York: Random House, 1992.
Moss, Hilary. *Schooling Citizens: The Struggle for African American Education in Antebellum America.* Chicago: University of Chicago Press, 2009.
Moten, Fred. *In the Break: The Aesthetics of the Radical Black Tradition.* Minneapolis: University of Minnesota Press, 2003.
Muhammad, Khalil Gibran. *The Condemnation of Blackness: Race, Crime, and the Making of Modern Urban America.* Cambridge, MA: Harvard University Press, 2011.
Munford, George Wythe. *The Code of Virginia: Including Legislation to the Year 1860.* Richmond: Ritchie, Dunnavant, 1860. Gale Cengage.
Nadis, Fred. *Wonder Shows: Performing Science, Magic, and Religion in America.* New Brunswick: Rutgers University Press, 2005.
Nash, Gary, and Jean Soderlund. *Freedom by Degrees: Emancipation in Pennsylvania and Its Aftermaths.* New York: Oxford University Press, 1991.
Nash, Richard. *Wild Enlightenment: The Borders of Human Identity in the Eighteenth Century.* Charlottesville: University of Virginia Press, 2003.
Natale, Simone. *Supernatural Entertainments: Victorian Spiritualism and the Rise of Modern Media Culture.* University Park: Pennsylvania State University Press, 2016.
Nelson, Alondra. *The Social Life of DNA: Race, Reparations, and Reconciliation after the Genome.* Boston: Beacon Press, 2016.
Nelson, Jennifer. *Women of Color and the Reproductive Rights Movement.* New York: New York University Press, 2003.
Newbery, John. *The History of Little-Goody Two Shoes.* London, 1765.
The New England Primer. Boston: Printed by S. Kneeland and T. Green, 1750. Readex.
"News and Notes." *Science* 17, no. 436 (June 1891): 352–55.
Nickels, Cameron C. *Civil War Humor.* Jackson: University Press of Mississippi, 2010.
Nielsen, Kim E. "Incompetent and Insane: Labor, Ability, and Citizenship in Nineteenth- and Early Twentieth-Century United States." *Rethinking History* 23 no. 2 (2019): 175–88.
———. *The Radical Lives of Helen Keller.* New York: New York University Press, 2004.
Nisbet, Richard. *The Capacity of Negroes for Religious and Moral Improvement Considered.* London: Printed by J. Phillips, 1789. Star Collection. John Hay Library. Brown University.
Noble, Marianne. *The Masochistic Pleasures of Sentimental Literature.* Princeton, NJ: Princeton University Press, 2000.
Nord, Paul. *Faith in Reading: Religious Publishing and the Birth of Mass Media in America.* New York: Oxford University Press, 2004.
Nott, Josiah Clark. *Types of Mankind: or, Ethnological Researches, Based upon the Ancient Monuments, Paintings, Sculptures, and Crania of Races, and upon Their*

Natural, Geographical, Philological, and Biblical History. Philadelphia: Lippincott, Grambo, 1854.

Nussbaum, Martha C. *Frontiers of Justice: Disability, Nationality, Species Membership.* Cambridge, MA: Harvard University Press, 2006.

Nystrom, Kenneth. "The Bioarchaeology of Structural Violence and Dissection in the 19th-Century United States." *American Anthropologist* 116, no. 4 (October 2014): 765–79.

———. "Postmortem Examinations and the Embodiment of Inequality in 19th Century United States." *International Journal of Paleopathology* 1 (2011): 164–72.

O'Connell, Dierdre. *The Ballad of Blind Tom.* New York: Overlook Duckworth, 2009.

Odell, Margaretta Matilda. *Memoir and Poems of Phillis Wheatley, a Native African and a Slave. Dedicated to the Friends of the Africans.* Boston: George W. Light, 1834. Massachusetts Historical Society.

Oertzen, Christine Von. "Science in the Cradle: Milicent Shinn and Her Home-Based Network of Baby Observers, 1890–1910." *Centaurus* 5, no. 2 (2013): 175–95.

Oldys, Alexander. *The Female Gallant.* London: Printed for Samuel Briscoe, 1692.

Oladipo, Gloria. "Republican Iowa Governor Rolls Back State's Child Labor Law Protections." *Guardian*, May 27, 2023. http://theguardian.com.

O'Neall, John Belton. *The Negro Law of South Carolina: Collected and Digested under a Resolution of the State Agricultural Society of South Carolina.* Columbus: J. G. Bowman, 1848. Gale Cengage.

Osterweil, Ara. "Reconstructing Shirley: Pedophilia and Interracial Romance in Hollywood's Age of Innocence." *Camera Obscura* 24, no. 3 (2009): 1–40.

Owens, Camille. "'Fine Discords': Anarranging the Archives of Philippa Schuyler." *American Quarterly* 73, no. 2 (2021): 205–31.

———. "'I, Young in Life': Phillis Wheatley and the Invention of American Childhood." *Early American Literature* 57, no. 3 (2022): 727–49.

Owens, Deirdre Cooper. *Medical Bondage: Race, Gender, and the Origins of American Gynecology.* Athens: University of Georgia Press, 2017.

Painter, Nell Irvin. *The History of White People.* New York: W. W. Norton, 2010.

———. "Soul Murder and Slavery: Toward a Fully Loaded Cost Accounting." In *U.S. History as Women's History: New Feminist Essays*, edited by Linda Kerber, Alice Kessler-Harris, and Kathryn Kish Sklar, 125–46. Chapel Hill: University of North Carolina Press, 1995.

Pascoe, Peggy. *What Comes Naturally: Miscegenation Law and the Making of Race in America.* New York: Oxford University Press, 2009.

Pasulka, Diana. "Somber Pedagogy—a History of the Child Death Bed Scene in Early American Children's Religious Literature, 1674–1840." *Journal of the History of Childhood and Youth* 2, no. 2 (2009): 180.

Pearson, Susan J. "'Infantile Specimens': Showing Babies in Nineteenth-Century America." *Journal of Social History* 42, no. 2 (2008): 341–70.

———. *The Rights of the Defenseless: Protecting Children and Animals in Gilded Age America.* Chicago: University of Chicago Press, 2011.

Pen.org. "The 10 Most Banned Books of the 2021–2022 School Year." December 21, 2022.
Penn Medical College, of Philadelphia. *Incorporated by the Legislature of the Commonwealth of Pennsylvania, and Approved by the Executive, February, 2d, 1853*. 1853. Readex.
Penningroth, Dylan C. *The Claims of Kinfolk: African American Property and Community in the Nineteenth-Century South*. Chapel Hill: University of North Carolina Press, 2003.
Perlmann, Joel, Silvana Siddali, and Keith Whitescarver. "Literacy, Schooling, and Teaching among New England Women, 1730–1820." Special issue on Education in Early America, *History of Education Quarterly* 37, no. 2 (Summer 1997): 117–39.
Perry, Claire. *Young America: Childhood in Nineteenth Century Art and Culture*. New Haven: Yale University Press, 2006.
Peterson, Dawn. *Indians in the Family: Adoption and the Politics of Antebellum Expansion*. Cambridge, MA: Harvard University Press, 2017.
Petry, Ann. "Smart Cat Does Tricks! Ifrit, Philippa Schuyler's Trained Persian." *People's Voice*, March 7, 1942. Readex.
Pettigrew, William. *Freedom's Debt: The Royal African Company and the Politics of the Atlantic Slave Trade 1672–1752*. Chapel Hill: University of North Carolina Press, 2013.
Phillips, Ruth B. "Aesthetic Primitivism Revisited." *Journal of Art Historiography* 12 (June 2015): 1–25.
Piepzna-Samarasinha, Leah Lakshmi. *Care Work: Dreaming Disability Justice*. Vancouver: Arsenal Pulp Press, 2018.
Pilkington, Ed. "Bones of Black Children Killed in Police Bombing Used in Ivy League Anthropology Course." *Guardian*, April 23, 2021.
Pleck, Elizabeth. *Domestic Tyranny: The Making of Social Policy against Family Violence from Colonial Times to the Present*. New York: Oxford University Press, 1987.
Plotz, Judith. *Romanticism and the Vocation of Childhood*. New York: Palgrave, 2001.
Ponce De Leon, Charles. *Self-Exposure: Human-Interest Journalism and the Emergence of Celebrity in America, 1890–1940*. Chapel Hill: University of North Carolina Press, 2002.
Popenoe, Paul. *The Conservation of the Family*. Baltimore: Williams and Wilkins, 1926.
Preston, Ann. *Cousin Ann's Stories for Children*. Philadelphia: J. M. McKim, 31 N. Fifth Street, Merrihew & Thompson, Printers, 1849.
The Pro-slavery Argument: As Maintained by the Most Distinguished Writers of the Southern States. Charleston: Walker, Richards, 1852.
Puar, Jasbir. *The Right to Maim: Debility, Capacity, Disability*. Durham: Duke University Press, 2017.
Putnam, Samuel P. *400 Years of Freethought*. New York: Truth Seeker, 1894.
Quashie, Kevin. *The Sovereignty of Quiet: Beyond Resistance in Black Culture*. New Brunswick: Rutgers University Press, 2012.
Radde, Kaitlyn. "Arkansas Gov. Sanders Signs a Law that Makes It Easier to Employ Children." *NPR*, March 10, 2023. http://npr.org.

Rafter, Nicole H. "Claims-Making and Socio-cultural Context in the First U.S. Eugenics Campaign." *Social Problems* 39, no. 1 (February 1992): 17–34.
Rankine, Claudia. "The Condition of Black Life Is One of Mourning." *New York Times*, June 22, 2015.
Ransby, Barbara. *Ella Baker and the Black Freedom Movement: A Radical Democratic Vision*. Chapel Hill: University of North Carolina Press, 2003.
Reagan, Leslie. "Monstrous Births, Birth Defects, Unusual Anatomy, and Disability in Europe and North America." In *The Oxford Handbook of Disability History*, edited by Michael Rembis, Catherine Kudlick, and Kim E. Nielsen, 385–406. New York: Oxford University Press, 2018.
Reed, James. "Doctors, Birth Control, and Social Values, 1830–1970." In *The Therapeutic Revolution: Essays in the Social History of American Medicine*, edited by Morris J. Vogel and Charles Rosenberg, chap. 5. Philadelphia: University of Pennsylvania Press, 1979.
Reinier, Jacqueline S. *From Virtue to Character: American Childhood, 1775–1850*. New York: Twayne, 1996.
Reiss, Benjamin. "P. T. Barnum, Joice Heth and Antebellum Spectacles of Race." *American Quarterly* 51, no. 1 (1999): 78–107.
———. *The Showman and the Slave: Race, Death, and Memory in Barnum's America*. Cambridge, MA: Harvard University Press, 2001.
Rezek, Joseph. "Transatlantic Traffic: Phillis Wheatley and Her Books." In Gillespie and Lynch, *Unfinished Book*, 289–302. New York: Oxford University Press, 2021.
Rhyne, J. Michael. "'Conduct . . . Inexcusable and Unjustifiable': Bound Children, Battered Freedwomen, and the Limits of Emancipation in Kentucky's Bluegrass Region." *Journal of Social History* 42, no. 2 (Winter 2008): 319–40.
Richards, Robert J. *The Tragic Sense of Life: Ernst Haeckel and the Struggle over Evolutionary Thought*. Chicago: University of Chicago Press, 2008.
Richardson, John G. "Common, Delinquent, and Special: On the Formalization of Common Schooling in the American States." *American Educational Research Journal* 31, no. 4 (Winter 1994): 695–723.
Riis, Thomas L. "Blind Tom: The Legacy of a Prodigy Lost in Mystery." *New York Times*, March 5, 2000.
Ritchie, Andrea, and Mariame Kaba. *No More Police: A Case for Abolition*. New York: New Press, 2022.
Roberts, Dorothy. *Fatal Invention: How Science, Politics, and Big Business Re-create Race in the Twenty-First Century*. New York: New Press, 2011.
———. *Shattered Bonds: The Color of Child Welfare*. New York: Basic Books, 2002.
Roberts, Kyle. "Rethinking the *New England Primer*." *Papers of the Bibliographical Society of America* 104, no. 4 (December 2010): 489–523.
Roberts, Samuel. *Tales of the Poor; or, Infant Sufferings: Containing, The Chimney-Sweeper's Boy; Sally Brown, the Cotton Spinner; The Orphans; and Mary Davis*. New York: Published by Samuel Wood & Son, 1821. Readex.

Roberts, Wendy Raphael. "'On the Death of Love Rotch,' a New Poem Attributed to Phillis Wheatley (Peters): And a Speculative Attribution." *Early American Literature* 58, no. 1 (2023): 155–84.

———. "'Slavery' and 'To Mrs. Eliot on the Death of Her Child': Two New Manuscript Poems Connected to Phillis Wheatley by the Bostonian Poet Ruth Barrell Andrews." *Early American Literature* 51, no. 3 (2016): 665–81.

Robinson, Norborne T. N. "Blind Tom, Musical Prodigy." *Georgia Historical Quarterly* 51, no. 3 (September 1967): 336–58.

Robinson, Victor. *The Don Quixote of Psychiatry*. New York: Historico-medical Press, 1919.

———. *Pioneers of Birth Control in England and America*. New York: Voluntary Parenthood League, 1919. National Library of Medicine Digital Collections.

Robinson, William. *Phillis Wheatley in the Black American Beginnings*. Detroit: Broadside Press, 1975.

Roediger, David. *The Wages of Whiteness: Race and the Making of the American Working Class*. New York: Verso, 1991.

Rollo, Toby. "The Color of Childhood: The Role of the Child/Human Binary in the Production of Anti-Black Racism." *Journal of Black Studies* 49, no. 4 (May 2018): 307–29.

Roosevelt, Theodore. "On American Motherhood." Speech delivered to the National Congress of Mothers, 1905.

Root, W. T. "The Intelligence Quotient from Two Viewpoints." *Journal of Applied Psychology* 6, no. 3 (1922): 267–75.

Rose, Jacqueline. *The Case of Peter Pan, or, The Impossibility of Children's Fiction*. London: Macmillan, 1982.

Rosen, Ruth. *The World Split Open: How the Modern Women's Movement Changed America*. New York: Penguin, 2001.

Rosenberg, Charles. "The Practice of Medicine in New York a Century Ago." *Bulletin of the History of Medicine* 41, no. 3 (May 1967): 223–53.

Rothstein, William G. *American Medical Schools and the Practice of Medicine: A History*. New York: Oxford University Press, 1987.

Rousseau, Jean Jacques. *Émile, or, On Education*. 1762. Edited and translated by Allan Bloom. New York: Basic Books, 1979.

Rudd, Annie. "Good Subjects, Bad Objects: Posing Devices and the Nineteenth-Century Commercial Studio." *Photographies* 13, no. 2 (2019): 195–218.

Rugemer, Edward. "The Southern Response to British Abolitionism: The Maturation of Proslavery Apologetics." *Journal of Southern History* 70, no. 2 (2004): 221–48.

Rusert, Britt. *Fugitive Science: Empiricism and Freedom in Early African American Culture*. New York: New York University Press, 2017.

Sacks, Oliver. *An Anthropologist on Mars: Seven Paradoxical Tales*. New York: Vintage, 1995.

Samuels, Ellen. *Fantasies of Identification: Disability, Gender, and Race*. New York: New York University Press, 2014.

Samuels, Shirley. *The Culture of Sentiment: Race, Gender, and Sentimentality in 19th-Century America*. New York: Oxford University Press, 1992.

Sánchez-Eppler, Karen. "Childhood." In *Keywords for Children's Literature*, edited by Philip Nel and Lissa Paul, 38–40. New York: New York University Press, 2011.

———. *Dependent States: The Child's Part in Nineteenth-Century American Culture*. Chicago: University of Chicago Press, 2005.

———. "Temperance in the Bed of a Child: Incest and Social Order in Nineteenth-Century America." *American Quarterly* 7, no. 1 (March 1995): 1–33.

Sandahl, Carrie, and Philip Auslander. *Bodies in Commotion: Disability and Performance*. Ann Arbor: University of Michigan Press, 2010.

Sanders, Charles W., and J. C. Sanders. *The New School Reader Fourth Book: Embracing a Comprehensive System of Instruction in the Principles of Elocution: With a Choice Collection of Reading Lessons in Prose and Poetry, from the Most Approved Authors: For the Use of Academies and the Higher Classes in Schools, Etc.* New York: Ivison, Phinney, Blakeman; S. C. Griggs, 1867. Gale Cengage.

———. *Sanders' Pictorial Primer, or, An Introduction to "Sanders' First Reader."* New York: Ivison & Phinney, [ca. 1856–58?]. Gale Cengage.

———. *Sanders' Union Reader Number Two: For Primary Schools and Families*. New York: Ivison, Phinney, Blakeman; J. B. Lippincott, 1861. Gale Cengage.

Sanders, Joe Sutliff. "Spinning Sympathy: Orphan Girl Novels and the Sentimental Tradition." *Children's Literature Association Quarterly* 33, no. 1 (Spring 2008): 41–61.

Santiago-Valles, Kelvin. "'Still Longing for de Old Plantation': The Visual Parodies and Racial National Imaginary of US Overseas Expansionism, 1898–1903." *American Studies International* 37, no. 3 (1999): 18–43.

Sappol, Michael. *A Traffic in Dead Bodies: Anatomy and Embodied Social Identity in Nineteenth Century America*. Princeton, NJ: Princeton University Press, 2002.

Saville, Julie. *The Work of Reconstruction: From Slave to Wage Laborer in South Carolina 1860–1870*. New York: Cambridge University Press, 1994.

Savitt, Todd Lee. *Medicine and Slavery: The Diseases and Health Care of Blacks in Antebellum Virginia*. Urbana: University of Illinois Press, 1978.

———. *Race and Medicine in Nineteenth and Early-Twentieth Century America*. Kent: Kent State University Press, 2007.

Saxon, A. H. "P. T. Barnum and the American Museum." *Wilson Quarterly* 13, no. 4 (1989): 130–39.

Sayles, John, and Henry Sayles, *Revised Civil Statutes and Laws Passed by the 16th, 17th, 18th, 19th, & 20th Legislatures of the State of Texas (2d ed.) 17*. Saint Louis: Gilbert Book Company, 1889.

Schafer, Judith. *Becoming Free, Remaining Free: Manumission and Enslavement in New Orleans, 1846–1862*. Baton Rouge: Louisiana State University Press, 2003.

Schalk, Sami. "Approaches to Disability Identity in Black Disability Politics." In *Black Disability Politics*, 129–39. Durham: Duke University Press, 2022.

———. *Black Disability Politics*. Durham: Duke University Press, 2022.

———. *Bodyminds Reimagined: (Dis)ability, Race, and Gender in Black Women's Speculative Fiction*. Durham: Duke University Press, 2018.
Schenck, Mrs. J. W. *The Rescued Child*. New York: American Tract Society, 1868. Gale Cengage.
Schuessler, Jennifer. "What Should Museums Do with the Bones of the Enslaved?" *New York Times*, April 20, 2021.
Schuller, Kyla. *The Biopolitics of Feeling: Race, Sex, and Science in the Nineteenth Century*. Durham: Duke University Press, 2018.
Schuyler, George S. *Black No More*. 1931. New York: Penguin Classics, 2018.
Schuyler, Josephine.
———. "Don'ts for My Daughter." *Crisis*, December 1933, 280.
———. "Fall of a Fair Confederate." *Modern Quarterly*, Winter 1930/31, 528–36.
———. "Looks at Books." *Pittsburgh Courier*, November 18, 1939. ProQuest.
———. "My Daughter Philippa." *Sepia*, May 1959, 8–12.
———. *Philippa, the Beautiful American: The Traveled History of a Troubadour*. New York: Philippa Schuyler Memorial Foundation, 1969. James Weldon Johnson Collection, Beinecke Rare Books and Manuscript Library.
———. [Published as Heba Janneth]. "The Salad Is Growing in Importance Says Nutrition Expert." *Baltimore Afro-American*, November 10, 1928. ProQuest.
———. "The Slaughter of the Innocents." *Crisis*, October 1934, 295–96.
Schuyler, Philippa. *Adventures in Black and White*. New York: R. Speller, 1960.
———. "Friends across the Border." *Calling All Girls* 5, no. 7 (March 1945): 15, 56–57.
———. "My Black and White World." *Sepia*, June 1962, 8–12.
———. *Nine Little Pieces*. New York: Copyright by Mrs. George S. Schuyler, 1938. James Weldon Johnson Collection. Beinecke Rare Book and Manuscript Library.
———. *Three Little Pieces*. New York: Copyright by Mrs. George S. Schuyler, 1938. James Weldon Johnson Collection. Beinecke Rare Book and Manuscript Library.
Schwartz, Marie Jenkins. *Birthing a Slave: Motherhood and Medicine in the Antebellum South*. Cambridge, MA: Harvard University Press, 2006.
Scott, David. *Conscripts of Modernity: The Tragedy of Colonial Enlightenment*. Durham: Duke University Press, 2004.
———. "Interview with Sylvia Wynter: The Re-enchantment of Humanism." *Small Axe* 8 (September 2000): 119–207.
Scott, Rebecca. "The Battle over the Child: Child Apprenticeship and the Freedmen's Bureau in North Carolina." *Prologue* 10, no. 2 (Summer 1978): 101–13.
Sears, Hal D. *The Sex Radicals: Free Love in High Victorian America*. Lawrence: Regents Press of Kansas, 1977.
Segal, Jacqueline Fear, and Susan D. Rose, *Carlisle Indian Industrial School: Indigenous Histories, Memories, and Reclamations*. Lincoln: University of Nebraska Press, 2016.
Selden, Steven. "Transforming Better Babies into Fitter Families: Archival Resources and the History of the American Eugenics Movement, 1908–1930." *Proceedings of the American Philosophical Society* 149, no. 2 (June 2005): 199–225.

Sexton, Jared. *Amalgamation Schemes: Antiblackness and the Critique of Multiracialism.* Minneapolis: University of Minnesota Press, 2008.
Shakespeare, William. *The Tempest* [1611]. Edited by Barbara Mowat and Paul Wernstine. Washington, DC: Folger Shakespeare Library, 2022.
Shalaby, Carla. *Troublemakers: Lessons in Freedom from Young Children at School.* New York: New Press, 2017.
Sharpe, Christina. *In the Wake: On Blackness and Being.* Durham: Duke University Press, 2016.
———. *Monstrous Intimacies: Making Post-Slavery Subjects.* Durham: Duke University Press, 2010.
Shaw, Gwendolyn Dubois. "On Deathless Glories Fix Thine Ardent View: Scipio Moorhead, Phillis Wheatley, and the Mythic Origins of American Portraiture in New England." In *Portraits of a People. Picturing African Americans in the Nineteenth Century*, 26–43. Andover, MA: Addison Gallery of American Art, 2006.
Sherbon, Florence Brown. *The Child; His Origin, Development, and Care.* New York: McGraw-Hill, 1934.
Sherrard-Johnson, Cherene. *Portraits of the New Negro Woman: Visual and Literary Culture in the Harlem Renaissance.* New Brunswick: Rutgers University Press, 2007.
Shields, David. "David H. Anderson." Broadway Photographs, University of South Carolina Library. http://broadway.library.sc.edu.
Shields, John C. *Phillis Wheatley and the Romantics.* Knoxville: University of Tennessee Press, 2010.
———. *Phillis Wheatley's Poetic of Liberation: Backgrounds and Contexts.* Knoxville: University of Tennessee Press, 2008.
Shiff, Richard. "From Primitivist Phylogeny to Formalist Ontogeny: Roger Fry and Children's Drawings." In *Discovering Child Art: Essays on Childhood, Primitivism, and Modernism*, edited by Jonathan Fineberg, 157–200. Princeton, NJ: Princeton University Press, 1998. 157–200.
Simmons, LaKisha. *Crescent City Girls: The Lives of Young Black Women in Segregated New Orleans.* Chapel Hill: University of North Carolina Press, 2015.
Sims, James Marion. "On the Treatment of Vesico-Vaginal Fistula." *American Journal of the Medical Sciences.* 1852.
———. *Silver Sutures in Surgery.* 1857. New York: Samuel S. and William Wood, 1858.
———. *The Story of My Life.* New York: D. Appleton, 1884.
Sinha, Manisha. *The Slave's Cause: A History of Abolition.* New Haven: Yale University Press, 2016.
Slauter, Eric. "Neoclassical Culture in a Society with Slaves: Race and Rights in the Age of Wheatley." *Early American Studies: An Interdisciplinary Journal* 2, no. 1 (2004): 81–122.
"Slavery as It Exists in America: Slavery as It Exists in England." Boston: J. Haven, ca. 1850. Library Company of Philadelphia.
Slovenly Kate: And Other Pleasing Stories and Funny Pictures. Philadelphia: W. P. Hazard, 1852.

Smith, Deborah B. [Hall]. *Friendship Album*. 1830–46. Library Company of Philadelphia. Manuscripts: Albums Collection.

Smith, Susan Lynn. *Sick and Tired of Being Sick and Tired: Black Women's Health Activism in America, 1890–1950*. Philadelphia: University of Pennsylvania Press, 1995.

Smuts, Alice Boardman. *Science in the Service of Children, 1893–1935*. New Haven: Yale University Press, 2006.

Smith, Valerie. *Self-Discovery and Authority in Afro-American Narrative*. Cambridge, MA: Harvard University Press, 1987.

Snorton, C. Riley. *Black on Both Sides: A Racial History of Trans Identity*. Minneapolis: University of Minnesota Press, 2017.

Soderberg, Laura. *Vicious Infants: Dangerous Childhoods in Antebellum U.S. Literature*. Amherst: University of Massachusetts Press, 2021.

Songs, Sketch of the Life of Blind Tom, the Marvelous Musical Prodigy, the Negro Boy Pianist, Whose Recent Performances at the Great St. James' and Egyptian Halls, London and Salle Hertz, Paris Have Created Such a Profound Sensation. New York: French and Wheat Printers, [1868].

Sorby, Angela. *Schoolroom Poets: Childhood, Performance, and the Place of American Poetry, 1865–1917*. Durham: University of New Hampshire Press, 2005.

Southall, Geneva. *Blind Tom: The Black Pianist-Composer, 1849–1908*. Lanham, MD: Scarecrow Press, 1999.

Spear, Jennifer. *Race, Sex, and Social Order in Early New Orleans*. Baltimore: Johns Hopkins University Press, 2009.

Spencer, Herbert. *Principles of Biology*. London: William and Norgate, 1864.

Spillers, Hortense. *Black, White, and in Color: Essays on American Literature and Culture*. Chicago: University of Chicago Press, 2003.

———. "Mama's Baby, Papa's Maybe: An American Grammar Book." *Diacritics* 17, no. 3 (1987): 64–81.

Stanley, Amy Dru. *From Bondage to Contract: Wage Labor, Marriage, and the Market in the Age of Slave Emancipation*. New York: Cambridge University Press, 1998.

Starr, Stephen. *The Social Transformation of American Medicine*. New York: Basic Books, 1983.

Stavney, Anne. "Mothers of Tomorrow: The New Negro Renaissance and the Politics of Maternal Representation." *African American Review* 32, no. 4 (Winter 1998): 533–61.

Stoddard, Lothrop. *The Rising Tide of Color against White World-Supremacy*. New York: C. Scribner's Sons, 1920.

Stoever, Jennifer Lynn. *The Sonic Color Line: Race and the Cultural Politics of Listening*. New York: New York University Press, 2016.

Stoler, Ann. *Carnal Knowledge and Imperial Power: Race and the Intimate in Colonial Rule*. Berkeley: University of California Press, 2010.

Stone, Deborah. *The Disabled State*. Philadelphia: Temple University Press, 1984.

Stone, Richard French. *Biography of Eminent American Physicians and Surgeons: Illustrated with Fine Photo-Engraved Portraits*. Indianapolis: Carlon & Hollenbeck, 1894. National Library of Medicine, Digital Collections.

Stowe, Harriet Beecher. *Uncle Tom's Cabin, or Life among the Lowly*. 1851. New York: Penguin, 1998.
Streeby, Shelley. *Radical Sensations: World Movements, Violence, and Visual Culture*. Durham: Duke University Press, 2013.
Streeter, Caroline. *Tragic No More: Mixed-Race Women and the Nexus of Sex and Celebrity*. Amherst: University of Massachusetts Press, 2012.
Stroud, George McDowell. *A Sketch of the Laws Relating to Slavery in the Several States of the United States of America*. Philadelphia: Published by Kimber and Sharpless, 1827.
Subramaniam, Banu. *Ghost Stories for Darwin: The Science of Variation and the Politics of Diversity*. Champagne: University of Illinois Press, 2014.
Sullivan, Dee. "Miss Beethoven in Bobby Sox." *Magazine Digest*, August 1945, 46–50.
Swingen, Abigail. *Competing Visions of Empire: Labor, Slavery, and the Origins of the British Atlantic Empire*. New Haven: Yale University Press, 2015.
Talalay, Kathryn. *Composition in Black and White: The Life of Philippa Schuyler*. New York: Oxford University Press, 1995.
———. "Philippa Duke Schuyler: Pianist/Composer/Writer." *The Black Perspective in Music* 10, no. 1 (Spring 1982): 43–68.
Tandy, Elizabeth Carpenter. *Infant and Maternal Mortality among Negroes*. Washington, DC: United States Children's Bureau, 1937.
Tanenhaus, David S. "Between Dependency and Liberty: The Conundrum of Children's Rights in the Gilded Age." *Law and History Review* 23, no. 2 (Summer 2005): 351–85.
Tarcov, Nathan. *Locke's Education for Liberty*. Chicago: University of Chicago Press, 1984.
Taylor, Diana. *The Archive and the Repertoire: Performing Cultural Memory in the Americas*. Durham: Duke University Press, 2003.
———. "Performance and/as History." *TDR* 50, no. 1 (Spring 2006): 67–86.
Taylor, Jane. *Physiology for Children*. New York: Saxton and Miles, 1846. National Library of Medicine, Digital Collections.
Ten Little Niggers. New York: McLoughlin Brothers, [1870–74]. American Antiquarian Society.
Terman, Lewis M. *The Measure of Intelligence*. Boston: Houghton Mifflin, 1916.
———. "Preface to the First Edition." In *Genetic Studies of Genius*. 2nd ed. Stanford: Stanford University Press, 1926.
———. "Traits of Gifted Children." In Terman, *Genetic Studies of Genius*.
———. "Were We Born That Way?" *Worlds Work* 44 (October 1922): 660.
Thomas, Tracy A. *Elizabeth Cady Stanton and the Feminist Foundations of Family Law*. New York: New York University Press, 2016.
Thompson, Lawrence. "The Printing and Publishing Activities of the American Tract Society from 1825 to 1850." *The Papers of the Bibliographical Society of America* 35, no. 2 (1941): 81–114.
Thorn, Jennifer. "Phillis Wheatley's Ghosts: The Racial Melancholy of New England Puritans." *The Eighteenth Century* 50, no. 1 (Spring 2009): 73–99.

———. "Seduction, Juvenile Death Literature, and Phillis Wheatley's Child Elegies." In *Atlantic Worlds in the Long Eighteenth Century: Seduction and Sentiment*, edited by Toni Bowers and Tita Chico, 189–203. New York: Palgrave Macmillan, 2012.

Tirak, Lita. "The American Grotesque: Free-Thought Idealism in Edward Bliss Foote's Science in Story." PhD diss., College of William and Mary, 2010. ProQuest.

Tise, Larry E. "The 'Positive Good' Thesis." In *Proslavery: A History of the Defense of Slavery in America, 1701–1840*, chap. 5. Athens: University of Georgia Press, 1987.

Todd, James T., and Edward K. Morris. *Modern Perspectives on John B. Watson and Classical Behaviorism*. Westport, CT: Greenwood Press, 1994.

Tommasini, Anthony. "He Was Born into Slavery but Achieved Musical Stardom." *New York Times*, March 3, 2021.

Tompkins, Kyla Wazana. *Racial Indigestion: Eating Bodies in the Nineteenth Century*. New York: New York University Press, 2012.

Tone, Andrea. *Devices and Desires. A History of Contraceptives in America*. New York: Hill and Wang, 2001.

Tortora, Phyllis G., and Keith Eubank. *Survey of Historic Costume: A History of Western Dress*. 5th ed. New York: Fairchild Books, 2010.

Trotter, James M. "Thomas Greene Bethune, Otherwise Known as Blind Tom, the Wonderful Pianist." In *Music and Some Highly Musical People*, 141–59. Boston: Lee & Shepard, 1880.

Trumpener, Katie. "The Modernist Picture Book in Three Dimensions." In Gillespie and Lynch, *Unfinished Book*, 166–82. New York: Oxford University Press, 2021.

Twadell, Elizabeth. "American Tract Society: 1814–1860." *Church History* 15, no. 2 (June 1946):116–32.

Twain, Mark. "Letters from Mark Twain: Special Correspondence." *Daily Alta California*, August 1, 1869.

Van Evrie, John. *Negroes and Negro Slavery: The First an Inferior Race: The Latter Its Normal Condition*. 1854. New York: Horton, 1861. Gale Cengage.

Varga, Donna. "Innocence versus Savagery in the Recapitulation Theory of Child Study: Depictions in Picturebooks and Other Cultural Materials." *International Research in Children's Literature* 11, no. 2 (December 2018): 186–202.

Vega, Tanzina. "Schools Discipline for Girls Differs by Race and Hue." *New York Times*, December 10, 2014.

Virtue in a Cottage, or, A Mirror for Children, Displayed in the History of Sally Bark and Her Family. Hartford: Samuel Babcock, 1795. Readex, Early American Imprints.

Vogel, Morris J., and Charles Rosenberg, eds. *The Therapeutic Revolution: Essays in the Social History of American Medicine*. Philadelphia: University of Pennsylvania Press, 1979.

Wakely-Mulroney, Katherine. "Isaac Watts and the Dimensions of Child Interiority." *Journal for Eighteenth-Century Studies* 39, no. 1 (2016): 103–19.

Wakeman, T. B. *In Memory of Edward Bliss Foote*. New York: Edward Bond Foote, 1906.

Walcott, Rinaldo. *The Long Emancipation: Moving toward Black Freedom*. Durham: Duke University Press, 2021.

Waldstreicher, David. "Anonymous Wheatley and the Archive in Plain Sight: A Tentative Attribution of Nine Published Poems, 1773–1775." *Early American Literature* 57, no. 3 (2022): 873–1052.

———. *The Odyssey of Phillis Wheatley: A Poet's Journey through American Slavery and Independence*. New York: Farrar, Straus, & Giroux, 2023.

Warren, Wendy. *New England Bound: Slavery and Colonization in Early America*. New York: W. W. Norton, 2016.

Washington, Harriet A. *Medical Apartheid: The Dark History of Medical Experimentation on Black Americans from Colonial Times to the Present*. New York: Doubleday, 2006.

Watson, John B. *Psychological Care of Infant and Child*. New York: W. W. Norton, 1928.

Watson, Victor. Introduction to *Coming of Age in Children's Literature*, edited by Margaret Meek and Victor Watson, 1–44. London: Continuum, 2003.

Watts, Isaac. *Improvement of the Mind, or, A Supplement of the Art of Logick*. London: Printed for James Brackstone, 1741.

———. *Logick or the Right Use of Reason*. London: John Clarke and Richard Hett, Emanuel Mathews, and Richard Ford, 1726.

Webster, Crystal Lynn. *Beyond the Boundaries of Childhood: African American Children in the Antebellum North*. Chapel Hill: University of North Carolina Press, 2021.

Weeks, Mary Harmon, ed. *Parents and Their Problems: Child Welfare in Home, School, Church, and State*. Washington, DC: National Congress of Mothers and Parent Teacher Association, 1914.

Weheliye, Alexander. *Habeas Viscus: Racializing Assemblages, Biopolitics, and Black Feminist Theories of the Human*. Durham: Duke University Press, 2014.

Weikle-Mills, Courtney. "Free the Children: Jupiter Hammon and the Origin of African American Children's Literature." In *Who Writes for Black Children? African American Children's Literature before 1900*, edited by Katharine Capshaw and Anna Mae Duane, 22–40. Minneapolis: University of Minnesota Press, 2017.

———. *Imaginary Citizens: Child Readers and the Limits of American Independence*. Baltimore: Johns Hopkins University Press, 2013.

———. "Learn to Love Your Book: The Child Reader and Affectionate Citizenship." *Early American Literature* 43, no. 1 (2008): 35–61.

Weinstein, Amy. *Once upon a Time: Illustrations from Fairytales, Fables, Primers, Pop-Ups and Other Children's Books*. New York: Princeton Architectural Press, 2005.

Welter, Barbara. "The Cult of True Womanhood, 1820–1860." *American Quarterly* 18, no. 2 (1966): 151–74.

Westland, Albert, and Edward Bond Foote. *Tocology for Mothers: A Medical Guide to the Care of Their Health and the Management of Children*. New York: Murray Hill, 1901.

Wheatley, Phillis. "Letter to John Thornton, 30 October 1774." In *The Collected Works of Phillis Wheatley*, edited by John C. Shields, 182. New York: Oxford University Press, 1988.

———. *Poems on Various Subjects, Religious and Moral. By Phillis Wheatley, Negro Servant to Mr. John Wheatley, of Boston, in New England*. London: Printed for A. Bell,

Bookseller, Aldgate; and sold by Messrs. Cox and Berry, King-Street, Boston, 1773. Massachusetts Historical Society.

Whipple, Charles K. *The Family Relation as Affected by Slavery*. Cincinnati: American Reform Tract and Book Society, 1858.

White, Charles A. "I'se Gwine Back to Dixie." Sheet music. 1874. Duke University Library. Digital Collections Online.

White, Deborah Gray. *Ar'nt I a Woman? Female Slaves in the Plantation South*. New York: W. W. Norton, 1985.

Wiggins, Thomas. *Specimens of Blind Tom's Vocal Compositions*. Columbus, GA: John G. Bethune, 1867. Geneva H. Southall Papers, series 2, box 14, Stuart A. Rose Manuscript, Archives, and Rare Book Library, Emory University.

———. *Vocal Compositions, Words and Music by Blind Tom*. 1881. Library of Congress Digital Collections.

Wilcox, Kirstin. "The Body into Print: Marketing Phillis Wheatley." *American Literature* 71 (March 1999): 1–29.

Wilderson, Frank. *Afropessimism*. New York: Liveright, 2020.

Williams, Heather. *Help Me to Find My People: The African American Search for Family Lost in Slavery*. Chapel Hill: University of North Carolina Press, 2012.

———. *Self-Taught: African American Education in Slavery and Freedom*. Chapel Hill: University of North Carolina Press, 2005.

Williams, Oscar Renal. *George S. Schuyler: Portrait of a Black Conservative*. Knoxville: University of Tennessee Press, 2007.

Williams, Rachel Marie-Crane. "A War in Black and White: The Cartoons of Norman Ethre Jennett & the North Carolina Election of 1898." *Southern Cultures* 19, no. 2 (Summer 2013): 7–31.

Williamson, Joel. *The Crucible of Race: Black/White Relations in the American South since Emancipation*. Oxford: Oxford University Press, 1984.

Willis, Deborah. *Van Der Zee: Photographer, 1886–1983*. New York: H. N. Abrams, 1993.

Willoughby, Christopher. "Anatomy and Anatomy Education." In *The Encyclopedia of Greater Philadelphia*, December 21, 2015. http://philadelphiaencyclopedia.com.

———. *Masters of Health: Racial Science and Slavery in U.S. Medical Schools*. Chapel Hill: University of North Carolina Press, 2022.

Wilmot Griswold, Rufus. *The Female Poets of America*. Philadelphia: Carey and Hart, 1849.

Wilson, Robert. *Mathew Brady: Portraits of a Nation*. New York: Bloomsbury, 2013.

Winterer, Caroline. *The Mirror of Antiquity: American Women and the Classical Tradition, 1750–1900*. Ithaca: Cornell University Press, 2018.

Wolff, Larry. "Childhood and the Enlightenment: The Complications of Innocence." In *The Routledge History of Childhood in the Western World*, edited by Paula S. Fass, 78–99. New York: Routledge, 2012.

Wood, Janice Ruth. *The Struggle for Free Speech in the United States: Edward Bliss Foote, Edward Bond Foote, and Anti-Comstock Operations, 1872–1915*. New York: Routledge, 2008.

Wordsworth, William. "Ode: Intimations of Immortality from Recollections of Early Childhood." *William Wordsworth: Selected Poems*, 157–63. 1807. New York: Penguin Books, 2004.

Wright, Nazera Sadiq. *Black Girlhood in the Nineteenth Century*. Urbana-Champaign: University of Illinois Press, 2016.

———. "Our Hope Is in the Rising Generation: Locating African American Children's Literature in the Children's Literature of the *Colored American*." In *Who Writes for Black Children? African American Children's Literature before 1900*, edited by Katharine Capshaw and Anna Mae Duane, 147–63. Minneapolis: University of Minnesota Press, 2017.

Wynter, Sylvia. "Beyond Miranda's Meanings: Un/silencing the 'Demonic Ground' of Caliban's 'Woman.'" In *Out of the Kumbla: Caribbean Women and Literature*, edited by Carole Boyce Davies and Elaine Savory Fido, 355–70. Trenton, NJ: African World Press, 1990.

———. "The Ceremony Found: Towards the Autopoetic Turn/Overturn, Its Autonomy of Human Agency and Extraterritoriality of (Self-)Cognition." In *Black Knowledges/Black Struggles: Essays in Critical Epistemology*, edited by J. R Ambroise and S. Broeck, 184–252. Liverpool: Liverpool University Press, 2015.

———. "The Ceremony Must Be Found: After Humanism." *boundary 2* 12–13, nos. 1–3 (Spring–Autumn, 1984): 19–70.

———. "1492: A New World View." In *Race, Discourse, and the Origin of the Americas*, edited by Vera Lawrence Hyatt and Rex Nettleford, 5–57. Washington, DC: Smithsonian Institution Press, 1995.

———. *On Being Human as Praxis*. Edited by Katherine McKittrick. Durham: Duke University Press, 2015.

———. "On How We Mistook the Map for the Territory, and Re-imprisoned Ourselves in Our Unbearable Wrongness of Being, of Désêtre." In *Not Only the Master's Tools: African American Studies in Theory and Practice*, edited by Lewis R. Gordon and Jane Anna Gordon, 107–69. Boulder: Paradigm, 2006.

———. "Race and Our Biocentric Belief System, an Interview with Sylvia Wynter." In *Black Education: A Transformative Research and Action Agenda for the New Century*, edited by Joyce E. King, 361–66. Washington, DC: American Educational Research Association, 2006.

———. "Unsettling the Coloniality of Being/Power/Truth/Freedom: Towards the Human, after Man, Its Overrepresentation—an Argument." *New Centennial Review* 3, no. 3 (Fall 2003): 257–337.

———. "Yours in Intellectual Struggle." In *On Being Human as Praxis*, edited by Katherine McKittrick, 1–8. Durham: Duke University Press, 2015.

Young, Jacy L. "G. Stanley Hall, Child Study, and the American Public." *Journal of Genetic Psychology* 177, no. 6 (October 2016): 195–208.

Young, Jennifer Rene. "Marketing the Sable Muse: Phillis Wheatley and the Antebellum Press." In *New Essays on Phillis Wheatley*, edited by John C. Shields and Eric D. Lamore, 209–46. Knoxville: University of Tennessee Press, 2011.

Young Ragamuffins. London: David Bogue, 1850. Osborne Collection of Early Children's Books, Toronto Public Library.

Zelizer, Viviana A. *Pricing the Priceless Child: The Changing Social Value of Children*. New York: Basic Books, 1985.

Zipf, Karin. *Labor of Innocents: Forced Apprenticeship in North Carolina, 1715–1919*. Baton Rouge: Louisiana State University Press, 2005.

———. "Reconstructing 'Free Woman': African-American Women, Apprenticeship, and Custody Rights during Reconstruction." *Journal of Women's History* 12, no. 1 (Spring 2000): 8–31.

Zorbaugh, Harvey, and Rhea K. Boardman. "Salvaging Our Gifted Children." *Journal of Educational Sociology*, October 1936, 100–108.

INDEX

Ableism, 8, 13, 89, 90–91, 174–175, 246n114; and eugenics, 186–187; and race, 8, 13–14, 90–91, 95, 174–175
Abolition, 29, 57, 66, 81–82, 89, 220, 246n6, 247n19
Adulthood, 38, 47, 59–60, 72, 141, 178, 180, 182, 199, 201–202
Adultification, 9
Adventures in Black and White (1960), 201–202, 262n91
African American children. *See* Black children; Childhood
African American family. *See* Black family; Family; Kinship
African American literature, 18–19, 35, 57, 81; African American children's literature, 18
Agassiz, Louis, 131–132, 251n94
Age, 3, 9, 17, 30, 72–73, 144, 153, 174, 187, 196, 205, 241n33
Alexander, Elizabeth, 220–222, 224
Als, Hilton, 211
Anagrammar, 12, 19, 21, 183, 210–211
Anarcha, 130–131. *See also* Betsey; Lucy
Anarrangement, 29, 177, 183, 210–212; definitions of, 210, 233n109
Anatomy, 10, 28, 114, 186, 249n78, 254n41; in medical education, 127–131; textbooks of, 17–18, 21, 28, 103–107
Ancestry, 147, 154–155, 178, 193, 194, 197–198; satire in *Black No More*, 193–194. *See also* Eugenics; Whiteness
Anderson, David H., 2–3, 145, 149, 253n16
Andrews, Ruth Barrell, 53–54
Angel of history, 214–216, 217. *See also* Benjamin, Walter
Angel of the house, 69, 70, 85, 195
Angelic children (representations of), 22, 36, 52–54, 69, 70, 85, 182, 189, 195

Angelus Novus (1920), 213–215, 217. *See also* Klee, Paul
Animal, the, 42–44, 48, 50, 127, 208
Antiblackness, 24, 28, 107, 108, 126–131, 199–200, 248n45; antiblack medical abuse, 28, 107, 127–131
Antislavery, 8, 22, 25, 45, 57, 104–105, 108, 231n62, 242n55, 245n49; depictions of enslaved children, 22, 66, 69, 81–84; politics of Dr. Edward Bliss Foote, 105, 246n6
Apple, Rima, 185
Archives, 5–6, 12, 40–41, 126–127, 138, 145–146, 149, 202–204; of childhood, 16–18, 20–21, 28–29, 40–41, 62, 218; legibility of, 5, 41, 63–64, 145–146, 166; of performance, 20–21, 68–69; of slavery and its afterlife, 5–6, 38–39, 40–41, 60–64; and social authority, 5, 29, 146
Audience, 2–5, 24, 52, 68–70, 84, 87, 109, 117, 145, 151, 162–163, 194–195; black audiences and press, 182, 187–189; enjoyment, 13–14, 70, 72–73, 77–78, 85, 144, 147, 151; of Oscar Moore, 2–4, 20, 151, 153, 159, 162–163, 165–167, 171, 174; sale of souvenirs to, 20, 68, 95, 145; of Philippa Schuyler, 177, 182, 205–206; of Phillis Wheatley, 33–35, 45; of Thomas Wiggins, 27, 67–70, 72, 77–80, 95
Authority, 6, 7, 11–13, 41, 71, 88–89, 105–107, 146, 168–170, 192, 219, 222; archival, 29, 146; in early America, 7, 11, 13, 41–44, 71, 75; narrative, 36, 38, 44, 55, 168–170, 201, 208; scientific, 105–107, 127, 154–155, 159, 178; white patriarchal, 4, 6–7, 11–12, 41, 43–44, 48, 71, 88–89, 91–92, 99, 134, 140, 222. *See also* Man; Patriarchy; White men

313

Barnum, P. T., 168, 257n110
Baumgartner, Kabria, 75, 229n31, 237n109, 241n39
Beatty, Barbara, 180
Benjamin, Walter, 21, 214, 217
Bernstein, Robin, 21, 24, 55, 126, 165, 194–195, 229n31, 234n27
Berquin, Arnaud, 124–125
Berry, Daina Ramey, 129
Bethune, Eliza, 92–94, 100, 150, 242n57, 245n98; suit for Thomas Wiggins's custody, 92–94
Bethune, James, 67–68, 71, 76–78, 80, 90–95, 98–100, 150; 1865 and 1885 lawsuits against him, 74, 76–78, 92–95
Bethune, John, 76, 90–94. *See also* Bethune, Eliza; Bethune, James
Betsey, 130. *See also* Anarcha; Lucy
Better babies, 139–141, 148, 158, 179–180, 185, 189
Binet, Alfred, 186, 187, 253n13, 260n46, 261n50. *See also* IQ (intelligence quotient)
Biological knowledge, 103, 106–107, 127–133, 156, 185, 246n10, 250n88; and child science, 185; extracted from black people's bodies, 107, 129–131, 156
Black childhood (construction of), 3–5, 9–13, 16, 75, 80–89, 108, 148–149, 164–165, 173–176, 187–189, 193, 195, 201–202, 210–212; contemporary, 9, 221–224; early American legal construction of, 1–13; Phillis Wheatley's contributions to, 36–37, 46, 55–57, 64, 66, 69; white imagination of, 22, 24–28. *See also* Black children; Child, the; Childhood
Black children (collective), 3–5, 8–14, 18–22, 25, 27, 30–31, 36–41, 126, 182, 187–189, 195–196, 200, 216–217, 222–224; aliveness, 221, 223; in archives, 5, 20, 38–39, 41, 60–64, 71, 224; discrimination against, 9, 70–71, 220–221, 241n39; indentures, 68, 71, 76–77, 84, 151, 168, 229n43, 240n17, 243n69; intellectual acts of, 4, 10, 14, 19, 21, 27, 30, 38, 44, 66, 142, 165–167, 217, 219; in nineteenth-century African American literature, 20–21, 81, 103–110, 113–114, 118–127; protection of, 14, 27, 39, 62, 66; vis-á-vis white children, 3, 9–11, 16, 18, 22–27, 36–39, 66, 81–87, 174–176, 180, 199–200, 220–222; and white men's power, 3–6, 12, 28–31, 66, 74, 76–77, 89, 100, 153, 173, 185–187; white possessive investment in, 3, 9–11, 14, 66, 70–71, 86, 100, 105–107, 143–148, 149–152, 168–175, 206–208
Black codes, 111, 240n17
Black family, 4, 13–15, 55–58, 59–64, 71, 74, 76, 93–94, 99, 151, 153, 155–156, 169, 241n38. *See also* Family; Kinship
Black men (individual), 29–30, 61–64, 74, 111, 136, 151–152, 175, 189, 197–198
Black No More, 29, 178, 181, 182, 192–195, 197–198. *See also* Schuyler, George
Black women, (collective and individual), 11, 15, 25, 35, 37, 62, 65–66, 85–87, 94, 130–131, 151, 173, 188, 199–202
"Black-a-moor" (caricature), 120, 122
Black-and-whiteness, 25, 70, 78, 85–87, 182, 193–195, 199; in Shirley Temple's repertoire, 192, 194, 210, 212; in Thomas Wiggins's repertoire, 69–71, 80
Blackening, 28, 117, 139–140, 158, 243n66; in nineteenth-century children's stories, 117–127
Blackface, 25, 124, 194, 212, 261n73
Blackness, 16, 18, 24–25, 31, 85, 131–134, 158, 187, 199–201; and disability, 68, 72–158, 168, 174; fungibility, 90, 94–95, 105, 117, 195; pedagogical uses of, 18, 108, 118–127; as resource to the human, 22, 25, 105, 107–108, 127–134, 158, 187, 220, 224; vis-á-vis whiteness, 25, 70, 127, 152, 158, 175, 193–195, 210–212
Blank slate, 7, 16, 18, 27, 41, 44, 58–59, 147, 163
Blind Tom, 67, 68, 147, 175; Blind Tom Combination, 77; Blind Tom Company, 77, 95. *See also* Wiggins, Thomas
Blindness, 2, 20, 67–68, 143, 150–151, 154, 163–165, 169, 174. *See also* Moore, Oscar; Wiggins, Thomas
Bluest Eye, The, 29, 210–213, 222–223, 262n81, 265n18. *See also* Morrison, Toni
Book-child relation, 17–19, 20, 38, 164, 183, 220, 222–223

Bourgeois family, 35, 69, 78, 88, 115, 124, 148. *See also* Family; Middle-class family
"Boy Who was Frightened at Soap and Water, The," 120–121
Boyhood, 2–3, 18, 72–73, 91–92, 96, 103–106, 109–110, 119–124, 135–136, 227n6; black boyhood, 18, 103, 174
Brady, Mathew, 3
Breedlove, Pecola (character), 210–213, 218. See also *Bluest Eye, The*; Morrison, Toni
Brewer, Holly, 7, 75, 231n62, 235n58
Brightness, 2, 10, 19, 20, 143–149, 151–152, 158–159, 176, 181; repertoire of, 159–167. *See also* Moore, Oscar
Brooks, Daphne, 87, 240n18
Brooks, Joanna, 35, 233n9
Brown, Gillian, 16, 228n17
Brown, Jayna, 21, 25
Brownies' Book, The, 188
Burnett, Frances Hodgson, 3
Butler, Octavia, 219–220, 223

Cadavers, 107, 114, 128–129, 249n78; use in medical school training, 128–131. *See also* Medicine
Cahan, Emily, 180
Caliban, 14, 114, 137
Campt, Tina, 204
Capshaw, Katharine, 18, 187–188
Care, 12, 30, 46–47, 63, 66, 128, 174, 185, 188–189, 223–224
Caricature, 8–9, 20, 72, 86–87, 122, 124, 126; of black children, 9, 22–24, 26, 194; of childlikeness, 8, 114. *See also* Picaninny
Carretta, Vincent, 41, 45
Cheapness, 22, 26, 39–40, 70, 197, 234n26. *See also* Value
Child, the, 4–7, 9–10, 26–27, 37, 40, 46, 48, 50, 56, 60, 66, 80, 95, 107, 118, 120, 133, 147–148, 158, 164, 181, 183, 185–186; development of, 4, 18, 20, 29, 42, 48, 52, 109, 117, 132–134, 143, 148, 157–158, 164, 178–180, 186, 202, 216, 224, 229n35; innocence of, 17, 22–25, 34–35, 40, 51–54, 69, 81, 118, 150; legal protection of, 9, 10–11, 60–64, 68, 74–77, 88, 91, 93, 221; as a measure, 5–7, 30, 46–49, 90, 93, 133, 157–158, 179, 181, 184–185, 187, 221, 223; mind of, 42, 54, 59, 141–143, 164, 178–178, 185–186; power of, 7, 37, 88, 91; and recapitulation, 132–133, 157–158; "tender years" of, 74, 76, 82, 241n33; vis-á-vis the human, 8–10, 17–19, 30, 133, 183; vis-á-vis Man, 5–8, 10, 15, 17, 19, 30–31, 44, 48–49, 127, 149, 224
Child, Lydia Maria, 81, 82, 242n55, 243n66
Child Labor, 7, 41, 60, 67, 70, 76, 82, 84, 150–152, 165, 167–169, 171–172, 244n80, 253n21, 264n12
Child Science, 4, 142, 147–148, 156–157, 174, 178–181, 184–186, 189, 193, 250n92, 254n47, 255n49. *See also* Psychology
Child Study Movement, 142, 147–148, 156–158, 164, 178, 180
Childhood, 3–9, 11–15, 16–17, 20, 30, 33–35, 46–49, 65–66, 78, 80, 148, 189, 193–194, 220–225; and ableism, 8, 13, 22, 89, 90–91, 174–175, 246n114; black childhood as resource to white, 9–10, 22–25, 30, 39, 70, 82–84, 108, 158, 175, 182, 194, 212, 221; cultural constructions of, 7, 20, 33, 50–57, 65–66, 69–70, 78, 80–88, 164, 189, 193, 200, 210–213, 221; enslaved childhood, 10, 37, 39, 40, 67–70, 74–75, 82; experts of, 156–158, 178, 180, 185, 255n48; futurity, 10, 15, 34–36, 49–50, 54, 66, 139, 141, 155–156, 158, 174–175, 178–183, 185–189, 220, 222; innocence, 17, 22–25, 34–35, 40, 51–54, 69–70, 85; legal constructions of, 11–13, 74–75; suffering, 24–25, 30, 66, 69, 78, 80, 81, 85, 86
Childlikeness, 4, 8–9, 28, 47–49, 60, 68, 71–73, 88–89, 101, 114, 126, 132–133, 158, 187, 213, 224; legal notion of, 91, 101; logic of, 4, 8–9, 47–49; in the measurement of IQ, 187; and recapitulation, 132–133, 158
Children's literature, 16–18, 21, 24–25, 51, 85–86, 103–109, 118–127, 177, 210–211; African American children's literature, 18–19, 189; bourgeois readership of, 40, 124; class politics of, 122–124
"Children's Number," 187–189. *See also Crisis* (magazine)

Christianity, 11, 34, 41, 44, 51–53, 55–57, 111, 234n35
Citizenship, 13, 16–17, 72–73, 110–113, 222, 231n63
Civil War (US), 3, 74, 84, 114–115, 122
Clevenger, Shobal Vail, 143–147, 154–159, 170–171, 174
Clinic for the Social Adjustment of Gifted Children at New York University, 186, 260n46
Coming-of-age (narrative), 17, 71, 110, 201–202, 231n70
Consent, 7, 47, 76, 151, 228n17; and rationality, 7
Contents of Children's Minds on Entering School, The (1883), 156, 158
Crain, Patricia, 17, 41–42, 163–164, 234n27, 234n38
Crisis (magazine), 187–189, 203
Cubber, Dinah, 61–63. See also Peters, John; Wilkins, Naomi
Custody, 5, 7, 68, 71, 74–77, 88, 90, 91–94, 98, 100, 150, 168, 239n5, 241n38; history of, 74–75
Cuteness, 194, 206, 210

Darwin, Charles, 106, 131, 185, 250n92
Daston, Lorraine, 13
Davis, Jefferson, 3
Dayton, Cornelia, 38–39, 58, 61–62
Dehumanization, 9, 24
Democratic government, 7, 15, 48, 231n62
Dependency, 5, 8, 15, 35–36, 57, 68, 88–91, 93–95, 100, 106, 127, 131, 146, 192, 194–195, 201, 235n58
Development, 4, 18, 20, 29, 42, 109, 114, 117, 143, 157, 164, 168, 178–180, 216, 224, 229n35, 232n70; eugenics and, 180, 184–185, 202; and recapitulation, 131–134, 158; unchecked (to "grow like Topsy"), 139
Dimples (1936), 194, 261n73
Disability, 13, 22, 28, 89–91, 95, 99, 175; black disabled subjectivity, 28, 95, 99; and prodigy, 13, 22
Discipline, 9, 59, 107–108, 125, 127, 136, 140, 158, 203–204, 206; in children's literature, 118–127; ink and, 120–127

Discord, 19, 21, 28, 71, 99–100, 183; in Philippa Schuyler's music, 183, 206; in Thomas Wiggins's music, 28, 71, 97–100
Dissection, 18, 114, 127–129, 141
Domestic sphere, 17, 36, 43, 46, 52, 54, 58, 66, 75, 78
Dorr, Gregory Michael, 181
Douglass, Frederick, 3, 30, 81, 221
Dr. Hubbs (character), 105, 108, 109, 111, 113–115, 134, 137
Du Bois, W. E. B., 175, 188–189, 203
Duane, Anna Mae, 18, 24

"Earthseed," 219, 223. See also *Parable of the Sower* (1993)
Education, 28, 36, 47, 59, 105, 108–111, 148, 157–158, 162, 164, 179, 185–186, 188, 221–222, 229n35; Early American, 38, 39–44, 47–48; for freedpeople, 108, 111; "gifted" education, 148, 186, 200; medical education, 127–130
Eliot, Charles, 51–53
Elway, 90–92, 96
Emancipation, 8, 15, 65, 68, 71, 74, 76, 100–101, 111, 117, 133–134; black Emancipation, 106, 108, 113, 134
Encyclopedia, 109; reference to Oscar Moore as, 162–165
Enlightenment, 6, 7, 48, 235n58
Eugenics, 8, 91, 137–143, 147–148, 173–175, 178, 186–189, 198–200, 214, 231n56, 259n15; black engagement with, 181, 188; promotion by Dr. Foote, 138–141; and recapitulation, 133–134; Schuyler family and, 178–179
Evolution, 8, 106–107, 131–133, 137, 158, 165, 175, 229n28
Exceptionality, 2, 4–5, 8, 10, 14, 22, 39, 59–60, 77, 147, 163, 165, 173–175, 186–189, 219–220; politics of black exceptionality, 174–175, 188–189
Exclusion, 7, 8–9, 20, 22, 66, 127, 137, 229n31, 249n73

Family, 4, 7, 8, 30, 46, 51–58, 85–89, 91–95, 99–101, 137–139, 151, 223–224, 234n29, 239n2; black family, 4, 11–12, 14–15, 27, 38, 56–58, 60–64, 68–69, 70–71, 75,

93–93, 98–100; family business, 68; family tree, 198–200; fictions of, 27–28, 58, 78, 80, 91–93, 170; law, 7, 10, 14, 15, 68–71, 74–77, 95; middle-class, 88, 124, 170; white family, 10, 15, 50–56, 68–69, 71, 74–75, 88, 90–94, 149, 152, 170
Fathers, 5, 7–8, 11–13, 15, 42–43, 56–57, 95, 169, 172, 219; authority of, 7, 74–75, 88–89, 99–100, 219; patrilineage, 11–12, 57, 90
Fauset, Jessie Redmon, 189
Feminism, 10–13, 28, 66, 131, 140, 223; black feminist critique, 10–13, 66; of Dr. Foote, 108, 134, 140; roots of, 108
Field, Corinne, 8
Fielder, Brigitte, 18, 139
Foote, Edward Bliss, 18, 28, 103–142, 173; as author, 104, 117; and eugenics, 134–137; feminist politics, 105, 108, 134, 140; legacy, 107–108; medical education, 127–130
Foote, Edward Bond, 138–141
Forsyne, Ida, 25–26
Foucault, Michel, 5, 228n12, 246n10
Fox-Genovese, Elizabeth, 88–89
Franklin, Benjamin, 33, 109, 126–127
Freedom, 4, 8, 10–15, 19, 56–57, 60–64, 68, 74, 93–101, 108, 110, 222, 224; black freedom, 4, 14, 19, 28, 45–47, 49–50, 60–64, 74, 81–87, 90, 93–101, 103, 108, 110–113, 117, 134, 140–141, 150, 188, 222, 224, 229n43, 230n49, 243n69; early African American freedom, 14–15, 46–47, 49, 65, 108; incompleteness of, 28, 100, 134; white anxieties toward black freedom, 86–87, 111, 134; of white children, 10–12, 15, 16, 27, 30, 36, 46–47, 49, 81–82, 88, 222, 224
Freedpeople, 74, 86, 104, 108, 110–111, 115, 243n69; and family law, 74; fictions of in *Science in Story*, 104, 110
"Friends of the negro," 108, 111, 133–134, 247n19
Fun with Dick and Jane, 210–212

Galton, Francis, 133, 259n23
Gammel, Hans Peter Neilsen, 28, 143–145, 149–152, 159–168, 170; account of Oscar Moore, 171–173; as "bookman," 168; as showman, 159–167
Garland-Thomson, Rosemarie, 22
Garvey, Ellen Gruber, 184
Gates, Henry Louis, Jr., 35
Gay, Roxane, 222
Gender, 3, 6, 10, 12, 13, 41, 88, 189, 222, 230n52, 264n12
Giftedness, 10, 29, 158, 178, 186–189, 194–196, 202, 204–206, 231n56; black engagement with, 181, 187–189; definition of, 148; "gifted and talented," 200; study of, 185–186
Gillespie, Alexandra, 21
Girlhood, 22–25, 41, 65, 84–85, 124, 188, 194, 196, 239n10, 241n39; black girlhood, 29, 82–84, 87, 173, 195, 210–212; white girlhood, 22, 41, 59–60, 65, 82–84, 85–86
Glatt, Carra, 58, 236n97
Glissant, Édouard, 146
Grammar, 10–12, 17, 19, 20, 30, 33–39, 44, 50, 56–58, 62, 65, 75, 77, 89, 96, 186, 208–213, 222, 223–224; "American Grammar Book," 10–13, 65, 224; anagrammar, 12, 19, 21, 183, 210; social grammar, 11, 19, 40, 50, 75, 89; subversion of, 12, 21, 29, 183, 208–210. *See also* "Mama's Baby, Papa's Maybe"; Spillers, Hortense
Grant, Julia, 180
Griffin, Farah Jasmine, 211
Gross, Tabbs, 74, 77, 240n30, 242n57
Gumbs, Alexis Pauline, 223

Haeckel, Ernst, 132–133, 250n92. *See also* Recapitulation
Hall, G. Stanley, 147, 156–159, 175, 180, 254n47, 255nn48–49
Hand-Book of the Wonderful Boy, a Few Things of What the Little Blind Two Year Old Boy, Prof. Oscar Moore, Can Tell You, 20, 29, 143–145, 159–168, 171
Hartman, Saidiya, 5, 24–25, 111, 146, 170, 173, 228n16, 230n53
Health, 108, 117, 128, 130–131, 137, 150–151, 156, 170, 180, 188, 189, 248n51; measurement of, 178, 180, 184, 185–186
Hoffmann, Heinrich, 118, 122–125. *See also Inky Boys, The*; *Slovenly Peter*

Home, 13, 42, 58–61, 64, 67–68, 88, 95–99, 126, 178, 195–196, 199, 259n11; black children in white homes, 25, 37, 45–46, 58–59, 65, 76–77; home instruction, 117; middle class, 148. *See also* Domestic sphere; Household

Household, 38, 45–46, 48, 60, 61–62, 71, 88–90, 92–93, 101, 113–114, 181, 189, 231n63

H. P. N. Gammel: Texas Bookman (1985), 171–174

Human, the, 4, 6–10, 13, 17–19, 22, 30, 38, 103, 126–135, 143, 154, 157–158, 201, 214–216, 218, 219–220, 224, 228n16; anatomy of, 17–18, 28, 109, 127; "being human as praxis," 219; biocentric reconception of, 28, 105–110, 175; black surrogacy with, 130–131; denial of black humanness, 131–132; future of, 134, 137, 141, 175, 179, 214, 224; hierarchy of, 120, 127, 132, 182, 186, 198–199; "human phonograph," 163; measure of, 4, 6, 30, 38, 48–49, 173, 224; science of, 28, 103, 127–128. *See also* Humanism; Humanness

Humanism, 6, 7, 9, 17–18, 24, 107, 133, 147, 220, 224; American humanism, 9; biocentrism, 6, 107–108; critiques of, 6

Humanity, 18–19, 25, 28, 108, 120, 127, 137, 220; "better specimens of," 137; "kindlier feelings of," 110, 117, 126

Humanness, 9, 17–18, 28, 103, 107, 126, 141, 158; "imposition" of humanness, 9; questioning of black humanness, 107, 127, 131, 134, 141

"Hybrid vigor," 181, 259n26.

Imagination, 14–15, 19, 27, 65, 182–183, 216, 218, 220, 225

Inclusion, 8–9, 20, 22, 25, 30, 229n31

Indenture, 10, 68, 71, 76–77, 84–85, 94, 149–151, 168, 229n43, 240n17, 243n69; of black children, 68, 71, 76, 85; of Oscar Moore, 150–151; of Thomas Wiggins, 68, 76–77, 84–85

Independence, 31, 57, 88–90, 99–100, 201–202, 228n17, 265n17

Indigenous children, 10, 229n35, 265n16

"Infant Prodigy, An" (1890), 154–159. *See also* Clevenger, Shobal Vail

Infantilization, 8–9, 228n27. *See also* Childlikeness

Inky Boys, The, 118, 120, 122–126, 140, 249n62

Innocence, 3, 17, 22–25, 27, 34, 40, 50–57, 69, 85, 118, 150, 194–196, 221; "racial innocence," 24–25

Intelligence, 4, 147–148, 152–156, 174–175, 184, 186–187, 189–190, 260n46; measurement of, 148, 175, 178–179, 187. *See also* IQ (intelligence quotient)

Interdependence, 30, 31, 57, 99, 202, 219

Interracial reproduction, 135–137, 140, 178–179, 181, 193

IQ (intelligence quotient), 29, 148, 175, 178–182, 186–189, 192, 194, 253nn13–14, 260n46; African American engagement with, 181, 188–189; IQ and eugenics, 179, 185–187

Ivy, Nicole, 130

Jackson, Zakiyyah, 9, 132, 228n16, 230n52

Jacobs, Harriet, 81

Jefferson, Thomas, 37, 48–50, 230n56

Juke, Margaret, 137, 139–140, 251n113

Juke Family, 137, 139, 251n113

Keller, Helen, 174–175

Keye, Elizabeth, 12, 229n43

Kinship, 12–13, 29, 65, 139, 153, 176, 223; black kinship, 12–13, 30, 37, 66, 99–100, 152, 173; "inventive kinning," 223; "kinfulness," 139; of Oscar Moore, 173–174

Klee, Paul, 213–215, 217

Law, 4, 7, 8, 11–15, 20, 38–40, 48, 56–60, 61–64, 68–71, 74–77, 88–89, 149; children's "best interests," 28, 66, 68, 74, 77, 88, 95, 101, 151; English common law, 43, 75, 91; family law, 7, 68–71, 74–77, 88, 90–95; *habeas corpus*, 74, 93; legal action on behalf of black children, 27, 39, 61–64, 66, 75, 241n39; *Partus sequitur ventrem*, 10–11, 15, 75, 222, 229n40, 229n43; of property, 12, 38–39, 60, 231n62; of slavery, 8, 10–12, 14–15, 27–28, 40, 56–57, 75–77, 222, 229n40, 229n43;

suit over Oscar Moore's indenture, 149, 168–169; suits for Thomas Wiggins's custody, 74–77, 92–94; Wheatley Peters family's action upon, 39, 58–60, 61–64
Lerer, Seth, 16
Levander, Caroline, 7
Lewis, Sophie, 223, 265n20
Lincoln, Abraham, 3, 110
Literacy, 16–18, 19, 20–21, 28, 36, 38, 48, 165, 201; alternate forms of, 21, 209, 223; early American, 39–40; enslaved literacies, 19, 41–44; lessons for freedpeople, 111
Little Eva (character), 22–25, 36, 69, 84, 118, 182, 194–195. *See also* St. Clare, Eva
Little Lord Fauntleroy, 3, 4, 25, 85, 227n6
Locke, John, 7–8, 15, 48, 50, 228n17, 231n62, 233n11, 265n17; pedagogy of, 40–42; theory of child's mind, 7–8, 16, 163
Logan, Angela, 181
Longshore, Joseph S., 128–131
Lucy, 130. *See also* Anarcha; Betsey
Lusu naturae, 143, 147, 155, 173, 252n9
Lynch, Deidre, 21

Major Bowes' Amateur Hour, 206–207, 263n110
"Mama's Baby, Papa's Maybe," 11–13. *See also* Spillers, Hortense
Man, 5–8, 13–15, 17, 19, 27–28, 48–49, 64, 96, 100, 120, 127, 134–136, 182, 199, 222, 224; "family man," 168; after Man, 224; as measure, 6, 14; overrepresentation of, 6; seat of power, 6, 182; transition from Man$_1$ to Man$_2$, 28, 100, 106, 107, 136, 138, 140–141; vis-á-vis the child, 5–8, 10, 15, 27, 30–31, 41, 100, 127, 149, 224
Manhood, 3, 4, 7, 28, 89, 100, 114, 117, 120, 133–136, 157, 173, 198, 206–207, 222, 230n51; rights of, 134, 222, 230n51; vector toward, 120, 133, 135. *See also* Man; White men
Manliness, 3, 114, 136, 247n22. *See also* Manhood; White men
Marriage, 7, 38, 58, 75, 95, 134, 136, 243n71, 245n98, 265n20
Martin, Trayvon, 220–221
McClintock, Anne, 8
McCurry, Stephanie, 88–89

McGill, Meredith, 146–147
McKittrick, Katherine, 126, 219, 228n16
McLoughlin Brothers, 122–124, 249n62
McMillan, Uri, 21
Measurement, 4–7, 30, 37, 91, 93, 99, 148–149, 173, 175, 221, 223–224; of children, 4–7, 14, 30, 47, 139, 143, 148–149, 154–155, 157–158, 175, 179–187, 193, 202; of gifted children, 148, 179–187; of the human, 6, 19, 30, 37–38, 143, 173, 183; of intelligence, 148, 156, 178
Medicine, 8, 28, 103–107, 110–114, 130–132, 135, 138, 141–144, 154–156, 192, 246n15, 249nn72–74, 249n79; authority of, 105, 124; medical school training, 107, 127–129, 246n15, 249nn72–74, 249n79
Memoir and Poems of Phillis Wheatley, 27, 38–39, 58–60, 111, 188, 236n97. *See also* Odell, Margaretta Matilda
Merish, Lori, 194, 262n81
Middle-class family, 88, 124, 126, 148, 181; African American, 175, 181, 188–189. *See also* Bourgeois family
Mitchell, Mary Niall, 82
Mixed-race, 140, 143, 152, 155, 178, 181–182, 192–193, 200, 212; in *Black No More*, 192–193; "hybrid vigor" theory, 259n26
Modernism, 173, 185, 213
Modernity, 22, 87, 100, 194, 231n70
Monaghan, Jennifer, 41
Monstrosity, 9, 13, 14, 22, 71, 100, 137, 140, 230n52; disability and monstrosity, 22; history of, 13–14
Montero, Felipa, 199. *See also* Schuyler, Philippa
Moore, Cora (Williams), 169, 173, 257n93
Moore, Fanny, 143, 149, 151, 169, 173
Moore, Henry, 143, 151, 168–169, 173, 257n93
Moore, Oscar, 2, 3, 4, 5, 10, 21, 25, 28, 29, 30, 31, 143–176; "Bright" Oscar Moore, 2, 3, 4, 5, 143–144, 152–153; brightness, 10, 21, 143–145, 153, 159–167; disappearance, 147, 167–169; examination of, 143–146; extraction of value from, 5, 144, 150–156, 158, 170–174; indenture, 150–151; memory, 155, 164, 167, 172; photograph of, 2, 3, 4, 20, 31, 145, 149, 164; repertoire, 20–21, 159–167

Morgan, Jennifer, 11–12, 16, 40, 230n49
Morrison, Toni, 18, 29, 105, 210–212, 262n81
"Mother Dear Mother, I Still Think of Thee" (ca. 1865), 78–80, 81, 84, 97, 100
Motherhood, 10–13, 58, 60–64, 71, 81–87, 88, 187; black motherhood, 10, 11, 37, 58, 60–64, 71, 78, 80; enslaved, 11–12, 14–15; white motherhood, 11–12, 74–75, 88, 184–185
Mothers, 10–13, 35, 37, 46, 61, 65, 70, 74–81, 92–93, 96–100, 169, 178, 184–189, 202–203, 208, 214, 216, 218, 220, 223, 239n8, 241n38. *See also* Motherhood
Murray Hill Publishing Company, 117, 138, 248n51

Natural selection, 106, 126, 132–133
Nature, 4, 7, 30, 34, 103, 132, 147, 220, 252n9, 255n52, 260n28; deviation from, 173–174; versus "nurture," 180–181, 187
New England Primer, 21, 42–44, 51, 118, 234n38
New Negro, the, 174–175, 181
Nystrom, Kenneth, 129, 246n15

Obstetrics and gynecology, 128, 130, 131
Odell, Margaretta Matilda, 27, 38–39, 58–63, 69, 111, 113, 188
Olamina, Lauren (character), 219–220. *See also* Butler, Octavia; *Parable of the Sower*
"Ontology recapitulates phylogeny," 132, 250n92
"Ordinary road, The," 36, 39–41, 44, 59, 233n11. *See also* Locke, John; Pedagogy
Orphans, 43, 81, 145, 194, 199, 210, 255n60
Owens, Deidre Cooper, 129, 130, 250n86

Pain, 24–25, 51, 80, 84, 244n79; and the suffering child, 87–88
Painter, Nell Irvin, 88–89
Parable of the Sower (1993), 219–220, 223
Parents, 2, 27, 45–46, 50–57, 62, 65–68, 74–76, 134, 148, 151, 197, 199, 216, 224, 241n39, 258n11, 262n90. *See also* Family; Fathers; Kinship; Motherhood; Mothers
Park, Katharine, 13

Parkland (massacre), 221–222
Partus sequitur ventrem, 10–12, 37, 75, 222–224, 229n43, 231n63
Pasulka, Diana, 51
Patriarchy, 3–4, 12, 35, 88, 92–95, 100, 110, 139, 198, 221, 223. *See also* Authority; Man; Manhood; White men
Pedagogy, 7–8, 10, 24, 30, 36, 40, 42, 51, 59, 104, 107–108, 128, 139, 147–148, 157–158, 174, 202, 210, 253n12, 255n48; Early American, 16–17, 39–44; for freedpeople, 108; home instruction, 117, 177, 184; late-nineteenth-century science of, 147–148, 157–158; Lockean, 39–41; Josephine Schuyler's pedagogical practices, 178, 184–185; scientific, 107; use of blackness in, 108, 141, 158
Penn Medical University, 128–130, 250n79
Performance, 2–4, 13–14, 20, 24–25, 67, 69–70, 81, 87, 107, 109, 126, 162–163, 169–172, 182, 189, 193–196, 197, 199, 204–206, 219, 225, 230n56, 238n3, 245n111; archives of, 20–21, 146, 164; of blackness and disability, 151, 168; books and performance, 20–21, 159–167; histories of, 3, 13–14, 21; of Oscar Moore, 144, 146, 159–167; Philippa Schuyler on piano, 204–207; sideshow, 21; Shirley Temple's repertoire, 194–195; Wiggins on piano, 67–68
Personhood, 4, 16, 19, 38, 44, 73, 95, 99, 101, 212
Peters, John, 38–39, 58, 60–64
Peters, Phillis Wheatley, 33, 58, 60–64. *See also* Wheatley, Phillis
Philandra, 33, 34, 38, 64–65, 237n124, 238n126. *See also* Wheatley, Phillis
Philippa, the Beautiful American (1967), 200.
Philippa Schuyler Middle School for the Gifted and Talented, 200
Picaninny (caricature), 5, 21–22, 26, 30, 69–70, 210; caricatures of Topsy, 22; etymology of, 26; picaninny choruses, 21
Plantation, 80, 88, 96–98, 100, 130
Poems on Various Subjects, Religious and Moral, 33–35, 39, 45, 51–57, 61. *See also* Wheatley, Phillis

INDEX | 321

Police, 85–87, 111, 220, 230n53, 243n71, 247n15
Polygenesis, 131–132
"Positive obsession," 219–220. *See also* Butler, Octavia
Preciousness, 15, 39–40, 52, 57, 66, 78, 85, 174, 180, 188–189, 192, 198, 221–222; of white childhood, 15, 36, 85, 221
Primers, 21, 27, 36, 118, 141, 162–163, 177, 208, 210–212, 220, 234n38; in Early America, 16–17, 38–44, 50–51; for freedpeople, 65, 108. See also *Fun with Dick and Jane*; *New England Primer*; *Wag and Puff*
Primitivism, 173, 213
Prodigy, 2, 4, 5, 8, 9, 10, 13–14, 26–28, 67–69, 104, 113, 127, 144–147, 154, 167, 189, 195–196, 200, 202, 219–220, 230n56; black prodigy, 4, 5, 9, 10, 13–14, 18, 20–22, 26–28, 30, 38, 59–60, 67–70, 72, 142, 144–145, 174–175, 195, 201–202, 205, 217; definition of, 13, 72, 219–220; and disability, 13–14, 22, 77, 174; history of, 5, 13, 14; white child prodigies, 13, 189, 196, 230n56
Progress, 4, 117, 128–131, 133–138, 180, 185, 188, 201, 214–216
Progressivism, 105, 107–108, 128–131, 137–138, 140; of Dr. Foote, 105, 107, 137–138; of Penn Medical University, 128
Property, 7, 10, 12, 15–17, 24, 37, 57–64, 90–95, 163–164, 182, 200, 212, 221–222, 224, 231n62, 234n29, 238n2, 239n5; book-child-property relation, 164; disputes, 38–39, 60–64, 90–94; enslaved children's status as, 12, 36, 39, 40, 45, 75; inheritance of, 12, 15, 27, 47, 60, 90, 93; learning proprietorship, 41; protection of, 15, 61, 221, 231n62
Proslavery, 8, 81–84, 89
"Proximate whiteness," 152–153, 175, 195, 212
Psychology, 147–148, 156–157, 165, 174, 178, 180, 185–187, 196, 250n92, 254n47, 255n49; and child science, 178, 180, 185; emergence of, 54n47, 147–148, 156–157
Puritans, 42, 44, 51

Race, 8, 10–11, 13–14, 16, 49, 82, 126, 148, 157–158, 174, 178–181, 182, 186, 192–194, 199; and ableism, 8, 89, 174–175; in *Black No More*, 192–193, 197; "critical race theory," 222; epidermal and reproductive organization of, 13–14; and eugenics, 134, 259n26; interracial sex, 11, 135–137, 193; polygenesis, 131–132; race improvement, 134, 138, 141; rearrangement of, 182, 186, 259n26; and recapitulation, 133–134, 157–158, 228n28
Racial capitalism, 30, 197, 219–220
Racial incorporation, 8–9, 17, 22, 25, 29, 49, 67–71, 80, 107, 127, 170, 175, 194
Racial power, 8, 88, 133, 182, 199, 200, 212
Racism, 122, 124, 136, 199; racial tolerance in *The Inky Boys*, 120–125. *See also* Race; Racial power; White supremacy
Radical Remedy in Social Sciences, or Borning Better Babies through Regulating Reproduction by Controlling Conception, The, 139–141
Rationality, 4, 7, 47–48, 91, 109, 135, 211. *See also* Reason
Reading, 19–21, 27–28, 33, 35, 50, 103, 110, 132, 135, 153–154, 162, 202, 222–223; black child readers, 18–19, 21, 43–44, 188–189; child readers, 16–19, 21, 39–44, 103–104, 108–114, 117, 164, 212; "dry reading," 105; intended readers, 43–44, 117, 122, 124, 126, 212; learning to read, 16, 17, 40–44; methods of archival reading, 19–21, 97–99, 146, 164–165, 177, 180, 182–183, 201–202; reader consciousness, 124–125. *See also* Literacy; Pedagogy
Reason, 4, 6–7, 91, 109, 135, 211; race and, 47–49
Recapitulation, 132–133, 142, 158, 228n28, 250n92
Repertoire, 14, 20–21, 24–25, 143–147, 159–167, 174–177, 204, 212, 217–218; of Oscar Moore, 143–144, 146, 159–167; of Philippa Schuyler and Shirley Temple, 192; of Topsy, 25–26, 28, 182, 194–196, 212; of Thomas Wiggins, 67–70, 78–80, 97
Reproduction, 10–13, 82, 131, 135, 137, 139–142, 171, 181, 189, 222–223; eugenic control of, 135, 139–142, 181, 189; social reproduction, 142, 189, 223. *See also* Eugenics

Rescued Child, The, 80, 84–87, 243n71
Roberts, Wendy Raphael, 53, 64, 234n29
Robinson, Bill "Bojangles," 194, 212, 261n72
Robinson, Norborne T. N., 91–92. *See also* Elway
Romanticism, 7, 8, 34–35, 52
Rousseau, Jean Jacques, 7–8, 228n24

Sandy Hook (massacre), 221–222
Sanger, Margaret, 140, 251n119. *See also* Foote, Edward Bliss
Sappol, Michael, 129, 247n15, 248n51
Savagery, 119, 158, 175; on G. Stanley Hall's theories, 157
Savitt, Todd, 129, 247n15
Schuyler, George, 29, 178, 183–186, 195, 197–200, 208, 259n11, 259n26; *Black No More*, 181, 192; conservatism, 199–200
Schuyler, Josephine Cogdell, 29, 177–179, 181, 183–189, 196–208, 210, 214–216; death, 200; ideas on eugenics, 198–199, 258n11, 259nn26–27, 260n29; ideas on motherhood, 185–187; mediation of scrapbook archive, 184, 197, 208, 214
Schuyler, Philippa, 5, 10, 29, 177–218; acts of looking, 29, 207, 213–215; anarrangements of, 196, 201, 203–204, 206–211, 213–216; compositions, 196, 203–204; giftedness, 10, 186, 195–196, 204–205; legacy of, 199–200; memoir of, 201–202; politics as adult, 199–200
Science, 8, 18, 103–111, 113, 117, 126–128, 147–148, 154–156, 193; of childhood, 4, 142, 147–148, 156–157, 174, 178–181, 184–186, 189, 193, 250n92, 254n47, 255n49; eugenic, 8, 28, 91, 133–135, 137–143, 147–148, 173–175, 178, 180–181, 186–189, 198–200, 214, 231n56, 259n15; evolutionary, 106–107, 131–133, 137, 158, 165, 175, 229n28; medical, 103–105, 107, 127–129, 246n15, 249n72. *See also* Child Science; Eugenics; Medicine
Science in Story: Sammy Tubbs, the Boy Doctor, and "Sponsie," the Troublesome Monkey, 18, 28, 103–142; publication context, 103–107. *See also* Foote, Edward Bliss
Scott, David, 17, 228n16

Scrapbooks, 21, 29, 177–179, 181–184, 189, 197–198, 201–202, 206–210, 212–217; as archive, 21, 177–178, 182–184; baby books, 185–186, 201; and narrative authority, 201–202, 208; Philippa Schuyler's subversions of, 201–202, 209–210, 214–216; tactility and haptic qualities, 204
Self-making, 6, 16, 19, 120, 172
Sentimental culture, 22, 24, 33–34, 36–38, 51, 59–60, 69–71, 85, 97–100, 109, 118, 195, 206, 218; anti-sentimentality, 28, 37, 70, 98–100, 206; and slavery, 37–38, 66, 67, 69, 87–88, 97–100; white childhood and, 22, 34, 36, 51, 55, 59–60, 69–71, 78, 80, 85, 87–88, 108, 118, 195, 218, 239n10; of white family, 51, 65, 78, 80, 91–93, 149, 152
Sentimental literature, 4, 17, 27, 36–38, 59–60, 65–66, 80, 85, 87–88, 118, 195; bourgeois readership of, 88, 108, 124; Phillis Wheatley's contributions to, 34, 36, 51–56, 65–66
Sexuality, 135–136, 181, 252n120; of Sammy Tubbs, 135
Sharpe, Christina, 209–210, 228n16, 230n52, 233n109
Shields, John C., 35
Showmen, 3, 28, 145, 159–168, 170, 227n5. *See also* Barnum, P. T.; Gammel, Hans Peter Neilsen
Sims, J. Marion, 107–108, 130–131, 250n84
Slavery, 3, 5, 8–10, 11, 12, 24–25, 36–38, 55–56, 66, 68–69, 71–77, 80–82, 84–85, 90–91, 99, 133, 150, 222, 229n43, 230n49, 231n62; afterlife of, 3, 5, 6, 73, 90–95, 99–100, 140; laws of, 10–15, 75–77; Phillis Wheatley's poetry on, 56–57; Phillis Wheatley's poetry on, 56–57; "white slavery," 82, 88. *See also* Abolition; Antislavery; Proslavery
Slovenly Peter, 118–125, 140
Snorton, C. Riley, 130, 230n53
Soderberg, Laura, 26, 223n107
Songs, Sketch of the Life of Blind Tom, the Marvelous Musical Prodigy, 68, 71, 78, 87
Specimens of Blind Tom's Vocal Compositions, 95–96
Spectacle, 4, 13–14, 143–144, 149, 158, 173, 212, 243n59

Speculation (evaluative or scientific), 81, 181, 250n88; about Oscar Moore, 143, 146, 149–151, 154–155, 167, 171; about Philippa Schuyler, 181, 197
Speculative reading, 44, 50, 146, 246n111
Spillers, Hortense, 10–13, 16, 30, 37, 65, 106, 228n16
Sponsie, 28, 103–105, 113–114, 117, 127, 135–137, 141–142. See also *Science in Story: Sammy Tubbs, the Boy Doctor, and "Sponsie," the Troublesome Monkey*
St. Clare, Eva, 22–26, 28, 36, 84, 118, 182, 194–195; Stowe's literary invention of, 24–25, 69. See also Stowe, Harriet Beecher; Topsy; *Uncle Tom's Cabin*
Stanford-Binet IQ questionnaire, 186, 260n46
Stowe, Harriet Beecher, 22–24, 69, 84. See *Uncle Tom's Cabin*
Subjection, 9, 24, 29, 46, 48, 57, 88, 132, 158

Tabula rasa, 16, 42. See also Blank slate
"Talented tenth," 175, 189
Tanner, Obour, 45–46, 57
Temple, Shirley, 25, 29, 175, 182, 189–196, 210, 212, 261n63, 262n81; in Morrison's *The Bluest Eye*, 29, 210–212; repertoire of, 193–196, 212; in Philippa Schuyler's archive, 189–190
Tenures Abolition Act, 75
Terman, Lewis, 175, 180, 186–187, 258n122, 260n46
Texas Bookman (1985), 171–174
Thaison, William, 149–153, 168–169, 171, 174, 253n15
Token for Children, A, 51–53
Topsy, 22–26, 28, 84, 118, 182, 194–197, 212, 251n117; to "grow like Topsy," 139, 148, 196–197, 251n117; repertoire of, 194–195, 212. See also St. Clare, Eva; *Uncle Tom's Cabin*
Trayvon Generation, The, 221. See also Alexander, Elizabeth; Martin, Trayvon
Trumpener, Katie, 21
Truth, Sojourner, 75, 241n38
Tubbs, Sammy, 10, 28, 103–142, 147, 158; character development, 109–110, 117, 134; invention of, 103–106

Unbinding, 20–21, 28–29, 146, 159–167, 170–174, 218; as method, 20–21, 28–29, 146; unbinding the *Hand-Book*, 146, 159–167
Uncle Tom's Cabin, 22–23, 25, 26, 194. See also St. Clare, Eva; Stowe, Harriet Beecher; Topsy
Uvalde (massacre), 221–222

Value, 6, 26, 39–42, 50, 66, 117, 158, 182–183, 187–188, 197–200; of black children to white Americans, 6, 9–10, 14, 22, 25, 36, 39–40, 66, 67–69, 74, 76–77, 84, 99–100, 144–146, 170, 175, 212, 217–218; of children to adults, 6, 29, 36, 67–69, 202, 221–222; claim of black children's cheapness, 22, 26, 36, 40, 197; of "proximate whiteness," 152–153; white children's preciousness, 15, 22, 36, 40, 221
Violence against children, 5, 9, 24, 26, 31, 62–63, 70, 80, 85, 88–89, 206–207; in children's play, 126; in contemporary US, 220–222; of slavery, 24–25, 39–40, 43–44, 70, 80, 84
Vocal Compositions (1881), 95. See also Wiggins, Thomas

Wag and Puff (1934), 177, 208, 210
Waldstreicher, David, 41, 60, 234n34
Warren, H. W., 150–152. See also Thaison, William
Webster, Crystal Lynn, 18, 75, 229n31, 238n135, 240n17, 241n39
Weikle-Mills, Courtney, 17, 234n27, 242n55
Wheatley, John, 39, 45, 47
Wheatley, Mary (Polly), 41, 44, 234n34
Wheatley, Phillis, 5, 10, 14, 19, 27, 33–66, 70, 75, 106, 111–113, 188–189, 210; births and deaths of children, 58, 61–62; in the *Brownies' Book*, 188–189; in *The Freedman's Third Reader*, 111–113; literacy, 38, 41–44; marriage to John Peters, 58–59; in Middleton, Massachusetts, 60–63; in Odell's *Memoir*, 59; poems on childhood, 51–57
Wheatley, Susanna, 39, 45–47, 47, 57, 234n34
Whipple, Charles, 81, 89

White children, 3–4, 11–12, 34–35, 42–44, 49, 51–56, 81–87, 117, 120–126, 141, 179, 182, 185, 220–224; attitudes toward, 8, 22, 34–36, 74–75, 81–82, 88–89; comparison to black adults, 8, 48–49, 89, 156; freedom of, 10–13, 15, 27, 30, 36, 47, 49, 81–82; as prodigies, 13–14; protection of, 9, 15, 74–75; vis-á-vis black children, 3, 10–13, 15–18, 22–26, 36–39, 66, 70, 81–87, 103–106, 158, 163–165, 170–173, 174–176, 192–193, 199, 202–212, 220–222. *See also* Child, the; Childhood

White family, 12, 15, 45–46, 51–55, 61, 65–66, 67–71, 74–77, 85, 88–95, 100, 139, 168, 170, 172–173, 221. *See also* Family

White men (collective and individual), 2–5, 11–12, 47, 100, 149–152, 154–158, 159–165, 168–175, 185–187; power of, 4–7, 15, 28, 70–71, 91, 100, 106–107, 131, 140, 170, 185; rights of, 7, 15, 75; vis-á-vis black children, 3–6, 10–11, 31, 36–37, 67, 70–71, 76–77, 86, 89–90, 143–146, 159–165, 168–175, 206–208, 214–217, 220–224. *See also* Man; Manhood

White supremacy, 4, 48–50, 108, 126, 192–193, 199, 223; John Birch Society, 199; satire of in *Black No More*, 192–193

White women (collective and individual), 10–13, 28, 35–36, 42, 45–47, 59–60, 91–94, 128–134, 183–189; and reproductive power, 108, 129–130, 135, 140, 185–187

White working class, 81–84, 88, 122–124

Whiteness, 10, 14, 16–18, 25, 44, 85, 132, 152–153, 187, 198–199, 212; of childhood, 25, 53–54, 70, 78, 82, 84, 221; classed representations of, 82–83, 122; as property, 16, 182, 200; protection of, 9, 200, 221–222; vis-á-vis blackness, 18, 22–25, 81–84, 127, 152, 175; white ancestry, 147, 154–155, 193, 197–198

Wiggins, Charity, 14, 15, 67, 76, 78, 80, 87, 241n42, 242n57; court filings, 71, 92–94; in Thomas Wiggins's songs, 97–99

Wiggins, Mingo, 67, 76, 241n42

Wiggins, Thomas, 10, 15, 27, 28, 67–101, 147, 150–151, 175; characterizations, 68, 70–71, 77, 90; commitment, 90; compositions, 27–28, 71, 72, 95–99; enslavement, 67; neurodivergence, 99; performances, 67–68, 72, 97–100

Wilkins, John, 60. *See also* Peters, John; Wilkins, Naomi

Wilkins, Naomi, 60–62. *See also* Peters, John

Williams, Heather, 19

"Wilt Thou Bring My Baby Home?" (1880), 27, 67, 71, 95–101

Woman, 11, 13, 65, 131, 137, 140. *See also* Womanhood

Womanhood, 35, 92–93, 108, 128–131, 217, 230n51, 239n10, 243n76; slavery and, 10–13; whiteness and, 10–13, 28, 90, 108, 127–134, 135, 140, 185–187, 218

Wordsworth, William, 8, 52, 228n25

Wright, Nazera, 18, 242n55

Wynter, Sylvia, 6, 28, 48, 106, 126, 137, 219, 246n14, 250n82

Zorbaugh, Harvey, 186–187, 260n46

ABOUT THE AUTHOR

Camille Owens is an assistant professor of English at McGill University. She received her PhD in American studies and African American studies from Yale University and was a junior fellow at the Harvard Society of Fellows from 2020 to 2023. Her work has appeared in *American Quarterly*, *Early American Literature*, and *Disability Studies Quarterly*.

www.ingramcontent.com/pod-product-compliance
Lightning Source LLC
Chambersburg PA
CBHW052011070526
44584CB00016B/1712